ONE FLESH

Rembrandt, *Adam and Eve*

ONE FLESH

Paradisal Marriage and Sexual Relations in the Age of Milton

> But O, selfe traytor, I do bring
> The spider love, which transubstantiates all,
> And can convert Manna to gall,
> And that this place may thoroughly be thought
> True Paradise, I have the serpent brought.
>
> Donne, *Twickenham Garden*

JAMES GRANTHAM TURNER

CLARENDON PRESS · OXFORD

Oxford University Press, Walton Street, Oxford OX2 6DP
Oxford New York Toronto
Delhi Bombay Calcutta Madras Karachi
Kuala Lumpur Singapore Hong Kong Tokyo
Nairobi Dar es Salaam Cape Town
Melbourne Auckland Madrid
and associated companies in
Berlin Ibadan

Oxford is a trade mark of Oxford University Press

Published in the United States
by Oxford University Press Inc., New York

© James Grantham Turner 1987

First published 1987
First published as Clarendon paperback 1993

All rights reserved. No part of this publication may be reproduced, stored in a retrieval system, or transmitted, in any form or by any means, without the prior permission in writing of Oxford University Press. Within the UK, exceptions are allowed in respect of any fair dealing for the purpose of research or private study, or criticism or review, as permitted under the Copyright, Designs and Patents Act, 1988, or in the case of reprographic reproduction in accordance with the terms of the licences issued by the Copyright Licensing Agency. Enquiries concerning reproduction outside these terms and in other countries should be sent to the Rights Department, Oxford University Press, at the address above

This book is sold subject to the condition that it shall not, by way of trade or otherwise, be lent, re-sold, hired out or otherwise circulated without the publisher's prior consent in any form of binding or cover other than that in which it is published and without a similar condition including this condition being imposed on the subsequent purchaser

British Library Cataloguing in Publication Data
Turner, James Grantham
One flesh: paradisal marriage and sexual
relations in the age of Milton.
1. Milton, John, 1608–1674—Criticism
and interpretation 2. Sex in literature
I. Title
821'.4 PR3592.S47
ISBN 0-19-818249-X

Library of Congress Cataloging in Publication Data
Turner, James, 1947–
One flesh.
Bibliography: p.
Includes index.
1. Milton, John, 1608–1674. Paradise lost.
2. Marriage in literature. 3. Sex in literature.
4. Bible in literature. 5. Bible. O.T. Genesis—
Criticism, interpretation, etc. 6. Marriage—History
of doctrines—17th century. 7. Sex—History of
doctrines—17th century. I. Title.
PR3562.T8 1987 821'.4 86-23864
ISBN 0-19-818249-X

Printed in Malta
by Interprint Ltd

Preface

This book grew from a concern with the following questions. What understanding of sexuality could be gained, in the early modern period, from the opening chapters of Genesis—the great authority from which all myths were thought to have derived, and 'in which all secrets were hid'? How did interpreters of Genesis, and the major poet who inherited their solutions and their problems, fill the silences of the text and reconcile its conflicting elements? How did they imagine the 'Love made in the first Age', and how did they relate it to the actual experience of desire, to the expression of romantic love, to the doctrine of marriage and the practice of sexual politics? Did the Paradise-myth reveal a positive form of Eros, allied to that celebrated in the Song of Songs and in Plato's *Symposium,* or did it show the fundamental evil of lust? In the terms of 'Twickenham Garden', was sexuality the 'True Paradise' or the destroying serpent?

One Flesh is thus not only a history of sexual attitudes, but also a history of exegesis—or more accurately of 'eisegesis', the process of reading meanings *into* a text, since the major significations of Genesis are normally based on the least valid interpretations.[1] It is part of a larger enquiry into ideologies of sex and gender as they relate to ethics, epistemology, and literature. As a cultural historian I want to provide a 'thick description' of the attempt to imagine Paradisal marriage, while as a literary critic I want to illuminate the specific paradox raised by Milton: while the central questions of sexual behaviour, gender, and human identity were for seventeen centuries referred to the biblical account of man's creation and fall, the Eden-myth produced only one important literary text, and that only when the interpretation of Genesis had, as I hope to show, entered a terminal crisis. *Paradise Lost,* which is both the culmination and the closure of the Genesis-tradition, has therefore been made the keystone of this study. I examine the various interpretations of Edenic sexuality and gender-relations available

---

[1] The useful term 'eisegesis', used, e.g., in John A. Phillips, *Eve: The History of an Idea* (San Francisco, 1984), p. xiii, is actually a barbarism, since *exegesis* means 'leading out' rather than 'reading out'.

as Milton wrote, defining his achievement by connecting and contrasting it with the exegesis of the Church Fathers, the Radical Reformation, Renaissance Platonism, and English Puritanism, with the various visionary, libertine, and sectarian tendencies of his own day, and with contemporary poems and dramas on the fall. I finish with a close reading of Milton's own writings on Paradisal marriage, from the intensely troubled divorce tracts to the mature epic, no less contradictory, but now filled with the lineaments of gratified desire.

Though this is not primarily a work of theory, it does deal with topics of great theoretical interest. Biblical studies have been increasingly allied to literary theory, by Northrop Frye and Paul Ricœur among others. The 'reception' of historically important texts, the inheritance of imaginative problems, and the responses of different readers—all these have provoked intense speculation by, for example, Harold Bloom, Hans Robert Jauss, and Stanley Fish. The conjunction of interpretation-history and 'histoire d'amour', again, has greatly preoccupied Michel Foucault and Julia Kristeva, just as in an earlier generation it preoccupied Georges Bataille. (Foucault's work on early Christianity, which would have been directly relevant to my first three chapters, unfortunately remained incomplete at the time of his death, and has not yet appeared in print.) My relation to these French histories of sexuality is not one of direct influence, however, but of shared concerns, parallel development, and distant respect.

The same is approximately true of feminism, except that the neighbourhood is inevitably closer. By and large this is a story of Fathers talking to Sons, passing on a husbandly eroticism and a masculine doctrine of female inferiority—and in the process severely distorting the original text, which I interpret in a more egalitarian light. There are a few vivid exceptions, however—such as Emilia Lanier, who submitted her own unorthodox exegesis for approval, not to the local curate, but to the Queen of England, or the nameless female parishioners of William Gouge, who confronted the Puritan sage with an argument for equality founded on a better reading of the creation-myth than Gouge's own. I show that the use of Genesis to legitimize dominion over women, far from being unequivocal, was contested by 'resisting readers' of both genders, and self-contradicted even within Pauline theology itself. In Milton's own mind, despite his embattled defence of patriarchy, I discover the ultimate triumph of sensibilities and values that he himself must have called female. But I have not attempted to reconstruct the Genesis-tradition from woman's point of view, or to organize my study around an anti-masculinist polemic. Much of what follows does expose the irrationalities and inconsistencies of using Genesis to support male suprematism; the aim is not denunciation, however, but rather an understanding of the 'limits of the thinkable' and a patient reconstruction of divided states of mind. Feminist criticism itself has already evolved in the same direction, of course.[2] I think there is a general interest in showing the cracks that run continually, and I would argue necessarily, through the monolith of patriarchy.

Though I have reservations about deconstruction as a general method—my preoccupations are closer to 'new historicism' than to deconstruction—I find it useful when analysing the disintegrative moment of the Genesis-tradition. My whole argument depends on an indeterminacy in Genesis: the sacred book is composed of texts that must be, and yet cannot be, read as one, and this creates an exegesis that paradoxically obscures what it intends to clarify, generating fresh problems with each solution. Sexuality appears in one place as a simple blessing and a central constituent of humanity, in another place as an abomination, while in the happy state of Eden—the core of the myth for Christian interpreters, and the foundation of their theories of happiness—sexuality is everywhere hinted but nowhere mentioned. This focus on indeterminacy is not, however, meant to suggest a radical indeterminacy in the act of signification itself. Far from it; if all meaning were indeterminate, the fruitful mystery of Genesis would lose its specificity, and this history would be diluted or invalidated. Nor do I believe, though I bring together many different kinds of text, that all discourses and all interpretations are equally valid links in an endless chain of signification, or that all exegesis, including my own, is merely eisegesis. I assume that certain readings and imitations of Genesis are more realistic, more legitimate, and more vital than others,

[2] For the emergence of a complex model of hegemony in feminist literary theory, cf. Elaine Showalter, 'Feminist Criticism in the Wilderness', *Critical Inquiry,* VIII (1981), pp. 179–205; Judith Kegan Gardiner, 'Gender Value, and Lessing's Cats', *Tulsa Studies in Women's Literature,* III (1984), p. 111; Judith Newton, 'Making—and Remaking—History: Another Look at "Patriarchy" ', ibid., pp. 125–6.

and of greater historical importance. The fact that arguments *can* be devised against these terms and assumptions, and that none has a simple uncontested meaning, does not seem to diminish their practical communicative value.

As in my earlier book *The Politics of Landscape,* I concentrate here on the shifts and fissures in the text and the thought-system, the discrepancies between representation and reality, and the antinomies or clashes of sensibility within each author. This whole study is grouped around problems inherent in the original text and exacerbated by the various Christian traditions—the conflict of redeemed imagination and fallen realism, of equality and subordination, of the blessing and the curse upon the flesh. This approach derives from the political analysis of ideology, applied to the more poetic and subjective areas that properly concern the literary specialist—though in the realm of gender, ideology and emotion are interwoven rather than distinct. Such a stress on contradiction carries the danger of anachronism, of importing into the past the twentieth-century view that only conflict should be taken seriously; in concentrating on the problematic, the eccentric, and the sensuous I have perhaps been led by a Whiggish desire to prove the emergence of a modern world-view. But the opposite heresy, the artificial unification of the past, is a more serious error, especially when dealing with a turbulent epoch and a notoriously schismatic religion.

This assumption of complexity and contradiction grows out of, and helps to determine, my characterization of Milton. A major canonical author is continually remade by each generation of critics and within each 'interpretative community'. Thus Fish stresses the self-consuming and reader-reforming Milton, Jean Hagstrum the celebrator of erotic friendship and castigator of Narcissism, Christopher Hill the revolutionary radical, Bloom the iconoclast and inhibitor of future generations. For others Milton is a rationalist, or a prophetic visionary, or an orthodox synthesizer of traditional opinions, or a proto-deconstructionist. Anti-misogynist critics have given us both a 'masculinist' Milton, following Virginia Woolf, and an egalitarian Milton. These selective revisions are often richly documented and brilliantly argued, and I am more indebted to them than can be acknowledged in one place; among other topics, this study explores Milton's reader-orientation, his masculinism, his radicalism, and (above all) his eroticism. But I do not think

Preface

that a single facet can adequately reflect his complex and divided mind, or that a single tradition or constituency can accurately place his affinities. My version of Milton thus shares the current tendency to stress his inconsistency and doubleness.

Milton's energetic confrontation with his precursors and contemporaries succeeds in solving some contradictions and deepening others, often in the same moment. I see him as a figure of abundance rather than inhibition, a heroic synthesizer of incompatible materials, continually engaged in the imaginative transcendence of conceptual limits. But I also show him deeply divided between radical and conservative mentalities, between Platonist idealism and psychological realism, between dualistic rejection and monistic acceptance of the physical world, and between patriarchal and egalitarian conceptions of Paradisal marriage. In Milton as in the multitude of poets and exegetes who inhabit the following pages, 'one flesh' breeds many meanings.

I am glad to acknowledge the John Simon Guggenheim Foundation and the American Council of Learned Societies for their support of this research, and the staffs of the Bodleian Library, the British Library Reference Division, the Department of Prints and Drawings at the British Museum, Doctor Williams's Library, the Alderman Library of the University of Virginia, the Huntington Library, the Kinsey Institute for Sex Research at Indiana University, Northwestern University Library, the Seabury-Western Theological Library, the Newberry Library, the University of Chicago Library, and the Folger Shakespeare Library. I am very grateful to the Trustees of the British Museum, the Curators of the Bodleian Library, the Museum of Art, Rhode Island School of Design, Providence, the Staatsgalerie, Stuttgart, and the Huntington Library, San Marino, California for permission to use the photographs that illustrate this book.

For encouragement and perceptive comments I would like to thank Margaret Atwood, John Carey, Margaret Doody, Marcy Edelstein, Stephen Fallon, Stanley Fish, Carolyn Forché, Arthur Kirsch, Janel Mueller, James Nohrnberg, Martha Pollak, Regina Schwartz, and Phyllis Trible. Irvin Ehrenpreis did not live to see the publication of the work whose completion he fervently encouraged. I am particularly grateful to Jean Hagstrum and David Loewenstein, assiduous readers of successive drafts, and to my parents, who watched the seemingly endless compilation of my research with toleration and amusement. This book is dedicated to the memory of my father, who died shortly before it went to press.

J.G.T.

ADDITION TO PREFACE

The opportunity to reissue this book as a Clarendon Paperback prompts certain questions, seven years after the first edition. What cover-image would best anticipate Milton's arresting, heterodox, and disturbingly erotic depiction of Paradise? Should I rethink the chapter-structure, which treats sexuality and gender as distinct but parallel phenomena? Should I update an already large text to acknowledge new renderings of Genesis and new interpretations of Judaeo-Christian antiquity, or recent work on seventeenth-century radicals and religious women—not to mention innumerable studies of Milton, sexuality, and feminism? When I began this work in the early 1980s most of the writings studied below, including Milton's divorce tracts, had been neglected as imaginative literature, reduced to intellectual and theological history, or mined for footnotes to *Paradise Lost*. Since then, abundant publications and conference papers have explored topics raised in *One Flesh*, from Aemilia Lanier's hermeneutics to the 'pornographic' in Milton.[3]

Hindsight suggested some changes in emphasis, but finally not enough to justify revision. I might have stressed Milton's almost light-hearted treatment of adultery as a factor in divorce, or explored political (rather than personal and developmental) explanations for the relation between the divorce tracts and the epic. But my central theses remain unchanged: the irrationality of the male-supremacist distortion of Eve; the violence needed to maintain that orthodoxy, and the continual presence of alternative readings that weakened it from the margins; the affinities between Milton and the libertines he envied and abhorred; the ungrounded or 'self-

[3] In the collection on *Politics, Poetics and Hermeneutics in Milton's Prose* I edited with David Loewenstein (Cambridge, 1990), two entire essays and half of a third deal with the divorce tracts, while several others tackle Milton's contradictory relation to biblical authority.

Preface

begotten' assertiveness of his scriptural interpretation; the crucial importance of the divorce-campaign in the process that led to *Paradise Lost*; the innovation of making Adam rather than God articulate the primal loneliness, interpreted as a fully sexual desire for a fully 'equal' partner. Eros generates Logos in Milton's vision of paradisal consummation, rather than vice versa.

I would like to extend my thanks to those who have invited me to present or rethink portions of this argument: the Newberry Milton Seminar, Diane McColley, John Knott, Richard Helgerson, Mary Ann Radzinowicz, and especially Annabel Patterson and Scott Elledge, for including parts of this book in the Longman Critical Reader *John Milton* and the Norton Critical Edition of *Paradise Lost*.

J.G.T.

Contents

List of Illustrations	xv
Abbreviations and Frequently Cited Authors	xvi
Introduction: Some paradigms of the response to Genesis	1

1 'This Great Mystery': Scripture and the problem of Paradisal sexuality ... 10
  1. The cracks in the foundation ... 12
  2. Eros, reason, and imagination: the exegetical dilemma ... 27

2 The Incorporation of Eros: Sexuality and the search for Paradise in Augustine, the Reformation, and the English Revolution ... 38
  1. 'A kind of imbracing': Augustine's reconstruction of Paradisal sexuality ... 40
  2. Theories of erotic feeling in Augustine, Aquinas, and Luther ... 49
  3. Eros redeemed? Plato, Solomon, and Paradisal marriage ... 62
  4. The radical revision ... 79

3 'The State of Eve': Female ontogeny and the politics of marriage ... 96
  1. Companionship versus procreation? ... 98
  2. Genesis and female subordination: the limits of the thinkable ... 106

4 The Crisis of the Imagination: Seventeenth-century visionary and libertine theories of primeval sexuality ... 124
  1. Literalism under fire ... 126
  2. The abomination of fiction: sexuality in the systems of Boehme and van Helmont ... 141
  3. Carnal knowledge and the libertine fall ... 156

5 Sensuous Poetics and the Ethics of Confrontation: Miltonic theories of the Word ... 174

6 The Intelligible Flame: Paradisal Eros and Old Testament divorce in Milton's prose	188
1. Patterning from the beginning: exegesis and the vision of perfect marriage	190
2. Love, sexuality, and hatred	194
3. Female usurpation: the act of bondage	215
7 Love Made in the First Age: Edenic sexuality in *Paradise Lost* and its analogues	230
1. Love and poetry in the state of innocence	232
2. Passion and subordination	266
3. The fall: 'casual fruition' and the problems of time	287
Index	310

List of Illustrations

Frontispiece: Rembrandt, *Adam and Eve,* London, British Museum
Reproduced by courtesy of the Trustees of the British Museum

1. Jan Sadelaer I after Martin de Vos, *Genesis 2* (detail), London, British Museum   36
   Reproduced by courtesy of the Trustees of the British Museum

2. Id., San Marino, California, Huntington Library (Kitto Bible)   36
   Reproduced by permission of the Huntington Library, San Marino, California

3. After medal of Mercantonio Passieri, *The Platonic Androgyne,* J. P. Tomasinus, *Illustrorum Virorum Elogia* (Padua, 1630), Oxford, Bodleian Library Douce TT. 166, p. 104   66
   Reproduced by permission of the Bodleian Library, Oxford

4. After J. B. Medina, *Book IX* (detail), in Milton, *Paradise Lost* (London: J. Tonson, 1688), Oxford, Bodleian Library Fol. St. Am. 61, pl. IX   259
   Reproduced by permission of the Bodleian Library, Oxford

5. Jan Gossaert Mabuse, *Adam and Eve,* Providence, Museum of Art, Rhode Island School of Design (Walter H. Kimball Bequest Fund)   293
   Reproduced by permission of the Museum of Art, Rhode Island School of Design

6. After Bartholomaeus Spranger, *Adam and Eve,* Stuttgart, Staatsgalerie (Kupferstichkabinett)   293
   Reproduced by permission of the Staatsgalerie, Stuttgart

7. Jan Sadelaer I after Martin de Vos, *Genesis 2,* London, British Museum (cf. Fig. 1)   294
   Reproduced by courtesy of the Trustees of the British Museum

Abbreviations and Frequently Cited Authors

Note: Patristic treatises and well-known literary texts will be cited by abbreviated title and numbered subdivisions, e.g. book, chapter, and paragraph, or canto and stanza. In the notes, the place of publication has been omitted if it is, or includes, London. I have silently modernized spelling and punctuation when the original would distract or mislead the reader unprofitably, and I have revised twentieth-century translations where necessary, though I retain their page numbering for convenience.

Agaësse St Augustine, *De Genesi ad Litteram,* ed. P. Agaësse and A. Soulignac, *Bibliothèque Augustinienne,* 48–9 (Paris, 1972).

Aug. St Augustine. Apart from *CG* and *Conf.*, the main works cited are *De Genesi ad Litteram,* tr. as *The Literal Meaning of Genesis* by John H. Taylor, *Ancient Christian Writers,* 42 (New York, 1982); *De Nuptiis et Concupiscentia,* tr. in *Anti-Pelagian Writings, A Select Library of the Nicene and Post-Nicene Fathers,* ed. Philip Schaff, 1st ser., V (New York, 1887); *De Bono Conjugali* and *De Incompetentibus Nuptiis,* tr. in *Treatises on Marriage and Other Subjects,* ed. Roy J. Deferrari (New York, 1955). All translations from Augustine have been checked against the standard Latin edition, i.e. *Corpus Christianorum Series Latina* (Turnhout, 1954–) where available, and otherwise *Patrologia Latina*.

Bayle Refs. are to the entry and remark in Pierre Bayle, *The Dictionary Historical and Critical,* 2nd edn. (1734–8), checked against the *Dictionnaire historique et critique,* rev. edn. (1702).

Calvin Unless otherwise indicated, refs. are to his commentary on Genesis, tr. John King (1847), checked against *Commentarii in Quinque Libros Mosis,* 2nd edn. (Geneva, 1573), cited by Biblical chapter and verse unless the section is unusually long.

Carey See M.

Cassuto Umberto Cassuto, *A Commentary on the Book of Genesis:*

Abbreviations and Frequently Cited Authors

	Part I, from Adam to Noah, tr. Israel Abrahams (Jerusalem, 1961).
CG	St Augustine, *The City of God*, tr. based on that of Henry Bettenson (Harmondsworth, 1972).
Conf.	St Augustine, *Confessions*.
DDD	*The Doctrine and Discipline of Divorce*.
DNB	*Dictionary of National Biography*.
Donne	Poems are cited by title and line from the standard Clarendon Press edns.; *Sermons* from the edn. by Evelyn M. Simpson and George R. Potter (Berkeley and Los Angeles, 1953–62).
Du Bartas	Joshua Sylvester, *The Divine Weeks [of] Du Bartas*, ed. Susan Snyder (Oxford, 1979), checked against Guillaume Saluste du Bartas, *Works*, ed. U. T. Lyons *et al.* (Chapel Hill, 1940–3).
ELR	*English Literary Renaissance*.
Fish	Stanley E. Fish, *Surprised by Sin: The Reader in Paradise Lost* (1967; paperback edn., Berkeley, 1971).
Fowler	See M.
FQ	Spenser, *The Faerie Queene*.
Graves	Robert Graves and Raphael Patai, *Hebrew Myths: The Book of Genesis* (1964).
Hagstrum	Jean H. Hagstrum, *Sex and Sensibility: Ideal and Erotic Love from Milton to Mozart* (1980).
Halkett	John Halkett, *Milton and the Idea of Matrimony: A Study of the Divorce Tracts and Paradise Lost* (New Haven, 1970).
Hill[1]	Christopher Hill, *The World Turned Upside Down: Radical Ideas During the English Revolution* (1972; rev. edn., Harmondsworth, 1975).
Hill[2]	Id., *Milton and the English Revolution* (1978; repr., New York, 1979).
HLQ	*Huntington Library Quarterly*.
JWCI	*Journal of the Warburg and Courtauld Institutes*.
Kirkconnell	Watson Kirkconnell, *The Celestial Cycle: The Theme of Paradise Lost in World Literature, with Translations of the Major Analogues* (Toronto, 1952).
KJ	King James's (Authorized) Version.

xviii   *Abbreviations and Frequently Cited Authors*

Leone	'Leone Ebreo', i.e. Judah Abarbanel, *Dialoghi d'Amore*, ed. Santino Caramella (Bari, 1929); tr. as *Philosophy of Love* by F. Friedeberg-Seeley and Jean H. Barnes (1937) (parenthetical refs. will be to both texts, with the Italian first).
Luther	Unless otherwise indicated, refs. will be to vol. and p. of *Lectures on Genesis, Luther's Works*, ed. Jaroslav Pelikan, I–VII (St. Louis, 1958–) checked against *In Primum Librum Mose Enarrationes* (1544), ed. G. Koffmane and O. Reichert, in *Werke*, Kritische Gesamtausgabe (Weimar, 1883–), XLII (1911).
LXX	Septuagint.
McColley	Diane Kelsey McColley, *Milton's Eve* (Urbana, 1983).
M	Milton. Prose is cited from the Yale edn., *The Complete Prose Works*, ed. Don M. Wolfe *et al.* (New Haven, 1953–82), with the Latin text further located in the Columbia edn., *Works*, ed. F. A. Patterson *et al.* (New York, 1931–8). 'Carey' and 'Fowler' refer to the notes in *Poems*, ed. John Carey and Alastair Fowler, *Longmans Annotated English Poets* (1968).
MS	*Milton Studies.*
OED	*Oxford English Dictionary.*
OT	Old Testament.
PL	*Paradise Lost.*
PR	*Paradise Regain'd.*
Prose	See M.
RQ	*Renaissance Quarterly.*
RR	George Huntston Williams, *The Radical Reformation* (Philadelphia, 1962).
RSV	Revised Standard Version.
SA	*Samson Agonistes.*
SEL	*Studies in English Literature, 1500–1900.*
Smith	Nigel Smith (ed.), *A Collection of Ranter Writings from the 17th Century* (1983). The writings of Coppe and Clarkson are quoted from Smith for convenience, but have been checked against the originals.
SR	*Studies in the Renaissance.*
Sylvester	See Du Bartas.

Introduction

SOME PARADIGMS OF THE RESPONSE TO GENESIS

> The Garden's quit with me: as yesterday
> I walked in it, today it walks in me.
> (Joseph Beaumont, 'The Garden')

In 1608, the year of Milton's birth, a controversy raged in Oxford on the subject of wife-battering. The academic dramatist William Gager had argued in a public debate that women were worthless and ineducable, and could lawfully be beaten by their husbands; this flippant display of learned casuistry so outraged a Lady M. H. in the audience that she commissioned a formal reply—*An Apologie for Women*, by the Revd. William Heale. Heale marshalled an impressive mass of resources for his project—no less than an ontological, sociological, and theological definition of 'Woman' as a being equal and in some ways superior in value to 'Man'— and his interlacing of Biblical and Patristic authorities, Classical mythology and Renaissance love-poetry, natural history, Sidneian 'Apologie', and Arcadian romance, reveals the characteristic *bricolage* of the seventeenth-century English mind. Most interestingly for the concerns of the present study, this whole assemblage builds up towards a detailed rereading of the story of Paradise, an imaginative and emotive expansion of the text, enriched with descriptive passages from Ovid and du Bartas, in which the traditional blame and demotion of Eve is replaced by a vision of the female as a higher being, who enhances and completes the male 'by a strange kinde of *Metamorphosis*'. Reproducing the relation of Adam and Eve in his own text, Heale begs his patroness to teach his 'harsh lines' a 'better language', and so to soften and vivify 'this little bodie of my apologie'.[1]

Genesis provides not only the constitutive norms of gender and sexual love, but also the shaping principle of Heale's treatise. The

---

[1] (Oxford, 1609), *passim*, esp. f. A2 and p. 52; cf. Falconer Madan, *Oxford Books*, I (Oxford, 1895), p. 75.

whole book is conceived as itself a journey in this direction, a 'pilgrimage to Paradise'. In the earlier chapters, human institutions are defined and framed by the analogy of Paradise: marriage 'is a state which either imparadizeth a man in the Eden of felicitie, or else exposeth him unto a world of miserie'; the relations of men to women must be gentle and respectful because 'they are one flesh, one minde together with us'. As he enters his crowning chapter, having worked successively through Nature, 'Morality or Civill Pollicie', and law, he feels the relief of the traveller at his goal: 'now here towards the evening of the day and end of my journey I . . . sit me downe in the bloomy shade of *Paradise*, and contemplate the monuments both of womans first creation, and first institution of her marriage.' From this contemplative journey he returns with authority to denounce the petty tyrannies and incitements to violence that underlie misogynistic wit. And this larger connection allows Heale to turn the attack on brutality into a didactic and constructive occasion: he will teach how to 'love women' and how to build a '*Temple* of *love*'—and his book will itself be a temple to which warring couples come on a pilgrimage of grace.[2]

In the 'little bodie' of Heale's treatise we may observe, undistracted by considerations of historical importance or literary reputation, the substance of this book: the network of connections, the pathways of association, that link Genesis and poetic myth, the temple of Love and the edifice of Scripture, moral exhortation and imaginative recreation, the everyday battles of the sexes and the original perfection of humanity. *Paradise Lost* is generated out of essentially the same materials. In Heale as in Milton we see the inherited possibilities and the inherited problems of the Eden-myth. Primeval happiness provides a standard and an ideal for married couples, and an inspiration for the writer—Genesis 'imparadizeth' both the relationship and the text into an 'Eden of felicitie'. But the incorporation of Paradise into the history and ethics of sexuality brings with it a double difficulty. Firstly, the painful loss of Eden may outweigh the original vision of happiness and destroy its normative value; in Donne, for example, the Paradise-myth only enters the world of Eros as an ironic counterpoint, a sign that the only authenticating mark of innocence is its own downfall:

[2] pp. 2 ('Many love not women because they know not how to love them'), 10, 25, 32, 52, 66. M also uses the traditional writing-as-journey topos, in *PL* III. 21: 'Thee [the light] I revisit safe'.

> And that this place may thoroughly be thought
> True Paradise, I have the serpent brought.

Secondly, even a more optimistic spirit like Heale, who combines Genesis and Eros into a model of primal unity untainted by 'predomination' and 'preheminence', cannot fulfil his own promise of translating ideal into reality. The text cannot escape the burden of interpretative tradition, and this tradition, though divided (as we shall see) between egalitarian and subordinationist readings, leans heavily towards the latter; not only does Heale preach submission to the wife, but he bases this ideology on a supposedly natural and primordial inferiority located in Genesis itself (3. 2. iii below). Heale thus reduces his own interpretation of Scripture, the diadem of his work, to fundamental incoherence.

To chart this problematic inheritance will be the task of the following chapters. Chapter 1 deals with the Biblical era itself, flashing forward to the age of Milton only to isolate the central issues: how can the different parts of Genesis be reconciled? Was sexuality included in the original God-given life of Paradise? Since the Word seems to contradict itself on this crucial point, how can the interpreter arrive at the truth? If Genesis declares the imagination 'evil', and if reason led to the fall itself, what part of the mind can be trusted? These questions are then pursued through the Christian era. Chapters 2 and 3, parallel studies of sexual feeling and sexual politics, begin with Augustine, move rapidly to the Reformation, and then examine in detail the Puritans, moralists, philosophers, and Radicals of Milton's lifetime. Chapter 4 explores the allegorists, visionaries, and facetious libertines of the mid-seventeenth century, using critical terms derived from Calvin, Donne, and Browne. Chapters 5–7 analyse Milton himself.

For the most part this narrative will stay within the confines of a genealogy, an internal history of interpretation; it identifies and explains the contradictions of the Genesis-tradition in terms of inherited problems, without offering an underlying social cause. To produce an adequate historical explanation would involve relating it to the events, technologies, and economic structures of two millenia—and all too often such attempts at large-scale explanation fall back on dubious and simplistic dichotomies (feudalism versus capitalism, the extended versus the nuclear family, matriarchy versus patriarchy). In the central decades of the seventeenth century, however, I do assume a general crisis in political, domestic, and religious authority which in turn precipitated a 'crisis of interpretation', marked by the collapse of an orthodox consensus and the simultaneous rise of both sceptic and radical-sectarian challenges to Scripture. The gestation-time of *Paradise Lost* was also the age of the *libertins érudits* and *esprits forts* in France, Holland, and Sweden, and an age when Henry More in England felt himself swamped, not only by crazed 'Enthusiasts' of every description, but by 'many hundreds of thousands of *Atheists*'.[3] In Milton's case the eruption of civil war and political activism intensified his own personal crisis—the collapse of his rash marriage and the energetic but futile campaign for divorce—but opened up a teeming multiplicity of possibilities from which he forged a new ethics of confrontation. The great achievement of his maturity, likewise, took shape in the 'darkness and dangers' of the Restoration, standing out against a culture of worldliness and scepticism.

This will thus be a study in historical hermeneutics, tracing the dilemmas and contradictions involved in the reconstruction of Edenic marriage, as they are intensified by Reformation and Revolution, or concentrated in minds of unusual sensibility and power. My approach is both reader-oriented and author-centred, and among authors I choose a representative range of genres and reputations; I examine Heales as well as Miltons, commentators as well as poets. The artist and the exegete join in a common pursuit, however different their means; they are both producers of the Word, engaged in a struggle to articulate a response to Genesis, and this makes them at once readers of a higher text and creators of their own. I will show the processes of reading that generate fresh discourse, using as far as possible the words of the readers themselves, and I will emphasize that the confrontation with Scripture was conceived in terms not purely intellectual, but *dynamic* (reading becomes a movement or 'journey'), *dialectic* (the text also moves towards, enters into, and transforms the reader, sometimes by a process of resistance and struggle), and *vitalistic*: the Word is apprehended as a living being, a movement and a presence, and the response is correspondingly 'alive'—as much emotional and energetic as ratiocinative. When I turn to Milton in chapters 5–7 I will show how thoroughly he realizes the poetic implications of this

---

[3] Cf. ch. 4 n. 22 below. A measure of the waning of Genesis is that after *PL* no important literary work, and no major treatise on human history or psychology, began with the Biblical account of the creation and fall.

response to the text; but it is by no means confined to the great poet.

[*ii*]

If the author—and the reader, caught up in the same meditation—moves through a network of associations from the immediate occasion to the Paradisal text, it is also true that the Genesis-myth moves forward to inhabit and inform the present moment. This paradigm of the reading-process may be illustrated from another neglected writer of the period, Joseph Beaumont. (We will encounter Beaumont later as the author of an epic on the fall, an illuminating parallel to Milton.) In 'The Garden' (1652), the lyric poem from which the epigraph to this Introduction is taken, he analyses the thoughts and feelings forced upon him by the first chapters of Genesis. To reread the Eden story is first to 'walk' in that garden, and then to have the text return to 'walk' within the mind: 'through all my memorie / It sweetly wanders.' But this pleasant repossession in turn forces him to relive the suffering of Adam and Eve and their 'sad and dangerous' expulsion. The reader is now painfully 'haunted' by the Spirit that returns to walk in him, and he feels banished, not just from Paradise, but from himself; only Christ, Beaumont concludes, can relieve the dread of 'barricadoed Eden'.[4]

The confrontation with Genesis may thus be a 'sad and dangerous' venture, a disturbing reminder of the exclusion from Paradise and the deficiencies of spirit and language that encourage the feeling that the human condition is 'fallen'. (Even Pascal, who lamented that he could not form the slightest idea of the state of innocence, still took his bewilderment and alienation as evidence of the essential truth of the fall-myth.) The text is both demanding and silent, insufferably remote and uncomfortably present. Despite the inaccessibility of Paradise, for Protestants as for introspective Catholics like Pascal the 'barricades' that prevented comprehension could never become an excuse to ignore the founding Scripture: the Word remained the only source of ultimate understanding, and the Word began with Genesis. And those who emphasized the possibilities of regeneration, those contemporaries of Milton who burned with zeal for the 'restitution of all things' in practice as well as in imagination, naturally felt impelled to seek out the

[4] *Minor Poems*, ed. Eloise Robinson (Boston, 1914), pp. 450-1; for Beaumont's allegorical epic *Psyche*, cf. 7. 1. iii below.

experience of Paradise—in Jakob Boehme's striking phrase, to 'force through the Fire-sword, and see with divine eyes'.[5]

The contradictory response to Genesis—a troubling mixture of urgency and incomprehensibility—is articulated not only by visionaries, poets, and moralists, but by the founders of Protestant exegesis themselves. Calvin, like Augustine before him and Pascal later, bewails his inability to grasp the meaning of Genesis, to 'explicate' or unfold the story of the creation and fall in terms equal to its dignity, and at times he gives up his own interpretative role in despair: 'how inexplicable is the cupidity of man!' But he still insists on the power and immediacy of the Word—suitably restored, of course, by his own interpretation. Calvin's stylistic analysis reveals the rhetoric of God, who 'invites us to himself', 'demonstrates' the things necessary for salvation and 'almost compels us to behold them', 'admonishes' us for having lost Paradise, and 'excites in us the desire of its recovery'. The exegete is thus raised to the role of God's collaborator, promoting and intensifying the painful confrontation of Scripture and the individual conscience, even in the text that declares his own inadequacy.[6]

Luther, again, frequently testifies to the powerful emotions inspired in him by the loss of innocence, and frequently laments the impossibility of even imagining the unfallen state, let alone capturing it in words or actually regaining the experience. The splendour of pre-lapsarian sexuality can be conceived only negatively, by contrast with 'the evil which we have with us': 'not only have we no experience of it, but we continually experience the opposite, and so we hear nothing but bare words.' Fallen sexuality becomes a hideous inversion of Platonic Eros, aborting rather than engendering true Logos. Attempts to break this cycle of unknowability, and to clothe these 'bare words' with vivid imagination, only deepen the catastrophe; the futile effort to imagine innocent sexuality only confirms the terrible judgement delivered by God in Genesis 6:5 and 8:21—'the imagination of man's heart', the entire effort of the human heart and mind, 'is evil from his youth.' And yet, as we shall see in chapter 2, Luther does brave the perils of lust and embarrassment to portray his ideal of Paradisal marriage, and he does find in married sexuality the most vivid

---

[5] Pascal, *Pensées* (Lafuma) 431, 423 (and cf. 110), 117, 122, 131; cf. Acts 3:21 and ch. 4 n. 36 below.

[6] 'Dedication', 'Argument', 1:27, 2:8, 3:6; for Augustine see 1. 2. ii below.

evidence, the least diminished trace, of Paradisal bliss. He shares Heale's egalitarian vision of the first created state—though we shall see in chapter 3 that both men contradict their own ideal quite openly—and like Heale he locates in marriage the possibility of an 'Eden of felicitie'.[7]

Despite the grievous problems of fallen epistemology, Reformation exegesis did manage intermittently to connect Scripture to the particular lived experience of the sexes. To read Genesis was to be 'invited' as well as 'admonished'; it allowed the faithful to move between the immediate cruelties and raptures of marriage and the vast collective history of humanity, to draw upon the resources of a Paradise not wholly remote and 'barricadoed', but to some degree pervaded with familiar feelings—evidence of the continuity and essential rightness of the blessing on 'one flesh'. Genesis sanctions 'wedded love' and is in turn made comprehensible by it. In this dialectic, as it was realized by divines and preachers in the generations before Milton (2. 3. iii below), the sexual experience of marriage became not just a survival but a re-enactment of the original 'ordinance' of Genesis, bringing the Holy Spirit into the act of love itself; the text was, as it were, reinserted into practice.

Genesis could thus inspire wildly different conclusions and consequences, ranging from quietism to activism, from restitutionist fervour to alienated despair. No consensus or doctrine emerged to regulate this unpredictable variation—a lack which helps to explain the unstable, schismatic quality of Christianity, especially in the seventeenth century. These multiple responses are brought to a head in Milton. In the divorce tracts and other prose works studied in chapter 6, for example, he creates a passionate and vivid image of ideal sexual love by fusing Genesis and Platonic myth, and he demands that his vision be translated into practice by the legislature. If the love of husband and wife does not re-enact, 'at least in some proportion', the original creation of Eve-Eros in the Garden, the marriage should be immediately dissolved. And yet, despite this astonishingly idealistic demand, Milton's case for divorce is founded on the futility of applying the Paradisal dream to fallen humanity: we should not 'fondly think within our strength all that lost Paradise relates'. This radical disjunction in Milton's argument reflects and deepens the fundamental division, in all responses to Genesis,

[7] I. 61-3, 72, 90, 104, 106, 113, 117, 143-4, 168, II. 123; cf. 2. 2. iii and 3. 2. iv below. The comparison with Plato is mine, not Luther's.

between the remoteness of 'barricadoed Eden' and the immediate experience of Paradise, 'walking' within the reader.

[*iii*]

This book, then, will study the interplay of various hermeneutic, ideological, and artistic problems inherent in the application of Genesis to sexuality. Each chapter will explore an important cluster of contradictions, some enabling, some limiting, in the tangled skein that I call 'the Christian tradition' more for convenience than from any conviction of its unity. I see this tradition as profoundly and incurably restless, condemned perpetually to shuttle between dichotomies that it must raise but cannot solve: between a beatific and a tragic sense of life, between constructive and destructive impulses, between a lapsarian and a non-lapsarian view of human nature, between a redemptive and a diabolical vision of sexuality, between the hopeless remoteness of Paradise and the urge to 'force through the fire-sword', between the equality of all believers and the ratification of hierarchy by the 'Father', and above all between two meanings of 'one flesh'—evil substance, divine incarnation.

The scope of this study may be defined in the way Foucault defines the final stages of his own *History of Sexuality*: it 'analyzes, not behaviours, nor ideas, nor societies ... but *problematizations* ... and *practices*', and its approach is 'genealogical' and 'archaeological'.[8] It differs from Foucault, however, in its focus on the individual poetic sensibility of many diverse figures, in its concern with ideology, and in the dominant status it grants to the literary presence of Milton. Milton will not appear in every region of the 'map of misreading' that follows, but he will be frequently invoked to frame an episode, to define a problem, or to point a contrast of character—with Augustine, for example, whose timid speculations about innocent sexuality are fulfilled and transcended in *Paradise Lost*, or with Boehme, who sacrifices all realism to the visionary imagination, or with Bayle at the opposite extreme, who denies all connection between reason, imagination, and faith.

Milton will thus emerge from this study as a troubled but monumental figure; whether he is a Colossus guarding a busy harbour of trade and invention, or a shattered Ozymandias in a desert of folly and obscurity, the reader must decide. He is given this dominant status, not just because of his achievement in the

[8] *L'Usage des plaisirs, Histoire de la sexualité*, II (Paris, 1984), pp. 17-19.

divorce tracts and *Paradise Lost*, but because he embodies the problems of art and exegesis with particular intensity, sometimes falling victim to them, sometimes transcending them by an astonishing leap of imagination. He towers above his contemporaries both radical and conservative, but he is not remote from them. He is a critical and dynamic reader, often contemptuous of 'common expositors' and commonplace poets, but always ready to respond to hints and to meet challenges from contrary opinions. His own conception of the engaged reader and the confrontatory reading-process, expressed not only in *Areopagitica* but throughout his prose, leads him to create an equally involved reader for his own epic, bound to the Genesis-myth not just by guilty complicity in fallen emotion, but by the capacity to share 'in some proportion' the erotic dream of Paradise.

1
'This Great Mystery'

SCRIPTURE AND THE PROBLEM OF PARADISAL SEXUALITY

> Moses writ this, but is gone from me to thee; if he were here, I would hold him, and beseech him for thy sake to tell me what he meant.... But from whence should I know that he said true? Or when I knew it, came that knowledge from him? (Augustine, *Conf.* XI. iii. 5)

It is ironic that the brief, cryptic, and discouraging tale of Adam and Eve should have come to bear so large a weight of signification. The industry of exegesis, eloquent on the horrors of the fall and the fiery sword, nevertheless turned the Eden-myth into an oracular authority for the most urgent questions of human nature and its most essential institutions. John Donne, comparing the brevity of Genesis to the 'volume scarce lesse than infinite' of commentary, bewailed the grovelling impotence of the human mind (*Sermons*, IX. 48). For those of us who do not believe in supernatural authorship, on the other hand, the interest of Genesis lies precisely in the historical production of its meanings—the vast, ramshackle edifice of interpretation. This incessant labour testifies to the restless 'walking' of the Paradise-myth, its power to generate discourse even though its ostensible lesson is the wretchedness of the fallen mind, the evil of the imagination, and the poverty of 'bare words'. We may think of another of Donne's paradoxes: that 'true Paradise' can only be constituted in words that bring in the serpent.[1] Within the chosen field of this book—the history of sexuality—important questions emerged from this tragicomic struggle between a resisting text and a hermeneutics hungry for universal explanation. How could the first version of the creation-myth ('male and female created He them', 'increase and multiply') be reconciled with the subsequent creation of a single woman from a 'rib', and the apparent postponement of sexual reproduction until after the fall?

[1] Cf. title-page and Introd. i above.

1. *This Great Mystery*

What was the meaning of the terms that God and Adam apply to Eve—'help meet', 'bone of my bone', and 'one flesh'—and what light did these throw on the relation between man and woman? What kind of knowledge was conveyed by the forbidden tree, and how did it relate to the sense of genital nakedness, the subsequent curse of painful childbearing, and the carnal 'knowledge' that led to the birth of Cain? These questions in turn contributed to a larger question: should human sexuality and human gender-relations, as they are actually experienced, be considered an integral part of human nature as originally created and blessed, and if not, in what way should they be changed to conform to that pre-lapsarian ideal? The original text derives its mythic power from cloudy intimations of these questions, numinous hints that somehow approach the essence; but it provides no answers.

Nor did these questions exist in isolation. Attitudes to sexuality, perhaps influenced by the Platonic linkage of Eros and Gnosis or the Hebraic concept of 'carnal knowledge', were intimately connected to other issues of interpretation and understanding. This will be illustrated historically in the following chapters, culminating in *Paradise Lost*, but we may frame the discussion by citing representative opinions from later Protestant interpreters. For Adriaan Beverland, for example, the conviction that the fall-story referred to the discovery of sexual intercourse led him to divide and desacralize the text, treating it with a blend of textual scholarship, historical anthropology, and libertine mockery (ch. 4 n. 81 below). Pierre Bayle, on the other hand, denied any kind of sexual component in the Eden-myth, whether in the state of innocence or in the fall, and castigated those who speculated in such areas: 'None but those who are more guided by their own Imaginations than the Authority of Scripture will deny that *Adam* and *Eve* came out of the Garden without any carnal Knowledge.' Sexuality and imagination are thus ranged together as enemies of piety and truth. But Bayle's apparent defence of orthodoxy actually led him to the brink of scepticism or fideism, since the arguments marshalled on either side of the question of Edenic sexuality are equally absurd ('Abel' A, 'Eve' B). Differing from both these extremes, a great twentieth-century traditionalist can find in the story of Adam and Eve a promotion, rather than a denial, of sexuality:

Men are simply male and female. Whatever else they may be, it is only in this differentiation and relationship. But as the original form not only of man's confrontation of God but also of all intercourse between man and man, it is the true *humanum* and therefore the true creaturely image of God. Man [*der Mensch*] can and will always be man before God and among his fellows only as he is man in relationship to woman and woman in relationship to man.[2]

Milton himself is closer to the twentieth-century Barth than to the seventeenth-century Bayle; he insists on a full sexual life for the unfallen Adam and Eve—bringing it to life as fully as his poetic resources allow—and thus demonstrates the constitutive role of Eros in human ontology. His Protestant worship of marital sexuality comes into conflict, potentially, with his iconoclastic suspicion of 'imaginations'.

To understand how the plain tale of Eden could generate such divergence, we should turn to the interpretative traditions themselves, to the successive forms of eisegesis and the modes of reading that underlie them. Where does this history begin? We must examine the founding texts, first in isolation and then in relation to other passages in the Bible and contemporary writings. Even in Scripture, however, we will find inconsistency, discursive multiplicity, and commentary mingled with original narrative.[3] It should be recognized that the interpretation-history of Genesis has always been a struggle between disintegrative and unitary readings, and that the latter, far from achieving the seamless unity they intended, have actually intensified the contradictions of the text.

1. The cracks in the foundation

The interpretation of the first three chapters of Genesis must cope with two sources of potential disintegration—internal contradiction between parts of the narrative, and incompatibility between the text and the doctrinal significance it is called upon to support. Nothing is said in the text, for example, about the angels worshipping Adam, a scene frequently repeated in the Koran, or about Satan acting within the serpent, the first principle of Christian theories of evil; nor, *pace* later theories of a 'protevangelium', is there any

---

[2] Karl Barth, *Die Lehre von der Schöpfung*, tr. as *Church Dogmatics*, III. i, *The Doctrine of Creation* (Edinburgh, 1958), p. 186.

[3] M assumed that Gen. 2 is actually 'a commentary on the first', making God Himself an exegete (*Prose* II. 594).

promise of a Messiah or redeemer. And if Genesis is silent on these supernatural events, when it comes to the nature and origin of mankind it speaks with a double tongue, for the first four chapters contain redundancies and inconsistencies which have stimulated commentary and provoked revision since before the Christian era.

Whether or not one accepts the nineteenth-century historicist division into 'Priestly' and 'Jahwist' segments, it is obvious that the story of the Six Days of Creation (1:1–2:4a) differs considerably from the story of the Garden of Eden (2:4b–4:1). Each represents a different narrative mode, one being an orderly hymn to creation, the other a set of interlocking aetiological fables explaining the origin of thorns and edible grains, of embarrassment, of labour, of snake-phobia, of birth-pains, of female subjection, of clothing. The second piece is constructed round a series of verbal and situational puns, playful at first but successively grimmer as we approach death, the 'cherub', and the fiery sword.[4] The God of each part is correspondingly different—one the grand artist who speaks the cosmos into existence, whose works progress as steadily as the liturgical language that describes them, and one the cunning artisan Jahweh, a God of tests and boundaries and missing counterparts. And the human being likewise appears differently in each version.

In the first chapter humanity is created as a species, an indeterminate number of males and females who are instructed to rule the earth and fill it with their offspring. Humankind, like the 'Elohim' in whose image they are made, is assumed to be male and female, procreative and plural; the creation-passage refers to 'them' in every phrase, except once where 'him' is substituted to avoid cacophony.[5] 'Man' is plural in God's own statement of His purpose ('Let us make man [*'adam*] in our image, after our likeness; and let them have dominion . . . '), in the act of creation ('male and female He created them') and in the benediction, when 'God blessed them, and God said to them, "Be fruitful and multiply"' (1:26–8). No restrictions or prohibitions are put on them (though it is implied they should be vegetarians) and nothing is mentioned of their relationship to one another, even though their absolute rule over

---

[4] Verbal puns connect, for example, Adam/earth, Eden/pleasure, cunning/naked/curse, help/adviser, Eve/snake/life, birth-pain/labour/tree, and the plants of 2:5 and 3:18—the last two examples are unearthed by Cassuto, pp. 100–2, 165.

[5] Cassuto, p. 58. Biblical quotations will here follow modern scholarly reconstructions, particularly Cassuto's, rather than KJ.

other species is heavily stressed (they are to 'trample' them).[6] In the 'Priestly' Genesis of 1:1–2:4 we see the divine image of Biological Man, just as in a similar passage, 5:1–3, we see Genealogical Man. 'Adam' is the species-name of both male and female, and the same ceremonial phrase—'in his own likeness, after his image'—is used for human procreation and for divine creation.

This first, 'Priestly', chapter assumes an untroubled relationship between humanity and God. Genesis 1 does not depict a radically altered world: nothing in it (except perhaps the implied vegetarianism of verses 29–30) suggests any alteration or falling-off between primordial existence and universal experience. The vision is essentially non-lapsarian. The reader—any healthy man or woman who appreciates the beauty of the cosmos—effectively shares God's aloof but benign regard, His satisfaction at having created a 'very good' universe.

In the more ancient 'Jahwist' creation-story the picture is quite different. The reader is forced to be aware of the fabulous differences between the obedient and the 'fallen' state. Man is here defined in terms of individual consciousness rather than species-function, and enters into difficult reciprocal relationships rather than simply dominating and procreating. He is conceived not as a collective mass but as a single figure, an 'earth-human' or *'adam* moulded from the soil (*'adamah*), a cultivator of the land, for whom Jahweh creates in turn a garden, an obedience-test, a series of animal companions (whom *'adam* names) and finally—after the lack of human fellowship has been remarked upon several times—'a help [or adviser] corresponding to him'. He appears to be male, but the narrator—surprisingly, in a patriarchal culture—does not actually use the sexually differentiated term *'iš* (male) until after the creation of woman from his side, and after 'Adam' has recognized her as *'išša*, female.[7]

---

[6] Gerhard von Rad, *Genesis: A Commentary*, tr. John H. Marks (Philadelphia, 1961), p. 58.

[7] Cassuto, pp. 127, 171; Phyllis Trible, *God and the Rhetoric of Sexuality* (Philadelphia, 1978), ch. 4, esp. pp. 97–104. Trible points out that *'adam* can be interpreted differently at different stages of the narrative: humanity is first genderless, then reciprocally distinguished into equal sexes, and only later reduced to the state where 'human' and 'male' are considered synonymous. The narrator does, however, use *'adam* and *'iš* interchangeably at times, and 'taken from *'iš*' (2:23) does seem to indicate a temporal sequence in which the male existed prior to the creation of woman; Trible discovers a discontinuity between this verse and the rest of the narrative, as does Walter Brueggemann, 'Of the Same Flesh and Blood (Gn 2,23a)',

Adam receives his companion with a joyful recognition of identity; human language, hitherto confined to cataloguing animals, blossoms into erotic poetry:

> This, at last, is bone of my bone
> and flesh of my flesh.
> This shall be called 'female'
> because from 'male' was taken this.

Then he appears to merge his personality into hers. Though he is 'with her' in the adventure of the serpent (a detail suppressed by many translators and by virtually every commentator)[8] he makes no effort to assert authority or raise objections, but simply accepts the fruit from her hands. The serpent addresses woman in the plural, and she assumes without demur the role of spokeswoman and interpreter of the law. A difference in the moral capacities of man and woman is also suggested by the questions and answers at their trial. He is asked 'who told you that you were naked' and 'have you eaten the fruit', whereas she is required to define 'what' she has done; she categorizes the fall in moral and intellectual terms, admitting her mistake ('the serpent beguiled me'), while Adam describes it as mere action and thrusts away the blame—'the woman whom Thou gavest to be with me, she gave me fruit of the tree' (3:11-13). Adam and 'Eve' both have the child's unawareness of nakedness—not broken until both have eaten the fruit—but they resemble two different kinds of child, or perhaps two stages of childhood: they are somewhat like an articulate nine-year-old and her five-year-old brother, who can name objects and frame simple excuses.[9]

Catholic Biblical Quarterly, XXXII (1970), 538. I am grateful to Prof. Trible for this reference, and for many helpful comments. (For a detailed critique of Trible, see Mary Nyquist, 'Gynesis, Genesis, Exegesis: The Formation of Milton's Eve', forthcoming in a volume edited by Margaret Ferguson provisionally entitled *Re-membering Milton: New Essays on the Texts and the Traditions*: I am grateful to Prof. Nyquist for an earlier version of this paper, delivered at the English Institute in 1985.)

[8] McColley has nevertheless found several Renaissance commentators who assume that Adam was present during the temptation (p. 181 n. 1); Cassuto claims that 'with her' means 'associated in a venture with her' (p. 148).

[9] Adam and Eve were occasionally identified as children in earlier exegesis: cf. Irenaeus, *Adversus Haereses* II. xxii. 4; Norman P. Williams, *The Ideas of the Fall and of Original Sin* (1929), pp. 41-3, 193, 203; Cassuto, pp. 112-13. My interpretation of Eve's leadership and development obviously differs from the conventional view, which can be found even in the most persuasive radical critics of the Christian tradition; cf. Mary Nyquist, 'Reading the Fall: Discourse and Drama in *Paradise Lost*', *ELR* XIV (1984), 214 ('the devaluation of female speech that is inscribed in the

Otherwise we know little of their relationship. Woman, being created from living flesh rather than clay, is presumably a higher being than other creatures—she certainly proceeds from a higher level of skill in the artificer, since Adam and the animals were 'formed' and Eve 'built up'—and her leadership and intellectual ambition are obvious from her dealings with the serpent. Her role as 'help' suggests a higher being descending to rescue man from his predicament—those translators who later reduced Eve to a 'helpmeet' or assistant fail to recognize that the word *'ezer* (help) is most frequently applied to God, as in Psalm 70: 'Thou art my help and my deliverer.'[10] And yet there is insufficient evidence to say that woman is the superior, especially since her initiative leads to transgression; her only explicit identification is as a counterpart and help against loneliness. She is certainly not an inferior, however. There would be little point in announcing her subjection to her husband as a dire consequence of the fall—'your desire will be for your husband, and he will rule over you' (3:16)—if she were already a subordinate.

This much, then, can be conjectured about the human figures in the Eden myth. In one crucial area, however, the narrative is ambiguous, and the reader experiences, not the typical clarity and concreteness of fable, but vague apprehension. It is impossible to tell how far sexuality enters into the story, whether Adam and Eve had sexual intercourse before the fall, or whether the procreation first announced at 4:1 is part of the post-lapsarian curse. This uncertainty greatly troubled later commentators, for whom every nuance and omission in the text held vast implications for the human race. They claimed Genesis as an authoritative guide to

opening chapters of Genesis itself'). For other refs. to the Eve-myth as unequivocally misogynistic, cf. Jane Marcus, 'Still Practice, A/Wrested Alphabet: Towards a Feminist Aesthetic', *Tulsa Studies in Women's Literature*, III (1984), 83, and Hilda Smith, 'Feminism and the Methodology of Women's History', in Berenice A. Carroll (ed.), *Liberating Women's History* (Urbana, 1976), p. 377.

[10] Trible, p. 90; cf. the LXX *boēthos*, also used for divine redemption in cases (e.g. Exod. 15:2) where KJ does not use 'help' at all. Von Rad, however, clings to the identification of *'ezer* as 'assistant' (p. 80), as does Barth, whose entire existential analysis of these lines rests on the Pauline assumption that woman is 'for' the man exclusively (e.g. pp. 203, 301-9); for criticism of Barth, cf. F. Peczenik, 'Fit Help: The Egalitarian Marriage in *Paradise Lost*', *Mosaic*, XVII. i (Winter, 1984), esp. p. 47. Claus Westermann (*Genesis 1-11: A Commentary*, tr. John J. Scullion (1984), p. 227) shows that *'ezer* is normally applied to God and that the normal feminine form *'ezerah* is deliberately not used here, but elsewhere he falls into the standard Pauline/Barthian suprematism (e.g. p. 262).

sexual morality and the conduct of marriage; they actually found there a free play of powerful but contradictory suggestions.

The text itself encourages, then undermines, a sexual interpretation. 'They were naked' may be a euphemism for intercourse. Adam's joy at first meeting woman is followed by a comment linking their union to the later history of sexual bonding—'therefore a man leaves his father and mother, and cleaves to his woman, and they become one flesh' (2:24). (The translation of *'iššā* as 'wife' further ties this line to marriage, here apparently matrilocal.) The creation of Eve from Adam's side would thus be a mythical explanation of the strength of the erotic bond and its strange predominance over every other obligation—rather like the allegory of the divided protohumans in Plato's *Symposium*. But this verse, as a modern Hebraist points out, is an aetiological aside by the narrator rather than the words of God or Adam, as later translators have often made them. It is not clear what 'father and mother' could mean in the Garden of Eden, or, if the line is Adam's vision of the future, why sudden prescience should be granted here and not elsewhere. In normal Biblical usage, moreover, Adam's own words 'bone of my bones and flesh of my flesh' would suggest kinship rather than sexual union.[11] Another interpolated allusion to motherhood, indeed, suggests that sexuality was a post-lapsarian phenomenon. After the fall and the punishment, Adam renamed the woman Hawwah or Eve 'because she was the mother of all living' (3:20); this naturally implies that motherhood was unknown before.

Eve's punishment in 3:16 specifically focuses on reproduction: 'I will greatly multiply your suffering and your childbearing; in pain you will bring forth children, yet your desire will be for your husband.' But this still does not solve the problem of pre-lapsarian sexuality. Does it mean that her childbirths, like Adam's tillage, have hitherto been easy but must now become painful, or that now the whole agony of reproduction will be visited on her? The words themselves suggest the former, but neither intercourse nor offspring are mentioned in the text, and the beginning of the next chapter (if it belongs to this story at all) suggests that the first impregnation and childbirth were very memorable events: 'Now Adam knew Eve his wife, and she conceived and bore Cain, saying, I have created

[11] Cassuto, p. 135; for an interpretation that stresses covenantal loyalty rather than blood ties, cf. Brueggemann, pp. 532–42.

a man equally with the Lord' (Cassuto's version). Eve will experience 'desire' for her husband, which suggests that sexuality, like bodily shame, is something new. But this does not necessarily mean that she did not desire him before: she must now long for him despite the pains that will follow, and despite the 'rule' that he opposes to her love. (An alternative theory suggests that the Hebrew word means 'desire to dominate' rather than sexual desire.)[12] But whatever the precise reference, the obstetric focus of her punishment, like the institution of male circumcision in Genesis 17, does suggest some particularly intimate relation between sexuality and original sin.

The story of the forbidden tree is similarly ambiguous. Since the first mention of copulation in 4:1 uses the word 'know', it is natural to assume that the Tree of Knowledge whose fruit makes Adam and Eve know they are naked, and cover not their faces but their genitals, was in some way associated with sexuality. We feel, though we cannot prove, that the story conceals the traces of an extinct sexual religion, a worship of the mother and the serpent—the name 'Eve' contains shadows of both these significations.[13] Later in the

[12] Bruce Vawter, *On Genesis* (NY, 1977), pp. 84-5. Trible is on firmer ground when she points out that *tešuqa* ('desire') occurs only three times in the OT—here, in a very similar phrase about Cain's sin (4:7), and in the unmistakably erotic S. of S. 7: 10 (pp. 128, 159-60, 164 n. 18). Edmund Leach goes to the opposite extreme from Vawter: 'the latter part of iii.16 is later repeated exactly (iv.7), so Cain's sin was not only fratricide but also incestuous homosexuality' (*Genesis as Myth* (1969), p. 15). A useful perspective on this issue is provided in Joel W. Rosenberg, 'The Garden Story Forward and Backward: The non-narrative dimension of Genesis 2-3', *Prooftexts*, I (1981), p. 17.

The question remains whether 3:16 is a prescriptive punishment or a sorrowing description of the consequences of sin. Trible makes the important point that the Hebrew verb-form normally translated as 'shall' does not necessarily carry any sense of futurity or prescription—all depends on the context. Here, however, the context is clearly that of a legal trial, and the sentence of female subordination, though manifestly not a 'curse', is surely intended as a penalty for breaking the command. Westermann identifies the language of 3:16 as typical of legal sentences, then hastens to point out that Eve is subordinate both before and after her sentencing, and that woman always did and always will 'achieve the fulfilment of her being ... by belonging to her husband and being a mother'; he even toys with the idea that the second half of the verse, dictating husbandly rule, is a blessing rather than part of the punishment (pp. 261-3).

[13] Evidence for a 'depotentiated' sexual religion, and an Aramaic pun on 'snake', can be found in Williams, p. 41 n. 1, Cassuto, pp. 170-1, von Rad, p. 58 (though on p. 93 the snake-pun is dismissed as implausible); cf. also Joseph Coppens, 'La Dame-serpent du Sinaï', *Ephemerides Theologiae Lovanienses*, XXIV (1948), 409-11. John A. Phillips bases his *Eve: The History of an Idea* (San Francisco, 1984) on the thesis that Eve is a displaced goddess once worshipped as 'the mother of all living'.

Old Testament, serpents and whoredom are linked by association with false religion. The whole configuration of nakedness and transforming fruit has an erotic flavour, especially when read in conjunction with other narratives that were later combined into the book of Genesis: the discovery of the vine, in a chapter beginning with God's renewed injunction to 'increase and multiply', leads directly to the homosexual incest of Noah and Ham; an aphrodisiac plant plays an important part in the story of Leah and Rachel; wine makes possible the incest of Lot and his daughters.[14] But whether the fall refers to the discovery of sex, or to a transgression that spoiled their innocent sexuality, or whether their crime of disobedience is conceived as only *analogous* to sexual pollution, is difficult to determine. However strongly we sense a sexual core to the story—what Sartre would call a hairy mass[15]—it remains virtually impossible to resolve the details.

These dilemmas multiply when both 'Jahwist' and 'Priestly' versions are read as a single text. For if Adam and Eve *are* the species-couple made to 'increase and multiply', and if the anxious magician of the garden *is* the all-powerful creator of a 'very good' cosmos, then God must have either suspended His commandment and frozen the biological processes He had just created—whether by preventing copulation or by hindering conception—or else the whole story must have taken place in the few hours between creation and bedtime: human happiness, according to later orthodoxy, lasted only six hours. This cannot but appear, to our fallen minds, cruelly or absurdly short; the sequence of events is so rapid that we assume, by a sort of mental reflex, some causal connection between the creation of woman and the loss of innocence. The Jahwist story, which in itself enjoys the timelessness of the fable, thus falls into temporality, constrained by its Priestly neighbour.[16]

M is typically comprehensive; his Adam appears to know both etymologies, but only brings out the 'serpent' connection after he has fallen: 'Out of my sight, thou Serpent, that name best / Befits thee with him leagued' (*PL* X. 867-8).

[14] Gen. 9:1, 7, 20-5; 19:30-6; 30:14-17; Ham 'seeing his father's nakedness' is clearly a sexual euphemism—Noah himself 'knew what his youngest son had done to him'. The fruit of Gen. 2-3 was 'like clusters of the vine' according to 1 Enoch; cf. J. M. Evans, *Paradise Lost and the Genesis Tradition* (Oxford, 1968), p. 28.

[15] *Les Mots* (Paris, 1964), p. 41: 'sous la surface lumineuse de l'idée [of Love], je pressentais une masse velue.'

[16] For a subtle analysis of the time-scheme of Gen. 1-4, using Rashi's idea that 'knew' in 4:1 is a pluperfect, see Andrew Martin, *The Knowledge of Ignorance* (1985), pp. 20-1.

Subsequent accretions make increasingly greater demands. In time, the serpent-story came to be ranged among other aetiologies of trouble—the first murder, the sexual transgressions of Noah, Lot and the Sodomites, the failure of Babel. Above all it was combined, and later identified, with the episode that became the principal myth of the origin of Evil in pre-Christian times—the fatal coupling of male angels and female humans in Genesis 6:1-2.[17] This sexual fall in turn was juxtaposed, as if causally, with God's terrible repentence at having made man—'for the imagination of his heart is evil from his birth'—and His duplicate curse on the earth for man's sake. The ground is thus prepared for the idea of 'the Fall', a general catastrophe—dimly linked to sexual abomination—that swept over the human mind and body because of the transgression in the garden.

In general, however, the compilation of Genesis and its incorporation into the historical, poetic, and prophetic books threw little new light on the story of Adam and Eve, since most Old Testament writers were entirely unaware of Eden and its inhabitants. The only other episode set in Eden, Ezekiel 28:12-17, derives from an almost totally different version, where the garden is filled with jewels and fire, and the perfect man, somehow also identified with the cherub, is expelled for infatuation with his own beauty. These half-remembered myths of transgression were not thought to constitute a single, irreversible 'fall' that altered the human condition. Other Old Testament accretions, moreover, may even eliminate the original sin and reverse these suggestions of evil.

The blessing of 'increase and multiply', for example, is reiterated later in Genesis, and in the story of Noah is used to frame the moment when God gave permission to eat meat, thereby lifting the one restriction implied in the first chapter (8:17, 9:1, 9:7). The births of Cain and Seth are celebrated as equivalent to the divine creation, with no mention of pain or wifely subordination. Adam does not die on the day he disobeys, but lives almost a thousand years. The curse on the earth, redoubled in God's anger before the Flood, is withdrawn afterwards when His nostrils smell the pleasant savour of Noah's first sacrifice (though He still pronounces the human imagination constantly and unalterably evil); would not the other

---

[17] Cf. Williams, pp. 20-31, 77-8, 112-17, 121-2. The original reads only 'sons of God', but Cassuto clearly identifies this as a reference to angels, and the Greek codices Alexandrinus and Vaticanus read *aggeloi*.

curses on Adam and Eve be equally suspended in this covenant? The land of milk and honey redeems the loss of Eden. The unashamed eroticism of the Song of Songs, set in another garden of delight (the punning meaning of 'Eden'), seems to undo the bond of female desire and male possessive lordship established in Genesis 3:16; in a rare echo of the earlier text, Song of Songs 7: 10—'I am my lover's and for me is his desire'—inverts the very words of the sentence on Eve. The new covenant of Hosea exalts the erotic bond between God and humanity and abolishes the language of husbandly dominance.[18] And would not the advent of Christ—whom Paul identified as the second Adam come to undo the damage of the first—sweep away the Old Testament order in a general redemption?

[*ii*]

In the apocalyptic, Rabbinical, and philosophical writings of Judaism the Eden-myth takes on a new importance, but this promotion generates new problems of consistency and credibility. Fragments of the text, though never the complete story, are invested with deep moral and prophetic significance. The serpent, for example, turns into a vehicle of Satan, and, by fusion with the angelic copulations of Genesis 6, the transgression of Eve becomes a sexual seduction, as a result of which she conceived the evil seed of Cain and his descendants. Adam (in 4 Esdras) and 'woman' (in Ecclesiasticus) are now blamed as the source of a catastrophic and irreversible sin. This fall, 2 Baruch declares, brought pain, death, sexual desire, and 'the begetting of children' into the world, and is reiterated in every subsequent individual: 'each one of us has been the Adam of his own soul.'[19] The way is open for a redemptive 'second Adam' and 'second Eve', and for a psychological, inward application of the myth; the garden, in Beaumont's phrase, walks again in every reader.

In a more practical vein, the Rabbinical commentators converted the Genesis-myth into a school of marital relations and a fund of

[18] Trible (ch. 5) deals extensively with S. of S. as a return to the egalitarian and unembarrassed Eros forfeited by the fall (though 8:1–2 contains a hint of the shame that attends fallen sex); cf. Hos. 2:16–20.

[19] Graves, pp. 82–5; Williams, pp. 77–8; Evans, pp. 29–36. Another apocryphal text, the Armenian Book of Adam, shows how the psychologization of the Eden-myth could lead to a tender and domestic version of the fall that strikingly anticipates Milton (Graves, p. 77).

sexual lore. The creation of male and female together, and the subsequent building of Eve from Adam's side, led some rabbis to assert that the human form was originally a double hermaphrodite or 'androgyne' (the Greek loan-word suggests a Platonic origin for this idea). Others reduced the 'side' to a rib, and spun various meanings out of the operation—that 'death should come to man by his wife', that she should be modest and covered up rather than loud and mobile, or else that she would be stubborn as a bone, and a source of pain and revulsion to her husband. Her extraction was supposed to make her ancillary to Adam—quite illogically, since the same argument would make Adam subordinate to the earth from which *he* was made. Some commentators invent another consort for Adam, either before the creation of Eve or during the long period of abstinence before she is ready to procreate; this first spouse, Lilith, refused to accept a subordinate position in the household and in bed, and was therefore replaced by the more compliant Eve, but she still haunts the marriage-bed as a succubus, provoking nocturnal emissions and disasters in childbirth. It is also reported that Adam tested the animals by copulating with them as he named them.[20]

Other Rabbinical commentators stress the normal married life of our first parents. They describe the wedding in sumptuous detail, and insist that Adam and Eve did consummate their marriage on the first afternoon, and that the serpent grew jealous watching them make love. (In later Islamic legend this pre-Cainite conception was to produce a race of untainted humans from whom the Prophet descended.)[21] Others suppose that Adam was not present when the serpent spoke to Eve, having succumbed to post-coital slumber. She then gave Adam the fruit to prevent him from living happily with another wife. Others read into God's rebuke to Adam, 'you have heard the voice of your woman [rather than the voice of God]', a primal hierarchy in which Eve should have remained subordinate not to the Lord but to Adam. (The English translation, 'you have listened to the voice of your wife', is even more domestic.) Eve is sometimes assumed to be herself the serpent's mate or mirror-image (a fancy often depicted by later painters), or the archetype of the

[20] Graves, pp. 65-9; Evans, pp. 32, 43-5; Phillips, pp. 32, 43-50. For Adam's first spouse, Lilith, see also James Nohrnberg, *The Analogy of the Faerie Queene* (Princeton, 1976, corr. edn. 1980), pp. 228-39.

[21] Graves, pp. 86-7; Evans, pp. 45-6; Peter Lindenbaum, 'Love-making in Milton's Paradise', *MS* VI (1974), 302 n. 2.

dangerous temptresses denounced in Proverbs and in the Q'mran scrolls.[22]

More Hellenistic commentators like Philo assume that the entire story is allegorical, often drawing explicit analogies with philosophical myths such as those of Pandora, the Golden Age, the divided androgyne, or the birth of Eros in the garden of Zeus (the last two from Plato's *Symposium*). This mode of reading is suggested by the text itself, with its generic names and its trees of Knowledge and Life. Indeed, the whole Hebraic association of 'knowing' with sexuality could be interpreted in the light of Socratic Eros—the upward-tending Aphrodite Ouranos being the contemplative happiness of Adam, and the base Aphrodite Pandemos being the fall into physicality with Eve. And the Gnostics, who likewise could not see true knowledge as a curse, assume that the Serpent is the real divinity, and that 'Jahwe' is in fact the evil demiurge who seeks to trap humanity in the toils of materiality. For the allegorists, Eve represented the lower, sensual, or physical plane of existence, while for the Gnostics she is either the divine Wisdom who warns Adam to escape from Eden, or the demon who activates the most insidious of all the demiurge's snares—the urge to 'increase and multiply'.[23]

The text of Genesis is thus paradoxically fragmented and magnified, charged with a host of doctrinal and prophetic meanings. The process is intensified by occasional references in what would become the Christian New Testament—such as Christ's quotation of 'they become one flesh' to solve a marriage-dispute, or St. Paul's

[22] Graves, pp. 85-9 (p. 87 includes some practical hints for dealing with lustful serpents); Evans, pp. 48-50; Ecclus. 25; Roland M. Frye, *Milton's Imagery and the Visual Arts* (Princeton, 1978), pp. 103-5. A poem from Q'mran, cave 4, on display in the Dead Sea Scrolls Museum, Jerusalem, describes the female temptress in terms almost identical to Prov. 5-7 (I owe this reference to Carolyn Forché).

[23] Cf. Philo, *De Opificio Mundi* 76, *Quis Rerum Divinarum Haeres* 164 (*Philo*, Loeb edn., I and IV); Origen, *Contra Celsum* IV. 39-40 and *In Genesin* I. 15; Eusebius, *The Preparation of the Gospel*, ed. E. H. Gifford (Oxford, 1903), III. 632-4. For Gnostic and Manichaean interpretations of sexuality in Genesis, see Graves, p. 102; Irenaeus I. xxx; Bayle, 'Abelians', 'Cainites', and 'Manichees' B and D; A. V. Williams Jackson, *Researches in Manichaeanism* (NY,1932), pp. 248-9; Hans Jonas, *The Gnostic Religion*, 2nd edn. (Boston, 1963), pp. 204-5, 227-30; Elaine Pagels, *The Gnostic Gospels* (NY, 1979), pp. 54-6. The Gnostic Eve may sometimes be enlightened, self-sufficient, and creative, but she may also represent an extreme debasement and denial of the female; it is unwise to argue that Gnosticism represents a model of liberation in contrast to the rigid Pauline tradition (Christine Froula, 'When Eve Reads Milton: Undoing the Canonical Economy', in Robert von Hallberg (ed.), *Canons* (Chicago, 1984), pp. 149-75).

use of the same phrase to hint at the 'great mystery' of Christ and his church. Genesis must now announce the Messiah, expose the machinations of Satan, justify the subordination of women, channel the collective yearning for a vanished time of happiness, explain the origins of evil, and throw light into every corner of the human condition. In particular, it must be consulted in order to understand the *agon* of individuals with their God, and the struggle of 'one flesh' and divided spirits that raged between man and woman. A subtle but slender fable of the origin of domestic troubles now gasps under a gigantic weight.

[*iii*]

The earliest Christian writings clearly reflect and embody this glossolalia or proliferation of interpretations within Judaism. Christ, who seems quite unaware of the story or the concept of the fall, nevertheless retrieves a fragment of Genesis when confronted with the problem of divorce. Jude and the author of 2 Peter allude to the sexual fall of the angels in Genesis 6:1-2, as does St. Paul himself when he prescribes the veil for women 'because of the angels'. The Pauline epistles imply several times that Eve was sexually seduced, and that sin therefore came into the world through woman and not through man—though elsewhere Paul identifies Adam as the source of sin and death, a lone male counterpart to Christ the second Adam.[24] New Testament interpretations of Genesis are thus as varied and unsystematic as the Judaic beliefs they synthesize.

Christianity, of course, developed a system of Messianic and Scriptural authority to fix this fragmented, shifting field. When Christ or St. Paul adopt a particular line of the Old Testament they invest it with a double truthfulness. The scripture is now 'fulfilled'; old and new readings combine in a definitive trajectory, a fixed path directed towards a future state of salvation or damnation.

But Christ and Paul are themselves inconsistent in their interpretation of the lines most crucial to the understanding of sexuality. Christ proved by quoting Genesis 2:24 (transferring it in the process from Moses to God himself) that marriage was founded in Paradise, and should conform to the Paradisal ideal rather than to the hard-hearted Mosaic Law; but though he also uses 'Paradise' for

[24] Williams, pp. 114, 121-2.

the state of blessedness after death, he insists that 'in the resurrection they neither marry, nor are given in marriage, but are as the angels of God in heaven,' and he appears to praise those who 'have made themselves eunuchs for the kingdom of heaven's sake' (Matt. 22: 30, 19:12). (This in turn is offset by Hosea 2:19, 'I will marry thee unto me for ever', which flowered into the Marriage of the Lamb in Revelation.) St. Paul uses the same verse of Genesis ('they become one flesh') to express the *magnum mysterium* itself, the nuptial union of Christ and the Church (Eph. 5:31-2), but he also applies it to the crudest physical conjunction: 'know ye not that he which is joined to an harlot is one body? for two, saith he, shall be one flesh?' (1 Cor. 6:16) His attitude to marriage correspondingly varies between grudging contempt and fervent praise: marriage is sometimes a mere concession to physical desire, and sometimes a sanctified condition ('honourable in all, and the bed undefiled') in which husbands should love their wives 'even as Christ also loved the church', cherishing them as their own flesh. On the one hand he asserts that 'it is good for a man not to touch a woman'; on the other hand he claims the 'power to lead about a sister, a wife,' and lists 'forbidding to marry' among the 'doctrines of devils' — a text most memorably combined with God's original 'increase and multiply' in the great hymn to wedded love in *Paradise Lost*.[25]

The story of the fall, too, suggests different conclusions to Paul at different times. In Romans 5:12-19 and 1 Corinthians 15:21-2 sin and death came into the world through Adam alone, so that one man's transgression can be atoned by one man's sacrifice, but in 1 Timothy the blame seems to rest principally on Eve. In a curious blurring of fallen and unfallen features, this culpability of Eve is combined with her original creation to prove the necessity of 'subjection':

I suffer not the woman to teach, nor to usurp authority over the man, but to be in silence. For Adam was the first formed, then Eve. And Adam

[25] 1 Cor. 7:7, 9, 25; Heb. 13:4; Eph. 5:25, 28-9; 1 Cor. 7:1 and 9:5; 1 Tim. 4:1-3; *PL* IV. 748-9. Modern scholarship denies the Pauline authorship of Hebrews and ascribes Colossians, Ephesians, and 1 Timothy, all of which contain crucial pronouncements on sexuality and gender, to later followers (cf. Wayne A. Meeks (ed.), *The Writings of St. Paul* (NY, 1972)); during the period covered by this book, however, they were taken as the work of a single author, and I therefore discuss them in that light. Cf. also Elizabeth S. Fiorenza, *In Memory of Her* (NY, 1983), pp. 206-41 (ambiguities in Paul) and Milton, *Prose* II. 271 n. 5 (true reading of 'due benevolence').

was not seduced, but the woman being seduced was in the transgression. (2.11-14)

A similar interpretation of female aetiology leads him in 1 Corinthians 11 to demand the veil for women: 'the man is not of the woman, but the woman of the man; neither was the man created for the woman, but the woman for the man.' Here again Paul uses pre-lapsarian evidence to justify a condition explicitly imposed as a punishment after the fall. Woman is thus defined in terms of three passages in Genesis, but they have been interpreted in a strange and tendentious way: the 'image of God' is denied to her (woman is even called 'the image of man'), her raw material makes her secondary and derivative, her divine *'ezer* or 'help' is reduced to that of an assistant, and she represents a sexual danger 'because of the angels'.

Further implications of the creation-story tend to undermine this masculine-separatist reading, however. If Genesis teaches that the fleshly configuration of man and woman should determine their relationship, and that authority should depend on priority of generation, then all men apart from Adam should be subject to motherhood. So after the blame of woman in 1 Timothy Paul continues 'she shall be saved in childbearing' (2:15), and after the 'veil' passage in 1 Corinthians he offsets his own suprematism by pointing out that 'as the woman is of the man, even so is the man also by the woman' (11:12). Here he sways back towards the 'Biological' assumptions of Genesis 4 and 5, where childbirth is seen as 'creating a man equally with the Lord'.[26]

As the Pauline epistles came to represent the definitive key to Genesis, his suprematist prescriptions were enshrined at the heart of Christian doctrine and repeated in every marriage-service, while his self-qualifications went largely unheard. In one area, however, he did establish an egalitarian rather than a hierarchical model. In sexual relations Paul recommends a reciprocity of power and surrender entirely at odds with the subordination he calls for elsewhere:

let the husband render unto his wife due benevolence (*eunoia*), and likewise also the wife unto the husband. The wife hath not the power of her own

---

[26] Paul also abandons the hierarchic model when he contemplates regeneration and resurrection; cf. 1 Cor. 15:24, 2 Cor. 3:18.

body, but the husband: and likewise also the husband hath not power of his own body, but the wife (1 Cor. 7:3-4).

It is ironic that Paul should dissolve his usual suprematism in an area—procreation and childbirth—specifically linked to subordination by the punishment of Eve in Genesis. We can perhaps attribute this to the influence of the Song of Songs. In Ephesians Paul drew on the allegorical interpretation of the Song to grasp the meaning of 'one flesh', and derived from this union of Solomon and Genesis a vision of hierarchical love that he applied both to Christ and to the husband. Here he makes the same equation, but on the literal level, and his reading is astonishingly egalitarian. In love-making man and woman regain an erotic mutuality that reverses the fall: 'my lover is mine and I am his . . . I am my lover's and his desire is for me.'

In the supreme authorities of Christianity, then, the story of Adam and Eve could support strikingly different valuations of marriage, and remarkably varied ideas of the proper distribution of power between man and woman. St. Paul's remarks on 'one flesh' and 'due benevolence', in particular, allowed Christians to see the marriage-bed as an autonomous realm, where a mysterious mutual blending replaced the strict hierarchy normally required in the household. And yet the same authority interpreted 'one flesh' as an ignominious pollution, and marriage as a sordid 'burning'.

2. Eros, reason, and imagination: the exegetical dilemma

In early Christian writings a fissured text combines with a fragmented and intuitive hermeneutic. But the theologians of the early Church could not be satisfied with inspirational randomness; their debates, commentaries, and '*enarrationes*' aimed to produce a consistent Scripture and a unified scheme of salvation. The Word cannot contradict itself and cannot speak in vain. Every detail of the Eden-story was now construed as an explanation of evil or a glimpse of 'Paradise', the transcendent and consummatory state to which all human concerns must lead. The remoteness and internal contradiction of the text must now be read as a deliberate stratagem, God's own way of stimulating the pursuit of truth. This view was held not only by occultists and allegorists, but by those who, like Augustine, gradually came to accept a concrete and literal interpretation, constrained by logic, natural probability, and formal realism.[27]

A great deal therefore hinges on the narrative problem of pre-lapsarian intercourse—a problem created by the necessity of reading the original cluster of myths as a single commanding voice. It will be useful to restate it as clearly as possible, then. If Adam and Eve consummated their marriage before the fall, why was there no conception? If they did not, what was the reason?

Explanations are of three kinds. The Gnostics assumed that 'increase and multiply' is a snare set by the evil demiurge; humanity can only regain its true nature by expunging the material world, whether by extreme asceticism or by intense sexual activity of a non-reproductive kind.[28] Orthodox Christianity provided two theories. Either man is properly an asexual being, and originally would have fulfilled the commandment to 'increase and multiply', if at all, by some non-genital means that we can no longer imagine—though the 'overshadowing' of the Virgin Mary by the archangel gives us a faint hint; according to this school, the creation of 'male and female' was a touching foresight on God's part, who knew that after forfeiting immortality Adam and Eve would need organs of generation. Or else man would have propagated by the normal means if the fall had not come so suddenly. It may have seemed cruel and absurd that the six days' work was destroyed in a few hours, or that the fall follows the creation of Eve almost immediately, but it was still easier to accept these difficulties than to explain why, after a longer stay, Adam would not have known his wife nor she have conceived.

Augustine, for example, as he shook off the influence of Manichaean antiphysicality and Platonist allegory, became convinced that genital intercourse and physical procreation had been intended from the start. He points out that a woman could not possibly have provided companionship or practical help for Adam, and that Eve must therefore have been created exclusively for child-rearing; and since the whole body will be saved in the resurrection, the sexual apparatus must have been included in God's design. Why, then, was it not set in motion by the command to 'increase and multiply'? Augustine offers two reasons. Adam

---

[27] *CG* XI. 19; for Aug.'s gradual assumption of a literal reading of sexuality in Gen., see Agaësse II. 516–21.

[28] Bayle, 'Manichees' B; Jonas, pp. 227–30, 271–4.

and Eve were probably waiting for an explicit and less general command—an easy task when the genitals were still entirely in the control of the will, moved as easily as we move our fingers. And in any case the fall came 'as soon as the woman was created', so they would not have had time to make love.[29]

For the majority who follow Augustine, in fact, the question of sexuality provided conclusive evidence for the brevity of the time of innocence: as one seventeenth-century commentator explained, 'it must necessarily be granted that Adam fell before ever he knew his wife, otherwise Cain had been conceived without sinne, because presently after the Man and Woman were made, God said, *Increase and multiplie*'—the fall therefore took place on the same day that man was created (22 April). This 'necessary' consensus was ready to break apart, however. A few years later, the same writer decided that such a rapid fall was impossible, since God pronounced the whole creation 'exceedingly good' at the close of the sixth day. The matter is thus left suspended between two equal but opposite certainties.[30]

We see, then, that the problem of Edenic sexuality precipitated the 'fall into time', and exposed the limits of a rationalistic hermeneutic. Mainstream commentators of the seventeenth century were unwilling to imagine a sexless humanity, but not yet ready to make this reluctance the basis for a kind of erotic ontogeny, as Milton did and as Barth was later to do. Nor could they accept the possibility of pre-lapsarian intercourse; the doctrine of Original Sin apparently meant that Cain, the first-born, was conceived after the entrance of evil. They were thus forced to fall back on one of two absurdities—an almost instantaneous fall, or an Eden of perpetual virginity. Bayle's synthesis of this exegetic tradition, as we have seen, led him to the same aporia. In a secular mood he proclaims that sexual passion is entirely natural and beneficial to mankind, and pours scorn on Augustine's bizarre theories of Adamic copulation; but he cannot modify his interpretation of Genesis accordingly. He sees 'very strong Objections' to the theory of a rapid fall, but the logical, emotional, and narrative problems of ascribing a sexual life to the unfallen Adam and Eve, thus reconciling the biological and the theological as far as possible,

[29] *De Genesi ad Litteram* IX *passim* (e.g. iv. 8, vii. 12); cf. 2. 1. ii below.
[30] John Swan, *Speculum Mundi* (Cambridge, 1635; 2nd edn., 1644), p. 497; (4th edn., 1670), pp. 455–6.

are insurmountable for him; the great spokesman of Protestant rationalism is thus forced to accept either that the fall was virtually instantaneous, or that virginity is the natural condition of man ('Abel' A). The 'hairy mass' of Genesis does not tempt him: he remains absolutely opposed to the one move that would dissolve his *reductio ad absurdum*—the admission of normal sexuality into the unfallen state ('Eve' B). This would be a surrender to Rabbinical fantasy, to private dreaming, to 'Imagination'.

The first three chapters of Genesis thus become a place not only for the struggle between innocence and experience, or between conflicting 'Priestly' and 'Jahwist' texts, but also for the conflict of reason, imagination, passion, and faith. Bayle pretends to operate within the normal ground-rules of exegesis, defending faith and 'casting down imaginations' by rational analysis of the text. Biblical theology assumes at least a working relation between reason, faith, and emotion, since the heart as well as the head must be schooled to receive grace—and it is also surprisingly dependent, as we shall see, on bare words and evil imagination. Bayle's remarks on Paradisal sexuality, however, effectively deconstruct the whole enterprise by refusing to accept any connection between these four epistemological realms. Augustine, the major architect of their synthesis, is dismissed as a lunatic and a dreamer. Bayle knew Milton only as a writer of republican prose; if he had read *Paradise Lost*, where the first couple live for weeks in Paradise enjoying full sexual intercourse without pregnancy, he would surely have been horrified.[31]

Bayle's rationalism may be destructively exaggerated, but his positions are themselves quite orthodox. The exegetical consensus did indeed believe that consummation only happened after the expulsion, that the fall came within a few hours of the creation of woman, and that Satan assailed a weaker and subordinate Eve during a period of separation from Adam. How could these improbable opinions, unfounded in the text and incompatible with each other, gain such assent? Clearly the extreme gullibility of the commentators, in matters that discredit woman, must be part of the explanation. But we should relate this to an underlying fear of indeterminacy, and a deep uncertainty about the value of imagination and emotion, particularly sexual passion.

[31] 'Augustine' G; despite 'Milton' G, where he notes that M's epic was held in such high esteem that Dryden made a play from it, Bayle had clearly not read *PL*.

[*ii*]

Whatever the level of irony in Bayle's rationalistic orthodoxy, there can be no doubt that he genuinely loathed emotional and visionary hermeneutics; Protestant iconophobia combines with the scepticism common in generations that follow persecution and religious war. He draws on a long-established suspicion of the 'evil imagination' or 'heart's cogitation' denounced in Genesis, the 'abomination of fiction' (in Boehme's phrase) that led man to disbelieve God's prohibition, and the rebellion of passion that made Adam and Eve rush to hide their genitals. These disreputable faculties must at every turn be quelled by the forces of truth—the privileged combination of human reason and divine revelation. In the attempt to discover the primordial status of sexuality, however, both these authorities led to bewilderment and contradiction. And the major exegetes themselves, even those who most vividly evoke the anxious state of indeterminacy and confusion, turn for hermeneutic redemption to precisely those scandalous subrational modes— emotion, imagination, and Eros. In so doing, they bring exegesis closer to art. I hesitate to invoke the vocabulary of deconstruction, but in this case the exegetic tradition does seem to dethrone or subvert its own hierarchy of values.

The exegetes at times explicitly declared their concern, not only with intellectual questions of content and consistency, but with the psychology of response, with the interpreter's own 'mood' and 'emotion', with the capacities and limits of imagination, and with the problems of finding adequate language—all concerns shared by the artist. St. Ambrose, for example, evokes the seething agitation (*aestus*) excited by the prospect of investigating and explaining Paradise.[32] Genesis was received as the rhetoric of God, inscribing dread and desire upon the human heart; and emotional persuasion, of course, was considered an essential function of both rhetoric and poetry.

It is in Augustine that we see most clearly the emotive and speculative core of exegesis. At a poignant moment in the *Confessions*—used as the epigraph to this chapter—he grieves over the task of understanding the first lines of Genesis; the intellect soon fails him, and he longs to be able to 'hold' the vanished Moses and entreat him to reveal the truth. But even as he mourns the departure

---

[32] *De Paradiso* I. i: he goes on to compare the desire to know what Paradise was like to the rapture of St. Paul in 2 Cor. 11.

of authoritative truth, Augustine feels a new certainty imparted by grace, an internal and emotional apprehension of the text, independent of reason and almost of language itself: 'for within me, within me there is a truth, not Hebrew, not Greek, not Latin, not barbarous; which without organs, without noyse of Syllables, tels me true, and would enable me to say confidently to Moses, *Thou say'st true.*' (Donne, a poet-exegete like Luther and Milton, attached great importance to this episode, and it is his translation I quote; he praised Augustine's ability to make exegesis 'liquid and pervious', and made his own words correspondingly lyrical.) The experience of understanding Genesis, for Augustine, is a dialogue between the emotion 'within' the reader and the truth concealed in the text; the deep calls to the deep.[33] A cryptic, contradictory, and yet all-inclusive Scripture necessarily stimulates the pursuit of truth, and when he himself faces the challenge of pre-lapsarian sexuality, he proclaims his conjecture to be at full stretch (*CG* XIV. 26, XXII. 21). This response springs not from some cerebral detective faculty, but from the 'deep desire' that Henry More would later call 'the deepest act, / The very selfhood of the soul' (ch. 2 n. 80).

As Augustine explains in his *enarrationes* of the Psalms, this internal capacity which lets us 'hold' the otherwise inaccessible truths of the divine world proceeds not from reason but from love: 'thy affections are the steps, thy will the way; by loving thou mountest, by neglect thou descendest.' Passion and sensuousness play an important part in this ascent. Though they should not be 'enjoyed' (*fruitus*) or loved for their own sake, they should be 'used' (*usus*) or loved as a vehicle for apprehending the deity; thus 'by means of what is material and temporary, we may lay hold on that which is spiritual and eternal.' Earthly experience is made transitive, but it is not abandoned: 'to every one converted to God, his delights and pleasures are ... not withdrawn, but are changed.'[34] In Augustine's Christianization of Platonic Eros, the love-impulse is a force at once erotic, hermeneutic, and ontological. He thus manifests the general contradiction or paradox that would later be crystallized in Pascal's opposition of *la raison* and *le coeur*: Christianity officially subscribes to the hierarchy of reason over passion, but it apprehends its deepest truths in emotion.

---

[33] *Conf.* XI. ii. 5 (and cf. *CG* XI. 19); Donne, *Essays in Divinity* ed. Evelyn M. Simpson (Oxford, 1952), pp. 15–16; *Sermons*, X. 350–2.

[34] *Enarrationes in Psalmos* LXXXV. 6; *De Doctrina Christiana* I. iv. 4; cf. H. A. Deane, *The Political and Social Ideas of St. Augustine* (NY, 1963), pp. 264–5, nn. 5 and 11.

[*iii*]

There is an obvious sense in which Genesis is not art, and the exposition of Genesis, with its second-order status and didactic intention, would appear to be even further from the aesthetic condition. Nevertheless, commentary borders on literature, not only in its concern with emotional response and rhetorical persuasion, but in its verbal and psychological inventiveness. Luther may lament the inadequacy of 'bare words', but this does not prevent him (and countless others) from expanding the spare lines of Genesis into dramatic scenes, and subjecting the characters to close psychological analysis, often inventing motives and sometimes transcribing them back into the text; the dialogue of Eve and the serpent was a particularly fruitful ground for malicious embroidery.[35] The very title of Augustine's *Enarrationes* on the Psalms, or Luther's on Genesis, suggests that interpretation is a 'telling out' of cryptic truths.

Thus the artist and the exegete, however different their projects, may share a concern with passion, invention, and psychological realism. But art itself may also serve as a model for the interpreter. For Augustine, understanding God's plan means learning to read it as a supreme work of art: he defines the ultimate joys of heaven as aesthetic transformations of erotic delights, as we shall see in the next chapter, and he attempts to reinterpret human history itself, from God's point of view, as an artistic arrangement, with evil providing 'the kind of antithesis which gives beauty to a poem'. The communication of God and man may be conceived as a kind of elevation to artistic inspiration, particularly in the state of original perfection. Thus Luther, himself a sublime hymnodist as well as a commentator, conjectured rather wistfully that every one of us in the unfallen state could have composed hymns even loftier than the 148th Psalm; these powers have been replaced by the 'evil imagination' of fallen man, but in rare cases of inspiration this corruption can be suspended, and God's own imagination may flow through the fortunate author.[36] Luther could not—within his own terms—have denied Milton's own claim to divine inspiration, had he been able to hear the morning-hymn of Adam and Eve in

---

[35] Cf. Luther, I. 61, Calvin, I. 148-51; both Calvin and Luther (I. 155) suspend their usual scrupulous Hebraic scholarship and accept the Vulgate reading of Gen. 3:3, which has Eve soften the prohibition by adding 'perhaps'. On this tendency in the commentators, cf. also Nyquist, pp. 216-17.

[36] Aug., *CG* XI. 18; Luther, I. 105, II. 123.

the fifth book of *Paradise Lost*, a sumptuous expansion of precisely the Psalm that Luther had chosen for his conjecture. One poet-exegete fulfils the speculation made by another, not by added speculation, but by the practice of his art. The artistic achievement of primeval humanity, manifested in Adam's first outpouring of love for Eve, could thus become a model for the highest pitch of interpretation.[37]

Throughout the history of interpretation, then, we find an alternative value-system which erodes, though it could not displace, the pessimistic doctrine of the evil imagination. To one who views the Christian tradition from the outside, as I do, the whole edifice is of course one supreme fiction; but the builders of that edifice themselves defined imagination in many different ways, some to be welcomed and some rejected. It was seen sometimes as a combinatory mechanism and sometimes as a creative capacity, sometimes as a subordinate 'fancy' but sometimes as the 'cogitation of the heart' that brings humanity closest to God. The Hebrew word translated as 'imagination' denotes not mere fantasy but the entire 'impulse', 'resolution', or 'fashioning' of the human spirit, including the reproductive urge and the constructive arts: thus Rabbinical commentators could arrive at the paradox that 'the evil imagination is good, for without it man would not build a house, nor marry, nor beget children' (nor, we might add, compose arduous commentaries and Biblical epics).[38] Luther perhaps recognizes this when he translates the word as 'Dichten', which includes the positive idea of poetic creation; following Luther word for word, Tyndale then introduces 'imagination' into the English text. The term was both complimentary and pejorative: each good meaning was attended by its evil twin, at best an 'airy nothing' or empty fiction, at worst delusive, idolatrous, and Satanic—hence the Protestant zeal for 'casting down imaginations' (2 Cor. 10:5).

[37] Some examples of Adam and Eve's work apparently survived: in the 3rd century AD Jehoshua ben Levi saw some red and purple cloths woven by Eve (Graves, pp. 71-2); two of Adam's writings are reprinted in Johannes Eusebius Nierembergus, *De Origine Sacrae Scripturae* (Leiden, 1641), pp. 46-8. Bayle ('Adam' K) suggests that Nierembergus believed completely in Adam's authorship of these pieces, but p. 49 shows him to have some reservations. Ps. 91 was also ascribed to Adam, according to Bayle's source (Gaspar Schottus, *Technica Curiosa* (Nuremberg, 1664), p. 556), and Jonson's Sir Epicure Mammon owned 'a treatise penn'd by Adam' (*Alchemist* II. i. 85-6).

[38] Cf. Williams, pp. 59-67; the LXX, followed by the Vulgate, translated the Hebrew as 'the thoughts of the heart', and St. Paul in 2 Cor. 10:5 wrote of casting down 'reasonings' (*logismoi*).

Even if thought itself, now converted into 'Dichten' or 'imagination', continued to be condemned by Genesis, this was undermined by the growing Renaissance faith in art. The Protestant Sidney, for example, explicitly invokes Genesis to justify his high claims for creativity. Only in poetry, 'the highest point of man's wit', does humanity retain the divine creative power originally given in Paradise. This evidence of man's continued unfallen powers, Sidney continues, will convince 'the incredulous' that man is indeed fallen, since in witnessing the golden world of the poet a gulf will inevitably open between the 'erected wit', that 'maketh us know what perfection is', and the will 'infected' by the fall of Adam.[39] The thesis of a catastrophic fall is thus validated by what appears to disprove it—Donne's paradox again. Art here subsumes the functions of exegesis, and converts the pessimistic inheritance into an affirmation of the power and autonomy of creative 'wit', making it the equivalent of the Paradisal state itself.

But the affinity of art and exegesis consists as much in shared problems as in shared procedures of illumination. The text of Genesis itself exacerbates these problems, and as it were hinders its own realization. Pre-lapsarian sexuality is only one of many cruxes. The extreme simplicity of the original story makes it difficult to 'tell out' without importing anachronistic assumptions. Explicating God's motives, bringing them into the realm of realism, may make them seem more dubious.[40] The innocence of Adam and Eve is a fragile state, moreover, and one not likely to be strengthened by exploration. Ordinary humanity cannot look at Adam and Eve as they first looked at each other, naked and unashamed—or rather, neither naked nor clothed, since this opposition of concepts did not yet even exist. Artistic representation

---

[39] *An Apology for Poetry*, ed. Geoffrey Shepherd (1965), p. 101 (and cf. p. 159 for parallels in Calvin). The preface to Loredano's *L'Adamo* (ch. 7 n. 26 below) carries this notion a stage further: '*Adam*, in my opinion, will receive no lesse grace from these lines, than from the ruddy earth of which he was formed; yea, so much the greater, inasmuch as then he was a sinner and mortall, and here he is revived, sanctifyed and immortall' (f. A3v).

[40] The Jahwist God, for example, expels Adam and Eve because of an understandable concern for security; if they were to eat the Tree of Life they would indeed become formidable rivals, since His principal sanction would be dissolved by their new-found immortality. Later commentators including Calvin (3:22) and M (*PL* XI. 84-97, V. 735-6), believing that an omnipotent deity could not really fear such a move, make him speak these lines in derision; one human feature is thus removed, only to be replaced by a less creditable one—and the expulsion is still not accounted for (for a demurral, cf. ch. 4 n. 33 below).

1. Jan Sadelaer I after Martin de Vos, *Genesis 2* (detail), London, British Museum

2. Id., San Marino, California, Huntington Library (Kitto Bible)

may itself impose a fallen consciousness, reducing every Paradise-scene to an expulsion; the visual artist—or the owner of the work, as in Fig. 2—may be forced to supply premature figleaves, and thereby negate the very act of representing the unfallen state. And Edenic innocence is no less vulnerable to the resources of serious literature, which has always been concerned with knowledge of good and evil, the opening of the eyes, the transformation of the mind through new concepts and new experience. When God asks Adam 'who told you you were naked?' He appears to assume that some voice, some authority, could have shattered his innocence simply by *telling*.

We will encounter this pessimistic current at many points in the following study, but it will not have the last word. I will trace, not merely the chronological sequence of interpretations, but the recurrent attempt to breach the 'barricades' and 'force through the fire-sword' to repossess the garden. My analyses of Milton himself and his predecessors, of Augustine and Luther, the Spiritual Libertines, the Adamites and Ranters, Boehme and van Helmont, pay tribute to the perverse but enduring vitality of human inventiveness, which grants a kind of fictive restitution even to those thinkers whose theology would not allow it.

Sometimes, of course, this ingenuity creates obstacles as well as dissolving them: my prime example is the collective delusion of male primacy, which ignores the supposed inconceivability of Eden, and rashly mingles 'unfallen' and 'fallen' evidence, in its desire to prove that Eve was subordinate from the first (chapter 3, *passim*). The barricade is thrown down, only to be replaced by a Priapus. But many interpreters did overcome such obstacles and realize, at least in some proportion, their 'dream of other worlds'. And in some cases creative interpretation combines with scepticism or political militancy to generate resisting readers—like those feminists who challenged the subordinationist reading, or like Winstanley and Beverland, who were so troubled by the inconsistencies of Genesis that they refused to accept the unity and authenticity of the text, or like Milton himself, who attempts to demolish Christ's teaching on divorce in the light of a radical new interpretation of Genesis, and who violates the universal consensus of the commentators, not to mention the laws of biological probability, when he gives Adam and Eve a full but infertile sexual life in Paradise.

2
The Incorporation of Eros

SEXUALITY AND THE SEARCH FOR PARADISE IN AUGUSTINE, THE REFORMATION, AND THE ENGLISH REVOLUTION

> into their inmost bower
> Handed they went, and eas'd the putting off
> Those troublesom disguises which wee wear,
> Strait side by side were laid, nor turnd I ween
> *Adam* from his fair Spouse, nor *Eve* the Rites
> Mysterious of connubial Love refus'd:
> Whatever Hypocrites austerely talk
> Of puritie and place and innocence,
> Defaming as impure what God declares
> Pure, and commands to som, leaves free to all.
> Our maker bids increase; who bids abstain
> But our Destroyer, foe to God and Man?
> Hail wedded Love, mysterious Law, true source
> Of human offspring, sole proprietie
> In Paradise of all things common else....
> Farr be it, that I should write thee sin or blame,
> Or think thee unbefitting holiest place,
> Perpetual Fountain of Domestic sweets,
> Whose bed is undefil'd and chast pronounc't,
> Present, or past, as Saints and Patriarchs us'd.
> Here Love his golden shafts imploies, here lights
> His constant Lamp, and waves his purple wings,
> Reigns here and revels.
> (*PL* IV. 738-52, 758-65)

Montaigne was perhaps unkind to compare the exegete to a silkworm, incessantly obscuring the text he hopes to clarify with a tissue spun from his own bowels.[1] The greatest interpreters went beyond rationalistic pedantry to the emotional and existential core of the text. Commentary also seeks to emulate the splendour of the creation 'at least in some proportion', to redeem the 'evil

[1] *Essais*, III. 13; *Complete Essays*, tr. Donald M. Frame (Stanford, 1958), p. 817.

2. The Incorporation of Eros

imagination' by inspired conjecture, to bring the reader to the gates of Paradise. For Sidney it is the artist, and not the philosopher or the historian, who simultaneously demonstrates and transcends the fall by creating a golden world beyond the reach of the 'infected will'. By filling the text with redemptive possibilities, and reconstructing a pre-lapsarian happiness whose traces can still be felt in fallen sexuality, the exegetes pursue the same aspiration.

Thus 'every commentator', as Voltaire said perhaps more wisely than he knew, 'makes his own Eden'.[2] The myth of the garden does not remain a simple fable, but 'walks' restlessly through the minds of successive interpreters, provoking increasingly complex and fertile analysis. The theme of Paradisal sexuality in particular, associated in some obscure but powerful way both with God's supreme blessing and with the most terrible transgression, comes to inspire intense speculation and anguished scrutiny of fallen experience. As forbidden lust or 'carnal knowledge', the sexual drive could be virtually equated with the fall itself, and with the 'evil imagination' punished by the flood; but as divine Eros or Wedded Love it could be the 'perpetual fountain' of God's continued favour, itself able, as Raphael puts it in *Paradise Lost*, to 'refine / The thoughts' and serve as 'the scale / By which to heavenly love [we] may ascend'.[3]

The possibilities of such a fusion of divine Logos and earthly Eros are latent in the original text, but obscured by ominous associations: sexual procreation is blessed in Genesis 1:28, and equated with 'knowing' in 4:1, but in between falls the grim possibility that such 'knowledge' might be the fruit of disobedience and death. During the course of interpretative history, however, the Paradise-myth had been woven into a network of association with the founding texts of the literature of Eros, the Song of Songs, and Plato's *Symposium*. The Song was read as an analogue of Paradise, while Classical literature was believed to have descended in garbled form from the mouth of Adam himself, and gaps in the Genesis-narrative could therefore be filled with the poetic myths of Greece and Rome.[4] Once Adam is established as the original

---

[2] *Dictionnaire philosophique*, 'Genesis'.

[3] VIII. 589–92; cf. *Symposium* 211C, and cf. 7. 2. iii below.

[4] For this idea in Origen and Eusebius, see ch. 1 n. 23 above: Calvin also believed it, and compared the rib-story to Plato (2:24), the fall to the Titans, and the punishment to Prometheus (I. 153, 177). The use of the Greek loan-word 'androgyne' in Rabbinical Hebrew suggests that the debt is actually the other way round.

transmitter of Plato's erotic myths—the Garden of Zeus and the primal hermaphrodite—then Eros itself, the upward-seeking fusion of desire and knowledge, becomes a vehicle for the recovery of Paradise; this is the central principle of Augustine's theology and the driving force of his commentary on Genesis. The way was thus opened to a kind of Christian eroticism, applied either to the joys of holy matrimony, or to the mystic rapture of the Spiritual Libertines and Ranters, at once ascetic and orgiastic.

The relation between Christian visions of sexuality (whether unfallen, fallen, or resurrected) and Platonic Eros is an uneasy one, however. It is not simply that Christian exegetes were uncertain how far to assimilate pagan philosophy and Greek homosexuality into their religion, nor that Platonism itself is inconsistent in its attitude towards gender and the flesh. What confused the theologians, and inhibited the emergence of an erotic-ontological world view, was a larger uncertainty. How did normal human sexuality relate to divine love? How far could the physical world, and the praxis of daily life, be immanent with Godhead?

1. 'A kind of imbracing': Augustine's reconstruction of Paradisal sexuality

The most influential attempt to solve the contradictions in the first chapters of Genesis, and to evolve from them a Christianized theory of Eros, is that of St. Augustine. In his first commentaries on Genesis he did not face the problem, since he still held to the allegorical reading. But in later treatises (*De Genesi ad Litteram*, *De Nuptiis et Concupiscentia*, and above all *The City of God*) he attempted to rehabilitate the literal, physical meaning of the fall-story; only by understanding the bodies of Adam and Eve, and the 'important and knotty problem' of unfallen sexuality, could one begin to grasp the *magnum mysterium* itself—the resurrection of the flesh.[5] And if 'increase and multiply' revealed the kind of sexuality that unfallen humanity would have enjoyed, a prefiguration of heavenly bliss, then the fall itself, with its sudden impulse of genital shame, could help to explain the 'lust' that had bedevilled Augustine's own pre-Christian life.

[5] *CG* XIV. 1, XXII. 21, and cf. ch. 1 n. 27 above. The resurrected body will be finer than the original state of perfection in the same ratio as the Paradisal state was finer than fallen misery; the pre-lapsarian body is thus an indispensable middle term in the process of imagining future bliss.

2. The Incorporation of Eros

Augustine's emphasis on sexuality reflects and intensifies the paradoxical Christian attitude to the flesh. He appears to hate the normal processes of sexual intercourse, especially the penile erection and the 'almost total extinction of mental alertness' during orgasm (*CG* XIV. 16), and yet he would not abandon the search for the paradisal state of 'one flesh'—promised to Adam and Eve, but forfeited by sin—in which erotic delight and conscious piety would have been combined. Edenic sexuality may never be experienced directly, but it is the closest analogy to the 'love' that should motivate all Christian activity. When he imagines the embraces of God, for example, Augustine explicitly 'lays hold on' transcendent emotion by means of the sensory delights, with sexuality conspicuously at their head:

When I love thee, what kind of thing is it that I love? Not the beauty of bodyes, not the order of tyme; not the cleernes of this light which our eyes are so glad to see; not the harmony of sweet tongues in Musique; not the fragrancy of flowres, and other unctuous and aromatical odours; not Manna, nor any thing of sweet and curious tast; not carnall creatures which may delightfuly be imbraced by flesh and blood.... And yet I love a kind of *Light*, a kind of *voyce*, a kind of *odour*, a kind of *food*, and a kind of *imbracing*, when I love my God: the *light*, the *voyce*, the *odour*, the *food*, and the *imbracing* of my inward man.[6]

This beautiful passage, which Milton was later to imitate in Eve's outpouring of love for Adam, depends on the apprehension of heavenly love as a 'kind of' earthly sexuality. And when God in turn replies, He does so by implanting 'a new desire driving out the old, by Caritas overcoming Cupiditas; the sweetness of pleasure must be vanquished by something yet sweeter.' Indeed, 'the love of things temporal would not be expelled but by some sweetness of things eternal.'[7]

Augustine accepts Plato's law that 'as a man's desires tend, [so] does every one of us come to be,' and makes desire the central constitutive element of the individual, as Spinoza and Freud were later to do. He also assumes, like many of the speakers in Plato's *Symposium*, that human desire is analogous or even identical to

---

[6] *Conf.* X. vi. 8, quot. here from an anonymous tr. of 1620; for 'laying hold', see ch. 1 n. 34 above.

[7] Anders Nygren, *Agapē and Eros*, tr. Philip S. Watson (1953), p. 521, summarizing *Conf.* IX. i. 1; Aug., *De Mus.* IV. 18. See Nygren, pp. 520-40 for a fuller account of Aug.'s theory of love.

the great forces of the cosmos: 'fire tends upward, a stone tends downward; they are propelled by their own mass, they seek their own places.... My weight is my love.' And he evolves his own version of the Platonic dichotomy of downward- and upward-oriented Eros: all desires that ascend in stages to God are *caritas*, while all desires for earthly things are *libido* or *concupiscentia*, and lead only to embrutement and imprisonment.[8] The essence of things is their vector. All human phenomena exist in two forms, one directed towards man, the other towards God, and all can be comprised under the category of Love. 'The properly directed will is good love, the misdirected will is bad love: *recta voluntas est bonus amor et voluntas perversa malus amor.*' This is precisely the dichotomy of Socratic love transferred to Christian divinity—the 'right' way leading upward to the celestial Aphrodite, the wrong way leading out into the milling crowds of the City of Man, the realm of Aphrodite Pandemos.

But Augustine cannot simply equate Platonic Eros and Christian love. Christ himself spoke of 'one flesh' as a real conjunction of bodies, and promised that in the resurrection 'not a hair of your head shall perish'—words which Augustine repeatedly interprets to mean that, apart from repairing genetic defects, accidents and old age, Christ will restore our bodies completely as they are; the command to 'increase and multiply' shows that sexuality cannot be considered an accident or defect (*CG* XIII. 20, XXII. 12, 14, 15). This theology of the flesh, Augustine points out, goes far beyond any Platonic apotheosis of the soul alone. And he insists that, even in the fallen state, 'flesh' and 'spirit' must not be reduced to the dualism of physical and mental substances—'flesh', in the true Pauline sense, refers not to the body, much less to a particular organ, but to a self-centred rather than God-centred mode of being; indeed, 'anyone who exalts the soul as the Supreme Good, and censures the nature of the flesh as something evil, is in fact carnal alike in his cult of the soul and in his revulsion from the flesh, since this attitude is prompted by human folly, not by divine truth' (*CG* XIV. 5). The body was created good, and would remain good if all its functions were disposed towards divinity. Since the fall, of course, mankind is helpless to make this turn without election and

---

[8] H. A. Deane, *The Political and Social Ideas of St. Augustine* (NY, 1963), pp. 44 and 265 nn. 5 and 7; Aug., *Conf.* XIII. ix. 10, and cf. his Ep. 55 as used in Donne, *Sermons*, X. 376.

grace.[9] But the command to multiply (and thereby to produce the pre-ordained number of the elect) is still in effect, however grotesque the body we now inhabit, weighed down by physical necessity and wrested from our control by the unpredictable ravages of lust.

[*ii*]

Augustine's theory of pre-lapsarian sexuality must encompass this paradox: sin must be interpreted as an apostacy of the will and not as a physical condition, but the supreme manifestation of fallenness, the 'law within the members', the immediate horror that caused Adam and Eve to rush to the fig-tree, the immemorial taint that sends new-born babies to the depths of hell—was sexual arousal. (The problem can be traced via St. Paul to Hebrew semantics, where *basar*, 'flesh', can mean both the whole human being and the erect penis.)[10] He therefore makes the all-important, though precarious, distinction between lust (*libido, concupiscentia*) and sexuality itself.

The immediate result of eating the forbidden fruit, Augustine believes, was a sudden and conspicuous inflation of the erectile tissues; it is this involuntary priapism which made Adam and Eve aware of their nakedness. But Original Sin must not be equated with sexuality nor even with *libido*; when the will is properly directed, Augustine maintains, all amorous words—even *libido* and *concupiscentia*—may denote the love that brings us closer to God. Even in its fallen ithyphallic form, sexual passion may be redeemed by a good marriage (since the lawful use of a wicked thing is not in itself wicked) and may thus be 'not accounted sin in the regenerate'.[11] Nevertheless sexual arousal was inflicted as a *sign* or *paradigm* of the fallen condition, and as a *means of transmitting*

[9] Aug. several times explains (e.g. *CG* XIII. 20, 23, XXII. 21, 30) that the new body will be spiritual because its flesh will serve the spirit, in the same way that mental qualities are 'carnal' when they serve the flesh; the resurrection would not exist unless both substances participate. Indeed, they actually *entail* one another: 'if there is such a thing as an animal body, there is also a spiritual body' (XIII. 23).

[10] Ezek. 23:20, Rom. 7:23, *De Gen. ad Lit.* IX. iv. 8; Aug. assumes that Paul's struggle with his 'members' refers to sex. St. Paul's usage is explored in John A. T. Robinson, *The Body: A Study in Pauline Theology* (1952).

[11] *CG* XIV. 7 (cf. *De Nupt. et Conc.* II. xxx. 52); *De Bono Conj.* XVI. 18; *De Nupt. et Conc.* I. xxiii. 25 and xxv. 27. In a passage that found its way into canon law, Aug. even seems to contradict his own procreationist bias and accept marriages cemented by erotic love; cf. Henry A. Kelly, *Love and Marriage in the Age of Chaucer* (Ithaca, 1975), p. 248, and contrast *De Bono Conj.* V. 5.

original sin. As a judgement on human disobedience of God, the human body refuses to obey the will. Tumescence is thus a grim parody of their own sinful aspiration to autonomy, and leaves them aghast rather than excited. It is a sort of fifth column, an alien intrusion which destroys the integrity of the personality as well as the body: Adam was ashamed because his members 'were being moved not by his own will (*ad arbitrium voluntatis eius*) but by the instigation of libido as if they had a will of their own (*arbitrium proprium*)'.[12]

It follows that the essence of 'lust' and the source of sexual shame is not sexuality *per se*, but the unpredictability and autonomy of the penis. (Augustine speaks with some understanding of male experience, but though he assumes that Adam and Eve were equally engulfed in post-lapsarian shame, he never explicitly mentions the erectile nature of female sexual response.) The moment when the first couple's 'eyes were opened' corresponds to the moment in the *Confessions* when Augustine's father notices in the baths that his son is 'pubescentem'; the pagan-humanist father rejoices, in anticipation of grandchildren, at the physical signs of his son's sexual 'intoxication'—though the Christian mother is filled with grief.[13] But the effects of the fall are equally strong in sexual failure:

not even the lovers of this pleasure ... are moved when they want to be. Sometimes the impulse is an unwanted intruder, sometimes it abandons the panting lover, and desire cools off in the body while it is at boiling heat in the mind (*cum in animo concupiscentia ferveat, friget in corpore*). (*CG* XIV. 16)

With a mature irony that runs through much of his discussion of sexuality, Augustine dismisses the Cynic attempt to perform copulation in full public view, not because it is wicked, but because it could never have worked.[14] *Libido* is thus manifested as much

---

[12] *De Gratia et Peccato Originale*, quot. in Agaësse II. 522. See also *CG* XII. 13 and XIV *passim*; *De Nupt. et Conc. passim*; Deane, pp. 269-70; Peter Brown, *Augustine of Hippo* (1967), pp. 38-91. By removing sexual arousal from the realm of will, Aug. falls into a problem: does he not thereby remove it from the realm of ethics? In *CG* XIV. 23 he advises us to control the circumstances likely to lead to arousal, if not the response itself.

[13] *Conf.* II. iii. 6. For other examples of Aug.'s understanding of pagan masculinity, see *De Incomp. Nupt.* II. 8 and 20.

[14] *CG* XIV. 20. For Aug.'s amusing account of a pagan wedding, see VI. 9; Deane (p. 54) and Hagstrum (p. 30) rather overstate Aug.'s disgust, though Hagstrum does recognize some comic verve in the description (n. 12). Brown points out (pp. 390-1) that paganism also led to an asceticism compared to which Aug. is quite moderate.

2. The Incorporation of Eros

by embarrassment, detumescence, and frigidity as by successful arousal.

But if the tragicomic mechanism of erection came with the fall, how would humanity have reproduced in the state of innocence? If they had not fallen first, Augustine deduces, Adam and Eve would have made love consciously and deliberately, moving the genitals as we move our hands or our faces; sexual emission would have been exactly like the voluntary discharge of urine (a process that fills him with wonder).[15] Thus they could have combined the biological imperatives of Genesis 1 with the theological duties of Genesis 2. They would have sowed the 'genital fields' as a farmer sows his seed—the phrase from Virgil's *Georgics* suggests wholesome seasonal labour.[16] Augustine frequently uses the strength of athletes and the agility of craftsmen to imagine the delights of our original bodies, and it is clear that he conceives this controlled love-making as a marvellous skill rather than a perfunctory act; indeed, he proves his hypothesis by comparing this primeval genital control not only to the motility of craftsmen but to the freakish abilities of performing artists, who can weep or move their ears at will, swallow large objects, imitate birdsong, play music with their farts, and enter a yogic trance in which they feel no pain (*CG* XIV. 23-4). Augustine recounts these survivals of Adamic power in a tone of fascinated enthusiasm.

To these examples of bodily 'art', which had evidently captured his imagination, Augustine adds another association of deep personal resonance. When he describes how 'without the enticing spur of burning passion, in tranquillity of mind and with no corruption of bodily integrity, the husband would have been poured into the lap of his wife (*infunderetur gremio maritis uxoris*),' he deliberately echoes Virgil's description of Venus making love to her husband—the very '*vers de Vergile*' that Montaigne was later to praise as the supreme expression of sexual feeling in literature.[17]

---

[15] *CG* XIV *passim*, *De Nupt. et Conc.* II. xxxi. 53.

[16] *CG* XIV. 23; *Georgics* III. 136. *Contra Julianum* 14 uses the identical phrase—cf. James Nohrnberg, *The Analogy of the Faerie Queene* (Princeton, 1976, corr. edn., 1980), p. 527.

[17] *CG* XIV. 26; *Aeneid* VIII. 405-7 (cf. 'optatus dedit amplexus, placidemque petivit / conjugis infusus gremio per membra soporem'); Montaigne, *Essais*, III. 5 ('Sur des vers de Virgile'). With this interpretation contrast Peter Lindenbaum, 'Love-making in Milton's Paradise', *MS* VI (1974), 280, and Hagstrum, p. 30; cf. also John J. O'Meara, 'Virgil and St. Augustine: The Roman Background to Christian Sexuality', *Augustinus*, XIII (1968), 307-26.

In the *Confessions* Augustine accused himself of being so besotted with the love of Dido, as he read the *Aeneid*, that he neglected those things that would have led him to the love of God (I. xiii. 20-1); here he repays the debt, reconsecrating Virgil to the Lord. But Augustine does not only define pre-lapsarian sexuality by finding parallels in the art of others; he also draws on the resources of his own imagination. ('The imagination of man's heart' may be evil, but in the service of the City of God it is evidently redemptive.) Though he frequently laments the difficulty of conceiving our former happiness, particularly in this delicate area, he still presses on with further details: Adam and Eve would have felt no *labor* or *tarditas* as they copulated—just as the resurrected body will experience no *tarditas*—and it is even possible to believe, though we cannot prove it by experience, that

> the male seed could have been dispatched into the womb of the fertile wife with no loss of female virginity (*integritate*), just as the menstrual flux can now be produced from the womb of a virgin with no loss of virginity. For the seed could be injected through the same passage by which the flux is ejected. Now just as the female viscera might have been opened for parturition by a natural impulse when the time was ripe, instead of by the groans of travail, so the two sexes might have been united for impregnation and conception by an act of will, instead of by a lustful craving. (*CG* XIV. 26; cf. XIII. 20)

Far from exhibiting what a recent scholar calls 'a shrinking reluctance to contemplate a joyful union of opposite sexes in Eden itself',[18] Augustine here sets his imagination at full stretch; as he remarks himself, the problem calls forth his utmost powers of conjecture (*coniciamus ut possumus*).

But he works against a grievous obstacle. The fall itself imposes an embarrassment on this particular subject so intense that it spoils even the lawful embraces of man and wife, and paralyses even the godliest author as he tries to reconstruct the state of innocence; since the fall, we cannot think of coitus without also thinking of the turbulent lust that now comes with it (*CG* XIV. 26). Sexuality is, as it were, not only Paradise but also the flaming sword that keeps us out. But no Christian could ignore the urge to think about Paradise, however disturbing the agitation it inspires. Even while admitting that his own flights are severely crippled by post-lapsarian

[18] Hagstrum, p. 30; as I argue in 2. 2. i below, Aug. did imagine a joyful erotic (but non-tumescent) union of the sexes in the pre-lapsarian state.

shame, Augustine still makes some attempt to recreate the Edenic state in his conjectures. And he is aware that the same drama will be re-enacted in the fallen reader: in the state of innocence Modesty could have found no fault with a detailed discussion of sexuality like this one, and even now the regenerate may read it with profit; but if this fourteenth book should incite the reader to lascivious thoughts, let him blame the dreadful consequences of Adam's sin, and not the nature of the body as God made it (XIV. 23).

Augustine's meditation on shame leads him to some of the contradictions at the heart of sexual experience. Some he reveals unwittingly, and some he articulates clearly. In one place, for example, he will discuss *libido* as the paradigm and flagship of all passion, but at other times he treats it as a unique, specific phenomenon; the difference consists in shame—no other passion seeks to hide itself, and a man is far less ashamed to be seen wrongfully venting his anger on another man than legally and wholesomely copulating with his wife (*CG* XIV. 15, 19). This shame that engulfs even lawful wedded sex, inhibits even the most pious authors, and prompts even the Indian yogis to cover their genitals, is sometimes treated as proof of the damage done by original sin, sometimes as an innate, natural and excellent modesty, 'retained' from the state of innocence (XIV. 16, 17, 20, 21). The sexual life of the godly married couple is regarded sometimes as an evil made 'venial' by good intentions, and sometimes as a good in itself, a 'right action', 'by nature right and proper (*quod deceat ex natura*)' (XIV. 18). But even the most optimistic and generous evaluation makes no difference to the legacy of shame: the instinct for privacy is equally intense in those who pursue illegal perversions, in those who use legal prostitutes, and in the chastest and purest married couple. All the guests at a wedding know how the day will end, all were born of such an act, and all approve its expression in marriage—but consummation still shrinks from their gaze, and even the children of that union will be forbidden to witness it. Augustine's dissertation on Eros leads him to this epistemological knot: as a good thing or 'right action' sexuality longs to be known, 'craves for recognition in the light of the mind's understanding'; but as a legacy of the fall it none the less blushes to be seen. It '*appetit sciri*,' but '*erubescat videri*' (XIV. 18).

Thus even the most fallen aspect of human sexuality—the shame that pervades every attempt to imagine or perform the sexual act—

turns out to be a complex amalgam of turpitude and virtue. Sexuality still retains a cognitive impulse; something in it longs to be known, to manifest redemptive traces of the 'right Eros' it should have been. The blessing of 'increase and multiply' was a vital element of the unfallen state, nor was it rescinded by the punishment of the fall, but rather reiterated in later chapters of Genesis; current experience must therefore not be dismissed or ignored when reconstituting the original state of innocence. The elaborate conjectures on sexual ontogeny in *The City of God* are designed not only to ease the disparities of the text, but also to mediate between the fallen and unfallen condition of humanity.

Augustine's imaginative solution to the question of pre-lapsarian sexuality proved remarkably acceptable to later exegetes. As a recent scholar judiciously remarks, his voluntaristic hypothesis 'not only avoided the possible blasphemy of viewing God as dependent upon man's sin to accomplish his ends, but also neatly side-stepped the similar difficulties implicit in the idea of an unfruitful act of intercourse commanded by a God who wished to see man increase and multiply.' Furthermore, 'it enabled Christians to hold to the doctrine of original sin and thus account for Cain's evil nature, and at the same time to accept even carnal sexuality with a gratefulness proper to man when approaching any of God's gifts.'[19] We might add that it manages to reconcile the fable of Adam and Eve with the command to increase and multiply without entirely abandoning realism—since Paradisal copulation would have used normal human sexual anatomy, and since the extraordinary idea of voluntary genital movement is demonstrated by analogy with the most familiar bodily movements and functions.

But however skilfully Augustine steers between the astounding and the familiar, the reader will not 'lay hold on' the Edenic state unless some account is given of the feelings of the primal couple. Whatever the precise mechanics of their union, Adam's repeated cry of welcome shows that he has a strong emotional response to the newly-created woman, and the rapidity of his fall suggests, to Augustine and others, that the same bond of love led him to eat the fruit (*CG* XIV. 11). Without creating an analogous but redemptive bond, the myth of Eden could not 'walk' again within the reader. A neutral, anaesthetic sexuality would inspire no

---

[19] Lindenbaum, pp. 280-1.

empathy or identification, no Paradisal 'agitation', and no impulse of love towards a higher state.

2. Theories of erotic feeling in Augustine, Aquinas, and Luther

Though Augustine is not reluctant to imagine the details of pre-lapsarian copulation, to a modern reader his elimination of erection and orgasm will seem peculiarly anxious, perhaps even grotesque and inhuman. One recent theologian, indeed, sees little difference between Augustine's obsession with voluntary control and the calculated seductions of *Les Liaisons dangereuses*.[20] Without the semi-autonomous mechanism of arousal, and its powerful desire and shame, sexuality is no longer itself. Correspondingly, Augustine's description of fallen sex—

> lust disturbs the whole man when the mental emotion (*animi affectus*) combines and mingles with the physical craving (*carnis appetitus*), resulting in a pleasure surpassing all physical delights, so intense ... that when it reaches its climax there is an almost total extinction of mental alertness (*CG* XIV. 16)—

will probably seem like an unintended tribute to the ecstasy it condemns. His intention, of course, is to separate natural, God-given sexuality from its man-made perversion, lust. But in practice the distinction is so precarious that the narrow concept of lust widens to swallow every aspect of sexual experience—even when, as in *De Nuptiis et Concupiscentia*, he is explicitly defending the thesis that pleasure and concupiscence themselves exist in a blessed as well as a wicked form, that 'pleasure can be even honourable', and that 'concupiscence is sometimes a thing to be proud of, since there is a concupiscence of the spirit against the flesh' (II. ix. 22, x. 23, and cf. xii. 25, vii. 17). Nevertheless, I believe it is misleading to describe Augustine's Paradise as 'austere and largely sexless'.

In the *De Nuptiis* Augustine saw himself fighting two extremes, and he appears to be caught between their jaws. He argues in theory for the excellence of sexuality, against the Manicheans, but he argues far more intensely against the Pelagian idea that contemporary married life could approach the Paradisal ideal. Thus he sweepingly condemns '*ardor*', 'pleasure', and 'the emission of

---

[20] Charles Davis, *Body as Spirit* (NY, 1976), pp. 50-1, 141; cf. also Hagstrum, p. 30 (Prof. Hagstrum's comments have helped me to clarify this point, though I do not share his conclusion that Aug.'s Paradise is 'austere and largely sexless'). Aug. refers to sex as an 'anxius ardor' in *De Gen. ad Lit.* IX. iii. 6.

seed', and equates his enemy's vision of marriage with libertine perversity; nor does it occur to him to identify the natural sexual urge with pleasure in the service of the Lord.[21] But in the fourteenth book of *The City of God*, at one remove from these controversies, he reconstructs in considerable detail the warm emotions that would have accompanied primordial love-making. What he describes is not sex, in the modern sense, but neither is it sexless; it is a cluster of feelings specific to the loving conjunction of man and woman.

Emotion for Augustine is good or bad according to the direction of the will; the impetus to love, the central constitutive desire of the human spirit, becomes *caritas* or *libido* according as it is centred on God or self. Man is by definition a being centred on the transcendent Other, and any self-centredness, whether voluptuous or ascetic, is evil; animals, on the other hand, are quite properly centred on themselves, and they serve God by loving their own sexuality to the full (*CG* XI. 23). All feeling (*motus, affectus*) can be explained as variants of attraction (desire, love, appetite, joy) and repulsion (fear, grief, hatred, offence); Adam and Eve may have been spared the latter, but they experienced the joyful appetites, as long as their minds were directed towards God, in a 'blameless and even praiseworthy' form. They had the continual enjoyment (*gaudium, fruitio*) of a 'great love' placed equally in God and each other (XIV. 9). This 'enjoyment' is both general and particular. They would have experienced a general felicity in their whole being, and not just in spirit or body alone, and it would have steadily increased as their offspring grew more numerous. But there is also a 'felicity' particular to procreation; when Augustine says that the errors of Manichaean contempt or over-spiritual allegorization come from being 'unaware of the *felicitas* that existed in Paradise', he refers specifically to the interpretation of 'increase and multiply' and to the joys of procreation that he has reconstructed to explain it. As they made love Adam and Eve would not have felt the fierce desire that blanks out thought, but they would have felt the joy of the artist or performer, an exhilarated and effortless agility, an 'alertness' of body as well as mind, a trusting love, and a benevolent warmth. They would have come together in a blaze of holy love ('flagrabat caritas'), sustained by the *societas* that grows from *honeste amore*. And their copulation would end, as we have seen,

[21] II. xxxi. 52-3, xxxv. 59; cf. Brown, pp. 382 and (for later outbursts against the sexual 'Paradise of the Pelagians') 396.

in a 'pouring out' of the man into the woman that evokes the climactic embrace of Vulcan and Venus in the *Aeneid*. These are not neutral pieties, but recognizable and desirable emotional states.

Amorous emotion, then, is intrinsic to the Paradisal state provided it can be centred upon God. Even '*libido*', as we have seen, may be opened towards transcendence by turning the will aright, and even the strictest asceticism may be an expression of carnality. It is probably hard for us to think of the dominance of the will except as an ugly and repressive dichotomy; but though Augustine fully recognizes such painful divisions—the fallen state is a constant warfare between reason and appetite—they are not essential to his definition of human sexuality. Emotion and will are fundamentally identical, and both are ultimately determined not by the self-controlling mind but by the action of divine grace. Only in the fallen state must reason fight to subdue libido, rein it in, call it back, shackle and confine it. In Paradise passions such as hunger and sexual desire were not *vitiosae*, and were not 'set in motion in defiance of a right will'; this means, however, not that such feelings were absent, but that the division between reason and emotion, and the repression that is necessary to live morally in the fallen world, did not exist. Fallen self-control 'entails coercion and struggle (*cohibando et repugnando*), and the situation does not represent a state of health in accordance with nature (*sanitas ex natura*), but an enfeebled condition arising from guilt (*languor ex culpa*).' Augustine here makes the remarkable assertion that pre-lapsarian sexuality differs from sinful lust not in being more neutral or ethereal, but in being more healthy and vigorous (*CG* XIV. 19, and cf. 6, 7).

The hypothetical delight of Adam and Eve is still conceived in rather diffuse terms, unlike the precise description of their genital mechanism. This vagueness may inhibit, but it does not negate, the declared goal of Augustine's speculations: to imagine the experience of pre-lapsarian humanity, and the bliss they might have enjoyed if they had not sinned, in order thereby to 'lay hold on' the promised happiness of the resurrection. We have seen that, to arrive at the mysteries of unfallen sexuality, he set his imagination and ingenuity at full stretch—'let us conjecture to the utmost of our ability (*coniciamus ut possumus*)'. Likewise to conceive the '*gratia*' of the resurrected body, a joy that forces us to speak even though it is unknowable and indescribable, we must assemble in our minds all the beauties and excellences of this life and project them towards eternity: 'from God's gifts in this life we can conjecture, as much as possible (*coniciamus ut possumus*), the blessings we have not yet experienced and are unworthy to describe' (*CG* XXII. 21, and cf. XI. 28, XIV. 26). Augustine puts this long-announced principle into action in the twenty-fourth chapter of his final book, a swelling panegyric to the splendour of the universe and the brilliance of human culture. At the head of this list of blessings comes the original blessing, 'increase and multiply', and he celebrates in the human body precisely the craftsmanly agility, functional efficiency, and dignity that made pre-lapsarian sexuality so wonderful. And yet he falls short of what his whole method implies; he never ascribes a transcendental, 'sacramental' kind of sexuality to the angelic or resurrected state. On the authority of Matthew 22:30 ('in the resurrection they neither marry nor are given in marriage') he eliminates Eros completely from our future happiness (XXII. 17). Given Augustine's emphasis on sexuality and his debt to Platonism, this omission is bound to seem contradictory.

We should not simply attribute it to negligence or 'shrinking reluctance', however. Augustine in fact concentrates on bodily experience when he discusses Eden in Book XIV and the resurrection in Books XIII and XXII; his intention, as we have seen, is to refute the anticorporeality of Platonism while keeping its sublime ascent to the ideal. However wretched this earthly life has been, to be disembodied is actually a punishment compared to the joy of receiving our own bodies again, 'spiritual' even though made of the same flesh, freed of any physical necessity, incapable of death or pain, and more perfect even than Adam fresh from the hand of God. Why then should higher states of being—angels, or resurrected humans—not enjoy an exalted kind of erotic delight?

Augustine's conception of 'sacramental' physicality may be illustrated by the parallel case of eating. Adam enjoyed the perfection of animal life, but was still constrained by physical necessity: he had to take in normal food and drink to prevent the *molestia* of hunger and thirst, and he had to eat the Tree of Life to remain immortal. Angels, on the other hand, eat and drink real food only as a voluntary act, a kind of theatre put on for the benefit of mortals; and resurrected human beings will find their flesh so obedient to the spirit that they too will have that power to 'eat only if they wish to eat' (*CG* XIII. 20, 22–4). It is assumed, however, that such a 'wish' will occur—that necessitous desires will persist in a voluntary, transfigured form. Augustine would thus agree with Milton that angels eat neither 'seemingly . . . nor in mist, the common gloss / Of Theologians,' but he would absolutely deny that, as Milton goes on, they feel 'real hunger' and 'need / To be sustain'd and fed'.[22] For Augustine the essence of resurrected, 'sacramental' bliss is that volition resumes its empire over some organic function previously resigned to necessity.

If Augustine would have been shocked by the hunger of Milton's angels, what would he have thought of their sexual life? The poet is virtually unique in ascribing active eroticism, not only to the unfallen Adam and Eve, but to angels both fallen and unfallen. 'Spirits' in *Paradise Lost* 'when they please / Can either Sex assume, or both,' and as they couple without the 'restrain'd conveyance' of limbs they 'enjoy in eminence' every erotic sensation that Adam can feel in his unfallen body (I. 423-4, VIII. 622-8). Augustine entertains no such ideas, of course; but this may derive, paradoxically, not from reluctance or disgust but from the special status he gives to sexuality in the pre-lapsarian state. For copulation in Eden would not have been precisely analogous to eating and drinking: though it was absolutely necessary to God's plan for the human race, it was not immediately necessary for daily survival, and though it was a physical function shared with the animals, it was not then *initiated* by a physical appetite. Eating and drinking in Paradise were not essentially different from our own, but sexuality, as Augustine establishes in Book XIV, was different in kind as well as in degree, because it was voluntary. Pre-lapsarian sexuality, in comparison to fallen libido, is already at the resurrected stage. If therefore we can brave the perils of embarrassment to follow Augustine's speculations, we will be better equipped for the difficult task of imagining how our actual fleshly bodies could be 'spiritual'.[23]

Once it has served as an analogy, the genital function may either be abandoned or translated to a higher level still. Augustine chooses

---

[22] *PL* V. 414-15, 434-6. M's heaven does contain 'sacramental' or non-necessitous versions of earthly phenomena—cf. V. 628-9 'Wee have also our Evening and our Morn, / Wee ours for change delectable, not need.'

[23] This difficulty is discussed in Leopold Damrosch, *Symbol and Truth in Blake's Myth* (Princeton, 1980), p. 171. The idea that archangels enjoy vigorous sexual activity appears in Boccaccio (*Decameron* IV. ii), but it is evidently comic and fraudulent.

the latter: even though he excludes sexual reproduction from the resurrected state, he deliberately includes the erogenous zones in his vision of a higher beauty. We will rise again as fully formed men and women; since 'woman's sex is not a defect', but is 'natural', it is heresy to maintain that the blessed will all be male. In this future non-reproductive state, however, 'the female organs will not subserve their former use; they will be part of a new beauty (*decor novus*), which will not excite the lust of the beholder.' Woman's genitals will inspire gratitude for the divine wisdom and compassion that has freed humanity from corruption—their fallen lustful function is thus present in the new response, but only as a remembrance of evil past.[24] And this response is not only theological but aesthetic; the body will radiate a *decor*, a graceful and appropriate beauty. Even now, certain parts of the body excite a pure aesthetic feeling, divorced from any *necessitas* or biological function—the nipples of the male are Augustine's main example, suggesting a trace of Socratic sensibility. In the future state, the entire body will be equally beautiful, and 'we shall enjoy one another's beauty for itself alone, without any *libido*'. Furthermore, it will be radiant with immanent deity; God will be seen 'face to face' as St. Paul promises, but He will be visible in the bodies of others rather than in His essence, and He will therefore be sensed as immediately as we now sense the livingness of our own bodies. In the final chapter of the entire *City of God*, Augustine realizes that he dare not even define, and is not worthy to conceive, the full *motus* and *pulchritudo* of these resurrected bodies—their *motus* comprising not only their exhilarating lightness of movement but their power of emotion, and their beauty deriving, as we have seen, from transfigured sexuality.[25]

Milton's description of angelic love, like Augustine's, is explicitly offered as a model for human ascent, and is similarly created by converting Platonic Eros to the monism of resurrection theology. Milton's bold assertion—that the higher state will include the most intense erotic delight—flatly contradicts Augustine, of course; but the poet's speculations rest nevertheless on Augustinian principles.

[24] *CG* XXII. 17; on the memory of evil in the celestial state, see XXII. 30. Montaigne alludes to Aug.'s theories of female resurrection, but with an interesting distortion; he appears to think that Aug. is refuting the idea that women must be resurrected as men so that their naked bodies will not be tempting (*Essais*, III. 5).
[25] *CG* XII. 24, 29, 30; note that in the resurrected state corporeal beauty can be 'enjoyed' (*fruamur*) rather than having to be 'used' as a vehicle for something else.

In 'working up to spirit', as Raphael promises they will if they remain obedient to the limitations imposed by God, humanity will approach the angelic. The sexual function in man is created pure but still tied to what Augustine called 'the necessity of intercourse and childbirth' (*CG* XXII. 17). In angels it is transfigured into a purely volitional delight, performed 'when they please'; it is a 'work of love' for the greater glory of God. This is the 'sacramental' vision of Augustine applied to the full, and purged of Augustine's incomplete separation of lust and sexual desire; here *libido* is converted into *caritas*, and bodily experience is projected towards the absolute—with no diminution of God-given physicality.

[*ii*]

Milton's poetic realization of Augustine's erotology was not an isolated leap of the imagination, however. Though none believed that angels enjoyed sexual delight (a heresy generally associated with Islam), several later theologians had developed Augustine's speculations on what Adam and Eve would have felt if they had not fallen. Their efforts provide a precedent and authority for imagining Paradise, as Milton did, thoroughly infused with 'the spirit of love and amorous delight'. Aquinas, for example, whose codification of Augustine's beliefs installed them at the heart of Western theology, had already gone some way towards redeeming sexual desire, if not in the angelic, then in the primordial human state.

Like Augustine, Aquinas asserts that Adam and Eve did not actually consummate their marriage in Paradise, because 'once the woman was fashioned they were in next to no time (*post modicum*) thrown out of Paradise for sin'—the reason that Bayle was later to pronounce 'the most substantial'.[26] But he infers, again like Augustine, that the first couple would have used their genital organs even in the state of innocence, and would have moved them voluntarily, as we move our face and hands. Alternative theories of quasi-angelic multiplication, held by the early Greek Fathers Gregory of Nyssa and John Damascene, are rapidly dismissed. But though he stresses that pre-lapsarian intercourse would have been entirely without libido or embarrassment, Aquinas is not content

---

[26] *Summa Theologiae* Ia, Quot. 98 (I have used the Latin-English Blackfriars edn., 1964–); Bayle, 'Abel' A.

to define it by privation alone; he insists that Adam and Eve would have experienced a special form of sexual delight.

He had already argued, in Questio 95, that primeval man experienced *passiones animae* in his *appetitu sensuali* (art. 2); the difference between innocence and the fallen state is that such desires before the fall were devoid of fear, confusion, and the struggle between flesh and spirit. (Here, too, Aquinas draws heavily on the fourteenth book of *The City of God*.) Perfect moral virtue does not eliminate the passions, but *ordinat eas*, directs them; true temperance is an Aristotelian principle, 'to desire (*concupiscere*) as is proper and what is proper'. Now he applies this theory to erotic passion. He recognizes that the 'vehemence of the delight' and the *foeditas* of fallen copulation might reduce man to the level of the animals, but he insists that the problem lies not in the natural act itself but in the relation between physical desire and reason. In the state of innocence, he argues, there would have been no desires unmoderated by reason; but this 'moderation' or 'direction' does not involve suppression. Aquinas is quite explicit about this:

the pleasurable sensation would not have been any the less intense, as some say, for the pleasure of sense would have been all the greater, given the greater purity of man's nature and sensibility of his body.... It is not demanded by this empire of reason that the pleasurable sensation should be any the less, but that the pleasure-urge (*vis concupiscibilis*) should not clutch at the pleasure in an immoderate fashion.[27]

The authority for this admission of *delectatio sensu* and *vis concupiscibilis* into man's highest earthly state is Augustine.

Those who retain the memory of *De Nuptiis et Concupiscentia*, where erotic sensation is unmistakably condemned to the category of fallen lust, will find this assertion surprising; but Aquinas goes instead to the heart of *The City of God*, where he finds that 'Augustine's words [in Book XIV] do not exclude intensity of pleasure from the state of innocence, but impetuous lust (*ardorem libidinis*) and disturbance of mind'. We should recall that for Augustine the sexual climax of fallen man involves, not just the overthrow of the mind's agility, but the active, explosive co--operation of *carnis appetitus* and *animi affectus*. It is remarkable that when the leading theologian of the Roman church comes to

[27] *Summa* Ia, Quot. 98; the argument is then driven home by an analogy with eating. Bonaventure and Alexander of Hales had both argued that erotic feeling would have been weaker, Albertus Magnus that it would have been stronger.

develop Augustine's Paradisal ideal, he should imagine a similar cooperation of mind and body—a fusion of reason with an erotic desire more intense than anything we can experience.

Aquinas's conjectures allowed later medieval interpreters to link the Paradisal ideal more closely to the actual practice of married love. Augustine had described the physical mechanism of prelapsarian copulation, and had testified to the delights that Adam and Eve would have enjoyed; but the precise relation between these two areas had remained suggestively vague. Aquinas now tied Augustine's descriptions of Paradisal joy to a specifically sexual emotion. A recent historian of 'love and marriage in the age of Chaucer' has noted how erotic delight *per se*, distinct from considerations of procreation, could sometimes be accepted as a valid and sinless part of marriage—in some cases by using 'increase and multiply' as evidence of God's blessing on the whole phenomenon of sexuality.[28] Because it was instituted in the state of innocence, the more liberal medieval theologians believed, marriage had the power to transform the 'water' of corporal delight into the 'wine' of good works; they thus revived the Pelagian view of the intrinsic goodness of sexual pleasure that Augustine denounces in *De Nuptiis et Concupiscentia*.

The lay imagination, too, would sometimes assume that, because marriage was instituted by God between Adam and Eve, there is no sin in copulation. This sense of divine sanction, declared in Genesis and still manifest in the delights of the marriage-bed, is expressed by the '*Gawain*-poet' in *Cleanness* (ll. 697-708). God Himself, while denouncing the unnatural Sodomites, declares His own pride in personally creating for man a natural method ('kynde crafte') of sex, and infusing this 'play of paramores' with a delight so intense, a nocturnal flame so hot, that all the troubles of the world cannot slake it: 'Bytweene a male and his make such merthe schulde come, / Wel nygh pure Paradys moght prove no better.' In content if not in form, these lines anticipate the great hymn to wedded love in *Paradise Lost*.

[*iii*]

But Milton did not derive his vision of wedded love from Aquinas and the Middle Ages, which he regarded as a dark superstitious period lit only by the star of Wyclif. It was 'our Writers', the

[28] Kelly, pp. 251, 256-61, 272.

Reformation commentators on Genesis, who developed Augustine's anatomy of desire.[29] They explored more deeply the contradictory tangle of feeling inherited from 'our first parents', in which shame, disgust, and fury contend with, but do not entirely obscure, the vestiges of Paradisal bliss. The Protestant effort to exalt the 'prime institution' of holy matrimony gave Eden a social dimension, moreover; in a representative figure like Luther, a complex of social and familial emotions are added to the definition of 'one flesh', the core of sexuality itself.

Luther's conception of pre-lapsarian sexuality resembles Augustine's in many ways. Adam and Eve fell, if not on the day or night they were created, yet on the next day, the Sabbath. (Luther does not explain why God then spent that day in satisfied repose.) Otherwise they and their descendants would have enjoyed normal animal procreation—though it would have been without the execrable lust and prurience of the flesh, and would always have been performed for the greater honour of God. This mammalian sexuality would in no way have detracted from the glory of humanity; we may have been created in contradiction, radiant with God's image and yet sharing the physical life of cattle, but this contradiction is itself shot through with beauty, since it shadows forth the Incarnation of Christ.[30]

Love-making would have been 'sacred', Luther tells us many times. The copulation of husband and wife would have been as honourable as banqueting, and would always have resulted in conception; pregnancies would have been borne as lightly as a garland of flowers, and new-born children would have walked immediately and fed on the abundant vegetation, praising the Lord. Any post-coital weakness would have been healed by the Tree of Life. None of the body's excreta would have stunk.[31] Even now, conception is a privilege, a blessing, a miraculous re-enactment in every woman of the original creation; in her the Word forms life out of chaos. Through procreation, even in the fallen state, we can

[29] *Prose* II. 596; ironically, M is praising 'our Writers' for *rejecting* Aug.'s interpretation of Eve (cf. 3. 1. ii below).
[30] I *passim*, esp. 83: 'the semen congeals in the womb and is given form in an identical manner[; there] is no difference between a pregnant cow and a woman with child'; and 86-7: the image of God, though 'invisible', is 'reflected' from the faces of Adam and Eve, and makes human incarnation into 'a very beautiful allegory, or rather ... an anagoge'.
[31] I. 133, 202; 72, 102, 117; 93; 110. Aquinas explored the question of whether Adam and Eve's excreta would have stunk in *Summa* Ia, Quot. 97, art. 3, obj. 4.

fulfil God's chief purpose in the world, by aiming to make up the pre-ordained number of the elect; thus our seed will bruise the serpent's head. Through this harmony with the divine plan, human sexuality was 'linked with the highest respect and wisdom'.[32]

As Augustine implies and Aquinas makes explicit, this separation of procreation from lust does not involve anaesthesia. Unfallen man, Luther maintains, would have experienced not just a 'transcendent decency' but a specifically erotic, intersexual drive: 'there would not have been in him that detestable lust (*foeda libido*) which is now in men, but there would have been the innocent and pure love of sex towards sex.' The original glory can still be recognized in 'the *appetitus* of the male for the female', though now it is encumbered with 'libido'—a term which Luther is careful to apply not to sexuality itself but to the extraneous frenzy, embarrassment, and post-coital disgust that sin has heaped upon it (I. 104). Indeed, Luther comes close to Aquinas's declaration that unfallen sex would have been more intense than ours: Adam's unembarrassed and godly erotic life proves the 'greater powers and keener senses' that came directly from the image of God in him (I. 62). Procreation was the most 'excellent' and 'admirable' natural activity, and would have been 'better, more delightful, and more sacred' than today, accompanied not only by the satisfactions of godly duty but by 'a noble delight (*honesta voluptas*), such as there was at that time in eating and drinking' (I. 117-19). Adam received his bride '*cum magna voluptate*, just as even now in this corrupt nature the mutual love of bridegroom and bride is extraordinary'; though their love is 'chaste' it is also 'delightful', and their 'most honourable and most sacred' union can only be grasped by thinking of, and multiplying, the fervour of newly-weds (I. 134). Nakedness would have been 'delightful', 'most beautiful', 'our greatest glory'— particularly in the female—and the genitals would have been the 'most honourable and noble' part of the body, 'looked upon with glory' (I. 139-41, 167).

The innocent couple may not experience the destructive intensity of fallen passion, but they are held together in one flesh by a cluster of emotions that include the natural desire of 'sex toward sex', the glory of holiness, and the intimate comforts of nestling and 'cleaving' to one another. The woman herself becomes 'a nest or home'—hence God 'built' rather than 'formed' her from the rib—

[32] I. 53, 71, 127; cf. III. 134.

in which not only the foetus but the husband can dwell in safety. Fresh families are repeatedly imagined forming their own *nidula* or 'little nests'.[33] Adam's 'greatest pleasure' comes when he recognizes Eve as bone of his bone and flesh of his flesh, that is to say 'as a building made from himself': this Luther calls 'an overflowing emotion of love', which can only be inferred from what remains of 'the bridegroom's delight and his love for the bride' after lust has been discounted (I. 136). Gazing at one another's nakedness, Adam and Eve would have 'felt safe in God's goodness (I. 143)'. Their marriage would have combined Love and holiness, social gathering and sexual congress, procreation and worship: they would have come together to beget children 'not urged on by that passion which is now in our leprous flesh but admiring God's dispensation ... just as we now come together to hear the Word of God and to worship Him' (I. 168). The sexual union of 'one flesh' becomes that most comforting image for Luther, a miniature congregation.

Fallen sexuality, on the other hand, is experienced as a more painful kind of contradiction, a fouler incarnation. Though its core is natural and good, a blessing in which, however dimly, we can still feel the force of the original 'be fruitful and multiply', it cannot be known apart from its pathological deformation. From the moment that Adam and Eve's eyes were opened, this blessing can only be discerned dimly and with great grief, crushed beneath lust, dread, bodily 'disobedience', and an embarrassment so strong that it intrudes even between husband and wife, and erupts into the solitary thoughts of the author whenever he mentions woman (I. 104-6, 118, and cf. 167). The 'leprosy of lust', which for Luther as for Augustine manifests itself in arbitrary prurience and the equally uncontrollable collapse of desire, places an unbridgable rift between procreation and 'respect and wisdom'. Contrasting the unembarrassed love-making of Adam and Eve to the 'great passion ... in the flesh, which is not only passionate in its desire but also in its disgust after it has acquired what it wanted,' Luther repeatedly comes back to the metaphor, or rather the diagnosis, of leprosy. The leper, he explains, bears a grotesque contradiction in his flesh: every faculty of his body is withered and numb except for his sexual drive, which rages in isolated fury—'in his leprous flesh everything

---

[33] I. 132-4, 139; cf. Dante, *Purgatorio* xxviii. 78, on Paradise as the 'nest' of the human race.

2. The Incorporation of Eros

is almost dead and without sensation, except that he is violently excited to lust.'[34]

Homo erectus is thus horribly divided within himself, and human sexuality likewise degenerates into a complicated and contrary system of perversity. This theme is elaborated throughout Luther's commentary on Genesis, but particularly in his remarks on 4:1 ('and Adam knew his wife, and she conceived and bore Cain'). Here began 'the execrable lust which is also the cause of sundry adversities and sins'—the sins of excessive desire and the equal but opposite sins of celibacy, the post-coital disgust, the hatred of one's spouse, the craving for perpetual sexual variety, the whoredoms and mass infanticides of the monastic orders. Luther thus anticipates and perhaps fosters Milton's sense, made explicit in the hymn to wedded love, that the Paradisal ideal was endangered equally by the libertinism of 'Court Amours' and the asceticism of religious 'Hypocrites'. 'How manifold', Luther concludes at the end of this catalogue of sexually generated sins, 'are the ways in which the weakness of the flesh displays itself!'[35]

In the act of conceiving Cain, however, he discovers both the origins of degradation and the seeds of regeneration. Adam's first sexual impulse came not simply from 'the passion of his flesh' but also from a pious desire to obey the injunction to increase and multiply, which 'had not been withdrawn, but had been reaffirmed in the promise of the Seed'. And Moses' use of the word *know* suggests a deep 'feeling and experience' that is closer to knowledge of the Lord's ways than to the forbidden Knowledge of the tree. The ravages of lust may be the primary evidence for the truth of God's terrible condemnation—'the imagination of man's heart is evil from his birth'—but they may also become a means of grasping Paradise, a kind of epistemological redemption. Firstly, though it can induce a torpor that removes all sense of sin, fallen sex generally creates a sensation of evil and frustration so vivid that it fuels the search for its opposite: 'in this way a very beautiful and very accurate picture of original righteousness can be inferred from the deprivation which we now feel in our own nature.'[36] Secondly, even

---

[34] I. 62; for other equations of sexuality with leprosy or epilepsy, presented as a medical diagnosis rather than a metaphor, cf. I. 71, 119, 207.

[35] I. 238–40; cf. 67, 118, 133–5, 168, and II. 119, 122—where the squalid contradictions of fallen sexuality become important evidence for the 'evil imagination' of Gen. 8:12.

[36] I. 240–1, 113, but contrast 166, where he says that our bodies and minds are

in its fallen state sexuality can help the search for Paradisal happiness in a more positive way.

Even after hearing her punishment, Luther believes, Eve's heart was glad because she had not lost her sex, her marriage, and her 'glory of motherhood'; even mired in lust and bickering, marriage remains a place of comfort, maternal protection, and nourishment, and it is a source of 'great pleasure and wonderment' to behold the instinctive deftness and grace of the female body, compared to which the father's movements are as clumsy as 'a camel dancing'. In such vividly imagined domestic scenes, where the joyful duty of procreation merges with the comforting solidarity of the maternal family,the original blessing, 'be fruitful and multiply', is still in force.

The contradictory emotional significance of sexuality, and its elusive relation to primeval happiness, often fills Luther with pessimism. The oxymoronic combination of God-given, wholesome sexual desire with 'the terrible ugliness of lust and the fearful pain of birth' not only generates shame and 'leprous' disgust, but actively destroys all faith in imagination and language (I. 104-6, 116, 118); I described this earlier as a grim reversal of Platonic Eros, in which sexuality becomes an anti-cognitive and anti-discursive force. Luther's gloomy assessment conceals an all-important exception, however, and one which carries him far beyond Augustine. For the experience of procreation—the natural 'appetite' or 'longing' of one sex for the other, the emotional 'knowledge' that Adam, even after the fall, could only derive from the consummation of his marriage, and the happiness of parenthood—still retains some vestiges, some 'small and pitiable remnants', of primeval bliss.

3. Eros redeemed? Plato, Solomon, and Paradisal marriage

There is a certain appropriateness in combining the *Symposium*, the Song of Songs, and Genesis into a single interpretative scheme. Since the process of *enarratione* or telling-out was believed to have begun in Genesis itself—the creation of Eve expanding the plain 'increase and multiply' of chapter 1—it was logical to enlarge the rudimentary fable of the rib with more elaborate accounts of Eros, provided they were themselves august and numinous. But this solution, as frequently happens in Biblical hermeneutics, creates its own problems. Whatever their tantalizing similarities, Genesis,

---

so habituated to the fallen condition that we can no longer recognize its sinfulness—a major example being the easy acceptance of fornication.

Plato, and the Song of Songs express a very different vision of the erotic. Reading them together could transform the brief lines of Genesis into an anatomy of desire and a map of primeval happiness, but it could also augment the problem that awoke such painful contradictions in Augustine and Luther—the unstable signification of physical sexuality itself.

In the garden of Eden Augustine found the roots of sexuality entangled with the roots of shame, transformed into an agonized desire that 'forces us to speak' and 'longs to be known', but 'blushes to be seen'; in the Song of Songs the same passion 'goes down as sweetly as wine, causing the lips of those that are asleep to speak' (7:9). It is perhaps a historical accident that Scripture came to include this poem of intimate, unqualified, and entirely secular eroticism; once it was received as an allegorical myth, however, every detail—the navel, the fingers running with myrrh, the 'joints of the thighs'—could be interpreted as an emblem of Jehovah's private dealings with Israel, or Christ's love of the individual soul.[37] The garden of Solomon becomes the connection between Eden and Gethsemane. Already in St. Paul, we have seen, the mutual surrender of the sexual partners has been enshrined as the rule of 'due benevolence', and the union of 'one flesh' has been transformed into an image, and a re-enactment, of Christ's love for the church. Christian typology carried this interpenetration of Solomon, Christ, and Genesis much further. In the Song of Songs the lover feeds on the breasts of his beloved like a roe among beds of spice and lilies; in Joseph Beaumont he becomes a naked God revelling in the bed of his own mother, while 'troops of *Cherubs*' bring 'all *Edens* flowers': 'Now Paradise springs new with you; / Old *Edens* Beauties all inclin'd this way.'[38] The shady tree where the woman swoons with amorous sickness, and feasts upon the 'apples' of her lover, becomes the Tree of Life, the Cross, and the marriage-bed.[39] When

---

[37] My contention, that unilateral submission and religious transcendence belong to eisegesis and not to the actual S. of S., deviates not only from earlier Judaeo-Christian tradition but from Julia Kristeva; cf. *Histoires d'amour* (Paris, 1983), pp. 84-98, esp. p. 86, where Kristeva lightly dismisses Phyllis Trible's non-patriarchal reading.

[38] *Minor Poems*, ed. Eloise Robinson (Boston, 1914), pp. 16-17; the title of the poem, 'Jesus inter Ubera Mariae: Cantcl. 6', shows that Beaumont builds on Cornelius a Lapide's suggestion that typologically the lover in S. of S. is the Virgin as well as the Church.

[39] These connections are thoroughly explored in Stanley Stewart, *The Enclosed Garden* (Madison, 1966), pp. 73-96, 207 nn. 83-4, 208 n. 89.

the lover declares, invitingly, that 'our bed is green' and 'flowery', he opens the way for the garden of Eden to become the nuptial bower of *Paradise Lost*. The most intimate and sumptuous dreams assume the authority of Scripture.

This interconnection of Genesis and the Song of Songs certainly gives substance to Augustine's sense that the delight of God is 'a kind of imbracing'—but what kind? What is the relation between earthly and heavenly eroticism? In his poem on the 'beds of spice', Beaumont conceives the incarnate love of God in terms that would be scandalous if translated into physical reality; but in 'Loves Monarchie', another poem in the same collection, he celebrates a single, universal 'Love' that includes divine love, the bonds of society, and the 'honest and genuine Fires' initiated by the command to '*Increase* and *Multiplie*' (pp. 94-7). St. Paul assumes that the mystery of 'one flesh' applies equally to human and divine relations; but Origen, in his influential commentary on the Song of Songs, places an absolute barrier between sexual metaphor and sexual reality—indeed, unless the reader has completely eliminated physical sexuality, it is dangerous for him to read the Song.

Charles Davis, the theologian who accuses Augustine of a quasi-libertine obsession with sexual control, has identified two different metaphorics within Christianity, two different methods of using erotic love to apprehend or 'lay hold on' the deity. In one, exemplified by Origen's comments on the Song of Songs, the tenor is exalted and the vehicle denied completely. In the other, which Davis finds to be the healthy and truly 'sacramental' way, divinity is immanent in the physical, and tenor and vehicle are 'connatural' and consubstantial. This second vision—characterized by 'a self-possessed openness to the plenitude of being' and a 'true interiority' which is 'correlative with sensuousness'—sustains the Song of Songs itself and its literal application to 'increase' and marriage (pp. 126-36). Such a vision is always possible within Christianity, though it always struggles with its ascetic opposite. Its fullest expression in the seventeenth century, as we shall see, is the redemptive eroticism of *Paradise Lost*, where Milton reaffirms his faith in his own 'sensuous and passionate' art and its power to 'repair the ruins of our first parents'. Even there, however, it is problematic, conflicting with an equally intense condemnation of passion and lust.

2. The Incorporation of Eros

[*ii*]

The Platonic influence, again, may serve either to enhance or to obliterate the phenomenon of sexuality. The dichotomy can be traced in Plato's own philosophies of love: *Phaedrus* presents the flesh in loathsome terms, but in the *Symposium* Diotima's vision of birth-in-beauty subsumes the physical and the spiritual into a single process, and needs physical desire as a 'step' towards true beauty. Hence Plotinus could admit marital love as a kind of true Eros, 'sowing towards eternity'.[40] Correspondingly, the Platonic reading may either support or deny the literal meaning of the text.

The inconsistencies of the first chapters of Genesis, which nineteenth-century philology later explained by dividing the text into Priestly and Jahwist originals, seemed to the Platonically inclined reader a deliberate invitation to mystery. We recall that chapters 1 and 5 show man created male and female at once, and seem uncertain whether to use a singular or plural pronoun, while chapter 2 says that the female was created separately and only after Adam's side or 'rib' was removed in his sleep; furthermore, God declares the entire creation 'good' in chapter 1, but in chapter 2 remarks that 'it is not good for man to be alone'. To solve this inconsistency, Philo Judaeus had asserted that Adam was at first created asexual or complete with both sexes—which means, in Philo's allegory, that mind and sense-impression were properly balanced—and that only at a later stage, after some diminution of his being or pre-existent fall, did God divide the female into a separate creature. The Biblical fall is thus a second and still lower descent. Origen took this allegorization still further, freely admitting that the literal story was absurd. Genesis must be interpreted as a philosophical myth, indeed as an earlier and less garbled version of Plato's *Phaedrus* and *Symposium*: the seduction of Poros by Penia in the garden of Zeus corresponds to the serpent-episode, which signifies a spiritual rather than a physical fall; the Expulsion describes the soul's loss of its wings, as told later in *Phaedrus*, and the clothing of Adam and Eve in animal skins refers to the soul's acquisition of a fleshly body—the last and most ignominious of a series of falls.[41]

---

[40] *Enneads* III. v. 1, which in turn derives from *Symposium* 206C.
[41] Ch. 1 n. 23 above, and cf. *Symposium* 203B-D, *Phaedrus* 248C; Origen stresses the Hebrew ancestry of Plato's philosophy because Celsus had accused the Jews of garbling the sacred myths of Hesiod. Richard A. Baer argues that there is no gender

Pico and Leone Ebreo were among the Renaissance philosophers who took this interpretation even further. For Leone the discrepancies in Genesis are 'so obvious as to seem deliberate'; Moses must have intended 'some occult mystery beneath the manifest contradiction'.[42] (Attempts by 'the ordinary commentators' to harmonize the literal text are considered but dismissed.) Like Pico, he therefore revives the Rabbinical notion that Adam was actually hermaphroditic in form, and this in turn allows him to Platonize the myth still further. Leone associates the first hermaphroditic Adam, punished by incarnation and separation as well as by the Biblical fall, with the Janus-headed and double-bodied androgynes described by Aristophanes in the *Symposium* (Fig. 3),

3. After medal of Mercantonio Passieri, *The Platonic Androgyne* in J. P. Tomasinus, *Illustrorum Virorum Elogia* (Padua, 1630)

who were sliced in two as a punishment for their hubristic attempt to storm Olympus, and condemned to perpetual erotic yearning for their severed halves.

The idea of a direct relation between Genesis and Platonic Eros is not entirely absurd. The Eden-story, with its allegorical trees and

whatsoever in Philo's perfect original state (*Philo's Use of the Categories of Male and Female* (Leiden, 1970)); Edgar Wind (*Pagan Mysteries in the Renaissance* (Oxford, 1968; rev. edn., 1980), p. 212 n. 64) believes that Philo refers to the androgynous Adam.

[42] 293/345; cf. Giovanni Pico della Mirandola, *Hexaplus* and *Commento*, quot. in Wind, pp. 213, 201, and n. 39; *Symposium* 189D-193D; Bayle, 'Eve' I.

generic names, invites comparison with the philosophic garden-myth of the *Symposium*; the creation of humanity 'male and female', and the subsequent division of one 'side' and its recombination in the joyful union of 'one flesh', certainly resemble Aristophanes' myth of the divided protohumans, as Rabbinical and Alexandrian commentators remarked. The fusion of human procreation and divine creation in Genesis 4:1 and 5:1 may be seen as a cruder version of the 'procreation-in-beauty' that Diotima reveals to Socrates. The erotic garden of Solomon invites comparison with the *Symposium*, and there is also a Platonic tinge to the New Testament: both St. John's Gospel and 1 Corinthians 13 are sustained by the vital connection between *logos* and *agapē*, not yet verbally distinguished from *eros*. But the detailed elaboration of these shadowy affinities only adds to the contradictions that already burden the interpretation of Genesis. To reconcile fundamentally different myths is often to demolish the literal text, and to destroy the 'connatural' bond between sexuality and spirituality.

The point of Aristophanes' fable is not to bewail the original punishment of man, but to praise the merciful invention of sexuality that followed the punishment. Our original ancestors—double-men, double-women and androgynes—reproduced by squirting seed onto the grass from organs at what would become the rear of their bodies; after the separation erotic yearning was therefore doomed to pine forever unconsummated, since the severed halves could not be fused into one flesh. Zeus kindly moved the genitals to the front of the body, so that couples would obtain some satisfaction according to their kind—heterosexuals could have children, lesbians could have pleasure, and manly homosexuals could be less distracted from business affairs. 'It is from this distant epoch', Aristophanes explains, 'that we may date the innate love which human beings feel for another, the love which restores us to our ancient state by attempting to weld two beings into one and to heal the wounds which human nature suffered' (191D).

Renaissance thinkers gave various meanings to this fable. Marsilio Ficino, undeterred by the strong sexual emphasis in Aristophanes' story, converts it into a pious allegory: he interprets Eros first as the desire for virtue and divine vision that begins in adolescence, then as the power which 'by restoring to us the wholeness we have lost when we were divided ... leads us back to Heaven', and finally as the divine *agapē* itself; but he does not regard it as consubstantial with sexuality.[43] Rabelais compresses Ficino's interpretation into a gesture both serious and comic, in the true Socratic manner: he has Gargantua adopt the Platonic androgyne as a cap-badge, with 'deux testes' and 'deux culz', but with a motto from 1 Corinthians 13 ("*ΑΓΑΠΣ ΟΥ ΖΗΤΕΙ ΤΑ ΕΑΥΤΗΣ*", love seeketh not his own).[44] Donne compares the good priest, an agent of divine love who connects the heavenly and earthly realms, to a 'blest Hermaphrodite'.[45] Other thinkers, however, bring Aristophanes' fable back to its original subject, deep sexual love between human partners. When Hugo Grotius dramatized Adam's speech of welcome to Eve, he translated 'bone of my bone' into this kind of Eros: God made the wife's flesh out of the husband's 'so that it might return whence it was born, to its own first principle (*suum ad primordium*)'.[46] Du Bartas praises the first couple as an 'amoureux Androgyne'; scholars since 1611 have noticed the connection with Plato obscured in Sylvester's translation ('sweet *Hee-Shee*-Coupled-One'), and have recognized the androgyne as an emblem of marriage.[47] The interpretation of erotic desire as a healing return to primal unity survives, shorn of its mythology, in Descartes's *Les Passions de l'âme* (1649) and in the libertine dialogue *L'Escole des filles* (1656). But the fullest treatment of the theme, and the fullest parallel between the *Symposium* and Genesis, comes in Leone Ebreo's *Dialoghi d'Amore* (1535).

Leone differs from many other Renaissance philosophers of love because he is prepared to accept physical sexuality between man and woman as an *effect* of the higher Eros, though he condemns it as a primary *cause* of love (51/56). He connects Genesis not only to Plato, but to the erotic love expressed in the Song of Songs (345-6/422-5). Leone combines neo-Platonism with a more literalist

---

[43] *Commentary on Plato's Symposium (De Amore)*, ed. and tr. Sears Reynolds Jayne (Columbia, Mo., 1944), pp. 63, 163.

[44] *Gargantua*, ch. 8; cf. 'Prologue', where he identifies himself with Alcibiades's description of Socrates, satyr or silenus without and god within (*Symposium* 215B, 216D). For the *two*-headed hermaphrodite, which Rabelais mistakenly assumes Plato describes, see A. Henkel and A. Schöne, *Emblemata* (Stuttgart, 1967), col. 1629; Bayle ('Sadeur' F) makes a similar mistake.

[45] 'To Mr Tilman after he had taken orders', l. 54; cf. Wind, p. 217. For hints of a more spiritual-erotic version of the hermaphrodite, see also A. R. Cirillo, 'The Fair Hermaphrodite: Love-union in the Poetry of Donne and Spenser', *SEL* IX (1969), 81-95.

[46] *Adamus Exul*, in Kirkconnell, p. 136.

[47] Du Bartas, *Œuvres* (Paris, 1611), I. 307; Sylvester, p. 291. Cf. Nohrnberg, p. 601 and n. 461.

tradition, deriving perhaps from his Rabbinical background, that applies Genesis and love-philosophy to the practical aspects of sexuality and marriage. Nevertheless, his conflation of Plato and the Bible reveals an inconsistency in this area, particularly when he explains the separation of the protohuman into Adam and Eve. He himself recognizes one major discrepancy: in Plato the division of man is, quite plausibly, a punishment for hubris, and love 'the remedy of the sin which led to one being made into two' (291/345); but in Genesis the division is an improvement on the original design, with sin and punishment coming later in a separate episode. Leone proceeds to harmonize the two versions in a double allegorical reading, but neither of his explanations (one moral and the other intellectual) faces the most pressing question—why should God create a being that needed such drastic changes?

In the happy hermaphroditic state, Leone explains, the male and female principles were joined in a way 'not conducive to coitus nor to generation'; their 'union [was] not of the flesh, but of human essence and intellectual inclination ... in order that they might be of greater help to one another.' This lofty definition of the Edenic bond anticipates Milton's identification of 'help meet' with spiritual compatibility. But Milton's divorce tracts, though they rage against giving too high a priority to physical sexuality, still include it among the ends of marriage; Leone here eliminates it entirely from the state of innocence. His attempts to reconcile this with the command to 'increase and multiply' reveal a deep inconsistency. He praises the benevolence of a God whose 'primary intent' is to divide the protohumans 'for their own good', and thus initiate sexual reproduction. But in the same breath he equates division with sin itself: 'sin may be said to spring from division, according to the version of the Scriptures, and division from sin, according to Plato.' The real meaning of the forbidden tree is 'carnal pleasure', as we learn from the urge to cover the genitals with fig-leaves; Augustine's theories thus reinforce the non-Augustinian doctrine that procreation is a purely fallen business, a duty enjoined as part of the punishment. Leone's moral allegory (296-8/351-3) thus obscures both the timing and the motivation of the division into man and woman, making it seem either incomprehensible or evil.

Leone's intellectual allegory (298-302/354-8) tends, paradoxically, to restore the status of physical sexuality. The fall-story concerns, not sexuality *per se*, but the way cognition deals with it.

In the hermaphroditic state the perfect 'male' intellect dominates the imperfect 'female' body, paying no heed to the tree of appetite. This state, though 'perfect', is also somehow defective: the pure intellect neglects the flesh entirely, forgetting to eat and to preserve the race—'for those who are wedded to a life of intellectual contemplation despise corporeal love and flee from the lascivious act of generation'. (This angelic aspiration is what Plato meant when he accused the androgynes of trying to storm heaven; Leone does not enquire whether he himself is also prone to this fault.)[48] God intends man to preserve a balance between spirit and matter, and He so divides the 'male' and 'female' that they will be connected by awareness and loving concern. It is the abuse of this legitimate concern that constitutes the fall. Sexual procreation is not in itself corrupt, even though the female is 'the cause of every kind of bestiality in man' (303/360). The original sin is a kind of libertine eroticism: the serpent represents 'carnal appetite' and sexual connoisseurship, giving them 'much subtle craft and cunning knowledge pertaining to lasciviousness and greed which before they lacked'. The eyes which open when the fruit is eaten are 'not those of the intellect, for those were rather firmly sealed, but the eyes of the imagination (*la fantasia corporale*), which serve the body in its carnal and wanton practices.' (The physical ills of the curse, correspondingly, refer to the diseases of debauchery.) The serpent even encourages them to see sex as a kind of divine creativity, and thus as a direct challenge to God.

Milton himself was clearly influenced by the Platonic account of love, and knew Leone's grand philosophical expansion of Genesis. In *The Doctrine and Discipline of Divorce*, as we shall see, he invents his own myths of Eros and his own method of equating Genesis and the *Symposium*. For Milton, however, the birth of Love from Penia in the garden of Zeus represents, not the pre-existent fall as it did in Origen and Leone, but the central mystery of human love and the crowning purpose of creation—the invention of woman as a cure for loneliness. His application of this mythology is intensely practical, moreover: if true Eros cannot be engendered, if a marriage cannot conform to and re-enact the ideal of Plato and Genesis 'at

---

[48] 305/362-3. 'Storming heaven' is given two incompatible meanings by Leone, since it also signifies the aspiration to 'be as gods' that motivated the sexual fall; Calvin later equated the fall with the Titans' attempt to storm heaven (3:5), but, as we shall see in 4. 3. i below, he rejected the sexual interpretation of the fall.

least in some proportion', then it must be legally dissolved (II. 252-3). Milton does consider Leone's idea of the hermaphroditic Adam in his own interpretation of Genesis 1:27, but only to reject it as a 'fable' reinforced by 'the accidental concurrence of *Plato's* wit'. The idea of primeval androgyny is quite foreign to Milton's literalism and his love of sharply differentiated genders. Nor could he accept the static ontological categories assumed by the allegorical division into 'male' and 'female': gender-identity is established by a strenuous, and in the earlier works even hostile, dialectic of 'growth and compleating'.[49]

In the writings of the divorce crisis, Milton rejects the theories of Leone because he wants to narrow the terms of Genesis 1:27 to exclude woman. In *Paradise Lost*, on the other hand, he departs from the Platonist in a different direction; rather than seeking esoteric meanings, he expands the possibilitites of the literal interpretation, and creates a more humanly realistic Eden, more 'open to the plenitude of being'. (Ironically, this would also be the last Biblical Eden in Western literature.) He does respond to elements in Leone's allegory, but he entirely rejects the anti-materialism and anti-literalism of the Platonist. Unlike his predecessor Leone and his friend Marvell,[50] Milton refuses to imagine a happier state before the creation of Eve, and he refuses to identify the fall with sexuality in any form; instead he takes the sexualization of Eden and converts it to a positive vision, in his uniquely erotic description of the state of innocence. And though he does not *equate* the fall with libertinism, as Leone did in his second allegorical reading, he does create a vivid scene of sexual connoisseurship and courtly seduction immediately after the primal sin, to show how far the first lovers have fallen from Paradisal Eros.

[*iii*]

Milton's defence of 'wedded Love' against the twin dangers of asceticism and libertinism, 'Hypocrites' and 'Court Amours', grows from his dialogue not only with the Renaissance philosophy of love, but with Reformation exegetes and their promotion of holy matrimony. Many commentators of the period, including the more

[49] II. 589; for 'growth and compleating' in *Areop.*, cf. II. 528. M's conceptions of Eros, passion, and gender are analysed at length in chs. 5–7 below; cf. also Marilyn R. Farwell, 'Eve, the Separation Scene, and the Renaissance Idea of Androgyny', *MS* XVI (1982), 3–20.
[50] 'Two *Paradises* twere in one / To live in *Paradise* alone' ('The Garden').

enlightened Roman Catholics, expanded upon the speculations of Augustine, Aquinas, and Luther; they assumed that Adam and Eve would have enjoyed an innocent and pleasurable version of normal sex if the fall had not come within a day of the creation, that Eve would have borne children without pain, that the consequences of the fall are wrapped up in corrupted sexuality, but that the original blessing, however marred, can still be faintly (and as it were painfully) regained in the joys of godly marriage. The idea that sexuality itself is a punishment for sin recedes into the past, or slides into the marginal realm of eccentrics and visionaries.[51]

Calvin, for example, celebrates the institution of marriage and the sacredness of procreative union, invokes shortness of time as evidence for the apparent lack of consummation in Eden, and asserts that women would have given birth in the state of innocence 'without pain, or at least without great suffering (*tanto cruciato*)' (3:6, 3:16). When he comes to Genesis 4:1 ('Adam knew his wife Eve') he praises God for not having abolished the blessing of increase entirely, and for having 'confirmed' Adam's heart so that he would not shrink from the full horror of fallen copulation, a *res per se pudenda*; he hastens to explain, however, that the *foeditas* or loathsomeness of sexual intercourse is one of the fruits of the fall, and not an intrinsic property of generation. The distinction is a fragile one: in Thomas Tymme's translation of 1578 the marginal note to this passage, where Calvin had carefully separated the 'filthines' of fallen sex from sexuality itself, reads 'Carnall copulation is one of the fruites of sin'. Calvin himself, on the contrary, regarded the procreative union of one flesh as 'the most sacred bond' from which all other social concords derive—as Milton was later to do— and apparently identifies it both with 'Nature' and with the higher Eros of Platonism. 'Man was formed to be a social animal', and since 'the human race could not exist without the woman ... therefore, in the conjunction of human beings, that sacred bond is especially conspicuous by which the husband and wife are combined in one body and one soul, as nature itself taught Plato' (2:18, 2: 24, and cf. 5:2).

[51] Cf. Arnold Williams, *The Common Expositor* (Chapel Hill, 1948), pp. 89–90, 130, and 137; this pioneering study must be used with caution, however—Williams does not recognize Aug. as a source for Pererius, for example, and he ascribes two contradictory time-theories to Paraeus. For the sexual interpretation of the fall, see 4. 3 below.

This erotic and companionate doctrine of 'one flesh' in Calvin and his followers has persuaded many Miltonists that there is a distinct progressive Protestant theory of marriage, or even a 'Puritan Art of Love' that flourished particularly in England.[52] It is certainly striking to find Calvin linking Genesis to the Platonic conception of Eros, which foreshadows Milton's own use of Platonic myth in the divorce tracts. Even if the English 'Puritans' did not evolve an art of love like that of Ovid, or a theory like that of Leone Ebreo, their marital applications of Genesis do dwell upon the importance of love—not just the love that should endear the performance of duties, but also the sexual love specific to the marriage-bed.

Thomas Gataker, for example, maintains that in their sexual intercourse the husband and wife re-enact the original separation of Adam and Eve in reverse:

> There is in most *men* and *women* naturally an inclination and propension to the *nuptiall conjuction*. *The man seeketh his rib*, say the *Rabbines*; and the *woman the mans side*. The *man* misseth his *rib*, and seeketh to recover it againe, and the *woman* would bee in her old place againe, under the *mans arme or wing*, from whence at first shee was taken.

The only obstacle to this tender union, Gataker continues, is the loss of self-control that Augustine identified as the immediate result of the fall.[53] Here as in Calvin, the radical Protestant tradition comes to resemble the Platonic philosophy of Eros. But the 'Puritans' often show a frank and comforting acceptance of practical sexuality, provided it is expressed within marriage, which distinguishes them both from the Platonist and from the Cavalier libertine. Gataker's exposition of the rib shares neither the sad yearning that underlies Plato's original fable, nor the perverse eeriness of Lovelace's adaptation of Genesis, in which men who desire skeletal mistresses attempt to 'incorporate with Aery leane, / To repair their sides, and get their Ribb again'.[54]

---

[52] The foundations of this approach are laid in William and Malleville Haller, 'The Puritan Art of Love', *HLQ* V (1942), 235-72, and Roland M. Frye, 'The Teachings of Classical Puritanism on Conjugal Love', *SR* II (1955), 148-59; cf. also Laurence Lerner, *Love and Marriage* (1979), pp. 111-21. A note of revisionist caution is sounded in Halkett, *passim*.

[53] *A Wife in Deed*, p. 37, in *A Good Wife Gods Gift, and A Wife in Deed: Two Mariage Sermons* (1623).

[54] *Poems*, ed. C. H. Wilkinson, single-vol. edn. (Oxford, 1930), p. 96. The poem is untitled; Wilkinson transfers the title 'La Bella Bona Roba' from the previous poem, but it bears no relation to the theme—the witty praise of fat mistresses over lean ones.

The 'Puritan' sense of marital sexuality is typified in William Whately's *A Bride-Bush* (1617). The sexual satisfaction of the partners is not given absolutely the first importance in this popular wedding-sermon, but it is still 'the best means to continue and nourish their mutuall naturall love', and problems in 'the society of the marriage bed' are still the greatest source of danger to the whole marriage. When he rewrote *A Bride-Bush* as a formal treatise two years later, Whately promoted sexual love even higher. 'Due benevolence', the Pauline duty of mutual sexual surrender, is now essential to the very existence of marriage, whereas love is important but not essential. Sexual refusal actually dissolves the marriage—a position that Whately recanted under pressure from his superiors, but continued to print in later editions. Copulation must be filled with love, sustained by moderation, performed 'seasonally' and without aphrodisiac provocations, Whately insists; and it must above all be 'sanctified' by a due sense of 'God's ordinance'—that is, of the original words of Genesis re-enacted in each act of love. But it is still copulation, and not piety, companionship, or child-rearing, that constitutes the true Adamic marriage: 'how else should they be called one flesh?' Remembering the Scripture in a prayer before copulation—sanctifying sexual congress as meat and drink is sanctified by saying grace—is a means of 'seeing God in it'.[55]

William Gouge also raises 'due benevolence' to a primary constituent of godly marriage, distinct from 'love' and distinct even from procreation—Gouge is quite emphatic that married couples should still make love during pregnancy, and probably during lactation. Again, Genesis and its New Testament echoes inspire this apotheosis of sexuality—an elevation refreshingly free of the sublimation usually associated with Platonism. 'The first, highest, chiefest, and most absolutely necessary' feature of marriage, Gouge insists, is that '*unity* whereby husband and wife do account one another to be *one flesh*'. And the supreme factor in achieving this unity, second only to the fear of God itself, is 'that husband and wife mutually delight each in other, and maintain a pure and fervent love betwixt themselves, yeelding that *due benevolence* one

---

[55] 1617 edn., pp. 43-5 (note that the discussion of sex comes at the climactic point of the sermon version); 1619 edn., pp. 14-27; 1623 edn., prefatory remarks. For the disciplinary action of the High Commission against Whately, see Haller and Haller, pp. 267-8.

to another which is warranted and sanctified by God's word, and ordained of God for this particular end.'[56]

These and other 'Puritan' writers, though intensely aware of the horrors of a bad marriage, still write about matrimony as if it is an achievable Paradise—almost as if, as one critic feels tempted to say, they 'do not believe we are fallen'. And they still regard sexual satisfaction as the chief means '(next to an awfull feare of God)' of achieving 'a kinde of *Heaven upon Earth*'.[57] Milton's own vision of marriage has a complex and troubled relationship to this radical Protestant tradition. He clearly has a deep respect for the sanctified matrimony ordained in Genesis, and his own radicalism has clearly borrowed many features from 'Puritan' traditions. But his divorce tracts admit copulation among the ends of marriage only as an 'inferior' subdivision of the lowest category of 'conversation', and only when it is 'an effect rather than a cause of conjugal love'—a position similar to Leone's. We will see that the whole thrust of his argument, far from being in sympathy with these pillars of the Puritan tradition, is directed against the high status they give to physical sexuality; his divorce tracts, sustained by an idealistic myth of Eros, may nevertheless be read as an indignant reply to Whately's rhetorical question, 'how else should they be called one flesh?'

The 'society of the marriage bed', then, should be a living witness to the 'ordinance' declared in Genesis and re-established in the New Testament. Present and past are thus connected by a network of Scripture.[58] The idea of 'one flesh', in particular, already defined the essence of marriage for both Christ and St. Paul, and the nuptial theology of Ephesians created a link not only between the original happiness of Genesis and the 'prime institution' of godly marriage, but also between married love and the rich eroticism of the Song of Songs. And since the Song was ascribed to Solomon, then all his other comments on marriage could also be used to weave onto the frame of Genesis a dense and realistic texture of amorous experience.

Gouge, for example, brought Genesis into his 'Exposition of Ephesians 5:28-9' to illuminate the resemblance and identity of the married couple, and to defend the 'Naturall affections' that God

[56] *Domesticall Duties*, 2nd edn. (1626), pp. 125-32.
[57] Lerner, p. 121; Gataker, quot. in Frye, p. 157.
[58] M stresses that Edenic 'wedded Love' is equally applicable to 'present, or past' (*PL* IV. 762).

had implanted and declared to be intrinsically good (pp. 44-7). Henry Smith draws on the Song of Songs when he describes Adam before the creation of Eve as 'like a Turtle which hath lost his mate'. Gataker derives his sermon *A Good Wife God's Gift* from Proverbs 19:14, which becomes the link between the present state and the unfallen past: 'it was God that first gave *Adam* his wife, and it is God that giveth every man his wife to this day.' Gataker's description of love comes straight from the Song of Songs, and his sense that love can neither be understood nor 'constrained' comes from commentaries on the Song—though we can also detect the popular wisdom of Chaucer and the *Roman de la Rose*: 'love will not be constrained by maistrie.'[59]

Many preachers, including the 'Puritans' Gouge and Whately and the less radical Nathaniel Hardy, enrich their accounts of married love by expounding Proverbs 5:18-19: 'rejoice with the wife of thy youth; let her be as the loving hind and pleasant roe, let her breasts satisfy thee at all times, and be thou ravished always with her love.' Gouge uses these beautiful lines, reminiscent of the Song of Songs itself, in his polemic against 'Stoick' repression of passion, and recommends a love so 'ardent' and uncritical that it seems like dotage or 'error'—the literal meaning of the Hebrew word translated as 'ravish'. 'Read the Song of Songs', Gouge adds,

and in it you shall observe such affection manifested by Christ to his Spouse, as would make one thinke hee did (with reverence in a holy manner to use the phrase) even erre in his love, and doat on her. A good patterne and precedent for Husbands.

Though this delight is not *exclusively* sexual, it is still grounded in the body as well as the soul, on 'the neere conjunction of mariage' as well as on the 'inward qualities' of the partner. Hardy likewise uses the Solomonic 'ravishment' as a paradigm of the love that should bind the husband and wife: this is partly a spiritual love for her as a fellow-Christian (which other women may inspire in even greater measure), partly a 'natural love' for her as a woman (which other women may also inspire, though less intensely), and partly an unconditional love for an irreplaceable individual. By earnest application of this model, derived from the 'ravishment' of Solomon

---

[59] Smith, quot. in Haller and Haller, p. 245; Gataker, pp. 9-11 (cf. marginal refs to S. of S. 8:6-7 and to St. Bernard's commentary); Chaucer, *Franklin's Tale*, l. 92. See also ch. 3 n. 19 below.

2. *The Incorporation of Eros*

and the 'one flesh' of Genesis, the godly couple can achieve an ideal fusion of two qualities that the world splits apart—*dignitas* and *voluptas*.[60]

Though it is fervently opposed to 'lust', the Protestant defence of marriage could sometimes lead to the promotion of sexuality that Milton fiercely denounced in his divorce tracts. On the one hand the husband is warned not to love the wife as if she was a mistress, as Adam had done; on the other hand he is encouraged to dote excessively on her with all the sensuous fervour of Solomon. 'Lust' may destroy marriage and turn it from a heaven into a hell, 'natural love' may be a feeble foundation of sand, and copulation may be an 'inferior' end;[61] but 'Due Benevolence' is a primary constituent of marriage, the main solvent of marital problems, and the principle source of the unity that God intended by making Eve and Adam one flesh. The very act of lust could be seasonal, natural, and sanctified, performed at the proper times of the month and without artificial stimulation, 'seeing God in it'. Sexual pleasure, which Aquinas thought would have been more intense in the unfallen state, still allows us to feel the original blessings of Genesis. This is not simply pleasure in godly offspring—at least not for those divines who recommended intercourse with pregnant or infertile wives—but real erotic pleasure, the flame described in *Cleanness* that 'burns so hot in the night that the trouble of the world recedes'.

The myth of Eden is thus transformed by the Song of Songs into an erotic dream, by the New Testament into a marital 'ordinance', and by Reformation Bibliolatry and primitivism into the 'first institution' of marriage and the standard of perfection that should regulate its practices and emotions. Some features of the unfallen state, like unconscious nakedness, have vanished completely; but others live on in diminished form, and marriage is the most vivid and least attenuated of these survivals. Consequently it is in godly marriage, rather than in the extremes of asceticism and mystic rapture, that mankind comes nearest to regaining the glorious state of 'one flesh' that God originally intended for them. When Milton

---

[60] Gouge, pp. 208–9; Hardy, *Love and Fear the Inseparable Twins of a Blest Matrimony* (1658), pp. 6–8, 11–12. Contrast Donne (*Sermons*, V. 120), who denies the role of sexual love in marriage completely; the husband must not feel 'a love *Quia mulier*, because she is a woman,' but only '*Quia uxor*, because she is my wife'.

[61] e.g. Frye, pp. 156–8.

shows Paradisal marriage rebuilt by the efforts of Adam and Eve after the fall, he is precisely reversing—as Diane McColley has shown—the ascetic steps proposed by a Greek Father such as Gregory of Nyssa. 'We ... are allowed to return to our earliest state of blessedness by the very same stages by which we lost Paradise,' Gregory believes: marriage is the last of a chain of misfortunes, instituted only 'as a compensation for having to die'; to return to Paradise, the adept must therefore abandon marriage first of all. 'In *Paradise Lost*,' on the other hand, 'marriage is the first thing to be repaired' (pp. 32-3).

In this 'Paradisal trace' theory of sexuality, developed out of Luther by generations of practical moralists, the barricades of Eden are partially breached. This reading was founded not on rationalism or a coherent erotic ontology, but on intuitive glimpses, fitful and problematic; but it established an emotional affinity between Solomonic and Edenic Eros, between present and past, and between the 'saints and patriarchs' and the provisional, miniature 'Paradise within' of the godly family. These are precisely the terms of Milton's great apostrophe to wedded love, placed at the moment when Adam and Eve are 'imparadisd in one anothers arms, / The happier *Eden*' (IV. 506-7, 762). And yet Milton felt himself at odds with the prevailing ethos of his day. The Milton of the 1640s, embroiled in his own disastrous marriage, and bursting with indignation at the practical consequences of this praise of 'the society of the marriage-bed'—that impotence and adultery could dissolve a marriage while mental incompatibility could not—indulged in exaggerated attacks on the bestiality of copulation. But the divorce tracts still defend the 'ravishment' and 'error' of Solomonic Eros, and bitterly denounce those false 'sages' who dismiss its relevance to marriage. And in *Paradise Lost*—in the same paean to wedded love—Milton attacks those 'Hypocrites' who are too 'pure' to admit real copulation into the state of innocence.

Reformation praise of holy matrimony created the impression that the Protestants, like many of the Rabbis, literally believed in pre-lapsarian consummation; as late as 1700, Bayle indignantly defended 'our Writers' against the accusation ('Eve' B). It was quite untrue, however. One Elizabethan commentator, Gervase Babington, enraged at the wickedness of those who decry matrimony by dating it after the fall, suggested that Adam and Eve might have consummated their marriage before the fall; but he backs off almost immediately.[62] Belief in the Paradisal trace was never strong enough to dislodge the orthodox position, that Adam and Eve were virgins at the expulsion; *Paradise Lost* is unique and isolated in this respect. Milton is thus both more and less 'Protestant' than the tradition of practical eroticism we have just examined.

4. The radical revision

We will not understand Milton's complex relation to contemporary Protestantism if we confine our search to the 'Puritan' establishment, however. The Reformation and the English Revolution generated many varieties of religious experience and many contradictory positions. Most of the faithful accepted some connection between Paradise, Solomonic rapture, and the idealized married state, but this combination could produce dramatically different visions and practices. Milton himself both intensifies and rejects the application of Genesis to contemporary institutions, arguing both that marriages must attain the Paradisal ideal, and that we should not 'fondly think within our strength all that lost Paradise relates' (II. 316). In the upheaval of Milton's own lifetime, as in the 'Radical Reformation' of the sixteenth century, the question of Paradisal marriage opened into the major dilemmas and controversies of the age: the status of the flesh, the legitimacy of existing institutions, the nature and application of Scriptural metaphor, and the relation between the other world and this.

The spiritual eroticism of the Song of Songs could generate a mystic and ascetic enthusiasm that had the effect of undermining, rather than reinforcing, conventional matrimony. Francis Rous's *Misticall Marriage*, for example, elaborates in rich and sensuous detail the theme of the 'chamber within us, and [the] bed of love in that chamber, wherein Christ meets the soule,' and promises that through this union Christ will 'make a Paradise within thee'; but his way to Paradise resembles the asceticism of the Greek Fathers:

To be without lust is a true Paradise, for man had not this lust when he was first placed in Paradise, neither could Paradise endure man, when this

---

[62] *Certaine Plaine, Briefe, and Comfortable Notes, upon Every Chapter of Genesis* (1592), ff. 21ᵛ–22; Babington's point (reiterated in the 1596 edition, 'perused again and enlarged') is that marriage is honourable whether or not it was consummated in Eden. For pre-lapsarian sex in two Dutch poets, and their differences from M, see 7. 1. i below.

lust was placed in him; therefore the true way to return to Paradise, (or the state of happiness whereof it was a type) is to put off this lust.[63]

'Lust' is clearly identified with the whole phenomenon of sexuality, which is practically equated with the fall; there is no place in Rous's vision for a redeemed marital sexuality, connatural with the Solomonic rapture and the love of Christ.

Nuptial and Paradisal theology was particularly fully developed among the radical separatists who flourished in Reformation Europe and again in England during the overthrow of Royalism, but the relation of these sects to the institution of marriage was typically problematic, and for conventional Protestants extremely scandalous. Johannes Campanus, for example, based his vision of 'the restitution of all things' on a reading of Genesis that, like St. Paul's 'one flesh', could apply equally to divine love and to real marriage. Genesis 1:27 reveals God to be male and female, a 'binity' of two persons united as intimately as man and wife, and this in turn transforms the experience of nuptial union: the simultaneous creation of Adam and Eve, and their reunion into 'one loving flesh in marriage and procreation', represented for Campanus 'the moment and the action in which creation mirrors the divine'.[64] But what kind of marriage would be appropriate for the new age? Campanus's vision was translated into practice by the Anabaptists of Münster, where we see acted out the paradox that characterized many radical sects in the sixteenth and seventeenth centuries: their spiritualism led them to renounce the flesh, but their nuptial, Paradisal, and eschatological theology led them towards sexual experimentation and new forms of marriage that seemed outrageously carnal to the more orthodox observer. Lewdness was forbidden during the Anabaptist rule of Münster, but polygamy was compulsory; both laws were enforced by the death penalty. Their programme came from a narrowing and intensification of Augustine: the overwhelming urge was to hasten the apocalypse by generating the pre-ordained number of the elect, and the dominant text, defining 'the only legitimate purpose of matrimony', was *increase and multiply*. To guarantee that all these children were true citizens of the New Israel, they had to be conceived in extreme purity, free from the lusts of the flesh. Only thus would the saints

[63] (1653), pp. 39–40, and cf. ff. A2^v–4, pp. 328–9. Rous's vision of the fall as a 'placing' of lust in Adam is influenced by Boehme (cf. 4. 2. ii below).
[64] George Huntston Williams, *RR* p. 324.

bring together the first and the last things, the nuptial consummation of genesis and apocalypse.[65]

The 'mystical marriage' is of course a standard topic of contemplative Christianity. Among the radical sectarians, however, this intense imagery of erotic rapture and surrender was transformed, and its metaphorical status thrown into doubt, by activism and subjectivism—the conviction that the Holy Spirit has risen again in the flesh of the believer, and that inward sensations alone could determine its presence. It was often unclear, even to fellow-separatists, whether 'nakedness', 'marriage', or 'fornication' refer to physical acts or to spiritual states conveyed in esoteric imagery.[66] Sectarian leaders often had to repudiate the idea, growing within their own ranks, that 'faith and love may do and permit everything' including 'the lasciviousness and self-indulgence of the flesh', that female saints could not enter the Kingdom of Heaven 'unless they do abominably prostitute and make common their bodies to all men', and that no one could be properly initiated, nor reach the mystic *acclivitas*, unless they performed sexual acts 'in a special way ... without the fear of God or the scruples of conscience'.[67]

[*ii*]

The sexual experimentalism of these anti-establishment sectarians, or 'Adam-wits' as Dryden would later call them, guaranteed them a place in the contemporary imagination far larger than their numbers would suggest. Most witnesses to their practices are hostile and unreliable, of course, but their exaggerations are based on

---

[65] *RR* pp. 371-8, 511-12, and cf. Leo Miller, *John Milton among the Polygamophiles* (NY, 1974), pp. 46-7.

[66] The Anabaptist Melchior Hoffman, for instance, was horrified to realize that Nicholas Frey, a disciple who shared his nuptial theology of redemption, had actually put it into practice by a bigamous marriage to his 'spiritual companion', proclaimed as the 'New Eve' (*RR* pp. 286-8). The case against the 15th-century Homines Intelligentiae of Brussels similarly hinged on the status of metaphor: they appeared to proclaim that intercourse outside marriage was no sin, and to crown their gatherings with an act of coitus 'equal in value to a prayer', equated with the 'Delectatio Paradisi' and the mystical *acclivitas*, but their defender claimed that all this was Pauline imagery for the freedom of the spirit, not to be applied to the flesh at all; cf. Étienne Baluze, *Miscellanea*, II (1675), 281-94. The leader of this group allegedly claimed to have 'a special method of coitus, yet not against nature, which he said was what Adam used to do in Paradise'.

[67] *RR* pp. 182, 202; Baluze, pp. 282-3; cf. Henry Niclaes, quot. in Jean D. Moss, 'The Family of Love and English Critics', *Sixteenth Century Journal* VI (1975), 49.

explicit doctrines and verifiable incidents—the enthusiastic nuptial and Solomonic imagery, the polygamy of Münster, the communism that occasionally included community of wives,[68] the attempt to translate Augustine's speculations into action by inventing a 'special form' of sexual union, and to reverse the fall, re-establishing Paradise in this life, by odd mixtures of asceticism and erotic experiment. It was all too easy for the orthodox, mocking and fearful, to play up the erotic and to devalue the ascetic elements, presenting the complex restitutionist impulse not as a decayed metaphysic but as simple lust. The secular diagnosis of 'Enthusiasm' as a genital disorder, that reached its height in Swift's *Tale of a Tub*, was already strong at the time of the English Revolution. Indeed, for some centuries charges of polygamy and orgiastic eroticism had been constantly levelled against even the most austere heretical and separatist groups, in terms that go back to the early Greek Fathers' attacks on the 'Adamites'.[69]

Thus the Loists or 'Spiritual Libertines', according to Calvin, obliterate the fall and dilute Grace by their facile belief in a return to Paradise in this life, mangle the Scriptures and subordinate the Word to their own fantasies, and indulge in reckless sexual adventures under the name of 'Spiritual marriage'. Excessive confidence in the Spirit leads them to replace the heavily guarded Paradise of Genesis with their own subjective raptures, which derive

[68] *RR* pp. 504, 507, 511-14, and for other verifiable sexual experiments 133-4, 181-2, 192-3, 357, 372-8, 481, 484, 505-8. The Hutterites, on the other hand, believed that living by Paradisal standards meant even stricter monogamy, even though they abolished private property; cf. *PL* IV. 751-2, where wedded love is the 'sole propriety / In Paradise of all things common else'. The Hutterite position was based, ironically, on the same Clementine epistle that other sects used as the inspiration for 'community of wives'.

[69] Theodoretus, *Haereticarum Fabularum Compendium*, I. 6 (incorporating Clement of Alexandria, *Stromateis* III. ii); Wilhelm Fränger, *The Millenium of Hieronymus Bosch*, tr. Eithne Wilkins and Ernst Kaiser (1952), p. 19 (a rare verifiable detail in a fanciful work); Robert Burton, *Anatomy of Melancholy*, III. iii. 4. 2; *The Family of Love*, in Thomas Middleton, *Works*, ed. A. H. Bullen (1885), III. 57-9; Bayle, 'Adamites', 'Picards', 'Turlupins'; *OED*, 'Adamites'; Williams, *Common Expositor*, pp. 218-19; *RR* pp. 208, 359, 675. Epiphanius refers cryptically to 'insatiable lust' as the motivation of the Adamites (*Adversus Haereses* 52), but neither he nor Augustine accuses the Adamites of sexual orgies; in fact 'they are averse to marriage, because Adam did not know his wife before he sinned and was expelled from Paradise—there would have been no marriage at all if they had not sinned' (Augustine, *De Haeresibus* 31). As Bayle points out, this is good evidence for their asceticism, since 'Fame seldom lets such Transactions die, when once it has them in her Power, unless they are found to be notoriously false' ('Adamites', Remark C).

from the most depraved of human desires. These lunatics ('bis ergo insaniunt Libertini') feel they have a Biblical sanction for their confusion of carnal and spiritual love, their 'mingling of heaven and earth', and they 'maintain the fiction that we are restored to the state of innocence whenever our judgement is suspended and we are carried away by our own libido'. They allegedly insist that to be born again is to return to that innocent state which Adam enjoyed before his eyes were opened, to 'cease making judgements', and to regain a childlike or ecstatic indifference to the knowledge of good and evil; instead of morality one must be led by the *sens naturel*. Every crime is condoned by 'to the pure all things are pure', and every sensual impulse is a 'calling' such as St. Paul recommends in 1 Corinthians 7. The original blessing of 'increase and multiply' is distorted into the *'loi naturelle'* that (in the guise of an eschatological union with Christ) allows them to 'couple with one another whenever it suits'; and this Genesis-inspired sexual freedom is amplified by imitating the raptures of the Song of Songs.[70]

Calvin presents no evidence for his accusations, which are mostly supplied from ancient heresiology; the supposedly Libertine pamphlet he quotes refers only to 'the true bond, made in the tree of the cross, which we call "marriage" ', and insists that we must put off rather than revert to the old Adam.[71] Nevertheless, Calvin believes that he is attacking a real misappropriation of Genesis: the Libertines base their vision on Genesis 1:27 ('male and female created he them'), but he thunders back with Genesis 2:24—two, and no more than two, shall become one flesh. Worse still, they

---

[70] Calvin, *Genesis*, 2:9, and *Treatises against the Anabaptists and against the Libertines*, tr. and ed. Benjamin W. Farley (Grand Rapids, Mich., 1982), *passim*, esp. pp. 263, 275, 279-81, 306. The 'Editor's Introduction' to the tr. of *Contre la secte phantastique et furieuse des libertins que se nomment spirituelz* (1545) has a useful account of Calvin's relations with this sect (though it fails to note the reference to the Libertines in his commentary on Genesis), and carefully distinguishes the Loist or 'Quintinist' Libertines, the object of Calvin's treatise, from the 'Libertins' in Calvin's own Geneva community. The tr. itself should be used with caution, as Prof. Farley's grasp of language sometimes deserts him; Calvin calls one tract a *coq à l'âne* (*not* 'a cock and bull story') whose elements 's'entretiennent aussi bien que crottes de chievres', i.e. are as coherent as goat-droppings ('are maintained in any event as goat dung', p. 299). I have referred where necessary to an edn. of the original in the Folger Shakespeare Library (n.p., 1547). For the Spiritual Libertines' relation to the cult of Love at the court of Navarre, see Hiram Haydn, *The Counter-Renaissance* (NY, 1950), pp. 94, 357, 559.

[71] *Against the Libertines*, pp. 306 and 312-13.

impose on marriage the Pauline distinction between spiritual and carnal, interpreting it to mean that 'a marriage that has been contracted and solemnized before men is carnal, unless there is a good compatibility of mind'; anger, disrelish, a failure to *se trouver bien avec l'autre*—these in either partner would be sufficient to dissolve a marriage.[72] Milton's doctrine of divorce, also inspired by a new reading of Genesis, had thus been anticipated by this somewhat disreputable group. But Milton would have shared Calvin's horror at their casual recouplings—though his disapproval, as we shall see in chapter 6, would have been tinged with wistful envy; and he would have vehemently denied that the female partner had any right to evaluate and dissolve her marriage by the standard of spiritual compatibility.

In mid-seventeenth-century polemic, too, radical 'enthusiasm' was associated with the abuse of Genesis and the attempt to recover an Adamite relation to the body. This was supposed to involve either naturalistic sexual freedom or ascetic hatred of the flesh, and sometimes both at once: one English 'Adamite' leader, according to *A Nest of Serpents* (1642), encouraged promiscuity among his congregation with the words 'increase and multiply', even though the sect hated marriage and claimed that Adam and Eve would have been sexless before the fall.[73] It is presumably 'Hypocrites' like these, or those lampooned by John Philips for exposing their genitals because the state of 'perfection' is now at hand, that Milton (Philips's uncle) had in mind when he attacked the current opinion of a 'pure' asexual Paradise.[74] Other Adamite sectarians enjoyed a more libertine image. The Ranters were supposed to 'go naked as [Adam] did, and live above sin and shame,' to 'say that for one man to be tied to one woman, or one woman to one man, is a fruit of the curse', and of course to launch communal orgies with the words 'increase and multiply', 'holding this lascivious action to be the chief motive of their salvation'.[75] A female Ranter, who

---

[72] *Against the Libertines*, pp. 279 and 281; 'bonne convenance d'espritz' is tr. by Prof. Farley as 'a spirit of mutual compatibility'. M's idea of divorce was similar to that of Martin Bucer, who was friendly to the Libertines (Farley, pp. 164-5), but he claims to have arrived at his views before discovering Bucer (*Prose* II. 435-6).

[73] pp. 3-5; cf. Hill[1], pp. 318-19. As in many attacks on 'Adamites', this group, which was formed in the Blakean location of Lambeth, were thought to call their meeting-places 'Paradise'.

[74] *A Satyr against Hypocrites* (1655), pp. 20-1.

[75] Hill[1], pp. 317-18; Smith, pp. 18-19; M. Stubs, *The Ranters Declaration, with their New Oath and Proclamation* (1650), p. 2. Stubs, an ex-Ranter himself, accused

claimed to be pregnant by the Holy Ghost, allegedly learnt from Genesis that 'Woman was made to be a helper for man, and ... it was no sin to lie with any man, whether Batchelor, Widdower, or married, but a thing lawful, and adjured thereunto by Nature.'[76] Most of these accusations can be matched in Calvin on the Spiritual Libertines, in medieval inquisitions of popular heresy, and in Patristic attacks on Gnostics and Adamites.[77]

What motives underlie this composite portrait of the Paradisal eroticist? Secular amusement plays some part, of course—plain bawdry, or the display of titillating perversions under the guise of righteous indignation.[78] We should also allow for the paranoid defence of beleagured orthodoxy, as in the anti-enthusiastic writings of Henry More, who saw all the sects—Adamites, Familists, Jorists, Spanish Illuminati, Ranters and Quakers, even Muslims—as a single sexually-driven 'Perfectionist' movement that threatened to engulf England in the years before the Restoration.[79] The sexual element in More's attack is particularly intense, I suggest, because

them of proclaiming that he who 'commits adultery, incest, or buggers the oftenest' is the most beloved of God (I owe this reference to Noam Flinker, who kindly showed me his forthcoming paper 'Ranter Millenarian Discourse: Canticles and the Jews in 1650').

[76] Author unknown, *The Ranters Monster* (1652), *passim*, describing the life, deformed child, and hideous death in prison of Mary Adams; for the idea of pregnancy by the Holy Ghost, cf. Bunyan in Hill[1], p. 317. Anne Hutchinson's deformed foetus, and that of her friend and patient Mary Dyer, were also described in lurid detail and interpreted as a punishment for Antinomianism (by John Winthrop, Governor of Massachusetts, among others); cf. Selma R. Williams, *Divine Rebel* (NY, 1981), pp. 185-8, and Anne J. Schultze, ' "Such monstrous births": A neglected aspect of the Antinomian controversy', *RQ* XXXVIII (1985), 85-106.

[77] A generation later the Ranters were lampooned in words stolen from Burton, themselves lifted from Theodoretus; cf. *The Parliament of Women* (1684), p. 15, and passages cited in n. 69 above.

[78] e.g. Thomas Hall, *Comarum Ακοσμια. The Loathsomnesse of Long Haire ... Naked Breasts, etc.* (1654), pp. 110-17; L. R., *The Ranters Ranting* (London, 1650), *passim* (and cf. ch. 4 n. 86 below). For a more authentic witness to the attractiveness and wide spread of Ranter sensuality, see Bunyan, *Grace Abounding*, ed. Roger Sharrock (Oxford, 1962), pp. 16-17.

[79] *An Explanation of the Grand Mystery of Godliness* (1660), esp. pp. xi, 158-9, 254, 365, 510. The founder of the Family of Love (Henry Niclaes), for example, is 'a Pimp or second *Sardanapalus*' who encourages orgies by 'lusty animadversions against Shamefacedness and Modesty in men and women'. Once they reach the 'state of full Perfection', More alleges, sectarians believe that 'they *cannot sin*, do what they will', and 'hold that there is no Difference of Good or Evil, and that Sin is but a Conceit [except] to those that know not their own Liberty'.

in the ant-hill of sectarian revolution he saw, grotesquely enlarged, the principle on which rested his own version of Christian Platonism: the religious and ontological centrality of Eros, the belief that, as he puts it in an early philosophical poem,

> deep desire is the deepest act,
> The most profound and centrall energie,
> The very selfhood of the Soul.[80]

And we should also recognize that More's association of 'Perfectionism' and sexual Antinomianism was not entirely unfounded, as we can learn from slightly less fanciful sources such as trial reports and the writings of the self-proclaimed prophets themselves.

Scattered outbursts of erotic frenzy, no doubt exaggerated by outraged opponents, actually did occur among the radical sects of Reformation Europe and in the convents of France during the great epoch of demonic possession, apparently on the principles of 'killing sin by sin' and returning to the Paradisal state of Adamite nudity.[81] Something similar happened in Shabbatistic Judaism in the 1650s and 1660s, with isolated resurgences of sexual Antinomianism even in the eighteenth century; Shabbatai Zevi himself promised to abolish the punishment of Eve when he began his reign as Messiah.[82] In England William Franklin and James Naylor believed themselves to be the Messiah, and their followers thought themselves incapable of sin. Gerrard Winstanley believed that his Digger movement would restore the pre-lapsarian 'law of righteousness' and establish man and woman on an equal basis. Some Quakers went naked for a sign, not as a public penance but because, as David Hume later put it, they 'fancied that the renovation of all things had commenced, and that clothes were to be rejected together with other Superfluities'. Some of the wilder adventures of the London Ranter gatherings probably did happen,

---

[80] *Antimonopsychia*, st. 36, in *Philosophical Poems* (1647), p. 294.

[81] Cf. *RR* in n. 68 above; Esprit du Bosroger, *La Piété affligée* (Rouen, 1652), pp. 169-70; R.-P. Desmarets, *Histoire de Magdelaine Bavent* (Paris, 1652; repr. Rouen, 1878), pp. 9-10; *L'Adamite, ou le Jésuite insensible* (Cologne, 1682), tr. as *The Adamite, or the Loves of Father Rock and his Intrigues with the Nuns* (1683), *passim*; Jules Michelet, *La Sorcière*, tr. A. R. Allinson as *Satanism and Witchcraft* (NY, 1946), pp. 192, 208-10; Roger Thompson, *Unfit for Modest Ears* (1979), p. 142.

[82] Gerschom S. Scholem, *Kabbalah* (NY, 1974), pp. 245-9, 255, 268, 274, 278, 282, 355. For a fuller account of Zevi, see Scholem, *Sabbatai Sevi*, tr. R. J. Zwi Werblowsky (Princeton, 1973); items 47 and 60-7 in Scholem's Bibliography show how knowledge of his messianic claims reached England.

including an enticing display of nakedness by a servant of Dr Paget, a close friend of Milton. Quaker women sometimes claimed to have given birth without pain, since the godly had re-entered a Paradisal state and the 'curse' on Eve had been dissolved. Quaker weddings eliminated the obedience clause, for the same reason.[83]

We can, then, speak of the radical Antinomianism of the age of Milton, not as a coherent programme, but as a series of paradoxical convictions that shine through the confusions of the record. Many militant separatists were motivated by the attempt to recover the sense of divine immediacy and by the belief that the Paradisal state could actually be achieved in this life, whether personally or through a charismatic New Adam or New Eve.[84] They depart from the comfortable Protestant faith in holy and civic matrimony, either to scorn marriage as a fleshly post-lapsarian impediment or to replace it with more intense and 'spiritual' arrangements. They are at once orgiastic and hostile to the flesh, ascetics and devotees of the Solomonic rapture that could release them from moral constraint and original sin. They aspired to the state in which, as Sebastian Franck put it, they could 'spitt out and vomitt up the knowledge of good and evil as poyson, and become as Adam was before his fall, Fooles and innocent Turtles.'[85]

This Paradisal Antinomianism, the belief that one has attained 'the image of *Adam's* holiness in his innocency' and therefore need not obey the law,[86] comes to the Radical Reformation from two sources: on the one hand, the Carpocratian or Catharist idea that what man conventionally calls good or evil are actually indifferent or 'natural', and that matters of morality are trivial compared with the transcendent mysteries of faith and love; on the other hand, the extreme Calvinist position that sin is indeed real, but that the elect are supernaturally prevented from sinning, whatever they do— 'to the pure all things are pure.' The latter conviction combines

---

[83] Hill[1], p. 134 (and cf. 233), 312, 316-17, 321; Hume, *History of England*, ch. 62; Smith, p. 183. Smith's forthcoming book (Yale University Press) will deal extensively with radical writings of this period.

[84] Cf. *RR* p. 7 and *passim*; Alistair Hamilton, *The Family of Love* (Cambridge, 1981), pp. 8, 24-5, 32; Christopher Hill *et al.*, *The World of the Muggletonians* (1983), pp. 19, 67.

[85] *Forbidden Fruit*, quot. in Joseph E. Duncan, *Milton's Earthly Paradise* (Minneapolis, 1972), p. 261.

[86] Duncan, p. 260. For Carpocratians, see Clement, *Stromateis*, III. ii; for practical Catharist morality, see Emanuel Le Roy Ladurie, *Montaillou*, tr. Barbara Bray (NY, 1978), pp. 157-9.

with another Gnostic idea, that the spiritual elect should actually perform the sinful act 'as no sin', working through the fleshly sins in order to annihilate them. Flesh is thereby converted into spirit, in living action rather than in mere contemplation. This tendency is reinforced by the sectarian hermeneutics of the spirit, which interprets everything according to internal sensations of holiness rather than external authority. Those who believe that 'God is in our flesh as much as in Christ's flesh', and that God's seed is 'apprehended by us to be risen in us', had literally no means of determining whether an impulse came from the spirit or from the libido.[87]

This assemblage of beliefs is expressed with unusual vividness in the writings of the authentic Ranters Abiezer Coppe and Laurence Clarkson, both 'turners of the world upside down ... to bring things back to their primitive and right order again'.[88] In his apocalyptic and visionary *Fiery Flying Roll* (1649) Coppe declared that 'Sin and Transgression is finished and ended'; to his contemporaries he appeared to maintain that sin exists purely in the imagination, that Heaven consisted in performing 'Murther, Adultery, Incest, Fornication, Uncleaness, Sodomie etc.', that wives should be enjoyed communally, that 'men please God as well when they sinne, as when they sin not,' and even that 'to act most sinne [is] the nearest way to perfection'. These accusations—revivals of older Gnostic and Adamite heresies—were doubtless a travesty of Coppe's teachings, but they came close enough for Coppe himself to recant them, at great length, after his imprisonment for blasphemy.[89]

[87] Hans Jonas, *The Gnostic Religion*, 2nd edn. (Boston, 1963), pp. 227-30, 271-4; Smith, p. 180; *RR* pp. 219, 377-9; Hill[1], pp. 188, 221.

[88] William Penn, quot. in Hill[1], p. 231; the Ranter Joseph Salmon described himself as 'posting most furiously in a burning zeal towards an unattainable end' (Smith, p. 204).

[89] Smith, pp. 81, 91 (*A Fiery Flying Roll*). Coppe lists and refutes or recants the charges against him in *A Remonstrance* (1651) and *Copp's Return to the Wayes of Truth* (1651), which includes letters to Hartlib's friend John Dury and M's friend Marchamont Needham (Smith, pp. 121, 133-4, 144-52, 156-7); the idea that 'to act most sinn' is the best way to perfection (p. 152) he claims never to have heard, much less believed—an evasion perhaps designed to protect Clarkson. For Coppe's lewd reputation at college and in his Ranter days see also Anthony à Wood, *Atheniae Oxonienses*, ed. Philip Bliss, III (1817), cols. 959-60, and for a sceptical account of his recantation, see John Tickell, *The Bottomles Pit Smoaking in Familisme* (Oxford, 1652), *passim*: Coppe was still 'very merry', preaching on 'there is a time to sing, and a time to dance', and alluding darkly to Hosea's whore (pp. 64, 86).

The impression of extremism was generated by Coppe's farouche personal demeanour and by his rapturous and intense Biblical rhetoric. From Hosea and Revelation he learned to create startling images of whoredom, from King David he learned to shock the 'precise' Puritans with wild displays of inspired folly, including kissing and fondling women in public, and from Solomon he learned to woo female disciples in the words of the Song of Songs and to 'have concubines without number'.[90] (These displays of Old Testament metaphorics were taken literally by his enemies, including Henry More, and Coppe found that he had to deny charges of multiple promiscuity.) From Genesis and St. Paul he learned to combine the 'one flesh' of primal innocence with apocalyptic expectations of the new age, when male and female will be confounded and the Christ-child will spring in his womb: to a female convert he declared that '*Man* is the *Woman*, and thou art the Man, the *Saints* are thy *Spouse*, our *Maker* is our *Husband*; *We* are no more *twaine*, but *One*.'[91] The Adamic 'Flesh of my flesh' and 'one flesh' also leapt into his mind when he encountered the lumpenproletariat, and rushed to embrace even the most wretched of them.[92] Above all, Coppe's entire work was designed as a chain of riddles that would discriminate between the fallen and the unfallen reader: the unregenerate—'you that eat of the Tree of Knowledge of Good and Evil, and have not your Evil eye Pickt out'—can see only evil in his outrageous statements, but true disciples have the Adamic vision that reveals the good. Coppe thus comes close to the ideal of Sebastian Franck or the Spiritual Libertines, the ecstatic pre-lapsarian state where good and evil are abolished—a state that hostile observers would brand as overexcited libido. He even describes the service of God as 'Perfect freedom, and pure Libertinisme'.[93]

[90] Smith, pp. 104, 106-7, 109, 111, 113, 120, 141.
[91] *Some Sweet Sips of Some Spiritual Wine* (1649), in Smith, p. 69, and cf. p. 112; the addressee is a Mrs T. P. of Abingdon, whose own rather Blakean account of a Genesis-like vision is included in Coppe's work (pp. 64-5). Holy bisexuality was a tradition among restitutionist prophets: Guillaume Postel, for example, after the spirit of his dead mentor and redemptress had come to dwell in him as a New Eve (July, 1551), felt that he was a male enclosed within a female (cf. Marion L. Kuntz, *Guillaume Postel, Prophet of the Restitution of All Things* (The Hague, 1981), esp. pp. 92-3, 102-8, 242), though as Michael Screech points out, this belief did not alter Postel's male suprematism ('The Illusion of Postel's Feminism', *JWCI* XVI (1953), 162-70).
[92] Smith, pp. 90-1, 105-6, 112, 115, and cf. 145.
[93] Smith, pp. 91, 86; for Franck, see n. 85 above.

Just as the Spiritual Libertines courted a bewildered and hostile response with their 'marriages', so Coppe's most important riddle is scandalously sexual. The desire to commune with 'flesh of my flesh' here combines with the desire to shock the Puritan establishment as David had shocked Princess Mical: 'I sate downe, and eat and drank around on the ground with Gypseys, and clip't, hug'd and kiss'd them, putting my hand in their bosomes, loving the she-Gipsies dearly. O base! saith mincing *Mical*, the least spark of modesty would be as red as crimson or scarlet, to hear this.' 'That notorious businesse with the Gypseys', as Coppe himself calls it despite his claim to be without sin, confirmed Henry More in the belief that all 'enthusiasm' was sexual in origin.[94] But this erotic Antinomianism turns out to be a paradoxical gesture of asceticism: 'by base impudent kisses (as I then accounted them) my plaguey holinesse hath been confounded[;] by wanton kisses, kissing hath been confounded.' Coppe intends the 'killing of sin by sin', the quasi-Platonic transformation of sexuality into *acclivitas*. His sexual foolings destroy his outward, hypocritical 'holiness', and fuel a vertical ascent 'out of Flesh into Spirit, out of Form into Power, out of Type into Truth'; thus 'externall kisses' become 'the fiery chariots to mount me swiftly into the bosom of him whom my soul loves', where Coppe dissolves in the raptures of the Song of Songs, 'kist with the kisses of his mouth, whose loves are better than wine'. Even lust itself, and 'concubines without number', become vehicles of transcendence.[95] Coppe arrives at his vision, the common goal of Christian contemplation, by joining Solomonic eroticism and the pre-lapsarian release from the categories of good and evil.

Clarkson or Claxton, the self-appointed '*Captain of the Rant*', took Coppe's system one stage further into radical activism, and confirmed Milton's observation that the most extreme sectarians ('that sort of men who follow *Anabaptism, Famelism, Antinomianism*, and other *fanatick* dreams') might be sexually motivated, since 'their opinions having full swinge, do end in satisfaction of the

---

[94] Smith, pp. 105-7; More, *Enthusiasmus Triumphatus* (1656; 2nd edn., 1662), p. 14. Coppe alludes to 2 Sam. 6:18-23 and 1 Chron. 15:29.

[95] Smith, pp. 43 and 108-9 (where he also expatiates on the horrors of lust). In a passage of Bunyanesque spiritual autobiography (pp. 134-5) Coppe himself later describes the 27-year period of obsessively strict 'holiness' that preceded his burst of Dionysiac Ranterism; despite all his mortifications (which included binding Scriptural quotations to his wrists), he could not shake off the conviction, beginning at the age of 13, that he was the 'chief of sinners' (contrast Wood, n. 89 above).

flesh'.[96] Like Coppe and the Spiritual Libertines, Clarkson claims to see with the '*Single Eye*' of unfallen vision, and to be transported into a Paradisal state of unity with the creature that grants him the privilege of sinning without sin—

for indeed sin hath its conception only in the imagination; therefore, so long as the act was in God, or nakedly produced by God, it was as holy as God: but after there is an appearance in thee, or apprehension in thee, that this act is good, and that act is evil, then hast thou with *Adam* eat of the Forbidden Tree, of the Tree of knowledge of good and evil.[97]

The polarized categories of sin and holiness only appear 'for want of this light, of this single pure eye'; for the illuminatus all things are 'a pure act' (p. 171). Notwithstanding this professed indifference to moral categories, Clarkson chose to demonstrate his divine purity by performing the most 'terrible' acts of blasphemy and sexual promiscuity. Indeed, he is tied to the very sins he seeks to confound: 'for my part,' he reveals at the crowning moment of *A Single Eye*, 'till I acted that so-called sin, I could not predominate over sin.'[98] This sense of release inspires rapturous declarations of his own personal impunity ('see what I can, act what I will, all is but one most sweet and lovely'), but they are framed by fiercely ascetic denunciations of the fleshly lusts and the 'evil imagination' of others, and particularly of those who attempt to follow his Antinomian path without inward assurances of the Holy Spirit.[99]

Clarkson's vision of unity, like Coppe's, derives from an incantatory fusion of Paradisal simplicity and Solomonic eroticism.[100] Like Coppe, too, he speaks only to specially enlightened disciples who are 'risen from title to act, from act to power, from power to His name,' and attacks the least sexual aberration in those who remain at a lower level. But where Coppe confines himself to

[96] Smith, p. 181; *Prose* II. 278. Calvin remarked that the Spiritual Libertines were 'carried away by their own libido' (n. 70 above).

[97] *A Single Eye All Light, No Darkness* (1650), Smith, p. 169 (and cf. 171-2). On Clarkson see also Barry Reay in Hill *et al.*, *Muggletonians* ch. 6, where we learn of further developments in his reading of Genesis; as a Muggletonian, he proclaimed that Satan had 'entered Eve to become the reprobate seed' (p. 181).

[98] Smith, p. 173, and cf. 169 ('Well Friends, although the appearance of God in me be as terrible to you, as it were to *Moses* in the mount, yet [I] rejoice . . . ').

[99] Smith, pp. 169, 170-1, 173.

[100] e.g. Smith, p. 170: '*Thou art all fair my Love, there is no spot in thee*. Observe, all fair my Love: in thee only is beauty and purity, without defilement: my love my dove is but one, thou one, not two, but only one, my love' (cf. S.of S. 4:7). Flinker (n. 75 above) explores the language of the Song of Songs in Ranter writings.

fornicatory metaphors and 'base impudent kisses', and later denies his Antinomianism or reduces it to 'insinuations' and 'suppositions', Clarkson translates his eroticism into 'pure act'; indeed, his doctrine and practice is based on the principle that 'without act' there can be 'no life, without life, no perfection, and without perfection, no eternal peace and freedom.' And his later recantation, far from denying his sexual activism, gives details of the libertine adventures on which his reputation was based.[101]

Taking as his inspiration the Song of Songs and Ecclesiastes, Clarkson joined a secret community in London of which Coppe was also a member, and which had given itself, presumably at Coppe's suggestion, the Paradisal name 'My One Flesh'.[102] Here at last he declared his doctrine that 'none can be free from sin, till in purity it be acted as no sin,' and here large numbers of female disciples (women in black vizard-masks, according to the commissioner who cross-examined him) came 'to make trial of what I had expressed'. In these multiple liaisons, as they are described in his later spiritual autobiography, Clarkson translated or uncoded the veiled raptures of *A Single Eye*: when he declared that 'with me, all Creatures are but one creature', he meant that 'till you can lie with all women as one woman, you can do nothing but sin'; indeed, 'no man could attain perfection but this way.' '*Solomons* Writings', he admits, 'was the original of my filthy lust, supposing I might take the same liberty as he did.'

[*iii*]

These Edenic experiments should probably be understood as extreme examples of the ethics of confrontation that inspired *Areopagitica*, Milton's most positive response to the sectarian uprising. As we shall see in chapter 5, Milton's revolutionary prose, as well as his mature poetry, insists on a purification that can only come by 'trial with what is contrary', a reparation of innocence by means of a deep, almost physical knowledge of fallen experience,

---

[101] Smith, pp. 43, 107, 173 (*A Single Eye*), 178–84 (*The Lost Sheep Found* (1660)). For Coppe's extenuation of his Antinomian blasphemies, which also includes a confession of spiritual drunkenness that associates him with Habbakuk (p. 129), cf. esp. pp. 137, 151, 156; Coppe's revised 'orthodox' position is still radically prophetic and denunciatory, however.

[102] Smith, pp. 180–5. Clarkson was referred to this clandestine group by Giles Calvert, the printer of many radical-sectarian writers including Coppe, Winstanley, and Niclaes; for a tenuous possible link with M, see Hill[2], pp. 135–6.

a systematic testing of the Pauline injunction to 'prove all things', and the reassurance that 'to the pure all things are pure'. It was Milton, and not Coppe or Clarkson, who declared that 'those actions which enter into a man, rather than issue out of him ... defile not' (II. 513). Milton and the Ranters both rejected external authority, both expressed their vision in intensely physical and poetic terms which they claimed as direct inspiration, and both held that virtue is only achieved by entering into some kind of intimate dialectic with sin. *Areopagitica* recognizes the conceptual interdependency of good and evil that makes book-censorship counter-productive ('look how much we thus expell of sin, so much we expell of virtue'); but Milton refers only to external prohibitions, which debar the warfaring Christian from his true task—pushing the vicarious knowledge of evil to 'the utmost', so as to be rewarded all the more for rejecting it (II. 527, 515). The Ranters, on the other hand, believed that sin had to be known in person before it could be transcended. For Milton, all things are good to read, for Clarkson, to act. Milton's imagination delivers a golden world, but he does not surrender to its dissolving power, as Coppe and Clarkson do; emotional apprehension and prophetic vision are qualified by an equally intense concern for discipline, authority, and reason. Milton's dialectic is meant to enhance moral distinctions, while Antinomianism seeks to soar beyond them.

Milton's relation to the 'Radical Reformation' was nevertheless an intimate one, and many contemporaries lacked the subtlety to distinguish his fervent imaginings from the '*fanatick* dreams' he denounces. (He himself implied that the all-important difference between 'liberty' and 'licence', in a free and open society, would be difficult to perceive.) His doctrine of divorce for incompatibility had been anticipated by the Spiritual Libertines and by the English offshoots of Familism, and his radical arguments—based on the principle that the true, spiritual essence of marriage, as God had ordained it in Paradise, might be better realized by breaking rather than keeping the current law—struck many readers as belonging to the sectarian underground.[103] The anonymous *Answer* to the first divorce tract seized upon this part of Milton's 'wilde, mad, and frantick divinitie', and caricatured his main criterion, the

---

[103] *Prose* II. 225, and cf. Sonnet 12, l. 14. For Familist divorce, see *RR* p. 789 and Hamilton, pp. 48-9; for M's Libertine and fanatic reputation, see W. R. Parker, *Milton's Contemporary Reputation* (Columbus, 1940), *passim*, and ch. 6 n. 21 below.

inward principle of 'love and peace', as an Antinomian call for lawlessness; the same impulse, he claims, inspires the outbreak of Familism among the women of the East End of London.[104] This gave great pain to the conservative side of Milton's mind—he had, after all, criticized the sexually disordered fanatics even in the first tract—and he responded by fencing the original arguments with disclaimers and distinctions, and deflecting the Familist accusation with a scornful jest.[105] And yet contemporaries were not entirely wrong to detect a radical and 'Libertine' undercurrent in Milton, an attraction to the hermeneutics of the Spirit, a hatred of the repressive 'Puritan' ascendency, an exaltation of erotic rapture, and a tendency towards 'Perfectionism'.

In later years Milton adopted as a personal motto 2 Corinthians 12:9, 'I am made perfect in weakness', applying the words of God to his own experience with almost the boldness of a Coppe or Clarkson (ch. 7 n. 89 below). The end of *Paradise Lost* holds out the possibility of achieving the 'Paradise within', and of rising 'from Shadowy Types to Truth, from Flesh to Spirit,' in the daily life of the regenerate. The Edenic state is suffused with a Solomonic eroticism far more intense than anything Augustine conjectured, a transfigured but connatural sexuality that has the qualities of prayer and *acclivitas*, yet with no ascetic renunciation of the flesh. As Adam describes the situation of the first couple, loved by a God

> Who formd us from the dust, and plac'd us here
> Full to the utmost measure of what bliss
> Human desires can seek or apprehend,

he bears witness to the centrality of desire, and endows it with a perceptive as well as an appetitive power.[106] But Milton's Paradise

[104] (1644), p. 36 (facsimile in Parker, pp. 170-216). The 'Maids of Aldgate' with whom M is scornfully equated are evidently Familists, since they use the catch-phrase 'godded with God'.

[105] *Prose* II. 750: 'the *Maids at Algate*, whom hee flouts, are likely to have more witt than the Servingman at Addlegate.' This hardly constitutes a 'defence', *pace* Hill[2], pp. 109, 313, and Maureen Quilligan, *Milton's Spenser* (Ithaca, 1983), p. 222. M was, however, tenderer than most conservatives in his allusions to 'Familists', Antinomians, etc., adding 'if we understand them not amisse' to his attack in the 2nd edn. of *DDD*, and earlier speculating whether the primitive Christians had been abused with similar labels (II. 278-9, I. 788).

[106] *PL* XII. 587, 303, V. 516-18; for *acclivitas* (the mystic ascent to God) as a name for ritual copulation see n. 66 above. M's Eden does border on the Land of Cokaigne at moments: the happy couple eat 'fruits which the compliant boughs / Yielded them' (IV. 332-3), and Eve 'Yielded' herself with 'sweet compliance' (IV. 309-10, 489, VIII. 603).

is no hedonistic fantasy or Antinomian Land of Cokaigne. Not only in the fallen world, but even in the original state of innocence, blessedness is achieved through struggle, patience, and the acceptance of weakness. 'Difficulty and labour' are virtues from the beginning, determining the 'growth and compleating' of the human character. Throughout his working life Milton condemned the radicals' confusion of Spirit and Libido, as he condemned all facile attempts to retreat from complexity and all 'ready and easy ways' to return to Paradise. The ascent to Spirit is the goal defined by Raphael in *Paradise Lost*, but it must be within a framework of obedience and human limitation. To obliterate the concerns and conflicts of daily life, and to indulge rash aspirations to 'spiritual' ascent, is to surrender to an 'empty dream'; this transcendental urge, in fact—as Milton surely learned from observing and responding to his radical Antinomian contemporaries—was precisely the original temptation and the motive for the fall.

3
'The State of Eve'

FEMALE ONTOGENY AND THE POLITICS OF MARRIAGE

> Every wife should be to her husband, as *Evah* was to *Adam*, a whole World of women; and every husband should be to his wife, as *Adam* was to *Evah*, a whole World of men.
>
> (William Secker)[1]

The reconstruction of Paradisal sexuality, then, could lead either to a world-renouncing spiritual libertinism, or to a new sense of holiness in the everyday business of matrimony. It brings out a paradoxical commitment to *praxis* in Christianity, which forces the Platonic doctrine of Eros, formulated in a spiritual and homosexual milieu, into the contested ideological arena of the sexes. For Luther, as for Christ and St. Paul, the text of Genesis is ever-present in the union of man and woman: indeed, the whole Eden-story was written 'not because of Adam and Eve (for they had long since been reduced to ashes ...) but because of ourselves, so that those who cannot contain themselves might live content with their own Eve' (4:1). The garden-myth 'walks' forward to meet the present day, bringing not just a sense of corruption but an optimistic, restitutionist impulse to create new social structures. The original happiness of Adam and Eve, the universal couple, could be regained in a new kind of marriage founded on mutual respect, reciprocity, and even—among the Quakers, at times—the equality of Eve before the 'curse'. But these visions of Paradise collided, in radical and conservative alike, with the traditional anti-feminist reading of Genesis.

The mutual-egalitarian interpretation was always a possibility in Protestant exegesis and Renaissance humanism, as this chapter will show; the application of Genesis to marriage, and to the status of woman, was by no means univocally patriarchal. But it would be Utopian to deny the overwhelming weight of the subordinationist

---

[1] *A Wedding Ring* (1658), p. 31.

3. The State of Eve

reading. Eve was not only blamed for having feebly given in to Satan when Adam would have resisted—ignoring the clear statement in 3:6 that Adam was 'with her'—but she was also given a secondary, obedient status before the fall. The punishment of subordination in 3:16 is thus translated into a universal or 'natural' condition that continues unchanged even after other Old Testament impositions, like circumcision and burnt-offerings, had been abolished by Christianity. Heedless of blasphemy, the exegetes swept away the essential distinctions between lapsarian and non-lapsarian elements, redeemed and fallen features; the weakness, inferiority, depravity, auxiliary status, and natural subordination of women were all proved by constant reference to this foreshortened and simplified 'Eve', forced upon both the original text and the female reader. It is clear, then, that exegesis of the creation of Eve depends on, and helps to determine, the politics of gender, and that the ideological inscription of 'Eve' into 'woman' was different in kind from that of Adam into man; women were even required to apologize for their 'grandmother Eve' in their personal prayers.[2]

The institution of marriage—what William Heale called 'that state which either imparadizeth a man in the Eden of felicitie, or els exposeth him unto a world of miserie'[3]—is political in the sense that it encloses and defines the woman, but in Reformation Europe and Revolutionary England it was political in another sense too: marital questions were directly involved in the agitation for social reform. Milton's first major engagement with the text of Genesis came with the great political campaign of 1643-5, when he harnessed all his skills as myth-maker, exegete, and polemicist to the cause of divorce—believing with Martin Bucer that 'it should be a Princes care that matrimony be so joyn'd, as God ordain'd; which is, that every one should love his wife with such a love as Adam exprest to Eve.'[4] Milton's agitation made him a 'resisting reader'; his fury is directed not against subordinationism, however, but against the overvaluing of 'due benevolence'—the purely physical sexuality

[2] Cf. Samuel Hieron, *A Helpe Unto Devotion*, 4th edn. (1613), p. 270. Antonia Fraser makes this point repeatedly in *The Weaker Vessel* (1984), e.g. pp. 2 ('Men in the seventeenth century were not, it seemed, descended from Eve'), 71, 247; it should be pointed out, of course, that men were required to examine and bewail the sins of the 'old Adam' in themselves.

[3] *An Apology for Women* (Oxford, 1609), p. 10.

[4] *Prose* II. 446. Though M claims him as a predecessor, Bucer is actually much less adventurous; his arguments apply only to pre-contracts, not to the marriage itself.

that, even according to the harshest suprematists, makes man and woman equal in the marriage-bed. Other revisionists, including Adam himself in *Paradise Lost*, demanded an equal partnership of man and woman in every aspect of marriage. Such energetic expansions of the myth, as we shall see, run the risk either of self-contradiction, as in Milton and Luther, or of some more drastic confrontation with authority. An extreme paradigm may be found in a grimly comic anecdote from Renaissance Germany: a printer's wife, outraged by 'that sentence of subjection to her husband' in Genesis 3:16, changed only two letters in the text—'he shall be thy master (*Herr*)' appeared as 'he shall be thy fool (*Narr*)'—and was put to death.[5]

1. Companionship versus procreation?

When Augustine set out to redeem the literal meaning of Genesis, none of the available interpretations could provide any reason for Eve to exist in Paradise. The earliest Church Fathers mostly assumed that sexual procreation has no part in the state of innocence, past or future. The literalists claimed either that there would have been no reproduction, or that it would have occurred in some unimaginable angelic fashion. The allegorists, following Philo, interpreted Adam as the Reason or the Soul and Eve as Sense-impression, initially repulsive to Adam, but later able to drag him down into corporeality by collaborating with the serpent Pleasure. Neither of these positions provides creditable motives for the creation of Eve. For the allegorists, the separation of Sense into a separate person actually *was* the fall, and for the literalists the creation of Eve has no meaning except in relation to the fall; since God knew that man would fall into mortality, He thought it would be useful to have some reproductive equipment on hand to help repair the loss. Or else God created the first Eve, a virgin who conceives evil by Satan, in order to manifest the glory of the Virgin Mary, the second Eve.[6]

---

[5] Isaac D'Israeli, *Curiosities of Literature*, 'Errata'.
[6] The concept of the Second Eve originates with Justin Martyr; cf. Norman P. Williams, *The Ideas of the Fall and of Original Sin* (1929), p. 174. The asexual theories of innocence that preceded Aug. are usefully summarized in Agaësse II. 516-18. Clement of Alexandria is one exception to the prevailing denial of sexuality; he maintained that Adam and Eve sinned by starting normal sexual relationships *too soon* (*Stromateis*, III. xvii).

3. The State of Eve

Augustine, as we have seen, redeems physical reproduction by showing that it would have taken place in the unfallen state; a trace of the Paradisal blessing, 'increase and multiply', may thus be felt in fallen sexuality. But in the process of reinterpretation he binds Eve once again into an exclusively procreational role: he cannot conceive of a woman providing any kind of 'meet help' other than child-rearing—and certainly not companionship. This at least is his opinion in the influential *De Genesi ad Litteram*:

> if then we ask for what fitting purpose this 'help' could have been made, the procreation of children is the only probable reason that comes to mind.... If not to help him produce children, what other sort of help could she have been made for? ... We could say that it was for solace, in case solitude were to grow boring. But how much more suitable for living together and talking together are two men friends, equally matched (*pariter*), than a man and a woman![7]

Why was consummation indefinitely delayed, if Adam and Eve had nothing to do together except procreate? Augustine's reason— that foreknowledge of the fall made God suspend intercourse until it was needed to repair mortality by offspring—is virtually the same as the old position he was trying to refute.

This literalist commentary also lays in place the cornerstone of the suprematist reading. In Genesis 3:16 God explicitly ordains subordination as a punishment for transgression, but Augustine, who elsewhere emphasizes the massive and comprehensive changes brought about by the fall, here derives male supremacy from both fallen and unfallen states, and mingles the boundaries of the two. God declares that Eve will be 'subject to your husband', and that 'he shall rule over you (*dominabitur*)', only after the fall. But 'we must believe that even before her sin woman had been made to be ruled (*dominaretur*) by her husband and be submissive and subject to him.' Why must we believe this? Augustine offers no direct evidence, and immediately contradicts his own thesis: 'it is not by her nature but rather by her sin that woman deserved to have her husband for a master.' He turns to St. Paul for confirmation of his 'pre-subordinationist' theory of Eve, but the Apostle typically proves a mixed blessing. Augustine wants to show that before the

---

[7] *De Gen. ad Lit.* IX. iii. 5, v. 9, vii. 13; cf. also vii. 12, ix. 14-15, xi. 19. The English editor attempts to soften Aug.'s crabbed opinion by pointing to his love for his mother and his mistress: *The Literal Meaning of Genesis*, tr. and ed. John H. Taylor (NY, 1982), II. 267 n. 24.

fall Eve submitted to Adam in a bond of love, whereas after sinning she became a slave; but he illustrates the remote pre-lapsarian past by quoting Paul on what *currently* should prevail between married Christians. Here, moreover, Paul is recommending, not his usual hierarchy of husband and wife, but a loving and egalitarian mutual submission. Augustine's only other proof-texts for Eve's 'natural' subordination, likewise from St. Paul, support a quite different kind of submission, applicable to the wife only. They derive, as we have seen in chapter 1, from a highly tendentious interpretation of Genesis—that woman is 'of' the man in some ontological sense, that the passive supply of the rib means that man, as Donne later put it, 'gives essence' to the woman and therefore can rule over her, and that the woman's 'help', contrary to common Old Testament usage ('my help cometh even from the Lord'), makes her an ancillary or employee. Augustine's unquestioning and unsubstantiated assumption of the Pauline misreading reveals the slightness of his case. The need to make women 'naturally' inferior simply hangs in isolation, beyond logic and beyond even the Logos, as a pure ideological imperative: *decet credere*; we ought to believe.[8]

Elsewhere, however, Augustine is less narrowly procreational and less dogmatically subordinationist. His application of Genesis to marital relationships is as complex and contradictory as St. Paul's. In *De Bono Conjugali* he gives a high value to marriage 'not just because of the procreation of children, but also on account of the *naturalis in diverso sexu societatis*,' the natural 'society of love' it establishes between the sexes; by creating Eve from the very flank of Adam God establishes man and woman as an 'equally matched' couple—*pariter*, the same word later applied to male friendship alone (III. 3, IV. 9). Some years later, in *The City of God*, he glosses Genesis 1 in terms that make it hard to reconcile with the unfallen subordination of Eve: 'He wanted rational man, made to His image, to have dominion over irrational creatures only, not man over man, but man over beast.' Here again he conceives marriage as an amorous *societas*, and he even suggests that the creation of Eve from a rib, and the reunion of 'one flesh', are God's sign that all subsequent human relationships should be affectionate, sociable, and harmonious. In other works he elaborates on the comfort and mutuality of marriage—precisely what, in *De Genesi ad Litteram*, he had eliminated from God's purpose in creating Eve: 'it is S.

[8] *De Gen. ad Lit.* XI. xxxvii. 50, and cf. VIII. xvii. 36; for Donne see n. 31 below.

Austen's counsel', wrote Heale, 'that such as we woulde have our wives appeare unto us, the same we should first approve ourselves unto them'; the marriage of Adam and Eve, built on this reciprocity, was 'a mysterie of union, a sacrament of love, a bonde of fidelitie, a paradise of content ... the truce of peace [in] this present life, and the way unto perfection in that better life to come'. Augustine was even prepared to accept, on one occasion at least, a marriage held together by pure erotic delight rather than the desire for godly offspring.[9]

It appears, then, that the marriage of Adam and Eve inspired two very different views—the 'narrow-Augustinian', which assigned Eve solely to procreation and denied the value of her companionship and resourcefulness, and the 'broad-Augustinian', in which she participates fully in a mutual society of love, a Paradise within Paradise.

[*ii*]

Augustine appears uncertain what role to ascribe to 'Nature' in his interpretation of Genesis; it was 'not in Eve's nature' to be subordinate, and yet any efforts to challenge her inferior position after the fall 'corrupt her nature still further'. By the time of Aquinas, however, Nature had been discovered to be coterminous with the writings of Aristotle, and the question of Eve's function could be determined on a firmer basis. Thus was established the 'scholastic synthesis' of Genesis and Aristotle, that continued to confirm the subordination of women long after scholasticism itself had come under attack.[10]

Aquinas comes out decisively for the narrow-Augustinian view. Seeking to reconcile Genesis and Greek biology, he argues simultaneously that woman is defective, and that she is not. *Qua* individual, she is naturally 'deficiens et occasionatum', a product of debility, indisposition, or accident, and thus 'naturally' in need of domination by a man—though before the fall this rule could have been gentle. But with regard to the species she is not defective, since all generation, Aristotle assures us, requires an active and a

---

[9] *CG* XII. 22, 23, 28, XIV *passim*, and XIX. 15; Heale, pp. 45 and 62; cf. ch. 2 n. 11 above.

[10] Cf. Ian Maclean, *Woman Triumphant* (Oxford, 1977), p. 23 and ch. 1 *passim*, and *The Renaissance Notion of Woman* (Cambridge, 1980), p. 10 and ch. 2 *passim*.

passive. Generation, then, is the sole function for which woman was created:

> It was absolutely necessary to make woman, for the reason Scripture mentions, as a help for man; not indeed to help him in any other work, as some have maintained, because where most work is concerned man can get help more conveniently from another man than from a woman; but to help him in the work of procreation.[11]

That *generatio* is meant in the narrow biological sense is clear when he distinguishes it from 'domestic life, in which are the other works of man and woman' (Quot. 92, art. 2), and the principle is driven home in Questio 98: copulation must have been intended even in the state of innocence, because 'for any other work a man could be more efficiently helped by a man than by a woman' (art. 2).

We have seen in chapter 2 that Aquinas's theories of voluntary pre-lapsarian sexuality derive from Augustine, and Augustine is again the authority here. But Aquinas fuses ideas from different periods of Augustine's thought into a single text; from *De Genesi ad Litteram* he adopts the narrow equation of woman with physical reproduction, denying her companionship and resourcefulness, but the details of primeval sexual life are derived from the fourteenth book of *The City of God*, where Augustine had evolved a more generous view of pre-lapsarian marriage as an amorous *societas*.

[*iii*]

The question of female ontology is no less embroiled in Renaissance and Reformation reconstructions of Genesis. The pivotal concepts are of course 'fit help' and 'one flesh', which could be interpreted either physically or spiritually. If 'increase and multiply' is taken as the dominant text, then the creation of Eve, and consequently the essence of woman, will be explained in physiological and naturalistic terms; if the interpreter stresses the immediate context in Genesis 2, Eve will be valued for her intimate society and emotional 'help' against loneliness.

The problem with the former of these views is that human biology was still largely dominated by the kind of Aristotelianism

---

[11] *Summa Theologiae* Ia, Quot. 92; the point about work is also made in the passage from Aug. quot. n. 7 above. The Blackfriars editors attempt to soften this by claiming that *generatio* is meant to include 'all the work of motherhood and of rearing a family [and] keeping house (XII. 36)', but this is explicitly contradicted by Aquinas.

[1.iii]   *3. The State of Eve*   103

that led Aquinas to label woman deficient and occasional. Though not all physiological determinists went as far as the preacher Paul Best, who denied woman a soul because Genesis does not mention that God ever breathed into Eve, they do unwittingly raise questions about God's reasons for introducing what the fallen Adam would call a 'fair defect' into the state of Nature.[12] So for example John Salkeld, in *A Treatise of Paradise* (1617), endorses Augustine's theory of pre-lapsarian sexuality because it is inconceivable that God could have created woman for anything but procreation — otherwise 'they might have both been created males'.[13] Again we see the paradox of the narrow-Augustinian position: the female is reduced to a reproductive organism in the very act of restoring reproduction to its original glory in the divine plan. To the authority of Genesis and Augustine Salkeld adds the voice of Aristotle, as Aquinas had done: 'generation is the most naturall action of life; yea then every thing is in his perfect estate, when it is powerfull to bring forth another like to it selfe.' But this testimony of perfection actually deepens the paradox, for Aristotle maintains, with the fervent support of Salkeld, that females are monstrous and defective, and would have formed only a minimal part of the population had the human race continued to multiply in the state of innocence. Even then, females would have been the result of botched copulation or 'defect of nature' (pp. 181-4).

An even more contradictory example is provided by the medical psychologist Juan Huartes. Contrary to the general opinion, Huartes actually believed that man would not have reproduced sexually at all if he had not sinned. Nevertheless, he founds his theory of human consciousness on reproductive physiology — his book teaches how to produce brilliant children by eugenics — and he provides an unusually detailed account of the bodies (and therefore the minds) of Adam and Eve, the perfect man and woman from whom we all

---

[12] Henry Neville, *The Parliament of Ladies* (1647), p. 3; *PL* X. 891. Donne liked to play with this paradox (e.g. in his own *Paradoxes and Problemes* and in his second verse epistle to the Countess of Huntington, which begins 'Man to Gods image, *Eve* to mans was made, / Nor finde wee that God breath'd a soul in her'), but in his sermons he recognizes that this opinion comes from 'the extravagancy of Paradoxes' and must be rejected (*Sermons*, IV. 241 and IX. 190); cf. also Keith Thomas, *Man and the Natural World* (1983), p. 43.

[13] p. 181. Though I continue to cite Salkeld's *Treatise* in this chapter, it should be pointed out that most of it is plagiarized from Benedictus Pererius, *Commentariorum et Disputationum in Genesin Libri IV* (Cologne, 1601); here, for example, from pp. 227-8.

deviate. The temperate and wise Adam would still have been threatened by the fierce heat in his testicles necessary for reproduction, the 'law in his members' that St. Paul had to contend with. (He assumes that Adam was so rapt in spiritual contemplation and in conversations with the asexual angels that he did not notice his own bodily conformation until his 'eyes were opened'.) Eve, whose entire frame is assumed to be designed for reproduction and therefore cool and moist, must therefore have been created mentally deficient, an ideal to which women are encouraged to aspire.[14] In this account, then, the benign foresight of God in creating man partially and woman entirely sexual, while placing them in a completely non-sexual state of blessedness, comes dangerously close to seeming incompetent.

Huartes's precarious theory can at least explain why no children were conceived before the fall. Salkeld, however—like all those who accept the possibility of pre-lapsarian sexuality, and who try to reconstruct a literal, consistent, and imaginable 'history of Paradise'—cannot explain Eve's non-pregnancy without falling into the paradox of time. On the one hand, he redeems sexuality and insists that it is the central motivation for creating male and female; on the other hand, he assumes that Adam and Eve never actually experienced the ideal, orderly copulation that God had planned, even though they were given seven full nights in Paradise. Any less time would not be 'sufficient for the experience of that happy estate'. But if God wished them to know the utmost happiness of the unfallen state—for the rather ghoulish purpose 'that they might better perceive the miserie into which they fell by sinne, by the knowledge and experience which they had of their former felicitie in Paradise'—why should He have withheld its most perfect experience, 'the most naturall action of life' and the thing for which above all they were created?[15]

These, then, are some of the problems of the 'narrow-Augustinian' concentration on woman's procreative function, which predominates among scientifically minded exegetes even when they deny that reproduction was intended in the state of innocence.

[14] *Examen de Ingenios* (1575; rev. 1640), tr. Edward Bellamy (1698), pp. 377–81 (and cf. 67–8), 401–2, 409–12, 456–65.

[15] pp. 227–9. Salkeld does not pursue his experiential model, but reverts to a typological argument: God postponed the fall for a week because He wanted all the major events of human history—the creation, the fall, and the Crucifixion—to happen on a Friday.

3. The State of Eve

Advocates of a more companionate interpretation of 'one flesh' and a more generous definition of woman took issue with this opinion, however, particularly as it is stated in Augustine's *De Genesi ad Litteram*; the broadening of his view of marriage is rarely noted.

Calvin, for example, had refuted Augustine's narrow interpretation by adding a social and spiritual dimension to the reproductive function. Rather than linking procreation only to Eve and spiritual companionship only to Adam, Calvin asserts that Adam and Eve were *both* created for procreation, and that Adam was only a half-person (*dimidium*) without his counterpart; he then treats this sexual union of 'one flesh' in terms that extend it far beyond the narrowly physical (1:27, 1:28, 2:21). As we have seen in chapter 2, he anticipates Milton in seeing the sexual core of wedded love as the 'fountain' of all social relationships, and as an ontological and transcendent force akin to Platonic Eros. Indeed, Calvin wonders whether 'help' ought to be extended to procreation at all, and interprets Eve as a kind of counterpart, mirror-image or equal—

and hence is refuted the error of some, who think that the woman was formed only for the sake of propagation, and who restrict the word 'good', which had been lately mentioned, to the production of offspring. They do not think that a wife was personally necessary for Adam, because he was hitherto free from lust; as if she had been given to him only to sleep with (*ad concubitum*), and not rather that she might be the inseparable associate of his life (2:18).

Thus Calvin opposes two reductive definitions of God's purpose in creating woman—as a means of propagating the race, and as a relief of sexual urges—to a fuller vision of Eve as a social companion in all the functions of life; but these social bonds are themselves to be transfigured by the sacred union of one flesh.

With a few striking exceptions—Luther and Peter Martyr, for example—this companionate interpretation of the creation of Eve prevailed among the more radical Protestants, and coloured their vision of marriage and 'the society of the marriage-bed'.[16] The Huguenot André Rivet, as Milton points out, took 'help meet' to 'pertain not only to procreation but to all the intercourse of life,

---

[16] For Luther, see 3. 2. iv below; for Peter Martyr (Vermigli), see V. Norskov Olsen, *The New Testament Logia on Divorce* (Tübingen, 1971), p. 90.

and to the uniting of habits, minds, and affections'. David Paraeus, a commentator who often influenced Milton, similarly juxtaposed the dismissive lines of *De Genesi ad Litteram* to a broader vision of the 'help' that woman can provide, and discovers all kinds of social and economic benefits in the marriage-bond and wifely help. Milton is certainly right to claim—in furious response to a critic of his *Doctrine and Discipline of Divorce*—that 'our [Protestant] Writers' often 'deservedly reject' the narrow-Augustinian view. At several points in his divorce tracts Milton himself attacks the 'rusticity' of *De Genesi ad Litteram* and its 'crabbed opinion' that woman could not provide amorous companionship and spiritual delight: 'there is a peculiar comfort in the married state besides the genial bed, which no other society affords.'[17]

2. Genesis and female subordination: the limits of the thinkable

What then would be the relation between man and woman in this society of one flesh? The general assumption, of course, is that the wife should be subordinate. The desire to enforce male authority clashes, sometimes conspicuously, with the desire to make holy matrimony a restitution of Paradise, founded on mutual respect and delight. We have seen that Augustine and Aquinas are prepared to violate the sacred Scripture itself in their effort to find the 'natural' inferiority of woman in God's original creation. But Genesis resists this interpretation. Even the 'pre-subordinationist' St. Paul, who based his male suprematism on the assertion that Eve was created as a secondary and ancillary being, and not directly in the image of God, recognized complete mutual surrender in sexual 'benevolence'; and his use of 'one flesh' as a synonym for copulation (even with a prostitute) suggests that, in some part of his mind, he believed that the erotic bond abolished all dominance and re-established primal unity.

The first two chapters of Genesis, as several commentators realized, do not support St. Paul's suprematist interpretation. Male and female are created together in God's image, and neither the 'Priestly' nor the 'Jahwist' creation-stories mention subordination; the story of Eve suggests, if anything, a higher though more precarious status for woman. This omission led Chrysostom and

---

[17] *Prose* II. 246, 596 and n. 26, 740; Arnold Williams, *The Common Expositor* (Chapel Hill, 1948), pp. 85–6, 92. For an even more elaborate list of the areas in which the woman is a 'help', see Henry Smith, quot. in Halkett, p. 87.

later Luther to insist that subordination was entirely a post-lapsarian condition, and even the pre-subordinationists paid tribute to the mutuality of Adam and Eve—Calvin, as we have seen, describes the help-meet as an 'equal' companion, a mirror of the self, the amplification and fulfilment of a previously unfinished Adam. The eroticism of the Song of Songs is likewise free of any hint of male supremacy or female inferiority. Genesis 3:16 does of course establish wifely obedience as a punishment for Eve's hubris, but this primal curse should have been softened or even abolished by redemption and regeneration, like all other strictures of the old Law. As Augustine put it, unconsciously weakening his own suprematism, Eve was punished by slavery and domination, but Christian husbands and wives can be joined in a gentle mutual subordination such as existed in the state of innocence. In the resurrection, Aquinas maintained, male and female would be absolutely equal because the punishment of Genesis 3:16 would be abolished; he seems to abandon his own earlier assertion, supposedly based on Genesis and biology, that woman was created intrinsically deficient and subordinate.[18]

Nor did the 'scholastic synthesis' absolutely dominate later medieval thought. Peter Lombard, for example, accepts the Augustinian-Thomistic theory of pre-lapsarian sexuality, but combines it with an egalitarian conception of 'one flesh': Eve was made from a rib, rather than from some higher or lower part, because she is to be neither an overlord nor a servant, but a companion. A recent scholar finds parallels to Lombard's interpretation in Jean le Meung's glorious vision of the Golden Age, when lovers enjoyed absolute equality and *amour* was never contaminated by 'maistrie'.[19]

The Pauline headship of the husband was accepted by all Reformation writers, but many of them insisted that he ruled over an equal and must therefore display all the more affection and consideration as a lover. Among the separatists, Campanus's vision of the simultaneous creation of male and female removed the argument from priority, a keystone of the supremedist interpretation;

---

[18] Chrysostom, quot. in McColley, pp. 49-50; for Aug. see n. 8 above, for Aquinas n. 11 above and contrast Maclean, *Renaissance Notion*, p. 14.

[19] Henry A. Kelly, *Love and Marriage in the Age of Chaucer* (Ithaca, 1975), p. 41, referring to the *Roman de la Rose*, ll. 8325-424, esp. ll. 8421-4 ('onques amor et seigneurie / ne s'entrefirent compaignie / ne ne demorerent ensemble: / cil que mestroie les dessemble'). Even though the Chaucerian tr. does not include this part of the *Roman*, Chaucer echoes these lines (ch. 2 n. 59 above).

in many radical sects women enjoyed considerable self-determination, and even assumed charismatic leadership. And given their general stress on patriarchal authority, English Protestants were surprisingly open to egalitarian readings of the unfallen state, and surprisingly willing to transfer that happiness to the present day. As we shall see, this leads them to many contradictiors.

Because Eve was made from Adam as 'woman of man, equall to him in dignity,' Daniel Rogers argued, marriages should now be 'true matches' and 'couples should be peeres'. William Secker insisted that the husband should be a 'meet help' to the wife as well as she to him—a suggestion apoplectically denied in Milton's divorce tracts. The Quaker Margaret Fell maintained, and later convinced her husband George Fox, that according to Genesis 1: 27 'God joyns [Male and Female] together in his own Image, and makes no such distinctions and differences as men do'—again, Milton's divorce tracts maintain the opposite.[20] And although some English radicals were reported to believe that woman had 'no more soul than a Goose', others like the Diggers recognized that, though humanity was given dominion over the natural world in Genesis, 'not one word was spoken in the beginning, That one branch of mankind should rule over other; and the Reason is this, Every single man, Male and Female, is a perfect Creature of himself.' The 'Rosicrucian' John Heydon and the rationalist François Poulain de la Barre likewise insist that in the beginning 'the *Scripture* speaketh not a word of Inequality'.[21] Far from being unthinkable, as Christopher Hill implies in his attempt to make Milton a progressive for his age, the fundamental equality of woman could certainly be conceived as part of the legacy of Genesis.

[*ii*]

Many Protestant exegetes, then, rejected the 'narrow-Augustinian' reduction of woman to a procreative device, and defined marriage as a fusion of the social and the erotic—'a pleasing combination of two persons into one home, one purse, one heart, and one

---

[20] Rogers, quot. in William and Malleville Haller, 'The Puritan Art of Love', *HLQ* V (1942), 259; Secker, pp. 23-4; for Margaret Fell Fox, cf. Hilda L. Smith, *Reason's Disciples* (Urbana, 1982), pp. 95-6, and Hill[2], p. 118. For M's views on masculine rule, see 6. 3 below.

[21] George Fox, quot. in Hill[1], p. 314; *The True Levellers Standard Advanced*, in Gerrard Winstanley, *Works*, ed. George H. Sabine (Ithaca, 1941), p. 251; Halkett, pp. 78, 80.

flesh'—in which subordination and equality were somehow combined.[22] Some more radical thinkers even argued for the prelapsarian state of equality, distinguishing it from the masculine rule imposed at the fall. The chief source of the egalitarian Genesis, however, is not the 'Puritan Art of Love' but the Renaissance tradition of learned wit.

The relative value of Adam and Eve, and their relative responsibility for the fall—the subject of striking contradictions in the New Testament—generated debate not only among Biblical commentators, but among learned humanists like Isotta Nogarola, who argued the female case with considerable eloquence.[23] The topic was also included in a larger genre, the 'apology for woman'. Heinrich Cornelius Agrippa, for example, composed an extensive proof of Eve's superiority in his *De Nobilitate et Praecellentia Foeminei Sexu*. Eve was the last, best creature, named after Life itself, 'built' by God from ensouled flesh in Paradise, which He had prepared as her palace; Adam was merely 'formed' by Nature out of the common earth whose name he bears. She was pre-eminent in delicacy, spirituality, and beauty, and consequently Satan, enflamed with ambition and desire, approached her not as the weaker vessel but as the greater prize. Woman received the blessing, but man—and only man—received the prohibition, since 'God wanted her to be free from the beginning'. Because man alone was forbidden the fruit, Eve's crime was far less; either she did not know the prohibition, or else she had no special reason to believe it since it came only from Adam. At most she was a deluded accessory to sin, whereas Adam knowingly broke the commandment and brought death upon us all. The punishment of circumcision confirms that the male is the greater sinner. Women were free and active in society until 'the *tyranny* of Men usurpt the dispose of all business, and *unjust Laws, foolish Customes*, and an *ill mode* of education *retrencht* their liberties.' Even more shamefully, religious leaders use the punishment of Genesis 3:16 (long swept away by

---

[22] William Whately, *A Bride-Bush*, 2nd edn. (1619), p. 31.
[23] 'De pari aut impari Evae atque Adae peccato', ed. and tr. in Margaret L. King and Albert Rabil, *Her Immaculate Hand* (Binghamton, 1983), pp. 57-69; as the editors point out, Nogarola's argument for Eve's relative innocence is premised on her weakness. For sexual abuse directed against Nogarola's attempt to continue an intellectual career, see ibid. 17; for a general context, see Patricia H. Labalme (ed.), *Beyond their Sex* (NY, 1980), esp. pp. 70-2, 96.

Christ), and the purely ceremonial dictates of St. Paul, to justify this continual oppression.[24]

The mingling of judicious and preposterous arguments suggests that Agrippa was concerned more to display his wit, and to placate his dedicatee Margaret of Austria, than to reform contemporary opinion; his *De nobilitate* is a conscious exercise in paradox, and thus confirms rather than undermines the assumption that male supremacy is normal and natural. Nevertheless his arguments were frequently repeated during the following century, sometimes for comic effect, sometimes as part of a formally balanced display of commonplaces, but sometimes in genuine earnest. The Agrippan theses, shorn of their facetious context, could be used to articulate deeper needs, and even modern scholars will occasionally refer to Agrippa as a sincere feminist.[25] Successive English versions of his treatise reflect this range of tone: that of 1542 is a straightforward translation; those of 1652 (one in prose and one in verse) are fervent and sincere arguments on behalf of women; that of 1670 is an expression of 'wit' and social banter, with many added reassurances of playfulness.[26]

---

[24] *Opera Omnia* (Lyons, n.d.), II. 518–42; *Female Pre-eminence, or the Dignity and Excellency of that Sex, above the Male*, tr. Henry Care (1670). The passage about ill education quoted here is added by this English translator (p. 76)—who does not, however, translate the idea that God wanted woman to be free from the beginning (cf. *Opera* II. 528).

[25] For later uses of the Agrippan Genesis, cf. Ruth Kelso, *Doctrine for the Lady of the Renaissance*, 2nd edn. (Urbana, 1978), p. 15; Maclean, *Woman Triumphant*, pp. 6, 26, 40–2; Labalme, pp. 138–9 (summarizing Arcangela Tarabotti's *Tirannia Paterna*); Linda Woodbridge, *Women and the English Renaissance* (Urbana, 1984), *passim*. McColley treats Agrippa as a sincere defender of women (pp. 42–3); Woodbridge, in the fullest and most sophisticated account of Agrippa, appreciates both the preposterousness of his arguments and their potential for genuine feminism, and notes a shift or *volta* towards serious historical argument later in the treatise (pp. 38–42). Woodbridge relates these effects to the Renaissance paradox-tradition (cf. n. 12 above and Rosalie Colie, *Paradoxia Epidemica* (Princeton, 1966), esp. p. 102). M's first divorce tract seemed (to Bishop Hall) to belong in this deliberately outrageous tradition: he 'supposed some great wit meant to try his skill in the maintenance of this so wild, and improbable a paradoxe', but soon 'those too-well-penned pages' revealed their dreadful truth—'the author was in earnest' (W. R. Parker, *M's Contemporary Reputation* (Columbus, 1940), p. 79). A late (1700) development of Agrippa's exoneration of Eve is recorded in Bayle, 'Eve' M: Eve was not even expelled from Paradise and continued to live there, paying the occasional conjugal visit to her husband.

[26] The English trs. are as follows: David Clapam, *A Treatise of the Nobilitie and Excellencye of Woman Kynde* (1542), reissued as *The Commendation of Matrimony* (1545); William Bercher or Barker, *The Nobility of Women* (1559), ed. R. Warwick Bond (1904); Edward Fleetwood, *The Glory of Women, or a Treatise Declaring the*

Agrippa's arguments, ambiguously poised between jest and seriousness, appear in many treatises on the nature of man and woman. Samuel Purchas's *Microcosmus*, for example, proves Eve's 'preeminence above the Masculine' from Genesis and from current observation, in both cases virtually translating the words of Agrippa: after arguing from the superior place, matter, and form of her creation, and her superior *'helpe in Generation'*, he also pronounces her 'Equall ... in her reasonable immortall Soule, equall in that Universal Inheritance of the Universe,' and an equal supporter of the household. Purchas follows this vivid encomium, however, with a no less eloquent condemnation, likewise based on Genesis and Nature.[27] But in Emilia Lanier's 'Eves Apologie' and in Heale's *Apologie for Women*, the Agrippan arguments for the equality or superiority of woman stand on their own merit, with no counterbalancing refutation.

Lanier's 'Apology' for Eve, a dramatic monologue by Pontius Pilate's wife in the narrative poem *Salve Deus Rex Judeorum*, develops the idea of the lesser culpability of Eve. She was 'simply good', motivated by 'too much love', and ignorant of the serpent's guile, whereas Adam had been given the prohibition directly, and failed to make any objection even though fully aware of what he was doing. If Eve did display a trace of intrinsic evil, it must have come from the material of which she was made. The subsequent crimes of men have been overwhelmingly more heinous than those of women, and now that men are about to put the Son of God to death—over the objections of women—the last remnant of justification for masculine rule is swept away:

> Then let us have our Libertie again
> And challendge to your selves no Sov'raigntie.

Conscious of her double role as poet and exegete, Lanier appeals

Excellency and Preheminence of Women above Men (1652); Hugh Crompton, *The Glory of Women, or a Looking-Glasse for Ladies, wherein they may Behold their own Excellency and Preheminence ... Now Turned into Heroicall Verse* (1652); Care, n. 24 above. The variations from one version to another warrant a separate study; among the additions in Care, for example, see ff. A1-2, which stresses the 'innocent paradox' and Quixotic 'generous folly' of Agrippa, and pp. 3 ('This may at first perhaps seem an *odd Assertion*, and *extravagantly Paradoxical*'), 14 (a Platonic/Erotic interpretation of the rib), 62 ('a pretty obliging wench'), and 78-83 (attacks on 'Poetasters' and pamphleteers of the Restoration, replacing the original religious conclusion).

[27] *Microcosmus, or the Historie of Man* (1619), pp. 473-5, and cf. 477-82; Purchas's biology is also derived from Agrippa (cf. *Female Pre-eminence*, p. 22).

to the Queen, her patroness and mentor, to approve her remarkable new thesis and 'judge if it agree not with the Text': if it does, how can men continue to blame and abuse women?[28]

Protestant exegesis and the theses of Agrippa combine with the Renaissance courtesy-tradition in Heale's *Apologie*, which defends a position similar to Lanier's with a greater wealth of evidence. His arguments from secular sources—courtesy books, Sidney's *Arcadia*, law, 'civil policy', and natural science—are crowned, as we have seen, by a detailed and rapturous reading of the creation of Eve. She was created last because she was 'the Queene of the world', and her palace needed to be prepared beforehand. The place, matter, and form of her creation make her 'nothing at all lesse than ... man, and in some things also farre beyond him'. She was made from a rib 'that thereby shee might appeare his equal', and from the side next to the heart 'to teach obdurate man that woman is the Goddess to whom he ought to sacrifice the love of his heart'. The creation of Eve was a mutual transfiguration: 'Woman therefore by the divine power of creation was made of man, and man by a strange kinde of *Metamorphosis* converted into woman'—after the hard rib was replaced by softer material, his heart and mind assume 'a natural mildness'. The first result of this transformation is Adam's proclamation of 'one flesh'—his 'morning-song', his 'Hymineal Song', and his first statute, expressing 'a *nescio quid* in marriage, some higher mysterie, and a relation more essential' that makes us leave our parents and 'live unto our companion who is our second selfe'. In this Golden Age the marriage-partners were no more distinct than the persons of the Trinity, and there were 'no wordes of rigorous predomination, no thoughte of unkinde preheminence'. And just as then God made Eve 'as an equal associate and fellow helper for man', so even now, in the secular world, the wife is considered 'thy familiar friend, thine equal associate, the Mistresse of thy house; to speake at once, the same person and *Individuum* (as it were) together with thee.'[29]

We shall see, however, that Heale's eloquent and no doubt heartfelt tribute to the egalitarian ideal, written at the request of a

[28] *Salve Deus Rex Judaeorum: The Poems of Shakespeare's Dark Lady* (*sic*), ed. A. L. Rowse (1978), pp. 43, 102-5. Lanier's prose introduction makes further use of Agrippan examples, particularly from Christ's ministry to women (p. 78, and cf. Agrippa, *Opera* II. 529-30).

[29] pp. 48, 53-62, and cf. Introd. above. For other 'Apologies' for women (not including Lanier's), see Woodbridge, pp. 74-81.

powerful patroness, in no way diminishes his faith in the superiority of the male in the original state of creation. His *Apologie* is a gesture of gallantry, a gracious play of arguments and authorities. For Lanier, on the other hand, the Agrippan revision, and the realization that an unjust interpretation of Genesis still dictated the everyday attitudes of men towards women, is a matter of serious and uncompromising concern.

[*iii*]

It might seem, then, that interpretations of Genesis can be arranged in a spectrum according to the political and psychosocial vision they sustain. On the one hand, the belief in companionate marriage, and the vision of woman as a fully human counterpart to man, leads towards an egalitarian or female-suprematist revisionism. The other extreme stresses woman's defectiveness in every function except procreation—the 'crabbed opinion' of Augustine and Aquinas—and interprets every detail of the fall-story to throw the behaviour of Eve, and consequently the nature of woman, into the worst possible light.

It is certainly often true that exclusively biological definitions of marriage go hand in hand with theories of female inferiority. The narrow-Augustinian Salkeld, for example, claims that the unfallen human race would have been almost entirely male—'because nature then being in a full perfection, would for the most part have produced the most perfect, which questionlesse is the male'. Salkeld believes so fervently in female deficiency that he is even prepared to sacrifice the logic of his argument and the integrity of his Paradise: wrestling with the difficult problem of how women could have been admitted into the state of perfection, he notes that 'the production of the female doth not proceede only, or rather not alwaies of the defect of nature', but sometimes comes about from a 'more remisse manner' of copulating, a failure of the imagination, 'and other like naturall defects' (pp. 182-4). Milton's Adam expresses similar opinions, but only at the depth of his fall into sin and despair; here they are fully sanctioned by Salkeld himself, King James's personal chaplain. At such moments we can feel the ideological imperative in full force.

A more gifted exegete would not necessarily arrive at a more generous view. Donne, for example, chooses as the text for his Nethersole wedding-sermon Genesis 2:18, the same verse on which

Milton founded his doctrine of spiritual companionship, and with great ingenuity deduces from it precisely the narrow-Augustinian position that Milton abhorred. To explain *it is not good that the man should be alone*, he distinguishes individual good, the good of the male sex, and the good of the species, and assumes that only the third is served by marriage. The stress is almost exclusively on procreation, and in every other respect the male is worse off for having a wife:

God did not say, *non bonum Homini, It was not good for man to be alone*; man might have done well enough in that state, so as his *solitarinesse* might have been supplied with a farther creation of more men.... *Quanto congruentius*, says *S. Augustine*, how much more conveniently might two friends live together, than a man and a woman?

Donne then proceeds to describe primal happiness in words that would seem like a libertine mockery if they had not been delivered from the pulpit: 'God doth not then say, *non bonum hominis*; man got not so much by the bargaine (especially if we consider how that wife carried her selfe towards him), but that for his particular, he had been better alone.' Donne praises God for introducing evil into Paradise; divine power overrides the good of Adam just as it can make the elements 'depart from their owne nature'. From this alarming principle he draws wholesome lessons for the bridegroom and the wedding-guests: 'be as liberall in thy mortifications as in thy excesse'; do not love your wife as a mistress, lest she suck away your vital bodily fluids and so hasten your death as Eve did Adam's; strive, fast, and pray for continence or the gift of celibacy, like those who *'make themselves Eunuchs for the kingdome of heavens sake'*.[30]

In keeping with this valuation of lifelong female companionship, Donne defines '*help*' largely in terms of procreation, though he does warn the wife that to 'governe' or to think that she can 'give essence to the man, essence to her husband' would be a failure in her duty to 'help'. His definition of meetness or 'fitness' likewise dwells on sexual continence. Moral and spiritual fitness, and 'the Harmony of dispositions', the corner-stone of Milton's definition of marriage, are mentioned only negligently, as 'a subject too

---

[30] *Sermons*, II. 335-47; on pp. 338-9 Donne quotes from the passage of Aug.'s *De Gen. ad Lit.* cited in n. 7 above—a quotation not noted by Simpson and Potter in their list of Augustinian borrowings (*Sermons*, X. 376-86).

mis-interpretable and unseasonable'; they are shuffled out of the way at the very end, in a tone of embarrassed haste.[31]

Donne thus appears to stand in sharp contrast to the 'Puritan' defenders of companionate marriage, in his praise of celibacy and mortification, in his exegesis of the founding texts, and in his promotion of the 'crabbed opinion' of Augustine. He defines 'help' as procreation; the Puritans define it as companionship in every function of life. Henry Smith finds that 'man is stronger by his wife'; Donne discovers in the creation of Eve from a rib that 'she was not taken out of the *foot*, to be trodden upon, nor out of the *head*, to be an overseer of him, but out of *his side*, where she weakens him enough.' Every commentator draws some significance from the rib, and many of them use a similar formula to Donne's, which is Rabbinical in origin. (We have seen the egalitarian application of this formula in Peter Lombard, reiterated by Heale.) But though the anatomy of the rib is occasionally used to prove the crookedness of the woman or the painfulness of domestic fighting, for the most part it becomes an emblem of erotic intimacy, affection, mutual respect, companionship, protection, and 'equality'.[32] In contrast to this entire tradition, Donne discovers in the creation of Eve nothing but a sinister depletion.

We should be careful not to draw the battle-lines too rigidly, however. Salkeld, for all his Aristotelian disparagement of female company, still insisted that woman as well as man was created fully in the image of God—a concession which Milton's divorce tracts, despite their demand for mental compatibility, refused to grant: in some cases, Salkeld points out, women's religious gifts make them reveal more of the image of God than men possess.[33] On the other

---

[31] *Sermons*, II. 337, 342, 346-7. Donne assumes that harmony of disposition is something only occasionally required, not essential to marriage, and applies the same phrase ('mis-interpretable') to non-sexual definitions of fitness and to the embarrassing subject of circumcision (VI. 190).

[32] Cf. Williams, *Common Expositor*, p. 91; Halkett, pp. 84, 88; Gervase Babington, *Certaine ... Notes upon Genesis* (1592), f. 12; Salkeld, p. 173; John Weemse, *The Portraiture of the Image of God in Man* (1636), pp. 266-7; John Swan, *Speculum Mundi* (1635), 2nd edn. (Cambridge, 1644), p. 494; Secker, pp. 16-17 (but cf. 23); Thomas Goodwin, quot. in Hill[1], p. 309. Feminist responses to Joseph Swetnam often asserted that Eve's creation from Adam's side (rather than his foot) demonstrated the equality of woman; cf. Rachel Speght, *A Mouzell for Melastomus* (1617), f. B2v, p. 10, and 'Esther Sowernam', *Esther Hath Hang'd Haman* (1617), pp. 1-4, 6, 21.

[33] pp. 103-6. For M's assertion that woman was not created in the 'image of God' at all, or only in a secondary and derived way, see 6. 3. i below; for the

hand John Heydon, who insists on pre-lapsarian equality and who sincerely endorses the companionate ideal, can only praise female friendship by denying its femaleness:

a woman with a wise soul is the fittest companion for man, otherwise God would have given him a friend rather than a Wife. A wise Wife comprehends both sexes; she is woman for her body, and she is man within, for her soul is like her Husbands.[34]

The terms of Heydon's praise effectively endorse the narrow-Augustinian 'crabbed opinion' that he attempts to refute. And Donne himself, who used the Nethersole wedding as an exercise in 'edification through mortification' and an opportunity to drive home the subordinate and procreational function of the wife, treats marriage quite differently in his next wedding-sermon, for Margaret Washington.

Here the text is Hosea 2:19—'and I will marry thee unto me for ever', in the version Donne chooses—and the 'secular marriage' of Adam and Eve is only one step in the rhetorical progression towards celestial marriage. Donne is now buoyant and brilliant, apparently exhilarated by this larger horizon. He showers the happy couple with eloquent and judicious blessings ('Lord . . . as thy mercies are new every morning, make them so to one another'), and exhorts them to 'true help and mutuall help'. And he defines that help in ways which, if properly applied to the original intentions in Genesis, would abolish wifely subordination entirely: subjects need the help of kings, Christians place their help in the Lord.[35]

Thus we find striking inconsistencies among the narrow-Augustinian defenders of female deficiency. On the other hand, many of the most eloquent praisers of equality, companionship,

---

ambiguity of the phrase 'not equal', which seems to qualify the proclamation in *PL* IV. 291-2 that the image of God shone in both Adam and Eve, see 7. 2. i and iii below.

[34] *Advice to a Daughter* (1659), quot. in Halkett, p. 79.

[35] *Sermons*, III. 244-7. In a third wedding-sermon Donne abandons the marital relationship altogether, except for a few sensible remarks on mutual tolerance and realistic expectations; instead he treats his audience of Egertons and Herberts to a grand display of rhetorical powers on a dazzlingly inappropriate text—'in the resurrection, they neither marry nor are given in mariage, but are as the angels of God in Heaven' (VIII. 94-109). The editors' remark on Donne's 'perversity' in the latter sermon (VIII. 10) shows little appreciation of his strenuous attempt to discover truth in the clash of contraries, nor do they recognize that the 'morbid' passage on the resurrection is in fact an expansion of Aug. *CG* XXII. 21.

3. The State of Eve

and mutuality—whether in present-day marriage or in the God-given state of innocence—contradict their own premises by subscribing to pre-subordinationism as well, sometimes within a few pages of their egalitarian pronouncements. Chrysostom, who takes God's silence on the question of subordination to mean that Adam and Eve were equal, nevertheless imagines her obedient to him, and not him to her. And Heale, who denied 'predomination' and 'preheminence' in the state of innocence, can still assert that 'my first ground shall be the superiority of husbands over their wives'.[36]

The foundation for these statements is sometimes surprisingly shallow, moreover. When Heinrich Bullinger explains that, because Eve was taken from Adam's side and not his head, therefore 'the husband is the head and master of the wife', he uses a syllogism for which he would have been birched at school. When Bunyan expounds Genesis 3:16 he raises considerable doubts about the effectiveness and intelligibility of Eve's punishment: her state of subjection before and after the fall was 'doubtless' identical, but 'that duty that before she might do as her natural right by creation, she must now do as the fruits of her disobedience to God'.[37] And when Heale lists the reasons for his suprematism, he supplies tendentious motives for the creation of Eve ('the woman was made of man, and for man, and given in tuition by God unto man'), and confuses human relationships and the biological dominance of mankind over the lower animals. Genesis 1 clearly says that dominion over the animals is granted equally to male and female, and clearly demarcates the realms of 'man' and nature; but for Heale, the tender-hearted Apologist for Women, the founding text is invisible beside the dazzling 'first ground' of male suprematism.[38]

The radical separatists were no less contradictory. Though Campanus harmonizes Genesis 1 and 2 on egalitarian principles,

[36] McColley, p. 26, and cf. 49; Heale, p. 31, and cf. p. 62.
[37] Bullinger, quot. in Smith, *Reason's Disciples*, p. 70, n. 38; John Bunyan, *An Exposition of the First Ten Chapters of Genesis* (1678), in *Complete Works*, ed. Henry Stebbing (c.1859), III. 390. Bunyan's commentary is a strange mixture of absurdity ('But how could he be naked, when before he had made himself an apron? O! the approach of God consumed and burnt off his apron!' (p. 385)) and an almost Miltonic psychological realism: '*And the woman said, the serpent beguiled me, and I did eat*; a poor excuse, but a heart-affecting one, for many times want of wit and cunning to defend ourselves doth affect and turn the heart of a stander-by to pity us' (p. 388).
[38] p. 31; see *DNB* for the contempt allegedly inspired by Heale's 'softness' with regard to women.

he still asserts that the husband is always higher than the wife, just as in the Godhead the Father is always superior to the Son. (This was to be Milton's position.) Bernard Rothmann, the ideologist of Münster, used 'increase and multiply' to exert authority over his own nine wives and those of the whole city: women 'everywhere have been getting the upper hand', and should now submit to man as man to Christ and Christ to God. The communist Hutterites believed that the husband who relinquishes 'lordship' repeats the fall itself. Thus these radicals of the 'equalizing covenant' approach the more conservative position of Calvin, who insisted that feminist wives 'invert the order of nature' and must be forced back to the subordination they enjoyed before the fall, or of the Presbyterian John Weemes, who 'proves' female subjection with a mass of dubious post-lapsarian evidence (including Aristotelian science and the customs of Islam), and then proceeds to claim that 'since the fall, this heavenly order is mightily inverted, when the woman claymes soveraignty over the man, and will not be subject to him.'[39]

Among exponents of the 'Puritan art of love' we find the same unflinching juxtaposition of evidence from the fallen and the unfallen state, and the same unquestioning application of the immutable principles of natural science. Thus William Whately uses arguments from 'God and Nature' to persuade the wife to consider herself 'a wel-broken horse' and to manifest her inferiority in every detail of her life and thought; sometimes he will refer this doctrine to the punishment of Eve in Genesis 3:16, but sometimes he will assert that 'you wives' should 'be content to be subject to your husbands, as it is sure *Evah* was before the fall at least, and probable after too.'[40] And William Gouge likewise derives female subjection from a hopelessly heterogenous collection of factors— the punishment of Eve, her creation '*after man, for mans good*, and *out of mans side*,' the exclusion of woman from the image of God, the 'eminence in the male over the female' in animals, and the clothes women wear.[41]

[39] George Huntston Williams, *RR* pp. 373, 377-8, 507, 517; Calvin, 3:16: Weemes, pp. 264-6. Weemes's one exception to universal male suprematism is the 'due benevolence' of sexuality (ch. 6 n. 36 below); Rachel's need to arouse her husband with aphrodisiac mandrakes (Gen. 30:15) appears to contradict this principle, but Weemes points out, more wittily than perhaps he realized, that in polygamous marriages 'One man cannot serve two masters, *Mat.* 6:24' (pp. 265-6).

[40] Whately, *A Bride-Bush* (1617), pp. 36, 43, and *Prototypes*, quot. in McColley, p. 50.

[41] *Domesticall Duties*, 2nd edn. (1626), pp. 158-9. Gouge adduces the 'natural'

3. *The State of Eve*

These arguments, elaborated with a dazzling display of logical evasion and circularity, are explicitly intended to quell a women's revolt in the Puritan community—the same impulse, perhaps, that led the women of Kidderminster to stone Richard Baxter for insisting on the original sin of infants.[42] Genesis is the source of this resistance. Gouge recognizes that the creation from the rib, and the blessing of 'increase and multiply' given to both sexes, persuades many wives 'that in all things there ought to be a mutuall equality'; it was precisely this militant feminist interpretation, widespread in his own parish, that forced him to spell out his doctrine so fully. And he admits that the supposedly 'natural' and 'God-given' subordination of women is in no way self-evident: 'till a wife be informed that an husband, by vertue of his place, is his wifes superiour, she will not be perswaded that her owne husband is above her.' Gouge thus arrives at a position that precisely reverses his older contemporary Richard Hooker's opinion, that the qualities that make woman 'inferiour in excellency' to man, even in Paradise, 'might be sooner perceived than defined'.[43] Either female inferiority can be seen but not put into words, or else it must be put into words because it cannot be seen.

The ideological imperative, the passionate desire to dominate the female, thus has the power to override the hermeneutic process itself. The original non-subordination of Eve, and the original immortality of man, are equally inferable from the text; and yet one is almost universally accepted, the other almost universally denied. God says 'let us create man in our own image ... male and female'; Thomas Taylor says that 'to crosse [the husband's] will, his speeches, his lawfull desires and commands, on which God hath stamped his image, is to cut off God's image and ordinance, and misse the end of being a wife.'[44] Gouge must train his female

---

male dominance of the animal kingdom here, but elsewhere denies the applicability of animal to human sexuality (p. 131).

[42] pp. 158-9; cf. Haller and Haller, pp. 249-50, and William M. Lamont, *Richard Baxter and the Millenium* (1979), p. 131 (Baxter had reported to his audience of mothers that Hell is paved with infants' skulls).

[43] Gouge, p. 158; Hooker, quot. in McColley, p. 22. Hooker goes on to relate this mystery to the ineffability of married love: 'and even herein doth lie the reason, why that kind of love which is the perfectest ground of Wedlock is seldome able to yeild any reason of it self' (ibid. 22-3, and cf. p. 26 for Hooker on the 'imbecility' of women).

[44] *Catechism*, quot. in Halkett, p. 46.

parishioners and readers in the 'schoole of subjection', and to this end he is prepared to sacrifice the very notion of a fall, by scrambling together evidence from the God-given state of innocence and the man-made condition of sin. Sometimes this operates *pro bono*, in fervent praises of the Paradise of matrimony, but more often *pro malo*, when female 'inferiority' and 'defect' are transferred from the fallen state to God's original intention. When defining the ontogeny of Eve, these writers not only loosen the distinction between innocence and sin, but mingle lapsarian and non-lapsarian modes of thought. This contradiction appears even in the conscientious and humane writings of Puritanism and the courtesy-tradition, and—as we shall see in our discussion of *Paradise Lost*—it dominates the literary treatment of Eve by Milton's contemporaries.

[*iv*]

The reading of Genesis—the 'Glasse' in which all wives were to learn whether they are 'a wife indeed', and from which all husbands were to learn the complicated duties of love and 'due benevolence'—could thus produce diverse and inconsistent reflections on the nature of marriage, the role of sexuality and the essential nature of woman.[45] There was no logical agreement between egalitarian and subordinationist interpretations of Eve, and no consensus on whether the biological, social, or spiritual definition of marriage should predominate, in cases where their requirements came into conflict. Milton's divorce tracts, as we shall see in chapter 6, grow out of precisely this flaw in Protestant thought, and in some respects deepen it further. But this divergence already appears very strongly in the two fathers of Reformation exegesis, Luther and Calvin.

Luther, like Augustine, assumes that the woman was created for procreation only, which aligns him with the 'rustic' and 'crabbed' opinion that Milton denounces. So important is the first blessing and injunction to 'be fruitful and multiply', Luther assumes, that all other gender-defining texts in Genesis should be subsumed into it: the female was not created as a companion, as a remedy for lust, or *ad voluptatem*, and fulfils her original purpose only to the extent that she contributes to parenthood (I. 161). And like Donne he distinguishes between the good of the species, well served by marriage, and the good of the individual male—coming close to a

[45] Cf. Thomas Gataker, *A Wife in Deed* (1623), p. 13.

blasphemous denial of the good in woman *per se*. Calvin, on the other hand, opposes this procreative interpretation of 'help meet' as strongly as Milton would later do, and stresses instead the inseparable companionship of marriage and the social meaning even of 'one flesh'. He also overrides St. Paul's assertion that woman was not created in the image of God, as Salkeld later did: the Apostle did not intend his remark to apply generally, since women are just as spiritually gifted as men, but only to one aspect of their lives—the politics or 'government' of the household (1:26, 1:27, 2:18).

In other parts of his commentary, however, Calvin undermines this assertion. Woman is created in God's image only 'in the second degree', since the first creation was of the male, the representative of the race, to whom woman is only an 'accessary' or a 'portion'; Calvin is evidently not impressed by the original creation of 'male and female' together in chapter 1 of Genesis. The mutual society of one flesh turns out to be far from reciprocal: the creation of Eve from the rib taught Adam 'to recognize himself in his wife, as in a mirror, and Eve, in her turn, to submit herself willingly to her husband, as being taken out of him.' The headship of the man in the domestic realm, the one instance in which the 'image of God' could be denied to women outright, is thereby translated into the state of nature. It is identified, not with the punishment of sin, as Genesis unmistakably declares, but with the original ontology of woman. Assertive wives 'invert the order of nature'. Eve 'had previously been subject to her husband'—though in a relatively gentle way, just as her childbirths would have been relatively free from pain—and now that she 'perversely exceeded her proper bounds', God sees to it that she is 'forced back to her own position' (2:18, 2:21, 3:16). The abasement of woman is therefore not a fall, but a restoration.

Luther, however, will have none of this. In all three of his commentaries on Genesis, though most fully in the posthumously edited *Enarrationes*, he fastens upon the implications of the curse of subjection. To allegorize Adam and Eve into 'higher' and 'lower' faculties is absurd, since Eve's exalted powers of mind and body were identical to Adam's, and she shared in the divine image just as fully. The human race is a unique species, more valuable than the sum of heaven and earth, and woman is 'the other part of humanity'; if she had not sinned, 'she would have been the equal

of Adam in all respects (*in omnibus parem . . . in nulla re inferior*).'
Adam named her, not simply wife, but *virago*—a 'heroic woman'.
If mankind had not fallen, Luther maintains, household tasks
would have been shared equally, and woman would have been a
free agent: she could have travelled freely, determined her own
name, and chosen where to live and whether to take a partner. The
government of the state as well as of the family would have been
equally divided between men and women.[46]

Now, however, woman is 'deprived' of rule and public life, and
must sit unwillingly at home 'like a nail driven into the wall'. But
she is still master in one area, and that is procreation. Luther
defines 'meet help' in procreative terms, then, not because he
seeks to reduce woman to a biological function, but because in
child-rearing he glimpses a remnant, however 'pitiable', of the free
agency and world-mastery she enjoyed before the fall.

Even this moving and boldly imagined vision of equality, however,
is framed by contradiction. Within a few pages Luther falls back
into the common ideological assumptions of female inferiority: Eve
is the 'weaker part', dependent on her husband, and hence the
obvious choice for temptation. She is 'less excellent', a derived
being as the moon is to the sun. This unacknowledged disjunction
within the text might be explained by multiple authorship; Luther's
final commentary on Genesis was a posthumous edition of lectures
that may have been worked up by his followers (I. ix–xii, 69, 151).
It is more probable, however, that a single mind could contain two
incompatible readings, two different intuitions about the status and
ontology of woman.

The radical urge of the Reformation strove to press beyond the
confines of time—to embrace the holy bridegroom promised in
Revelation, but also to press further back, not just to the ancient
forms that 'Saints and Patriarchs used', but past the flaming sword
and the tree of knowledge to the pre-lapsarian state itself. This
was a practical hermeneutic, moreover, generating not merely
contemplative understanding but new modes of relationship in
family, church, and state. In this drive two kinds of Eros, and two
interpretations of the primeval 'one flesh', came into conflict: the
nuptial love of Ephesians is strictly hierarchical, whereas the union
of Adam and Eve before the punishment of subjection, and the
'due benevolence' that still recaptures a shadow of that primal

[46] I. 66, 68–9, 115, 137–8, 185, 202–3, 219; cf. *Werke* XXIV. 102.

bliss, are fundamentally egalitarian. Milton himself, I will argue, incorporates both the egalitarian and the hierarchical model into his vision of Paradisal sexuality, with no attempt to reconcile them. Such attempts would in any case have been impossible. The more authentic response is to register the contradiction unwittingly, to fill the imagination with dreams of equality, and to leave the ideological imperative, the stubborn will to believe in female subordination, naked and unadorned.

4

The Crisis of the Imagination

SEVENTEENTH-CENTURY VISIONARY AND LIBERTINE THEORIES OF PRIMEVAL SEXUALITY

> As for those who proudly soar above the world to seek God in his unveiled essence, it is impossible but that at length they should entangle themselves in a multitude of absurd figments. ... What advantage is it to fly in the air, and to leave the earth, where God has given proof of his benevolence towards the human race? ... Doubly insane, therefore, are the monstrous Libertines, who maintain the fiction that we are restored to the state of innocence when we are carried away by our own libido. (Calvin)[1]

Throughout the interpretation-history of Genesis, the fundamental questions of sexuality and gender have been entangled with another problem of 'knowledge', the uncertain status of the mental faculties loosely called 'imagination'. Without the faculty of inspired conjecture, Augustine would not have persisted in his reconstruction of Paradisal happiness, and later commentators would not have devoted immense labours to 'making their own Edens'. Luther would not have dreamt of primal equality, and the vast majority would not have sustained the fantastic thesis of 'natural' subordination. But the fictive basis of the enterprise could not be acknowledged. Genesis had established the 'evil imagination' as part of man's fallen corruption, and though Luther believes it can be suspended in those who are inspired with the true prophetic strain, he warns that such divine intervention is extremely rare.

The personal conviction of prophetic inspiration—abundant in the seventeenth century, as we shall see in this chapter—was therefore treated with great suspicion. Much of the commentator's work consisted of exposing fiction, the false and fabulous inventions of monks and rabbis, while promoting the orthodoxy of his own interpretation. Exegesis could not question its own larger premises, but within them it developed an intense concern for realism and

[1] 'Dedication' and 2:9.

4. The Crisis of the Imagination

consistency. Augustine exposed the pernicious fantasies of earlier Greek and Hebrew exegetes, and Augustine was in turn accused of writing his commentaries 'in a Dream ... or even out of his Head'.[2] Traditional legends and wire-drawn speculations are paraded alongside the authentic truth in Sir Thomas Browne's *Pseudodoxia Epidemica*, in the vast footnotes to Bayle's *Dictionary*, and in the many Satanic fables woven into Milton's epic. The danger of unbridled imagination seemed particularly germane to Genesis, moreover; the overzealous interpreter could be guilty of the same sin that caused the original fall—the lust for knowledge as a means to attain the creative self-sufficiency of Godhead. When the subject of enquiry is sexuality this danger is doubled. 'Lust and Imagination' were coupled as twin effects of the forbidden fruit: between them they could generate what Leone Ebreo called *la fantasia corporale*, dealing in libertine wisdom and carnal knowledge, or else they could lead, as Calvin proclaimed, to the equal but opposite extreme of the Spiritual Libertines, swept away by an inspiration that is really (he insists) nothing but libido.[3] Imagination, for the seventeenth-century mind, could be the weak and parasitic 'fancy' that Satan tries to inject with erotic dreams, or the idolatrous delusion that Milton would combat throughout his life—even in his latest prose works 'casting down imaginations and everie high thing that exalts itself against the knowledge of God'.[4] But it may be the poetic force that led Sidney to sense the unfallen powers of humanity, or the celestial inspiration that gives Milton his supreme confidence as an exegete and poet, visiting other worlds, putting words into the mouth of God Himself, describing without demur the sexual life of men and of angels.

This chapter will explore some of the independent interpreters, religious leaders, and creative artists who sought alternatives to the standard fundamentalist reading of Genesis. I have been stressing the divergences or fissures that develop within the mainstream

---

[2] Bayle, 'Augustine' G; cf. John Tickell's attacks on Coppe and the Familists, intended to 'open ... their Chambers of Imagery' and expose their 'Phantastique preaching'—'when they speak on the account of Scripture Revelation, they will tell you ... that the Authentick Copy is their *Imagination*' (*The Bottomles Pit* (Oxford, 1652), t.-p., f. A4ᵛ, pp. 39–40).

[3] Cf. epigraph to this chapter, and 2. 4. ii above; on Calvin's sense of the symmetry of 'Spiritual' and secular extremes, see also 'Dedication', 'Argument', 2: 8, 3:6, and 3:23.

[4] *PL* IV. 801–3, V. 102–13; *Prose* VII. 257, quoting 2 Cor. 10:5 (I owe this reference to David Loewenstein).

under pressure from the difficult questions of sexuality. But there still existed a common assumption, from Augustine to the founders of Protestantism, that exegesis should be constrained by a principle of local realism, a concern to reconcile and rationalize the events of Genesis as far as the supreme fiction of salvation-history allows. The Word was presumed to speak plainly, of real events and institutions whose traces can be revived within each believer—even though the Scripture itself is manifestly inconsistent, cryptic, and magical. But other modes of reading, other assumptions about the origins of the text, had always been available, and in Milton's lifetime they proliferated. Could Genesis be itself a fictive or symbolic mystery, the work of a God who 'played' with transcendent Wisdom before the world was made (Proverbs 8:30), and who requires an equally agile interpreter? Or was it even the product of a particular society and epoch, worthy of no more or less respect than any other human artefact?

1. Literalism under fire

Already in the sixteenth century, the fundamentalist reading of Genesis had its enemies. Sidney's simultaneous defence of poetry and the fall-story was aimed at 'the incredulous'. Calvin encountered the objections of secular 'mockers' at every point in his commentary; they form the opposite wing to the 'Spiritual' mystics, but they are equally 'Libertine' in their attacks on the sacred Word. To the sceptic the formation of Eve from a rib 'may seem ridiculous, and some of these may say that Moses is dealing in fables (*fabulari*)'; like Luther, who had also faced this objection, Calvin retorts that the normal method of reproduction 'from putrid seed' would seem just as absurd if we were not used to it.[5] The annihilation of the human race in the Flood 'seems at first sight frivolous' (Calvin assumed, wrongly, that the crime of Genesis 6 was not miscegenation between women and angels, but only careless marriage between the elect and the profane). The order to circumcise the entire tribe of Israel, again, must seem 'truly absurd and ridiculous', for 'who could say that it is proper and fitting for the sign of such a mystery to be set in the shameful parts?' Nevertheless, 'as it behoved Abraham to become a fool in order to prove himself obedient to

---

[5] Sidney, ch. 1 n. 39 above; Calvin, 2:21 (cf. 'Argument' and 3:1); Luther, I. 84, 123, 125–8.

4. The Crisis of the Imagination

God, so whoever is wise will soberly and reverently receive what God seems foolishly to have commanded.'[6]

For a semi-libertine like Donne, poised between blasphemous wit and devotion, this impious but irresistible questioning of Genesis is itself a product of the fall, an intrinsic property of the text: the fruit itself contains, as it were, the seed of forbidden questions. In his *Paradoxes* and in his 'poema satyricon' *Metempsychosis* he lists these rebellious criticisms with obvious relish.[7] But while ostensibly rejecting heretical enquiries, Donne's poem itself, a risqué sexual history of Adam and Eve derived from Rabbinical and Apocryphal sources, contributes to the 'satyric' attack. Less flamboyant Protestants made more determined efforts to bridle the speculative appetite. Fulke Greville, for example, anticipates Milton's Raphael in his 88th sonnet: Adam is told by the archangel to 'Dream no more of other worlds', while Greville's fallen reader must 'dreame no more of curious mysteries', such as 'The first Mans life' and 'the state of Paradise'; as the heavens were to Adam, so Eden is to us.[8] Du Bartas, too, dissociates himself from heretical readings and hubristic questions; he will not allow the reader to 'think that *Moses* paints fantasticke-wise / A mistike tale of fained Paradice', nor does he consider any of the concrete details of Eden 'fantasicall', 'supposed', or 'poeticall'. This lands him in the dilemma of literalism. Du Bartas must persuade us that Paradise is utterly real, and yet wholly inconceivable and unexpressible—indeed, to enquire into the details of Adam and Eve's marriage would be to commit the same 'too-curious' fault that brought them and us to destruction. Despite this 'feare to faile', however, Eden is described at gigantic length, and many lines are devoted to the unlawful sexual questions stimulated by pre-lapsarian marriage—precisely those that most taxed the exegetes, as we saw in chapter 1. These descriptions and

---

[6] 6:1 and 17:11 (cf. Luther, III. 143—but Luther's answer to the charge of absurdity appeals to Divine Power rather than Divine Folly). Like Erasmus, Calvin draws on 1 Cor. 1:18-25 for his concept of folly.

[7] e.g. *Metempsychosis* (*The Progresse of the Soule*), st. 11: 'So fast in us doth this corruption grow, / That now wee dare aske why wee should be so. / Would God (disputes the curious Rebell) make / A law, and would not have it kept? Or can / His creatures will, crosse his? Of every man / For one, will God (and be just) vengeance take? / Who sinn'd? t'was not forbidden to the snake / Nor her, who was not then made; nor is't writ / That Adam cropt, or knew the apple; yet / The worme and she, and he, and wee endure for it.' Agrippa's thesis (3. 2. ii above) is thus included in this list of rebellious thoughts. For impious paradox see also ch. 3 n. 12 above.

[8] *Caelica*, Sonnet LXXVIII; cf. *PL* VIII. 175.

speculations, which transform the laconic Eden-myth into epic verse, are clearly in some way meant to be 'poeticall'.[9] In du Bartas, in Donne, and later in Milton we sense a conflict between the doctrine of human limitation and the imaginative drive to experience and recreate other worlds, and to tackle the most challenging questions. Donne himself, in his personal 'Litanie', recognizes this struggle in his own case, and prays to be delivered 'from seeking secrets, and Poetiqueness'.

Like Calvin, du Bartas, and Donne, Browne defends his own faith against hubris, fantastic distortion, and trivializing reduction, creating a cast of marginals and extremists who serve to define and recommend, by contrast, his own *via media*—the plain and literal truth that leads to salvation. Like Donne he draws up a list of trivial and impious questions arising from Genesis. Whether Adam or Eve sinned more grievously he will leave to the 'Schoolman', whether offspring conceived in innocence would have inherited sin he leaves to the Lawyer, whether Adam was originally a hermaphrodite he consigns to 'Pantagruel's library'. Two further lines of speculation are relegated to the Jewish 'Thalmudists': whether the whole story is an allegory of 'the seduction of the rational and higher parts by the inferior and feminine faculties' and 'whether the Tree in the midst of the Garden were not that part in the Center of the body in which was afterward the appointment of Circumcision in Males'. At the other end of the scale, questions such as whether Adam knew of the Redemption, and what would have happened if only Eve had eaten or if both had also eaten of the Tree of Life, are left to God.[10]

Browne's rejected questions were not always considered invalid or absurd, however. The relative blameworthiness of Adam and Eve, raised in the New Testament itself, was formally addressed by

---

[9] Sylvester, pp. 321, 334-5; du Bartas, *Works*, III. 5-6, 21-2 (note that Sylvester uses 'poeticall' to translate '*feint*'). The forbidden questions include how long they lived in Eden before the fall, 'What children there they earned, and how many, / Of whether sex: or whether none or anie: / Or how (at least) they should have propagated.'

[10] *Pseudodoxia Epidemica*, ed. Robin Robbins (Oxford, 1981), p. 8; *Religio Medici and Other Works*, ed. L. C. Martin (Oxford, 1964), p. 22. Browne is mistaken, as far as I can tell, in ascribing a phallic interpretation of the Tree to the Talmud; the mistake may derive from a misapplication of the microcosmic passages in the *Avot de-Rabbi Nathan* and other Rabbinical writings (cf. *The Fathers According to Rabbi Nathan*, tr. Judah Goldin (New Haven, 1955), p. 127, and Louis Ginzburg, *The Legends of the Jews*, tr. Henrietta Szold (Philadelphia, 1968), I. 49 and V. 64-5).

virtually every commentator, and generated impassioned debate, as we have seen, wherever Genesis was translated into doctrine for the sexes. Speculation about pre-lapsarian sexuality is a central force in *The City of God* as it is in *Paradise Lost*. Nor do Browne's questions rest on assumptions very different from his own, or those of the orthodoxy he defends. He censures futile curiosity about the innocent race that might have descended from Adam and Eve, and yet he entertains the equivalent belief, widespread in the period, that remote peoples had avoided the fall and still lived in the pre-lapsarian state: 'whole Nations have escaped the curse of childbirth, which God seemes to pronounce upon the whole Sex.' He dismisses the androgynous Adam as a Rabelaisian whimsy in one place, but in others he seems to accept the hermaphroditic theory on the authority of Plato and Leone Ebreo. And in a celebrated passage of *Religio Medici*, much quoted by later satirists of anti-sexual Utopianism, he gives way to the same distaste for sexual encounter that inspires the fantasy he condemns, the same desire to eliminate the female and to subsume the reproductive function: 'I could be content that we might procreate like trees, without conjunction, or that there were any way to perpetuate the world without this triviall and vulgar way of coition.'[11] The sentiment that Milton gave Adam only in the depth of fallen anger and despair, Browne promotes in his confession of faith.

The orthodox Christian reading of Genesis was in any case scarcely less fantastic than the 'Thalmudic' speculations that Browne condemns. None of the significations agreed upon by the exegetes— the presence of Satan, the promise of a Redeemer, the 'fall' and original sin, the notion that Adam and Eve represented the most perfect stage of humanity—has any basis in the text. The most stubborn of all these shadowy assumptions, the secondary status of Eve, is almost equally unfounded. Again, Browne shares and even intensifies this collective delusion. His dream of vegetable procreation is in fact a pronouncement on Genesis, and follows immediately on the suggestion that 'the whole world' (or in the manuscripts 'the whole woman') 'was made for man, but the twelfth part of man for woman: man is the whole world and the breath

[11] *Religio Medici*, pp. 35, 67, and cf. *Pseudodoxia*, pp. 227–9. For ironic refs. to Browne's reproductive desires, see among others *Religio Medici* [with] *Observations by Sir Kenelm Digby*, '8th' edn. (1685), p. 100; Bayle, 'Sadeur' E; Richard Ames, *The Folly of Love* (1691), p. 26; Edward Ward, *Nuptial Dialogues and Debates* (1710), I, f. A5.

of God, woman the rib and crooked piece of man.' (As in the case of reproduction, Milton's hero only utters these distorted opinions when he is at the nadir.) But not even Adam, who 'included all humane nature, or was (as some opinion) an Hermaphrodite,' could multiply from within himself as plants do; God therefore decided to make him a help meet, 'that is, an help unto generation, for as for any other help, it had been fitter to have made another man.'[12] Browne thus reiterates the 'crabbed opinion' of Augustine, but with an extra twist: woman is reduced to a sexual-reproductive mechanism, and sexual reproduction is impugned as unfit for Paradise.

By invoking the hermeneutics of common sense against esoteric enquiry, Browne ventured onto thin ice; the same sardonic mentality could be turned on his own most nourishing 'secrets'. Elsewhere, for example, he turns another esoteric question—whether Adam and Eve had navels—into a vivid meditation on the bond of 'umbilicality' between God and man (*Pseudodoxia* p. 378). Less than a generation later, all such questions would be declared self-evidently absurd. Among the devout, Pascal sensed that we can know nothing whatsoever about the pre-lapsarian state. Among the sceptics, Samuel Butler encapsulated the enthusiastic taste for 'seeking secrets' in Hudibras, whose wiredrawn theological speculations include not only such patently absurd 'facts' as whether the serpent spoke German, but also those questions that could lead to deeper truths, as the navel-speculation did for Browne. It takes some effort to realize that Butler's dry couplet—'What *Adam* dreamt of when his Bride / Came from the Closet in his side'—is another way of describing one of the supreme moments in *Paradise Lost*, when Adam revives his memory of the vision granted him while his rib was being removed.[13] In Butler as in Bayle, the restoration of reason brings with it a strongly anti-poetic and anti-imaginative sensibility. Milton's commitment to visionary poetics and 'the spirit of love and amorous delight' takes on new meaning when read as a product of this age.

---

[12] *Pseudodoxia*, pp. 206–7; *Religio Medici*, pp. 67, 267. Cf. *PL* X. 884–95.
[13] *Hudibras* I. i. 175–8 (cf. Jonson, *Alchemist* II. i. 87–90, and Richard Verstegen, *A Restitution of Decayed Intelligence* (1605), pp. 190–2, for evidence that Adam and Eve spoke German); *PL* VIII. 470–7. For Bayle, see 1. introd. above, and cf. his attacks on the theosophists—'they have fallen into the Gaities of Rhetoric and Poetry, and even into visionary Notions of this Matter' ('Adam' E).

[*ii*]

The allegorical and fantastic readings lightly dismissed by Browne actually had a long history and a valid purpose, as we have seen. Each in its different way, these alternative interpretative methods try to restore the integrity and credibility of Genesis. In order to reconcile the differing creation-stories, each discards one element of the orthodox Augustinian reconstruction: theories of primal hermaphroditism or magic asexual reproduction ingeniously preserve the literal meaning and the consistency of Genesis 1-3, but destroy the possibility that normal physical nature could be divinely blessed; allegorical readings create a timeless moral significance for the myth, and rescue it from pagan charges of absurdity, only by abandoning the literal.[14] It is a principle of hermeneutic economy, rather than wilful fantasy, that generates these approaches. Nevertheless, they were feared and attacked by Augustine, Luther, Calvin, and the mainstream commentators, who thereby keep them alive even in the act of denouncing them.[15] Origen had adopted the allegorical approach to Adam and Eve, at least in his earlier writings, because he agreed with his pagan opponent that the literal meaning is absurd, and wanted to defend Christianity on firmer ground; Calvin, however, attributes this Origenic tradition to Satan himself, who fosters it 'to render the doctrine of Scripture ambiguous and destitute of all certainty and firmness'. Salvation appears to depend on a kind of realism. To reject the literal, this-worldly meaning of Genesis is 'to fly in the air, and leave the earth,' to despise the God-given material world, and to disintegrate the Scripture; such etherial spiritualization does as much damage as the atheism and scepticism at the opposite extreme.[16]

In one respect, however, allegorical and literal readings were in harmony: they fed the insatiable hunger for evidence of female inferiority. Plato's myth of the divided humans, the origin of the

[14] Leone Ebreo, for example, uses the hermaphroditic theory to create a harmonious Gen. that is *both* literal (for Adam and Eve) *and* allegorical (for the later reader); cf. 297/352-3, 304/361, and 2. 3. ii above. For allegory, cf. Philo's claim that his symbolic reading of Gen. is closer to divine truth than the 'fictive myths' of poets (*De Opificio Mundi* 157; Loeb edn., *Philo* I).

[15] Cf. ch. 1 n. 27 above; Luther, I. 233; Arnold Williams, *The Common Expositor* (Chapel Hill, 1948), p. 70.

[16] Origen, ch. 1 n. 23 above; Calvin, 'Dedication', 3:6, 3:7, 3:10. For changes in Origen's later attitude, and for other examples of the allegorical approach, see Norman P. Williams, *The Ideas of the Fall and of Original Sin* (1929), pp. 191-2, 210-31.

hermaphroditic Adam, is in no way concerned with the definition of male and female: the two-headed, four-footed beings described by Aristophanes contain double males and double females as well as androgynes, and Eros, the all-consuming yearning for the 'other half', is precisely the same in lesbians, male homosexuals, and heterosexuals. (Though several speakers in the *Symposium* regard women with contempt, expressing the values of a homosexual aristocracy, Aristophanes is not one of them.) But in later fusions of Genesis and the hermaphrodite-myth, whether purportedly literal or avowedly allegorical, the female component is marked as inferior, weaker, more sensual, and less definitive—a junior faculty whose subsequent autonomy must be lamented. And sexuality itself, all too often, is equated with this dubious 'female'.[17]

The allegorical heresy did indeed flourish among sectarian radicals and proto-libertine sceptics, as Calvin had feared, and with it came the familiar anti-sexual and misogynist assumptions. In Jean Bodin's notorious dramatization of forbidden beliefs, the *Colloquium Heptaplomeres*—a manuscript of which Milton actually owned—the literal fall-story is declared fit only for children and the vulgar; every man is his own Adam, and he falls whenever he gives way to 'female' sensuality and the *voluptas* which, like a serpent, insinuates itself into the most secret organs of the body.[18] Similar interpretations circulated widely during the English Revolution. Though the *True Levellers Standard Advance*, the founding manifesto of the Digger movement, deduced from Genesis the primeval freedom and equality of 'every single man, Male and Female,' the Digger leader, Gerrard Winstanley, denied the truth and relevance of the literal Scripture on which this judgement is

---

[17] *Symposium* 189B–190B, 191B–D; cf. Marilyn R. Farwell, 'Eve, the Separation Scene, and the Renaissance Idea of Androgyny', *MS* XVI (1982), 3–20. The exceptions to this conception of the hermaphrodite are few: in one recently discovered Gnostic text 'Eve is the spiritual principle in humanity who raises Adam from his merely material condition' (Elaine Pagels, *The Gnostic Gospels* (NY, 1979), p. 31); and two late 17th century writers, one of whom was probably making a careless mistake, assert that Adam and Eve were *both* autonomous hermaphrodites (see Bayle, 'Adam' F, and n. 76 below). Cf. also Salomon, the representative of Judaism in Jean Bodin's *Colloquium Heptaplomeres* (*Colloquium of the Seven about Secrets of the Sublime*, tr. and ed. Marion L. D. Kuntz (Princeton, 1975), p. 94): another speaker had objected to the misogynist element in Scripture, which gratuitously alienates the female reader; Salomon points to the women praised in the OT, and deduces that the allegorical equation woman=flesh has no literal application to the genders at all.

[18] Kuntz, pp. lxix, 98, 392–3, 405.

4. The Crisis of the Imagination

based. '*Adam* is within every man': sinners are condemned not because of some ancient transgression, but because in their daily lives 'they have been led by the powers of the curse in flesh, which is the *Feminine* part, not by the power of the righteous Spirit which is Christ, the *Masculine* power.'[19]

The crisis of literalism, provoked by the resurgence of the radicals in mid-seventeenth-century England, may be illustrated from the work of their great opponent, Henry More. He fiercely denounces those enthusiasts who 'alternate all so into Allegories, that they leave the very Fundamentals of Religion suspected'.[20] Radical sectarians had adopted various heterodox beliefs—including the existence of men before Adam, allegedly proposed by Elizabethan crypto-libertines and certainly proclaimed by Clarkson in the 1650s—and many of them used the shortcomings of the text as a reason for dismissing the literal reading in favour of allegory: Winstanley even insisted that we must read the fall figuratively *because* the inconsistencies of the Bible reveal the existence of Pre-Adamites.[21] More does not counter these heresies with strict literalism, however, but with an allegorical scheme of his own—a tripartite revision of Genesis 1-3 into a 'Literal', a 'Philosophick', and a 'Moral Cabbala'.

More does not say that the events of Genesis never happened, but he does regard the literal story as a skilfully managed 'Politick' contrivance for the vulgar reader, designed for such worthy ends as inspiring pity for our first parents, strengthening the marriage-bond, and reducing sexual embarrassment by making it more understandable—an interesting example of the ameliorative spirit of Cambridge Platonism. Questions of truth do not much concern him in the 'Literal Cabbala', however, because it is no more than the 'Body' of the text, and the 'Soul' or proper meaning can only be found in the allegorical versions. Indeed, without

---

[19] Hill[1], pp. 143, 145, 221; ch. 3 n. 21 above; Farwell, p. 8. A similar allegorization is found among the radical Anabaptists (*RR* pp. 219-20).

[20] *An Explanation of the Grand Mystery of Godliness* (1660), p. 244.

[21] Alistair Hamilton, *The Family of Love* (Cambridge, 1981), pp. 118, 160 n. 24; Hill[1], pp. 144 and n. 163, 174, 263; Smith, pp. 18, 185; Winstanley, *Works*, ed. George H. Sabine (Ithaca, 1941), p. 210, citing the same inconsistency in the story of Cain that provoked Lapeyrère's inquiry (n. 31 below). An essential article—which does not, however, use the examples of English Familism, Winstanley or Clarkson—is Richard H. Popkin, 'The Pre-Adamite Theory in the Renaissance', in *Philosophy and Humanism*, ed. Edward P. Mahoney (Leiden, 1976), pp. 50-69, esp. pp. 60-1.

proper guidance the literal Old Testament can be positively harmful, for its historical parts encourage domestic violence (Jael and Sisera) and the intrinsic absurdity of its mythic parts 'has bred many hundreds of thousands of *Atheists*'. More's conjectures are designed to restore the dignity and credibility of the text, and to rescue it from both the Scylla of excessive radical allegorization and the Charybdis of popular scepticism and courtly facetiousness.[22] By defending Genesis on two fronts, against spiritual and secular extremes, More continues the tradition of Augustine and Calvin, but with one important difference: the unsupported literal meaning will no longer serve his turn.

The more he embraces the allegorical, however, the greater appears his confusion about the status of materiality, 'one flesh', pleasure, and sexuality; Genesis is thus further drained of the credibility he attempts to restore. In the 'Literal Cabbala' and in the first chapter of the 'Philosophick', the material realm is wholesome and delightful, but subsequent chapters make Paradise, Adam, and Eve purely spiritual. More's 'Philosophick' Adam is not made of earthly matter at all, but of fire and ethēr; at the fall he is therefore naked indeed, 'having neither the covering of the Heavenly Nature, nor as yet the Terrestrial Body'. But during the punishment-scene he feels himself sinking stupidly into matter, until finally he is clothed in animal skins—the body of flesh, as Origen thought. This sinister fall into flesh clearly contradicts the cheerful acceptance of materiality in the previous chapter.[23] Sexuality likewise bears contradictory meanings. On the one hand, the delight and contrivance of the genitals is singled out for special praise; on

---

[22] *Conjectura Cabbalistica* (1653), pp. 121-2, 129, 132, 109, 225; More retails an anecdote from Bodin, showing how a literalist preacher accidentally made the fall-story a laughing-stock, both among his lower-class parishioners and at Court. References to More's versions of Gen. 1-3 will be given by chapter and verse, which are the same as the Bible's, and distinguished as *Lit.*, *Phil.*, or *Mor.*; his longer Introduction and 'Defenses' will be cited by page.

[23] *Phil.* 2:8-9, 2:17, 3:7, 3:21, and cf. p. 168. More also has problems with God's motives for the fall and the expulsion. *Phil.* 3:21-2 makes light of the fall (God 'did but . . . play and sport'), since Adam had all along been intended as a terrestrial overlord, and merely precipitated what 'in due time might have faln to his share by course'; the fiery sword simply means that man has to rediscover the 'fiery Vehicle' or original non-terrestrial body. This extraordinary idea, which undermines More's description of the fall as debility and death, is 'better *Decorum* than to make God sarcastically to jeer at *Adam*' (p. 181.) In the 'Moral' version, however, God does jeer at the animal body ('Now get you gone for a couple of Brutes'); the fiery sword now represents Conscience, which prevents them from reconstructing an imaginary Paradise in their 'Bestial delight' (*Mor.* 3:21, 23-4).

4. The Crisis of the Imagination

the other hand, the pleasure of the flesh is problematic even in the etherial state, and comes to be identified with the fall itself.[24]

Throughout the *Conjectura Cabbalistica* More fights an unequal battle against the temptation to debase the 'female'. Having turned away from literalism, he finds himself straining to reconcile two different allegorical interpretations of Eve: one, deriving from Ficino, makes her the spiritual power by which the soul casts 'her *vital Energie upon the Body*'; the other, from Philo, identifies her as Sense-impression, the beginning of Adam's downfall, and identifies the serpent as the equally disastrous Pleasure that springs from her sexual union with Adam—Pleasure the *hetaira* who uses Eve as her pander.[25] Philo's version evidently prevails here, as it does when the curse on Eve's childbearing is given the meaning that 'Adam should descend down to be an Inhabitant of the Earth, and that he should not there indulge to himself the pleasures of the body, without the concomitants of pain and sorrow' (*Phil.* 3: 16). The distinction between Eve and the serpent practically vanishes at this point. More does make some effort to preserve it: in the 'Moral Cabbala', for example, Eve is '*the natural and kindely Joy of the Body*', whereas the serpent is 'the *inordinate Desire of Pleasure*' that insinuates itself into Eve and speaks from within her. But this is still a difference in degree rather than kind, which undermines More's own insistence that the serpent is properly a distinct person while Eve is an aspect of Adam who 'proceeds' from him without impairing his unity.[26] And after the fall the distinction melts away again. After being punished, Adam's 'Minde was straight way taken up again with the delights of the flesh ... dearly embracing *the Joy of his Body*, for all she was grown so inordinate' (3:20).

Eve thus has many meanings. She may be the '*divine Affection*' that puts down the rebellious 'Animal Life' of earth, or she may be the ordinary sensual 'Affections'—that is to say, the 'Natural Life' itself. She represents the normal joy and health of the body whose 'warrantable and free operation' will redeem mankind, but

---

[24] For the genitals, cf. *Phil.* 1:28; for the intensity of bodily delight in Paradise (the garden of 'Hedone'), cf. *Phil.* 3:13, *Mor.* 2:21, 22, 3:10, p. 170; for the evils of pleasure (even in the spiritual body), cf. *Phil.* 2:14, 3:6, *Mor.* 1:4–12, 17.

[25] *Conjectura*, pp. 170–1, and cf. 180; Philo, *De Opificio Mundi*, 151–2, 157–70, *Legum Allegoria, passim* (Loeb edn., *Philo* I).

[26] *Conjectura*, p. 175; the position is further complicated on pp. 228 (the serpent is an internal faculty) and 234 (the 'regulated *joyes of the body*' are Eve's offspring).

she is also Earth and Flesh in the most pejorative sense. She is intermittently identified with the serpent; and finally, by an unhappy irony, she is herself the very '*Earthly-mindedness*' of Adam that is set over her as a punishment.[27] Whatever else she might signify in the various interpretations of Genesis, Eve is always the mother of contradiction.

[*iii*]

More's revision thus contributes unwittingly to the process he attempts to reverse—the crumbling of Genesis into a multiplicity of unrelated myths. The space between the 'Jahwist' and 'Priestly' chapters is widened rather than dissolved, and the different levels of allegory seem to come from quite different mentalities: More is at once the darkly brooding moralist who finds tension and conflict even in the state of innocence, the fantastic theosophist who abandons the body of flesh, and the neo-Pelagian who anticipates the bland Latitudinarianism of the eighteenth century. To the modern reader this polyvocality may be a welcome development, but it undermines the traditional Protestant need for a unified, literal, and all-inclusive Word. Calvin, for example, would have been horrified by More's 'loosening' of the text, even though both commentators profess to attack the same enemies, popular radicals and free-thinkers.

Other thinkers on the Protestant fringe, however, were prepared to accept the principle that Genesis could only be redeemed by discarding its unity or its literalism. The most systematic of these precursors of the Higher Criticism was Isaac Lapeyrère, a Marrano who became first a Huguenot and then a Catholic monk. His *Pre-Adamitae* (1655), published two years after More's *Conjectura* but circulated in manuscript during the previous decade, maintains that the creation and fall of Genesis 2–3 are indeed literally true, but only for Adam and Eve and their descendants the Jews; for the vast majority of humanity, who existed long before the events of Genesis 2, the Eden-story has a moral but not a literal significance. Lapeyrère moved in the circles of the free-thinking *libertins érudits*, and gathered his arguments from anti-Calvinist radicals like Palaeologus and from the oral traditions of plebeian separatists; as we have seen, similar arguments surfaced among the English Diggers and Ranters, and they were still being denounced

[27] *Phil.* 3:16; *Mor.* 1:27, 2:17, 3:6, 3:15–16, 3:19.

4. *The Crisis of the Imagination*

by Bunyan years after the Restoration.[28] His own refinement of the Pre-Adamite theory produced fresh outrage in each generation, and his 'romantick System', like the allegorical heresy, was thus kept alive by successive attempts to suppress it.[29]

By ascribing the first chapters of the Bible to different epochs and different peoples, Lapeyrère may have initiated the speculative dismemberment of Genesis that grew during the eighteenth century and dominated the nineteenth. The discrepancies between the two versions melt away, he maintains, because they refer to two quite distinct acts of creation. Genesis 1 describes the original formation of mankind, who increase and multiply and fill the earth with various races and cultures—some of which have historical records demonstrably older than the Hebrew.[30] These Pre-Adamites had already populated the earth, invented tools, and built cities, so that when Cain expresses his fear of the vengeful multitudes, or when he establishes a city, the reader need not be dumbfounded (the same discrepancies, which had puzzled Lapeyrère since childhood, inspired Winstanley to reject the literal). From them are descended the virtuous pagans of antiquity and such newly discovered civilizations as the Chinese and the Inca. Lapeyrère does not idealize

---

[28] Popkin, *passim*; René Pintard, *Le Libertinage érudit dans la première moitié du XVIIe siècle* (Paris, 1943), pp. 355, 358-62, 420-4; *RR* p. 743 (and cf. 789-90); Walter Pagel, *Paracelsus* (Basle, 1958), p. 335; n. 21 above; John Bunyan, *An Exposition of the First Ten Chapters of Genesis* (1678), in *Complete Works*, ed. Henry Stebbing (c.1859), III. 392—Eve's title 'mother of the living' proves 'that there were none of the sons of men in the world before Adam, as some have not only vainly, but irreligiously and blasphemously suggested.' Leo Strauss points out that Lapeyrère retains *some* belief in Scripture: he divides the Bible into the parts that are necessary for salvation, and the parts that are not, claiming that the inconsistencies and absurdities occur only in the latter (*Spinoza's Critique of Religion*, tr. E. M. Sinclair (NY, 1965), p. 75; I owe this reference to Harold Stone).

[29] Joseph E. Duncan, *Milton's Earthly Paradise* (Minneapolis, 1972), pp. 97, 109-11, mentions thirty refutations of Lapeyrère (also spelled [de] La Peyrère, Peirerius, and Peyrière). Cf. esp. Willem Salden, *Otia Theologica* (Amsterdam, 1684), pp. 60-72; Bayle, 'Peyrère, Isaac La' B; Pierre Jurieu, *A Critical History . . . of the Church* (1705), I. 253-60; Simon Berington, *Dissertations on the Mosaical Creation* (1750), pp. 127-9. The last two authors both use the term 'romance' to characterize Lapeyrère's work.

[30] *Men Before Adam, or a Discourse upon . . . the Epistle of the Apostle Paul to the Romans* (1656), pp. 22, 60; *A Theological Systeme upon that Presupposition that Men were before Adam* (1655), f. F1, pp. 113, 122, 126, 130-2 (the human race created like grass in every corner of the earth), 137-40, 147-52, 158-9, 164-78, 213, 255-7, 275. Donne recognized that the writings of Zoroaster, and the historical records of Egypt, Chaldea, and China, are older than the OT, but dismisses such questions as belonging to reason rather than to faith (*Essays in Divinity*, ed. Evelyn M. Simpson (Oxford, 1952), pp. 12 and 18).

remote cultures, as did those contemporaries who thought that 'primitive' man could still be living in the Adamic state, nor does he speculate about a primeval race of innocents. The peoples of Genesis 1 were created as natural fleshly humans, with normal sexual reproduction and birth-pains, obeying 'that natural Law by which the nobler sex [male] hath dominion over the inferiour [female]'. But just as a house decays in time, however excellent its materials, so mankind, though created in the image of God, began to develop the natural sins and infirmities of the flesh.[31]

God therefore decided to create a special race. Genesis 2 and 3 thus refer only to the ancestry of the Jews, into whom all the rest of the human race must be 'ingrafted' if they are to receive grace. (Lapeyrère here reveals his Huguenot upbringing.) Adam and Eve were still subject to what St. Paul later called the 'law in their members', the pre-existent infirmities of the flesh which eventually— when Eve reached puberty—made them fall into the common lot of humanity. But they were still purer and stronger than their decayed contemporaries—as proved by their extraordinary longevity after the fall—and they were endowed with spiritual gifts far above the others. The punishments meted out in Genesis 3 do not refer to physical conditions, for these were already their normal lot throughout life, but to new spiritual sufferings commensurate with these special gifts.[32]

Lapeyrère's ingenious dichotomy of 'Natural' and 'Adamic' man solves many of the problems of Genesis, without removing those hollow cornerstones of orthodox exegesis, male supremacy and the necessity of salvation. The confusion of lapsarian and non-lapsarian elements, for example, is untangled, since the idea of a cataclysmic fall no longer applies to common humanity. The bewildering distance between the superhuman ideal and ordinary experience, which still troubles Milton as he struggles to apply Paradisal standards to real marriage and divorce, loses its urgency; if we are not all descended from the one primal couple, then their splendour and misery no longer 'walk' within us. The problem of time is

---

[31] *A Systeme*, f. F1, pp. 15, 18–28, 37 (where sinful mankind came to prefer 'their own lust to the knowledge of God'), 124, 149–54, 159, 177, 243, 276–81, 330–1, '248' i.e. 348; cf. also Bayle, 'Cain' A, and n. 21 above. For Lapeyrère's interpretation of stone axes, cf. Glyn Daniel, *A Short History of Archaeology* (1981), pp. 35–6.

[32] *A Systeme*, pp. 8, 10, 13–15, 27, 52, 54–5, 87–90, 112–15, 135–46, 215, 218, 292, 299–'302' i.e. f. Bb6r v, 305, 327–8.

4. The Crisis of the Imagination

likewise greatly eased: the sudden change from unimaginable innocence to overwhelming evil is now replaced by a remoter and more gradual decay (as regards the physical life of the species) and a purely spiritual fall (in the case of Adam and Eve). The problem of sexuality also becomes less urgent, since the physical reproductive life of Adam and Eve is irrelevant to their state of Grace. It is all the more striking, then, that Lapeyrère still blames the fall on 'concupiscence', and still associates it with the puberty of Eve.[33]

For the diminishing number of those who retained their faith in a literal, unified, divinely-inspired, and all-explanatory Genesis, where the entire human condition can be read in hieroglyphic compression, Lapeyrère's historicism was as dangerous as any allegorical or 'poeticall' reading. Against this background of interpretative conflict, in which the literal meaning was forced apart from the spiritual significance, and Natural from Adamic man, Milton is all the more remarkable for attempting to reintegrate the text and translate it into an imaginable universe. In the divorce tracts he was torn between the standards of common humanity and the 'prime institution' of Adam and Eve, uncertain which should determine the conduct of sexual love. But in the epic, Paradise itself is rendered more 'natural' because more erotic, dense with passions and conflicts through which the primal couple learn and grow. The radical realism of Lapeyrère, or his counterparts in revolutionary England, could have challenged Milton's imagination to create what the Pre-Adamite system rendered impossible—an Adam and Eve who are both paragons of blessedness and recognizably human.

[iv]

By the time Milton was writing *Paradise Lost*, the interpretation and representation of Genesis had entered its terminal crisis. The standard Protestant reading, literalistic, coherent, and universalized, conflicted with the very realism it had helped to engender. The rational component of exegesis conflicted with the emotional, and

---

[33] *A Systeme*, pp. 145, 305–7; Lapeyrère generally assumes that contingent events in Gen. are actually separated by a number of years, but in this case he makes an exception: Eve's puberty is described in lyrical terms borrowed from Ezek. 16:7–8 (not Matt.) ('thy brests swell'd, and thy hair sprouted; behold thy time a time of lovers'), and as a consequence 'the Lord brought *Eve* to *Adam*, I guesse that *Eve* being now of age, and ready for a man, was brought to *Adam* at that same time when *Adam* was of ripe age'; the fall took place immediately afterwards (p. 145).

imagination—declared 'evil' by even the most fantastic commentators—came under renewed suspicion, eroded first by the spirit of scientific enquiry, and later also by the reaction against visionary 'enthusiasm'. These problems had been endemic in the Genesis-tradition, especially when it embodied the Protestant urge to found a spiritual renewal on a fresh return to origins and a fresh production of the Word. But the seventeenth century threw them into higher relief.

The central decades of the century, Milton's working life, saw an upsurge not only of scepticism but of radical reconceptions of Genesis, 'extraordinary and singular' new applications of the Eden-myth (the phrase was applied by Milton to his own divorce-campaign), and fresh literary and artistic versions of the fall. Heretical interpreters like Lapeyrère, Winstanley, and More, as well as artists like Rembrandt and Milton, attempted to renovate or transform the standard reading by the force of their individual vision. The most vivid of these reconstructions (by seventeenth- as well as twentieth-century criteria) tackle the forbidden questions that orthodoxy had condemned, but only Milton attempts to create a new significance for the Eden-myth without reversing or abandoning the standard ideology of the text—the assumption of unity and literalism. Thus Lapeyrère divides Genesis into different epochs and levels of application, and More dissolves it into allegories that throw its material reality into doubt. The most powerful and original depiction of Adam and Eve in seventeenth-century visual art, Rembrandt's etching of 1638 (frontispiece), is likewise scandalously 'singular', intensely realistic, and obscurely related to the text.

Rembrandt bridges the gulf between Paradisal perfection and common humanity by giving the gestures of Adam and Eve to a couple with the physical features of decayed and uncouth Pre-Adamites, a pair of primitives so distinctively ugly that they seem to issue from a private obsession rather than from the contemplation of divine creation. This collapses the stages of the narrative: since Adam and Eve are supposed to be 'not only our Progenitors but our Representatives' (as Addison later put it), the viewer is forced to identify with them as fallen, brutalized humanity, even though the fruit has apparently not yet been eaten. We are drawn into an intimate and disturbing mixture of compassion and revulsion, not mitigated by any trace of idealization: it is surely wishful thinking to find in these pendulous and gaping torsos an affinity with the classical nude, as some critics have done. The image seems irreducible to any plastic or iconographic tradition, and makes sense only as a distinctly personal, 'Rembrandtian' vision. It is, in short, what Milton claimed his own enterprise to be, 'extraordinary and singular'—but individuality here conflicts with the exegetical norm. Yet it would be rash to say that Rembrandt neglects or travesties the original story. He has pushed beyond narrative consistency to the psychological core of 'fallenness', manifested not only in the ugliness of Adam and Eve but in the shock, akin to the first opening of the eyes in Genesis, with which we see their nakedness.[34]

2. The abomination of fiction: sexuality in the systems of Boehme and van Helmont

Artists and exegetes were alike engaged in the search for what Browne called 'Authentick Drafts' of Adam and Eve, but the criteria for authenticity, never wholly secure, dissolved in the crisis of the mid-seventeenth century.[35] At the opposite extreme from the sceptics, and distant also from those who attempted to reconcile the conflicting claims of imagination, realism, and exegetical fidelity, are the theosophical visionaries. These self-proclaimed prophets and mystics seize fervently on the very questions that Browne and Butler condemned, and supply astonishingly detailed answers. They accept the hermaphroditic theory and equate the fall with sexuality, and they therefore invent alternatives to the current form of the body and to normal methods of reproduction. They draw sometimes on the allegorical tradition of Leone Ebreo and sometimes on Gnostic or Cabbalistic scriptures, but their authority derives primarily from personal hallucinations and *idées fixes*. In the view of their enemies, both sceptic and orthodox, they abandon themselves entirely to what Johnson in his praise of Milton's epic would later dismiss as 'the licentiousness of fiction'.

As Donne recognizes in his own poetic 'Litanie', there is a deep affinity between 'seeking secrets' and 'Poetiquenesse'. The creative

---

[34] Cf. John T. Shawcross (ed.), *Milton: The Critical Heritage* (1970), p. 154; Milton, *Prose* II. 247; Kenneth Clark, *Rembrandt and the Northern Renaissance* (1966), p. 36; Christopher White, *Rembrandt as an Etcher* (Philadelphia, 1969), pp. 162, 177-9; J. B. Trapp, 'The Iconography of the Fall of Man', in C. A. Patrides (ed.), *Approaches to Paradise Lost* (1968), p. 257.

[35] *Pseudodoxia*, p. 376.

element in exegesis, particularly of Genesis, was regarded as a grave danger to devotion: Calvin denounces it in the Spiritual Libertines, and Donne prays to be delivered from it. Hostile reaction to the theosophists continued this tradition of denouncing the impiety of fancy, the airy nothing of poetic fiction. And yet, as we have repeatedly seen, inspired speculation is the driving force of exegesis. The visionaries should thus be located within the problematic we have defined, uneasily divided between 'poetique' and theological criteria. They are as 'extraordinary and singular' as Milton, they individualize the Genesis-myth as sharply as Rembrandt, and the scale of their imagining is genuinely epic. But unlike Milton, they make no attempt to relate their 'romantick systems' to the material human world, and recognize none of the 'feare to faile' that inhibited du Bartas. Nor do they confront and exploit the problems of 'fallen' mentality, as Milton was to do, but place unquestioning faith in their own sense of being personally inspired, filled with the prophetic Spirit that alone can redeem the 'evil imagination' of the flesh.

[*ii*]

Jakob Boehme, a favourite author of Hudibras, is the most influential of these mystic revisionists. In a highly idiosyncratic vocabulary that combines alchemical, mystic, Neoplatonist, Gnostic, and Paracelsan terms, Boehme describes the many invisible worlds that lie hidden within the material. Genesis is reinterpreted as a key to this occult universe. Boehme was fortunate enough to have been present 'in a *Magicall manner*' at the creation and fall of man; he can relate the true life of Adam because 'when I was in *Adams Essence*, I was there ... and therefore let none cry it out as a thing un-knowable.' He can thus establish a higher literalism, above the problems of fallen imagination and rationality. The carnal mind, 'which desireth only to eat and procreate', can never share these visions, but the spiritual adept may actually regain Paradise if, guided by Boehme's writings, he is bold enough 'to force through the fire-Sword and see with divine Eyes'.[36]

[36] *Mysterium Magnum*, tr. John Sparrow (1654), 9:1, 18:1, 10:2, 26:2. All references to Boehme, unless otherwise specified, will be to chapter and verse of this edn., with cross-ref. to his *Sämtliche Schriften*, facsim. ed. Will-Erich Peuckert, VII–VIII (Stuttgart, 1958). A tr. of Boehme's *Works* inspired by William Law's revival, mostly reprinted from Sparrow, appeared in 4 vols. from 1764–81; *Mysterium Magnum* is Vol. III.

Boehme's powerful sexual mythology, which includes theories of the hermaphroditic Adam, the double fall, and the magic procreation of spiritual children, is most fully spelled out in the *Mysterium Magnum* (1623), a detailed exposition of Genesis. Man was originally a contemplative and angelic being. His outward body was flexible, transparent and entirely without bowels or genitals, and never impeded his inward faculties; the body that we experience is not human at all, but a 'bestiall grosse property' imposed at the first stage of the fall—the creation of Eve (16:1–5). Between this first fall and the second (Biblical) fall, however, the 'vanity' of the flesh lies dormant, until it too is awakened by inordinate serpentine desires and 'shuts up' the holier capacities. In our present state, then, the '*true* Body', with all the other spiritual powers, lies hidden within the fallen flesh like gold in ore, and can therefore be ultimately reconstituted by reversing the fall: if the 'vanity' can be neutralized by the essence or 'Tincture' of holiness, then it too 'is holy and a *Paradise*, which shall open it selfe at the End of this world' (15:13). The purpose of Boehme's occult evangelism is to prepare for this imminent consummation.

The original Adam contained both male and female tinctures, and yet 'he' was neither man nor woman but a purified hermaphrodite or masculine virgin (*Jungfrau*). In the words of Christ, he neither married nor was given in marriage but was as the angels, that is, in the state to which we shall return at the resurrection. In the first Adam, as in Christ the second Adam, the tinctures were in perfect balance, so that neither gender manifested itself. Adam did, however, possess a *matrix*, from which he gave birth by magical means 'as the Sun through-shineth the water, and rends (or teares) it not'.[37] The female has a high order of importance in Boehme's spiritual world. God the Son is female, and woman (*die Weibliche*) is equivalent to the creative light and to the 'tincture of Venus' which forms the spiritual body in the first place; indeed, man's 'true lifes-Centre' is precisely this Venusian 'Love-desire', which turns after the fall into a wrathful fire, cold and hard. The female part of Adam is his creativity, his rose-garden and his womb, through which he 'imagines himself' and repeats his own creation by giving

---

[37] 18:2–3, 17:14, 18:10. Boehme's source may be the vision of the 13th-century Mechthild of Magdeburg, who reports that the love of Adam and Eve 'was to be immaculate and without sin and was to give them children as the sun playing on the water gives it sparkle, yet without breaking it' (quot. in Wilhelm Fränger, *The Millenium of Hieronymus Bosch*, tr. Eithne Wilkins and Ernst Kaiser (1952), p. 51).

birth to images.[38] It is all the more striking, then, that Boehme denigrates the Biblical creation of woman, and repudiates physical sexuality.

All the essences of Boehme's invisible world interact in a kind of sexual union, an ardent 'Penetration' in which all the properties become 'Tinctured with the *Sweet Love*, so that there was nothing but meer pleasing relish, Love-desire and delight (*Liebe-Begehren*) betwixt them.' Adam's '*Magicall* Impregnation' would have taken place in the same way, by penetration of tinctures stirring up desire (*Begierde*) and a love (*Liebes-Lust*) which actually creates substantial images. The same process, in fact, which created him would, if he had stood his trial, have allowed him to conceive and give birth with great delight by a process remarkably like fallen intercourse— a pleasurable conjunction of male and female tinctures in the womb. By the 'female', however, we are not to understand the Biblical Eve, but a higher principle, sometimes an aspect of Adam himself, and sometimes personified in the Gnostic figure of Sophia or Wisdom, his original bride, with whom he will be reunited at the end of the world. Sophia is taken away at the first fall, and the recalcitrant Eve—'*Venus's Matrix*' taken out of Adam and fashioned into a separate person—is her substitute.[39]

Eve, unlike Sophia, can no longer be 'a Mother without Generating', that is, 'manifesting' images rather than 'generating' fleshly children. She should have retained her magic procreative ability, for, as Boehme himself recognizes, Eve is 'the right magicall childe' and 'the *Matrix* in which the Love-desire stood in *Adam*'. But unfortunately the 'Lust and Imagination' of Adam had already destroyed the capacity for magic birth; even before the separation of Eve he '*an den Thieren vergaft*'—fell in love with the animals— and 'introduced himself into beastiall *Lust*, to eat and generate according as the beasts doe'; he thus transformed himself from a spiritual into an animal creature, complete with genitals. Responding to this inexplicable fall in Adam's imagination, God cut out his womb and in its place 'hung upon him the wormes-*Carkasse* with the bestiall members for propagation, of which the poore soule is

---

[38] 23:45, 17:21, 27; cf. 41:26 and 15:10 (Boehme calls this Venusian love-principle in the eternal world 'fiery' in 17:21, but this is a mistake, as 6:21 shows). See also Leopold Damrosch, *Symbol and Truth in Blake's Myth* (Princeton, 1980), p. 189 n. 71.

[39] 16:5, 18:8–11, 25:14; cf. Kathleen Raine, *Blake and Tradition* (Princeton, 1969), I. 208.

to this day ashamed, that it must beare a beastiall form on the body.' (*Madensack*, the word translated in the seventeenth century as 'wormes-*Carkasse*', would more accurately be rendered *maggotbag*.) Those who object to this un-Biblical transformation, which Boehme places just before the creation of Eve in Genesis 2, are quashed by citing the post-lapsarian Genesis 3, clear evidence of the shamefulness of the genital region.[40] And though at one point he endorses Genesis 2:18—'*it is not good that this man should be alone*'—he still equates Eve with the sexual fall: 'shee was created to this corruptible life, for shee is the Woman of this world ... figured after a bestiall forme.'[41] Eve is virtually created by Adam's revolting genital longings.

In Boehme's cosmology 'nothing was created *Evill*'; the light and the dark principles are ultimately united in a single Godhead. But sexuality seems to form a significant exception. Boehme's God, constantly engaged in erotic mingling of tinctures, nevertheless abhors 'the *bestiall* copulation and propagation' and had no intention of introducing them into Paradise.[42] The Biblical fall merely continues the descent into lust: infected by Adam even before the separation, the newly created Eve falls in love with the serpent and longs for it as a pregnant woman longs for unusual food—the same word, *sich vergaffen*, is used for all these emotions (19:25; 20:5, 22). Sin is therefore referred to as the serpent's bastard, and Eve's behaviour as whorishness (23:32-4; 26:68, 75). As usual in writers heavily influenced by Biblical prophesies, it is hard to distinguish Babylonic imagery from actual accusations of sexual depravity here. But on one point Boehme is quite explicit: the serpent, for all the veil of silence in Moses's text, obviously signifies sexuality itself, 'being it was the most subtle Beast among all the Beasts, and slew *Eve* her virgin-like chastity, that she lusted after the beastiall copulation' (23:24). It is Eve's reproductive tract,

---

[40] Raine, loc. cit.; *Mysterium* 19:8, 17:39, 19:25, 18:6, 19:19-20. The erotic nature of 'sich vergaffen' is obscured in Sparrow's translation—'did amuse himself on (or Imagine after)'.

[41] *Mysterium* 18:33-4 (and cf. 20:35, which confusingly suggests that Adam's genitalization took place in the inner essence); *A Description of the Three Principles of the Divine Essence* (1648), 17:10—in the original, though not in this tr., Eve is 'nach Thieres Gestalt aus dem Adam figuriret' (*Sämtliche Schriften*, II (1960), p. 239).

[42] *Mysterium* 18:5, 41:2—sex is 'an abomination before the holiness of God', only tolerated 'by divine patience'.

already corrupted by Adam but now put 'into *Act*', that receives the curse ascribed in the Bible to the serpent (23:27).

This paradox is thus found everywhere in Boehme: he abhorred sexuality, and rewrote the story of Genesis so as to eliminate it from God's original plan; but he conceives the emanations and interactions of the *mundus invisibilis* in highly sexual terms—'great ardent Longing desire', 'Loveplay', 'Matrix', 'Penetration', and '*Holy Generation*' (6:2, 18). (So pervasive is Boehme's use of *Lust* [pleasure] for both celestial love-desire and fallen concupiscence, that his English translator created a noun from the Latin 'Lubet' to convey the former sense devoid of carnal associations.) Correspondingly, every normal copulation re-enacts the fall, 'introducing the *Ens* of the Devill, and Serpent, insinuated into the *masculine Seed*, so poysonfull, into the *womans* matrix' (41:26); but redemption seems to depend on the same process. Circumcision, the precursor of baptism, hallows the bestial appendage of the male with a drop of divine fire. Once the female Holy Spirit has baptized the man with a female 'virgin-like Tincture' he can reciprocate by 'baptizing the womans essence in his Seed with the *fiery* and also divine Tincture' (41:33). The mechanism of fallen impregnation proves to be exactly analogous to the higher processes that flow down into it:

Like as the Father generateth the Son ... and as before, while the woman was in the Man, the fires Tincture penetrated into the lights Tincture, and loved it selfe therein, and as man and woman are *one* Body, so likewise the *fire*-baptisme of the Circumcision went forth out of the *mans fire*-Tincture into his *female* Tincture in the woman.

It is common for mystics to conceive the invisible world in terms of Eros, but few in Western literature have modelled it so precisely on physical copulation.

Boehme's confused hatred and awe of sexuality may stem from his high regard for the creative imagination, which he conceives in terms that might be called folk-Platonic. As in most religious adaptations of the philosophy of Eros, desire is the principal vehicle of transcendence, but all consubstantiality between tenor and vehicle is passionately denied. Sexuality is both a squalid imprisonment in the flesh and an ontological mystery that leads to a higher state of the soul and a higher form of procreation—the 'birth in beauty' that Diotima reveals to Socrates, the generation of mental images.

The maggoty business of copulation thus reveals a more exalted aspect. The couple experience not only the blessed union of 'one flesh', but the creativity of the artist or artisan (Boehme's own class), and in the process they attain an almost hermaphroditic interpenetration of genders: 'the woman hath her soul from the mans soul, and when shee is given to the man, then she is *one* body with him, and brings forth children to the man; she is his woman (*Maennin*), his instrument, an *half-man*, and the Man an *half-woman*' (41:29, 32).

In Boehme's mental universe, then, the ideas of the 'instrument' and the artistic production of images are interwoven with a sublimated form of sexuality. The concept of love-play, for example, which probably derives from the description in Proverbs 8 of the divine Sophia 'playing' before the Lord, combines erotic delight, wrestling, the 'pregnant harmony' of music, and creative play—the generation of images by means of another kind of '*Instrument*'. Just as woman becomes the 'instrument' of man by bearing children, so for the spiritual Adam the outer world and the outward body was 'an Image of the inward *viz.* an *Instrument* of the inward' (16: 14); the mind's inner conceptions would have been translated into reality by the penetrative processes of '*Holy Generation*'. Adam even shared in the act of creation with the 'Verbum Fiat' of his own thoughts and the magical birth that resulted. The reader is explicitly told, moreover, that such magic powers may be recovered through diligent study of Boehme's scriptures.[43]

Apostacy, however, is bad art. Lucifer aspired to return '*in magiam naturae* into the Originall of the Eternall Nature, and would be an Omniscient Artist (*ein Kuenstler und Allwisser*),' and Adam was carried away by 'the lust of *Pride* ... to know and prove evill and good, desiring to be like God, as the Devill also did, when he would be an Artist in the magicall birth; after which *Adam* heere also lusted.' Satan thus attempted to emulate the 'art' or creativity of 'birth', deluding mankind with the serpent of animal sexuality. Good 'art' comprises the whole programme of mystic vision, occult eroticism, magic, and alchemy that will lead the adept back to Paradise. Lucifer, on the other hand, created a grotesque parodic art, 'forged to himselfe a strange fooles-play (*Kitzel-Spiel*), where he can act his gulleries with his sundry Enterludes, and

[43] e.g. 17:43, 11:8; the result of this restitution of vanished powers will be a Paradise within (11:16).

disguizments.' He thereby 'entered into the Abomination of fictions'.[44]

[*iii*]

For the hostile reader, of course, Boehme himself was a prime example of the human desire to be an 'Omniscient Artist', a unique and self-willed visionary—to possess 'the Magicall *roote* of the Originall of Essences' as Adam desires, or to 'play with the Centre of the *Transmutation* of the Properties' as Lucifer did (9:15–16). Were not his visions a grotesque travesty of Scripture, a counter-art to orthodoxy? Did he not replace the true meaning of Genesis with the 'abomination of fiction'?

Contemporaries were divided in their response. Among Milton's State Papers is a proposal for a college devoted to the study of 'Jacob B[o]ehmen ... who had true revelation from the true spirit' and who had manifested 'the noble mind of man soaringe beyond the letter'. Others dismissed his writings as the work of an 'enthusiast', a 'novelist', a 'heretic', or 'a Man, who if he was not stark Mad, was yet highly disturbed in his Mind and Understanding,' and accused his followers of basing their cult on 'imaginary conceptions' and 'carnal inventions'. Boehme had a large following among English sectarians, but his enemies denounced his carnal inventions and discovered in his system the Titanic hubris of the fall itself: it is 'not Christian Theology', but 'rather a War of the Giants against Heaven'.[45]

The influence of Boehme is nevertheless a lasting one. Versions of his myth appear in the visionary and philosophical writings of Jean-Baptiste and Franciscus Mercurius van Helmont, Samuel and John Pordage, Jane Lead, Antoinette Bourignon, Thomas Tryon, William Law, and William Blake. He was an acknowledged influence on Schelling and Hegel, and Coleridge praised him highly, even

---

[44] 17:27 (summarizing 9:15, 17); 18:29 (30 in original); 19:19-20. Cf. 17:40—Adam's lust and imagination actually create the forbidden tree.

[45] Margaret L. Bailey, *Milton and Jakob Boehme* (1914; repr. NY, 1964), pp. 135, 160; John Anderdon, *One Blow at Babel, in Those of the People Called Behmenists* (1662), p. 2 (inaccurately quot. by Bailey (p. 99) as if referring to Boehme himself); *Hudibras* I. i. 536; Gerard Croese, *The General History of the Quakers* (1698), II.'759' i.e. 259, 262 (Croese softens the blow by attributing Boehme's works to a sect of crazed academics, to whom the words 'War of the Giants' actually apply, *pace* Bailey p. 179). Cf. Charles Webster, *The Great Instauration* (1975), pp. 200, 202, 492, and Tickell's account of Coppe in *Bottomles Pit*, f. A7.

though he did sometimes 'mistake the tumultuous sensations of his own nerves, and the co-existing spectres of his fancy, as parts or symbols of the truths which were opening on him'.[46] He continues to be read wherever obscurity is revered. His vision of Genesis has the perennial fascination of a powerful imagination working on stubborn materials, and for many fervent spirits of the English Revolution it was irresistible. The attraction of theosophy may even be felt in More's *Conjectura Cabbalistica*: though he devoted an entire treatise to demolishing the 'Teutonic Philosopher', and was always vociferously critical of 'Enthusiasm', private revelation, apocalyptic millenarianism, and alchemical mystery, More still praises Boehme for discovering the angelic body of Adam, still sees the cosmos as a dark struggle of animal and spiritual principles each 'shut up' in the other, and still denounces the false Paradise of 'Beastial delight'.[47] And in More as in Boehme, Eve is an unstable particle in the structure of signification, a celestial delight and a flaw in the creation, the vehicle of a divinely ordained Eros and the embodiment of an inexplicable sensuality; her creation is itself a kind of fall.

One of these theosophical systems, however, breaks out of the impasse that led to the bestialization of Eve. Milton was to give her an unprecedented complexity and dignity, but he still must present her weak, seducible, 'much deceived, much failing'; Jean-Baptiste van Helmont, revered in Commonwealth England not only as a physician and experimental scientist but as 'a spiritual leader like Jacob Boehme',[48] goes much further, absolving her from all debility and responsibility. Like More, van Helmont insisted that his philosophical exegesis represented the core of Scriptural truth and a bulwark against atheism, though unlike More he upheld the literal truth of his visions and regarded allegory as the tool of the

---

[46] Cf. Wilhelm Struck, *Der Einfluss Jakob Böhmes auf die englische Literatur des 17. Jahrhundert* (Berlin, 1936); Serge Hutin, *Les Disciples anglais de Jacob Boehme aux XVIIe et XVIIIe siècles* (Paris, 1960); Hegel, *Lectures on the History of Philosophy*, III. i; Coleridge, *Biographia Literaria*, ch. 9 (incorporating Schelling); Raine, *passim* (with caution); M. H. Abrams, *Natural Supernaturalism* (1971; repr. NY, 1973), pp. 170-2, 223, 245, 383. Blake's reference to Boehme in *The Marriage of Heaven and Hell* is well known, but it should be noted that Dante and Shakespeare are there described as infinitely greater teachers than him. The fullest attempt to capture the Boehmean Genesis in English verse is Samuel [and John?] Pordage, *Mundorum Explicatio* (1661).

[47] *Conjectura*, pp. 124, 127; cf. Serge Hutin, *Henry More* (Hildesheim, 1966), pp. 55-6.

[48] Webster, p. 277.

libertine. Like More he regarded God's warning not as a prohibition or a test of obedience but as pure advice—eating the fruit will bring certain irreversible physical consequences. The fall for van Helmont was not a crime but a free choice, and the transmission of sin and death was not a disproportionate punishment but a necessary function of human reproduction, which the fruit had changed from an asexual to a sexual process. Like Browne, van Helmont endorsed the Paracelsan-Boehmean vision of pre-lapsarian non-sexual birth, and speaks of gynaecology with more distaste than befits a scientist and healer. But he differs remarkably from his predecessors by making Eve, not a subordinate part of Adam or an embodiment of his corruption, but a higher being, 'the head, top, and ultimate Creature above the Man'.[49]

Though van Helmont's natural philosophy claims to be rooted in the physical world, his explanation of the fall shows little respect for normal sexuality. The apple contained the essence of seminal generation, originally implanted in animals but not in man; its immediate effect was aphrodisiac, and this carnal desire necessarily produced a 'seminal disposition' in the blood which in turn demanded a new kind of soul—a 'sensitive' or animal soul that mediates between mind and body (pp. 650-58). Previously the human mind had governed and 'quickened' the body with absolute directness and unimaginable efficiency, but this happy state is now crumbled into 'duality, alterities and vicissitude'.[50] Previously Eve would have conceived children not by 'carnal Copulation' but in a manner proper to Humanity, though now only known to us from the 'overshadowing' of the Virgin Mary; indeed, the clearest sign that '*Eva* was constituted above the Man' was her power to generate children painlessly and independently of man (p. 652). The foetus would have been formed from pure arterial blood in the heart, and then transferred to the unopened womb, as happened when Jesus was conceived, and as will happen to all who are spiritually reborn (pp. 661-5).

---

[49] *Ortus Medicinus* (Amsterdam, 1648), tr. by J. Chandler as *Oriatrike* (1662), pp. 649-54, 665, 683; cf. More, *Phil.* 2:17. All refs. will be to this English version, unless the Latin is quoted.

[50] Walter Pagel, *The Religious and Philosophical Aspects of Van Helmont's Science and Medicine*, Supplements to the Bulletin of the History of Medicine, 2 (Baltimore, 1944), p. 30. Pagel's useful summary is mysteriously silent on the subject of the sexual fall.

4. The Crisis of the Imagination

Van Helmont purportedly derives this theory of virginal reproduction from Augustine,[51] but he goes further than Augustine by eliminating from the pre-lapsarian state, not just the penile erection, but the entire presence of the male. The external form of the human body was originally the same as it is now, however; van Helmont has no subdivided hermaphrodites or superadded genitalia, and believed that 'the Instruments of Generation were given unto Man, because the Corruption of Nature, the necessity of regeneration in a Saviour, and the virgin Purity thereof, were foreseen' (p. 658). The difference between innocent and corrupt reproduction consists entirely in the seminal principle that transforms the blood and thence usurps the entire constitution and mentality. The effects of this seed-production were none the less disastrous, for 'the Adamical or Beast-like Generation of the Flesh from the Concupiscence of the Flesh, and its Copulation, doth naturally contain Death in it' (p. 655). The curses that follow the fall are thus not judicial punishments but natural morbidities, constant reminders of the original mistake. This includes menstruation, that 'bloody defilement' whereby 'the part wherein the Image of God ought to be conceived by the Holy Spirit, became a sink of filths'. Because Eve yearned to copulate after eating the apple, she and all her descendants—except the Virgin Mary, who treads the moon under her feet—are visited with 'the malignancy of a cadaverous or stinking Liquor', a 'Curse' that 'derives itself from the same Causes from whence Death happened to us'.[52] Van Helmont's zeal sometimes obscures his own contention that the consequences of the fall were natural rather than punitive.

The human mind was similarly corrupted; sexuality and epistemology are alike transformed by the fall. Once the animal principle had entered Adam, 'his Mind (for the suppport of the sensitive Soul) dispersed from it self, only a darksom Light, through the Mists of the Flesh, upon the Life of a new and impure Generation'; once he had begun to copulate, true Knowledge was obliterated and he fell into a Lockean nether world—'Man thereby was born a vain or empty Table' (pp. 711-12). The divine mind has now shrunk so deeply into the sex-drenched body that atheists

[51] e.g. p. 679, where he cites a range of passages from Aug. to prove his contentions, some of which, like *CG* XIV. 17, actually disprove them.

[52] pp. 678, 740-2; van Helmont ascribes supernatural curative as well as toxic powers to the menstrual blood, particularly recommending it for 'Swine which are inclining into the Leprosie'.

and libertines deny its very existence (pp. 664-6). When Adam and Eve's eyes were opened, they realized that they had exchanged 'radical innocency' (*innocentiam radicalem* (p. 660)) for 'the sordid Concupiscence of the Flesh'; indeed, 'their whole *knowledge* of *Good and Evil* is included about their *Shame*, and within their privy Parts alone' (pp. 664-5).

Van Helmont's interpretation of the fall is itself an outstanding example of this sexualization of the mind; he goes further than his predecessors in making the fall exclusively genital. We see again the paradox, that those who wish to eliminate sexuality from the definition of human nature install it at the very centre of their myths of human origin. Before the fall Adam and Eve '*were without shame*, that is, without the Concupiscence of the Flesh, like Children, because they wanted Seed,' but immediately afterwards they felt a genital shame never found among the animals, for whom copulation is natural.[53] Van Helmont suspends his own dislike of allegory, and interprets the 'tree of the knowledge of good and evil' as a euphemism for the sexual act itself.[54] Genesis 4:1 ('Adam knew his wife, and she conceived, and bore Cain') was generally thought to refer to the first copulation, but van Helmont proves that the actual defloration of Eve must have happened earlier, before the expulsion from Paradise. Why did the guilty couple retire into the bushes, if not to copulate? Why did Adam rename his wife 'mother of all humans'? How could God promise that the woman's 'seed' would bruise the serpent's head unless she already had seed and all the 'tickling' (*titillatione* (p. 655)) that comes with it? (The silence of the text on these shameful matters further confirms this interpretation.) The subsequent conception of Cain in fact disproves the orthodox view, since the first penetration is, like menstruation,

[53] pp. 656, 676, and cf. 680. Even the OT dietary laws are forced into conformity with this sexual definition of sin; the unclean animals are those that linger over their copulation (p. 677).
[54] p. 665. This fits oddly with his insistence on the literal truth of his account and on the actual physical operation of the fruit, which led him to deny that there was any prohibition or disobedience. This is part of a larger contradiction in van Helmont: as an Augustinian he stresses the intellectual and voluntaristic fall, and comes close to Calvin when he asserts that Adam and Eve's main fault was to disbelieve God's account of the consequences (p. 654); but as a physician he makes extreme claims for the inherent properties of the fruit, even saying that the fall would have happened if they had eaten the fruit unwittingly (p. 657). Note M's skill at reconciling these physicalist and mentalist approaches: he makes the fruit an aphrodisiac intoxicant, but with a short-lived effect and thus a peripheral significance (*PL* IX. 793, 1007-54).

a 'bloody defilement', and 'because it is bloody, doth not admit of Conception as a Companion' (pp. 659-60). From here it is a short step to equating the fall itself with violent and outrageous sexuality. Adam was actually 'banished for his whoredom', and his descendants were punished by circumcision (p. 668) as a perpetual reminder of the rape of Eve.

What could be the motive for this gratuitous outrage on the part of Adam? Eve, we recall, had originally been created as the superior, a 'help meet' only in the sense that a prince gives help to his subjects (p. 666), and procreation was to be arranged between her and the Holy Ghost without 'the will of Man'. The male is as superfluous in this version as the female is in some Church Fathers, and both these extremes differ in turn from the standard picture of Adam and Eve as the first married couple. In the matrimonial version of Genesis 'Adam did not ravish Eve, but receaved her, delivered unto him by God the father', as Vives points out; or in Luther's words 'Adam does not snatch Eve of his own will'.[55] In van Helmont's revision it is precisely the reverse. Though Eve becomes an accomplice later by virtue of the aphrodisiac fruit, and so deserves the pollution and subordination visited upon her, it is clear that the primal sexual act was Adam's fault alone, a violent rape (*stupra*) which represented both a sexual defilement and an offence against the hierarchy that had placed him below Eve. Even in the fallen world, where marriage is tolerated as a remedy against more Satanic kinds of sexuality, female virginity remains the highest and most blessed state—the most in harmony with the authentic nature of humanity, and the closest to God's original intention.[56]

[55] Both authors quot. in Cheryl H. Fresch, ' "And Brought Her unto the Man": The wedding in *Paradise Lost*', *MS* XVI (1982), 24-5. Laurence Clarkson and the Muggletonians interpreted the fall as Eve's sexual pollution, but the perpetrator was Satan rather than Adam; cf. Christopher Hill et al., *The World of the Muggletonians* (1983), pp. 25, 28, 31, 80, 181.

[56] Marriage is better than 'detestable Copulations' with elemental spirits (nymphs, sylphs, gnomes, and salamanders) and with succubi, the 'daughters of men' who couple with the upright 'Sons of God' in Gen. 6 and thereby provoke the Flood (pp. 680-2). Van Helmont's praise of·virginity is influenced by St. Teresa (Pagel, *Van Helmont*, p. 10) and by Hildegarde of Bingen, who anticipated many of his visionary-scientific ideas, including the sexual transformation of the blood of Adam at the fall; cf. Peter Dronke, *Women Writers of the Middle Ages* (Cambridge, 1984), pp. 170, 175-7, and Barbara Newman's study of Hildegarde and her influence, forthcoming from the University of California Press. Van Helmont combines this visionary tradition with a kind of modern empiricism: his own research into parish registers, he assures us, reveals twice as many female births as male, and twice as many male deaths in infancy (pp. 686-7). What could be clearer proof of God's

Adam's sexual urge even tries to emulate and subvert the creativity of God. The defilement of Eve, which stamps man's image in flesh, is intended to make him the 'competitor' of God, to 'overthrow' the 'holy and unpolluted production of mind', and so to rob the human race of 'eternal glory'. Adam thus becomes a Gnostic demiurge, deliberately initiating sexual reproduction in order to 'prevent and pervert the intention of the Creator, about the propagation of his own Image' (pp. 661–2). In Genesis, of course, the serpent tempts Eve to be as the gods, and Leone Ebreo had made Satan suggest a parallel between fallen sexuality and divine fertility. But only in van Helmont does the story centre on Adam's Titanic attempt to frustrate God's plan—a project doomed to perpetual failure since he can create only bodies and not souls—by 'generating the Image of God out of himself ... with the Whoredom or Ravishment of *Eve*' (p. 663).

[iv]

It is sometimes suggested that Milton himself was tinged with esoteric or Boehmean influence. There are certainly hints in his earlier writings of Hermetic and neo-Gnostic leanings, suggesting that his vision grew from the same soil as Boehme's or van Helmont's: *il penseroso* steeps himself in Hermes Trismegistus, Platonic invisible worlds and Paracelsan demonology, and in the divorce tracts the Divine Wisdom is said to have '*played*' before the face of God (as the wife should play before her husband) rather than 'rejoiced' as in the Authorized Version. The Platonic vision of Eros is an acknowledged influence on the prose works of the 1640s. One would like to know more about the tantalizing opinion expressed in *Areopagitica*, that Irenaeus (one of the main recorders of Gnostic beliefs) denounces as heresy what should be called 'the truer opinion'.[57] Certainly Milton is no more afraid than Boehme to brave accusations of novelty, or to invent on an epic scale, and the invocations to *Paradise Lost* associate human creativity with divine sexuality—a precise inversion of what motivates van Helmont's Adam. But the spirit of occultism is quite alien to Milton, whose imagination respects the conceptual bounds imposed

intention to people the world with virgins, and so to redeem the human race from the invasion of alien male seed?

[57] II. 252–3, 596–7, 518. Bœhme and More are discussed in relation to M by Duncan, pp. 258–60; J. M. Evans claims an intimate relationship between M and More in *Paradise Lost and the Genesis Tradition* (Oxford, 1968), p. 265.

4. The Crisis of the Imagination

by the Protestant exegetes even when it overthrows their conclusions, and thrives on a psychological realism that can only flourish when the full complexity of human emotion is accepted.

The hermaphroditic Adam was curtly dismissed even in the more Platonic divorce tracts, where he also attacks the 'Gnostics' of his day for their hatred of erotic pleasure. Boehme's invention of a magic pre-corporeal form, and his shuddering disparagement of human sexuality, would have struck Milton as a Satanic blasphemy rather than a Christian desideratum, especially when combined with Helmontian female suprematism. Boehme's 'childe-like' Adam, who eats and drinks in spirit only and flits between heaven and earth (18:12), must have seemed like a tawdry parody of the blessed state that Raphael promises Adam and Eve as a reward for maturity and patience. Ancient myths of Eve's marriage to the serpent are associated with Satanic propaganda in *Paradise Lost*. Indeed, the grotesque figure of Sin—whom Phineas Fletcher had made the daughter of Satan and Eve—may parody the excesses of neo-Gnostic myth-making. She plays in front of Satan before the world was made, delights him and is 'possessed' as well as 'begotten' by him, exactly like Sophia in Proverbs 8, and she is then involved in a series of fantastic sexual couplings between demonic essences. Sin's reproductive history runs the gamut from cerebral birth in fire to the swarming of snakes—perhaps the two extremes of Boehme's 'magicall birth' and 'wormes-*Carkasse*'. The invention of sexuality in Boehme is closer to the rape of Sin by Satan and Death than it is to the tender wooing and 'amorous delay' of Paradisal wedded love.[58]

When Raphael holds out the possibility of a temperate and obedient ascent to spirit, he is promising that the human form will eventually be a 'liquid Texture', transformable at will into 'either sex, or both', and totally responsive to desire. In the spirit state we 'limb ourselves', sculpting or perhaps limning the body to the requirements of the will; it is a state for which Milton could yearn both as a Christian and as an artist.[59] The visions of primeval, anti-physical sexuality considered in this section are fuelled by an impatience for ascent, a 'disobedient' refusal to accept the natural form of the human body and the limitations of the flesh upon the imagination. In the later sceptic and satiric reaction against

[58] *PL* V. 493–503, X. 578–82, II. 747–802, IV. 311; cf. ch. 7 n. 68 below.
[59] Cf. *PL* I. 424–8, V. 497, VI. 348–53, VIII. 622–9.

theosophy—in More himself, in Bayle, in Swift, and in Voltaire—we see not only a new suspicion of prophetic and spiritual 'Enthusiasm', but also the return to a Pascalian insistence that the present human condition, however wretched, is the only available locus for our thoughts on salvation. Milton attempts to reconcile these two movements—grounding his conception of Paradise in human realism even before the fall, without abandoning the ascent to spirit, the sense of privileged vision, the romantic 'dream of other worlds'. They cannot actually converge, but the attempt still generates the propulsive energy of his epic.

3. Carnal knowledge and the libertine fall

The 'Artists' of the esoteric tradition, freed from the bonds of literalism and hostile to the realm of the flesh, tend inexorably towards the hypothesis of a sexual fall. This idea has a long ancestry in apocryphal writings, and sometimes even in the most canonical texts. In the Hermetic *Poimandres* sexuality and death came into the world together with the command to 'increase and multiply'.[60] Many Rabbinical commentators maintained, following 2 Enoch, that the serpent had coupled with Eve to engender Cain, and St. Paul agreed that Eve had been 'seduced'; this idea was repeated, not only by the Catharist heretics (who add that the serpent penetrated Eve with his tail), but frequently by orthodox Christians. Some Rabbis held that the fruit was a powerful aphrodisiac—a belief confirmed for Christianity by the highly popular *Physiologus*—and Browne ascribes to them, probably wrongly, the belief that the 'tree' is the phallus. Philo Judaeus, who believed that the true fall came when female 'Sense' split off from male 'Reason', interpreted the serpent as the sexual pleasure generated by the union of these separated halves. Leone Ebreo explicitly equated the forbidden tree with 'carnal pleasure', and in this he was followed by Boehme and van Helmont.[61]

[60] Cf. Williams, *Ideas of the Fall*, pp. 20–31, 58, 77–8, 112–17, 224–7, 271–3; for Hermetic and Gnostic versions of the sexual fall, see Hans Jonas, *The Gnostic Religion*, 2nd edn. (Boston, 1963), p. 152, and ch. 1 n. 23 above.

[61] Cf. Evans, pp. 46–7; Williams, *Ideas of the Fall*, p. 204; Antonello Gerbi, *Il Peccato di Adamo ed Eva* (Milan, 1933), pp. 14–15, 61, 67–8, 71; Moses Barcepha, *De Situ Paradisi*, xix; Bayle, 'Eve' B and C; n. 10 and n. 25 above; 2. 3. ii above. See also Joseph Coppens, 'L'interprétation sexuelle du péché du paradis dans la littérature patristique', *Ephemerides Theologicae Lovanienses* XXIV (1948), 402–8, and XXXIII (1956), 506–8.

The paradoxical effect of these readings is to enlarge the importance of sexuality in the very act of diminishing and renouncing the flesh. A similar point is made in Calvin's defence of the literal Genesis. The Libertines, for example, repudiate the physical world and 'fly in the air' in pursuit of a wholly spiritual Paradise, but their real achievement is comically limited—they are driven only by 'their own libido'. Milton's Adam and Eve likewise fancy they are growing wings after eating the fruit, but actually experience 'far other operation', an aphrodisiac titillation (*PL* IX. 1009-13). A related and more widespread reading, denounced even more fervently by Calvin, is the sensual hypothesis, the theory that the fall was appetitive and sexual, caused primarily by Eve's gluttonous hunger for the fruit and Adam's infatuation with her erotic blandishments. This confusion of cause and effect, Calvin insists, is not only absurd, perverse, and sophistical, but *puerile*: 'they childishly err who regard original sin as consisting only in lust, and in the inordinate notion of the appetites'; it is a broader and deeper calamity which 'seizes upon the very seat of reason, and upon the whole heart'. Against these localizing and extenuating tendencies, analogous in their focus to Adam and Eve's ridiculous attempt to hide their shame with fig-leaves, Calvin sets his own sense of the gravity of the fall—an apostacy of the entire human being, centred on the intellectual crime of disbelief (3:6, 3:7). To draw the greatest significance from Genesis, he calls for an integrated, existential reading of the fall, neither unrealistically spiritual nor narrowly sexual.

[*ii*]

The sexual hypothesis had nevertheless been strengthened by Renaissance and seventeenth-century investigators. The clearest and most influential version of the theory is Cornelius Agrippa's *De Originale Peccato*. We have already encountered, in his 'feminist' revision of Genesis, Agrippa's quixotic penchant for the elaborate defence of an impossible thesis; his major work is a self-cancelling pair of treatises, one on the efficacy of the occult sciences, the other on the vanity of all sciences. His *De Originale Peccato* is a 'declamation of disputable opinion', and a self-confessed work of youth.[62] Nevertheless, it argues its one-sided case with vehement conviction and accumulative power.

[62] *Opera Omnia* (Lyons, n.d.), II. 556; cf. 3. 2. ii above.

Agrippa brings together the Hermetic distaste for generation, the pseudo-Rabbinical microcosmic allegory which locates the 'tree' in the middle of Adam's body, and his own pseudo-feminist deduction that Eve did not sin individually, but only by 'giving the fruit' to Adam. The serpent is an appropriate euphemism for the 'sensible *affectus* of the flesh', or rather for the member that provides this pleasure—'*membrum reptile, membrum serpens, membrum lubricum*', the tempter and deceiver of Eve. All this suggests that 'the original sin was none other than the carnal copulation of man and woman.'[63] The immediate consequences of the fall, and subsequent references to sexual issues in Scripture, make this hypothesis overwhelmingly probable. Adam and Eve hid their genitals, and God cursed childbearing; pubic embarrassment, like the blood of defloration and menstruation, are signs of His perpetual and universal disapproval. The sexual sins of Genesis 6 make Him repent of having created man and unleash a flood to destroy the entire species. Circumcision, and ritual purification after childbirth, further identify the peccant members. Job located Satan 'in the loins'. Only virgins and eunuchs are welcome in heaven, and God would only choose a virgin for His incarnation. St. Paul identifies the *stimulus carnis* as the root of all trouble, and states unequivocally that 'it is good not to touch a woman.' Agrippa thus arranges a formidable array of ascetic and anti-sexual texts, the conventional foundations of the doctrine of celibacy, as retrospective proof of his original contention.[64]

Agrippa's sexually-centred reading of the fall was propagated and complicated by Paracelsus, and introduced into seventeenth-century England, enveloped in an air of profound mystery, by Robert Fludd. Paracelsus maintained that Adam and Eve entirely lacked reproductive organs before the fall. Once Eve began to desire Adam, however, Satan took his cue, manifesting himself in Adam's shape but adding a conspicuous set of genitals which he placed at Eve's disposal. At the moment of the fall a similar transformation took place in Adam's body—'the first sign of monstrosity'—and the sexual organs grew 'like goitres'. The serpent, being hairless from head to tail, was a suitable image to convey this 'singular

---

[63] *Opera* II. 554-8. Cf. Charles G. Nauert, *Agrippa and the Crisis of Renaissance Thought*, Illinois Studies in the Social Sciences, 55 (Urbana, 1965), p. 58.

[64] *Opera* II. 553-64. The notion that circumcision shows the location of the original sin can be found in St. Zeno of Verona; cf. Coppens, p. 507.

arcanum'. Satan thus 'corrupted and polluted their virginity', but only by prompting deeply buried desires in Adam and Eve themselves: they were like adolescents exploring with their hands in forbidden areas, and 'Adam always longed for the apple of the garden, that is, the womb out of which he came.' In short, 'they were themselves the tree and the fruit.'[65]

In Fludd's more Manichaean system, Adam is originally a good Daimon, with a 'diaphanous or even luminous' body, while Eve, 'created not for carnal concupiscence but as a help and companion in the contemplative life', is 'colder, more opaque and more imperfect,' and therefore naturally fitter for Satan's temptation. Adam should have heeded the divine command to 'increase, grow up and multiply, and remember that bodily love is the cause of death'—the precise words of the Hermetic Scripture—but instead he abandoned spiritual propagation for the 'sphere of generation'; his fleshly eyes opened as his spiritual eyes closed, and he became an evil Daimon. The agent of this corruption, and the cause of all human misery, was of course the '*concupiscentia carnis affectus*' and its outcome, sexual intercourse with Eve. Fludd supports Agrippa's thesis with Agrippa's chain of Scriptural arguments, adding a few of his own. He notices, for example, that the sense of nakedness only occurred after both had sinned together, and that the 'serpent' as well as Eve herself is cursed in terms of 'the womb and seed of the woman'. He adds details from the Old Testament: Leviticus warns against the impurity of the sperm, Solomon praises virginity and paints a grim picture of sexual exhaustion. No one could deny, Fludd concludes, that Adam's carnal act is 'abominable to the heart of God'.[66]

Agrippa and Fludd both recognize the danger posed to their thesis by God's blessing of 'increase and multiply', and reserve this principal objection for the crown of their argument. If sexual procreation is an abomination, given at best as a 'concession' to alleviate frail mortality, then God must have meant some other kind of productivity, which must somehow be both spiritual and

---

[65] *De Generatione Stultorum* and *Liber Azoth*, quot. in Gerbi, pp. 98-100; cf. Bayle, 'Adam' G, and Robert James, *A Medical Dictionary* (1743-5), 'Menses', which attributes Paracelsus's detestation of sexuality and the female body to his having been accidentally castrated by a sow.

[66] *Tractatus Theologico-Philosophicus . . . de Vita, de Morte, de Resurrectione* (Oppenheim, 1617), pp. 85-97. Fludd and Agrippa are both recognized as proponents of the sexual hypothesis in Bayle, 'Eve' B.

physical, since the 'multiplication' of man was intended to fill up the numbers of the fallen angels. Agrippa then returns to the Greek Fathers repudiated by Augustine, interpreting the Old Testament metaphor of 'spiritual seed' to refer, not only to the growth of holiness in the mind, but to some mysterious process by which man would have given birth in the state of innocence.[67]

In *De Occulta Philosophia* Agrippa elaborates this theory and reveals its connection to verbal art. If the Logos informs our utterance, entering our minds 'as seed into the matrix for generation', our words can perform the miracle of univocal or perfect generation. Just as Buddha gave birth out of his side, and just as some Islamic 'Nefesogli' are supposed to be 'born by a certain occult manner of Divine dispensation without carnall copulation', so Christ can make the human reason 'bring forth gods', and can transform the faithful into 'sons of God, who are not born of the will of flesh, or of man, or of a menstruous woman'. Non-carnal birth among the infidels may be pure myth, but in Christ it is absolutely true. How then can we conceive by the light of His countenance? All members of the human body, Agrippa argues, 'represent something in God whose image they bear'. By keeping each one clean, it can be transformed into its divine equivalent; 'even in our passions we represent God ... by a certain Analogy.' It is thus a sublimated Eros that turns the adept into a matrix for holy generation: 'the image of God', for Agrippa, 'is man, at least such a man that by a phrensie from *Venus* is made like to God, and lives in the mind only, and receives God into himself.'[68]

Agrippa's astonishing vision is translated into practical science by Paracelsus. He proves his reading of Genesis, and his theory of non-genital procreation, from parallels in the natural world—the unicorn, the basilisk, and the thousand elemental spirits who throng the mines and mountain passes. He maintains that all generation is in fact a process of putrefaction and disintegration that began

[67] Agrippa, *Opera* II. 557-8, 563-4; Fludd, p. 95.
[68] *Three Books of Occult Philosophy*, tr. J. F. (1651), pp. 382-4, 461-4, 507-8 (*De Occulta Philosophia*, III. xiii, xxxvi, xlix). In his 'feminist' tract Agrippa also refers to the 'Nefesogli', as evidence that women can produce offspring without the help of men (*Female Pre-eminence*, tr. Henry Care (1670), pp. 26-8); Bodin refers to the same legend ('Nephlis ogli') when gathering evidence for virgin birth in nature (*Das Heptaplomeres des Jean Bodin*, ed. G. E. Guhrauer (Berlin, 1841), p. 235, mistranslated in Kuntz, p. 284). The word seems to derive from Turkish *nefes* 'breath' (or *nefis* 'soul' or 'self', from Arabic *nefes*) and *oğlu* 'sons' (I am grateful to Muhammad Eissa for advice on this point).

with the fall, and ascribes to menstrual blood, the quintessence of this degeneration, a wide range of venomous and magical powers. (Van Helmont was later to make fresh discoveries in this field of research.) The spiritual adept, however, provided he maintained absolute chastity, could begin to regain the procreative powers of the first Adam. Paracelsus himself had succeeded in this supreme experiment: he had grown a human being or *homunculus* from sperm, without the aid of a female.[69]

For Fludd, on the other hand, this physicalist application of 'holy generation' runs the danger of repeating Adam's original sin. The physical realm is nothing but a sordid and devilish entrapment, and man should confine himself to 'chaste generation' in the soul alone, in memory of the state of innocence when he would have produced 'spiritual children' from a 'spiritualized body'. The motive for Adam's sexual fall, in Fludd as in Leone and van Helmont, is the vainglorious emulation of divine creativity. *Creation* is the privilege of God alone; *generation* is appropriate to humans, but only in a spiritual form. Adam is invaded by the impious desire to turn generation into creation, by 'the appetite to fabricate beings similar to himself' as God had done. Thus he 'rebels against God's power and command' in the very act of copulation, not by reducing sexuality to lust, but by 'foolishly and ambitiously desiring to create other beings in the manner of God'. Genesis 4:1 and 5:3 would appear to confirm Fludd's interpretation, since the identical words are applied to God's creation and Eve's pregnancy, but understandably he does not make use of this evidence; the sacred text clearly refers, not to a demonic rebellion, but to the blessing of physical increase and the birth of the pious Seth.[70]

The fantasy of non-sexual reproduction is an aberration within Christianity, but an understandable aberration. If a large sector of the orthodox believe that Eve was created exclusively for procreation, and if every commentator agrees that, for whatever reason, there was no copulation in the state of innocence, it is all too easy

[69] Pagel, *Paracelsus*, pp. 87, 113-17, 149, 215-16, 291, 335; Gerbi, p. 99; cf. n. 52 above, and James, 'Menses'. Keith Thomas notes a 'claim made in 1533 by Edith Hooker of New Alresford, Hants, that she could enable women to conceive *sine virili semine*', which 'may have been a folk version of the alchemical attempt to create *homunculi*' (*Religion and the Decline of Magic* (1971; repr. Harmondworth, 1978), p. 222).

[70] *Tractatus*, p. 92; *De Supernaturali ... Microcosmi* (1619), quot. in Gerbi, p. 103. Fludd may later have softened his attitude to physical generation in the light of his scientific experiments; cf. *Mosaicall Philosophy* (1659), pp. 166-7.

to supply the missing term. As Alice Sutcliffe put it, expostulating directly with Eve on the pains of childbirth, 'The game which thou by that same fruit didst winne, / Thou now dost find to bee but little worth.'[71] And when sexual intercourse is universally identified as the *means of transmission* of an overwhelming and catastrophic Original Sin, if not exactly the sin itself, then it is difficult not to regard it as an abomination in the sight of God—particularly when Christ was born from a virgin. Aquinas explicitly states that if Adam or Eve had 'eaten the fruit' on their own (a question that Browne thought better left to God), sin would never have been passed on to their progeny.[72] For the credulous masculinist, moreover, Satan's ascendency with the woman must indicate some sexual complicity. Philip Camerarius, for example, explains the 'efficacie' of Satan over Eve by noting that 'many Authors affirme that Serpents ... desire the companie of women', that 'all the Rabbins are of this mind, that the devills ... have great power over one's concupiscence and privie members,' and that '*Philo* and the Hebrewes say that the Serpent signifieth allegorically, Lecherie.'[73] In such a climate of opinion the notion of holy asexuality was never far from the surface, and it recurred persistently in the visionary imagination.

Abnormal methods of procreation, devoid of carnal pollution, were sometimes proposed to explain the Immaculate Conception: Rabelais parodies them in the birth of Gargantua, who climbs out of his mother's left ear (the *conceptio per aurem* of the Virgin) while the midwives are occupied below with a false birth of collapsed intestines—a comic prefiguration of Milton's Sin.[74] Browne, though he rejects many of Paracelsus's claims including the creation of a homunculus, still yearned for the ideal state of masculine self-sufficiency and vegetable reproduction. Browne's wish for tree-like procreation was linked to the Paracelsan homunculus by later

[71] *Meditations of Mans Mortalitie*, 2nd edn. (1634), pp. 145-6.
[72] *Summa Theologiae* Ia-IIae, Quot. 81, art. 5. Aquinas's point is actually that sin comes from the male, so that normal sexual intercourse between an innocent Adam and a fallen Eve would not have transmitted original sin.
[73] *The Living Librarie*, tr. John Moll (1621), p. 249, referring to Bodin, *Daemonomania*, II. i. Rabbinical theories of Eve's copulation with the serpent were frequently recorded in the commentaries (e.g. Williams, *Common Expositor*, p. 141), and were revived by the Muggletonians (see n. 55 above).
[74] *Gargantua*, ch. 6; *PL* II. 752–802 (and perhaps IX. 1067–8, 'O Eve, in evil hour didst thou give ear / To that false worm'). For satire on theories of the Immaculate Conception, see A. J. Krailsheimer, *Rabelais and the Franciscans* (Oxford, 1963), pp. 154–5.

satirists, and Bayle associated it with the hermaphrodites in Gabriel de Foigny's utopian fantasy *La Terre Australe connue* (1676), whose 'children grow in their bowels as fruits do upon trees' and who believe 'that a creature could not better resemble [the supreme being] than by acting alone in its productions as he does, and that an action performed by the intercourse of two persons could not be so perfect as those that are performed by one and the same person.' De Foigny's 'Australians' also told a version of the Serpent-Eve marriage to explain the origin of the half-men or monosexuals—a myth which Bayle traces to the Gnostics.[75] Bayle further connects de Foigny and Browne to the mystic visions of Antoinette Bourignon, who—herself influenced by Paracelsus—describes the original Adam as a transparent hermaphrodite who produces human eggs from a mouth situated where fallen man has genitals; the division into 'two imperfect Sexes, unable to produce their like alone, as Trees and Plants do,' proves that after the fall we became 'Monsters in Nature' ('Adam' G, 'Sadeur' B). Francis Mercurius van Helmont, the son of the great medical visionary, proposed even at the end of the seventeenth century that Adam and Eve were both hermaphrodites, each capable of generating children from within their own bodies.[76]

So powerful, then, is the nostalgia for a sexless innocence, and the urge to rescue procreation from the abomination of physicality, that it can sway the judgement of a Browne as well as an Agrippa or a Bourignon. It prevails not only with the mystic and the utopian, but with the reasonable and even-tempered anatomist, the judicious Anglican forbear of Physico-theology, who discovered in every other feature of the material world the miracle of divine providence.

When Milton's Adam is at the depth of his despair, overwhelmed by the realization of sin but as yet incapable of self-analysis, he too bursts into an arraignment of procreation, and reveals in the process that the real target of such fantasies is not sexuality *per se*, but woman.[77] Though later readers have sometimes taken these as the author's sentiments, the whole speech must obviously be

[75] *Religio Medici and Other Works*, p. 35; n. 11 above; Bayle, 'Sadeur' D and E; de Foigny, *A New Discovery of Terra Incognita Australia* (1693), pp. 120-1.
[76] *Quaedam Praemeditatae et Consideratae Cogitationes super ... Genesis* (Amsterdam, 1697), pp. 48, 51, and cf. 77 (hermaphrodite animals).
[77] PL X. 888-95; cf. Sir Richard Steele (ed.), *The Ladies Library* (1714), I. 2-4, listing this passage as an example of the prevailing misogyny of literature, and McColley (ch. 1) for later versions of this error.

interpreted dramatically: Adam gives the cry of Euripides's Hippolytos or Shakespeare's Posthumus, directed as much against 'the woman's part in me' as against the divine creation. He questions the providence of childbearing just as Samson questions the design of the body when he rages over his blindness. Adam's shower of misogynistic clichés—woman came from a crooked rib, woman is the sole cause of the fall, woman was made only for childbearing—is Milton's epic expansion of the first fallen excuse, *the woman whom thou gavest to be with me, she gave me of the tree and I did eat.* The whole weight of *Paradise Lost* and of Milton's ethics pushes against these attitudes. Procreation, which had been actively pursued throughout the period of innocence, is urged by the fallen Adam himself once he has regained his self-control. The prose works defend the God-given usefulness of the passions and the Paradisal raptures of the married state, and refute the 'narrow-Augustinian' notion that woman was created unfit for anything but childbearing. And Gnostic fantasies of alternative methods of birth, memorably revived by Agrippa, Fludd, Boehme, and the van Helmonts, are put decisively in their place—the allegory of Sin.

[*iii*]

Agrippa's original formulation of the sexual-fall hypothesis hovers between religious asceticism and profane wit. It was expropriated in all seriousness by Hermeticists and theosophists as a focus for their impatience with the body and their horror of the female. But it also opened the way to a different kind of libertine reading, that gleefully emphasizes the potentially comic physicality that Calvin had denounced as puerile. The extremes of 'spiritualization' and secular mockery coincide, as Calvin had feared, in their urge to discover sexual references in the most fundamental texts of Scripture, and to equate the fall itself with some particularly scandalous form of desire. If Agrippa and Fludd suppress the biological vision of Genesis 1 in favour of the shadowy intimations of sexual abomination in the rest of Genesis, the jocular tradition does the reverse—but with strangely similar results.

'Increase and multiply' was reportedly used by the 'wicked Libertines' of Elizabethan London to justify their free and easy eroticism, and by the Adamites and Ranters to initiate their orgies; the flaunting of this text as a fornicator's motto was so widespread,

4. The Crisis of the Imagination

in mock-learned treatises as well as in tavern wit, that 'well-wisher to the mathematics' became a slang term for a whoremaster.[78] In a similarly carnivalesque spirit, the idea of the phallic serpent prompts Rabelais to create a whole erudite mythology for the Andouillets, the race of tripe-sausages or chitterlings liberated by Pantagruel: 'it is still maintained in certain Universities that the Tempter was that kind of chitterling called Ithyphallus, into which good Sir Priapus was once upon a time transformed—a great tempter of women in "Paradises", as the Greeks say, which are "gardens" in French' (IV. 38). (Browne was evidently quite accurate when he consigned such physical speculations to 'Pantagruel's Library'.) In visual art, we may find a hint of the 'Talmudic' or Agrippan interpretation in the Sistine Chapel *Fall*: Eve's obscene finger-gesture, visible only to the close observer, signals the possibility of a private sexual reference, and her kneeling posture close to Adam's groin suggests that at the moment of the fall she is poised between two meanings of 'eating the forbidden fruit'.[79] A parallel interpretation of the Tree of Life appears in Donne's Elegy 'Nature's lay Idiot': once his naïve mistress has been impropriated and 'refin'd ... into a blis-full Paradise', once he has 'Planted knowledge and lifes tree in thee', then the inevitable fall occurs, since her new sexual sophistication leads her to other men. In *Metempsychosis* the young Donne comes even closer to the Agrippan thesis. Though he does not openly equate the fall with sexual experiment, he implies this by making the immediate consequences erotic: the soul of the fatal apple enters an aphrodisiac mandrake, riddlingly described so as to suggest the genitals themselves, then a cock-sparrow who squeezes out his life in continuous copulation, and finally, after a number of other highly sexual episodes, returns into the womb of Eve. This story is interwoven with a scandalous secret history of Adam and Eve's family, and an ironic commentary on the emergence of typical human failings in the earliest years.[80]

---

[78] Phillip Stubbs, *The Anatomy of Abuses* (1595), p. 59; 2. 4. ii above; Edward Ward, *The Libertines Choice*, 2nd edn. (1709), pp. 8-9; [Daniel McLoughlin], *An Essay upon Improving and Adding to the Strength of Great-Britain and Ireland by Fornication* (1735), esp. t.-p. and p. 18.

[79] Leo Steinberg, 'Eve's Idle Hand', *Art Journal*, XXV (1975-6), 130-5; I owe this reference to Paul Barolsky. Steinberg's sexual interpretations of Renaissance painting should be approached with great caution, but in this case the evidence is persuasive.

[80] Donne pretends to find in the primeval age an innocent form of sexuality that

166   4. *The Crisis of the Imagination*   [SECT.

These 'satyric' tranformations of Genesis flourished in the seventeenth century, and continued well into the eighteenth, in learned treatises as well as more obviously comic genres. In de Montfaucon de Villars's urbane *Comte de Gabalis* (1670), the source of Pope's mythology in *The Rape of the Lock*, the Agrippan hypothesis is combined with a Paracelsan account of the spirits that Adam would have enjoyed in the unfallen state; the adept is promised a spectacular erotic life with the sylphs, gnomes, and salamanders—a prospect which gives new point to his devout and ascetic preparations. And in Adriaan Beverland's obsessively erudite treatises, the equation of original sin and sexual discovery is pushed to the limit. Drawing on an unparalleled knowledge of ancient erotic practices and Christian arguments for celibacy, he effectively demolishes the sacred text, by first equating the fall with Roman perversions and Middle Eastern phallus-cults, and then explaining away 'increase and multiply' as a corruption in the text. Beverland represents the fullest expansion of Agrippa's work, reproducing not only his arguments but his uncertain balance of religious fervour and outrageous wit: he mingles misogynistic and ascetic diatribes, apparently genuine, with obscene puns and Restoration lampoons.[81] In Agrippa the spiritual visionary seems to predominate, but in Beverland the hater of the flesh gives way to irreverence and scepticism; he belongs rather among *libertins érudits* such as Francis Osborne, who speaks scornfully of Eve as a 'Beldame' and a broken-down horse, or La Mothe Le Vayer, who delighted in juxtaposing Biblical exegesis, classical erotology, Renaissance paradoxes, and Rabbinical speculations about the sexual adventures of Adam with the animals.[82]

Milton was aware that his own sexualization of Eden in the divorce tracts, a genuine and heartfelt evocation of the Paradisal and Solomonic bliss of ideal marriage, could be received as a

---

did not need artificial stimulants, when 'Man to beget, and woman to conceive / Askt not of rootes, nor of cock-sparrowes, leave' (st. 22), but the prominence of the mandrake-root and the cock-sparrow in the poem—precisely these aphrodisiacs— throws an ironic light on this apparent praise of innocence.

[81] *Peccatum Originale* ('Eleutheropolis: Adae et Evae', 1678), reissued as *De Peccato Originale* (Leiden, 1679), *passim*; *De Stolatae Virginitatis Jure Lucubratio Academica* (1680), ed. and (unreliably) tr. Francis D. Byrne (Paris, 1905), pp. 6, 10–14, 56, 90–4, 113, 168, 178–92, 242, 267, 288–91.

[82] Osborne, *Advice to a Son* (Oxford, 1656), pp. 38, 47; Pintard, pp. 144, 230 (and cf. Bayle, 'Eve' H, for Adam's bestiality).

libertine gesture: 'the brood of Belial ... to whom no liberty is pleasing but unbridl'd and vagabond lust without pale or partition, will laugh broad perhaps, to see so great a strength of Scripture mustering up in favour, as they suppose, of their debausheries.' He recognizes the threat, in the mid-1640s, of a well-established libertine subculture with its own travestic mode of reading Scripture; and in *Paradise Lost*, written when the 'Sons of Belial' had truly gained the ascendency, he frames the most erotic passages with bold attacks on libertine sexuality. This precaution, meant to 'drive far off the barbarous dissonance' of the Restoration ethos, was particularly appropriate because, in the revolutionary 1640s, his own divorce tracts had indeed been taken as incitements to debauchery. Milton then suffered the ignominy of being simultaneously identified with both of Calvin's pernicious extremes, ultra-radical sectarianism and sexual libertinism.[83]

Milton's 'Sons of Belial' represent the coarse, Rabelaisian form of libertinism, 'laughing broad' at the sexual dimension in Genesis and the Song of Songs. But in lyric poetry the same paradoxical and irreverent wit developed into an art of sly refinement. In Cavalier evocations of the 'first Age', as we shall see in chapter 7, the sensuous imagination creates a happy picture of primeval sexuality, with many teasing hints of Genesis—a secular and illicit counterpart to Milton's Paradise of wedded love, and the precise opposite of the Agrippan interpretation. The fall is then cleverly simulated by sudden reversals of attitude, so that the 'noble dream' of untainted Eros is revealed as either an artificial Paradise or one already lost.[84] Or else the parallel with Scripture will be a decoy. Charles Cotton's 'Forbidden Fruit', for example, edges nearer and nearer to the scandalous Beverlandian interpretation of Genesis: the joy he desires is 'in your gardens centre placed'; his own 'tree of life' is 'arbuscular in dresse, / Yet not forbidden neretheless'; this fruit would tempt any man to forfeit eternity. But in the last stanza he shifts the reference, pretending that all along he had located his *double entendre*, not in the sacred garden of Eden, but in the pagan garden of the Hesperides.[85]

---

[83] *Prose* II. 225; *PL* I. 497–502, IV. 765–70, VII. 32–4; ch. 6 n. 21 below.

[84] 7. 1. iii below; cf. also the Elegy 'Variety', once attributed to Donne.

[85] *Poems*, ed. John Buxton (1958), pp. 211–12; M was to reverse this conceit by calling the fruits of Paradise '*Hesperian* Fables true, / If true, here only' (*PL* IV. 250–1).

The effect of these refinements is not merely to secularize and physicalize the myth, but to transpose it into the world of comedy. Eve becomes the perpetually seducible wife, Satan the maker of cuckolds, Adam the inadequate husband. Adam *cornutus* appears occasionally as a satiric theme in visual art; in Cranach's *Fall* in the Courtauld (Lee Collection), a stag's antlers conspicuously frame the genitals of Adam, who is rubbing the forepart of his head. Satan had been granted sexual jealousy by Rabbinical commentators, and his 'seduction' of Eve, so called by St. Paul, had been expanded into florid amorous rhetoric by medieval and Renaissance poets. Plebeian bawdry might occasionally aver that Eve cuckolded Adam 'because he knew / Not how to exercise the gifts / Which nature did indue' (this is part of a 'hymn' supposedly sung by the Ranters).[86] But the crystallization of these comic possibilities, the final appropriation of the sacred text for worldly amusement and the confirmation of secular attitudes, came with Jean-François Sarasin's sonnet, 'Lors qu'Adam vit cette jeune beauté'. With such a dazzling lover as Adam, Sarasin begins, we can be sure that Eve was not 'cruelle'. Surely here, if anywhere, 'The World had a Woman of Faithful Behavior'—especially when no other man existed to 'turn her innocent Heart'? Unfortunately not:

> Tho' *Adam* abounded with vigorous youth,
> Tho' Beauty and Wit did his Person commend,
> *Eve* yet was dispos'd new Admirers to get;
> And, being a *Woman*, chose rather to lend
> Her ear to the *Devil*, than not to coquet.

In this lyric—widely quoted, translated, and imitated from the 1650s onwards—Genesis is entirely transformed into an encounter between 'beautiful and witty' lovers, an engagement on the sexual battlefield of the beau monde, and the illustration for a teasing, cynical *maxime d'amour*.[87]

[86] L. R., *The Ranters Ranting* (1650), p. 3.
[87] 'Sonnet à Monsieur de Charleval', in *Poesies* (Paris, 1658), p. 61; both this edn. (vol. I of *Œuvres*, Paris, 1663) and *Œuvres* (Paris, 1694) have 'caqueter' in the final line, but the text in Bayle ('Eve' K), and in other citations and translations, reads 'coquet[er]'. Bayle denounces the profane wit of this sonnet and analyses the jealousy that motivates such accusations against the female sex, before going on in Remark L to make similar criticisms of Loredano (ch. 7 n. 26 below); both works had been included in a single volume, later tr. into English as *The History of Adam and Eve . . . Whereunto is Annex'd M. Sarrasin's Fine Epigram on Eve's Coquetry* (c.1720), p. 76, from which my text quotation is taken. The poem is also quot. and discussed in François Poulain de la Barre, *De l'égalité des deux sexes* (Paris, 1673),

4. The Crisis of the Imagination

Donne himself had continued to develop and refine the cynical paradoxes latent in the fall-story, and its sardonic lessons about the nature of sexuality. Even in the pious *First Anniversary*, and later still in his Nethersole wedding-sermon, he repeats with relish the outrageous proposition first made in the brash and youthful *Metempsychosis*—that 'the first wedding was our funeral', since Eve slew her husband, and since her daughters continue to kill us 'delightfully' by sexual depletion (ch. 3 n. 30 above). The most poised of these variations on the Agrippa-Beverland thesis, however, and the most brilliant crossing of the sacred myth with the conventions of the world of love, is the lyric that provides the first epigraph of this book—'Twickenham Garden'.

This poem is an exercise in what Marvell would later call 'love begotten by Despair upon Impossibility', and it is also a precise parallel to Donne's own verse letter in praise of the Countess of Bedford and her estate.[88] The final paradox of the letter—Lady Bedford is an angel, but an excluding angel, the 'Cherubin' of Paradise—is placed at the centre of 'Twickenham Garden'. Donne pays her the gallant tribute of pretending to be hopelessly in love with her, perpetually doomed to grieve because of her perpetual disdain. He conforms to the definition of the modern lover in 'Loves Deity', a slave to the 'custom' of adoring one who scorns him; in the first age, 'before the god of Love was born', such unnatural situations could never have arisen.[89] The garden setting evokes another and even earlier first age, however—the immediately post-lapsarian era of *Metempsychosis*. In 'Nature's lay Idiot' Donne had compared his liaison to the creation and loss of the garden of Eden; now he turns the private Paradise of Twickenham into an emblem of his amorous state.

It is a Paradise only known through its loss, however. The central concern of the poem is not amorous desire or pain but authenticity. The real fall, for Donne as for Hamlet, is the separation of seeming and being: 'Alas, hearts do not in eyes shine.' (Shakespeare expresses

---

p. 82 (*The Woman as Good as the Man, or the Equallity of Both Sexes*, tr. A. L. (1677), p. 63), and imitated in Bernard Mandeville, *The Virgin Unmask'd* (1709), pp. 129-30.

[88] 'To the Countesse of Bedford' [II] ('You have refin'd mee'), ll. 70-2; cf. Marvell, 'The Definition of Love'.

[89] This lyric from *Songs and Sonnets* is also a compressed version of a verse letter, 'To the Countesse of Huntingdon' [I] ('That unripe side of earth'), ll. 1-76—another of Donne's ironic reversals of the supposedly innocent primeval age.

the same unhappiness in Sonnet 93: 'How like Eve's apple doth thy beauty grow, / If thy sweet virtue answer not thy show!') Only Donne's tears have the authentic flavour, he protests, and only Donne's Petrarchan mistress is 'true': 'O perverse sexe, where none is true but shee, / Who's therefore true, because her truth kills mee.'[90] The poem thus closes with the theme of authentication-through-pain broached in the first stanza. Donne makes Twickenham garden into a true Paradise not by infusing 'amorous delicacies', and certainly not by planting his 'tree of life' there, but by destroying it: he brings with him 'the spider love', which converts manna to gall, and also—'that this place may thoroughly be thought / True Paradise'—the serpent itself. What is the 'serpent' that brings about this Satanic miracle? The lover's grief? The sense of irony that explodes the certainties of enjoyment? Donne's own phallic intrusion into the innocent world of Petrarchanism—another variation on Agrippa's equation of sex and the fall? The image is all the more powerful for being unresolved, for remaining a shadowy erotic implication. Donne's central insight is perfectly clear, however: the authenticating mark of Paradise is its own annihilation.

[*iv*]

These various sexualizations of the Paradise myth, developments of hints and shadows in the original text, are certainly not all as 'puerile' as Calvin thought; Donne's, in particular, is strangely serious despite its playful context. Within his own premises Calvin is right, however: they do localize the concept of sin, and they do diminish the possibility of a profound engagement of the whole being with the whole text. The allegorical-visionary tradition translates Genesis into intense but inaccessible private fantasies, and enlarges the gulf between the state of perfection and the concerns of common humanity. The libertine tradition drains the myth of tragic seriousness, and 'uncrowns' its sublime pretensions; Adam and Eve are stripped of their Paradisal splendour, and join us in a wry solidarity of the flesh. The fall-story becomes either

---

[90] 'Twickenham Garden', ll. 26-7. In the parallel verse letter to Lady Bedford, she is praised as an exception to the rule that 'good and lovely [are] not one' (l. 55); in the anti-Petrarchan letter to Lady Huntingdon, he reverses his equation of 'truth' with sexual rejection—'Who strives, through womans scornes, women to know, / Is lost, and seekes his shadow to outgoe' (ll. 65-6). When he praises his own tears in 'Twickenham Garden', Donne adds a further level of irony by impersonating a mountebank.

4. The Crisis of the Imagination

'fabulous' or mundane, a theosophic romance or an anecdote of the Way of the World.

Once again we find a crisis of divergence and diminution, a polarization of imagination and realism; we must again wonder how Milton's task might have been defined or channelled by this narrowing of the fall to 'carnal knowledge'. We cannot prove in every case that Milton is responding to contemporary movements—his connection with Boehme, for example, is only circumstantial—but there is still abundant evidence of his meditation on esoteric and libertine themes. The list of exploded 'fables' and 'empty dreams' in Milton's writings, in the divorce tracts as well as in *Paradise Lost*, is an index to the teeming multiplicity of interpretative possibilities, a map of sexual misreading. Nor does he merely refute; in keeping with the dialectic theories of *Areopagitica*, he 'tempers' these heteroclite opinions into 'useful drugs', expropriating and transforming them for the greater 'growth and compleating' of his vision.[91] He counters both 'carnal' and 'spiritual' reductiveness with his own bold resexualization, not only of the fall, but of the state of innocence.

By filling Paradise with 'the spirit of love and amorous delight' and the 'enormous bliss' of consummated sexuality, Milton breaks away from the standard interpretation; but unlike the equally adventurous 'Artists' of the esoteric tradition, his imagination flies *towards* rather than away from the 'sphere of generation'. Indeed, when he calls marriage the 'prime institution' and highest state of mankind, or when he makes sexual delight the 'sum' of Adam's happiness, he even approaches a different kind of libertine principle—that 'there is no heaven save woman'. Like the urbane Sarasin, he treats the encounter of Adam and Eve as a romantic *coup de foudre*, but with an epic seriousness and a heartfelt plenitude of sensuous delight that entirely eliminate the idea that Genesis might be a topic for light verse. (The Petrarchan convolutions of 'Twickenham Garden' are transferred to the seducer's rhetoric of Satan, and their association with loss and pain thereby translated from conceit into reality; the concern with fallen appearances is likewise deepened—on first encountering the 'naked majesty' of the genitals, Milton turns to denounce the 'mere shows of seeming pure' that have replaced true innocence.) Even Voltaire took *Paradise Lost* seriously as an amorous epic, enough to correct

---

[91] *Prose* II. 521, 528; see 5. ii below.

the 'smile' that appeared on every face when he described its subject-matter.[92]

Milton's ideal of wedded love is defended by vociferous contrast with both extremes, with libertine 'Court Amours' and with false ascetic visions of 'purity'. He rescues from esotericism its most profound idea—that we are analogous to God in our passions, that humanity itself, transfigured by 'a frenzy from Venus', is the image of God—but he rejects its fantastic denial of the flesh. The love that 'is the scale / By which to heav'nly Love thou maist ascend' is rooted in the love that binds 'our first Parents' and that is recreated 'in some proportion' in every true marriage. When Milton defends the necessity of passion in *Areopagitica*, he applies his words equally to the fallen Christian and to Adam in the state of innocence; without his desires and his imagination he would have been an 'artificiall *Adam*', a mere lifeless puppet.[93]

But Milton does not turn away from the uglier side of sexuality. He is not afraid to make Adam and Eve the first fornicators as well as the first couple locked in wedded love. At the very moment of the fall, as an immediate 'operation' of the fruit, before they are aware of nakedness and shame, they blaze with desire and copulate on the flowers—the 'seal' and 'solace' of their transgression. This aphrodisiac conception of the act of eating comes daringly close to Boehme, van Helmont, and Beverland; but the difference is all the more striking. Milton's Adam and Eve fall into lust, not from some etherial condition of magic asexuality, but from full and happy consummation; even in the state of guilt their love-making is not a rape, as it was in van Helmont, but a 'mutual' and pleasurable act.

Forbidden sexuality is not suppressed in Milton's epic, but vividly registered as a potentiality. All the most marginal and perverse legends of paganism, Gnosticism, and Rabbinical exegesis, everything that Beverland, Le Vayer, or Bayle would dredge up, can be found openly displayed in *Paradise Lost*, not to undermine the privileged ideal but to define it by dramatic opposition. The sexual abominations of Baal-Peor, Astarte and Belial, Pan and Sylvanus, are ranged against the 'Rites Mysterious of connubial Love'. The misogynistic yearning for 'some other way to propagate mankind' is revealed as a counsel of despair, inimical both to the eagerness

---

[92] *PL* IV. 316; Shawcross, pp. 249, 250, 252.
[93] Cf. n. 68 above; *PL* VIII. 591–2; ch. 5 below, *passim*.

of Paradisal Eros and to the more sober love that reunites the man and the woman, 'hand in hand', at the close of the poem. The possibility of Adam's coupling with the animals is raised, but only to define by contrast the kind of erotic companionship that only humans can enjoy. The legend of Satan's sexual jealousy is revived and promoted to a major dimension of his character, but its significance is reversed; rather than proving Eve's complicity and Satan's predominance over the 'privie members', his amorous daze makes him for a short while 'stupidly good'.[94] Milton's Paradise is not a blank space of negative innocence but a Borgesian 'garden of forked paths', dense with alternative possibilities; he treats them, however, not as a Borgesian (or Boehmean) fantasy, but as a series of concrete choices, a vital concomitant of freedom and responsibility.

[94] *PL* I. 412-57, IV. 707, IV. 742-3, VIII. 589-94, X. 894-5, XII. 648; 7. 1. iii below; cf. n. 73 above and Bayle, 'Eve' A and B. Bayle's contempt for those whose 'Imaginations' lead them to grant Adam and Eve an unfallen sex-life (1. introd. above) is particularly directed against those fabulists who maintain 'that *Eve* was no sooner created than she lost her Virginity, *Adam* enjoying her immediately as soon as he saw her'—precisely what M assumes ('Eve' B, and cf. H, where the idea 'that *Adam* carnally knew *Eve* the very day he was created' is considered as outrageous as Adam's copulation with the animals).

5
Sensuous Poetics and the Ethics of Confrontation

MILTONIC THEORIES OF THE WORD

Many there be that complain of divine Providence for suffering *Adam* to transgresse, foolish tongues! when God gave him reason, he gave him freedom to choose, for reason is but choosing; he had been else a meer artificiall *Adam*, such an *Adam* as he is in the motions. We our selves esteem not of that obedience, or love, or gift, which is of force: God therefore left him free, set before him a provoking object, ever almost in his eyes; herein consisted his merit, herein-the right of his reward, the praise of his abstinence. Wherefore did he create passions within us, pleasures round about us, but that these rightly temper'd are the very ingredients of vertu?

(*Areopagitica*)

We have seen in the previous chapters that Milton inherited a complex mass of problems when he attempted to understand, evaluate and recreate Paradisal marriage. Some of these problems, we saw, were inherent in the text and its original incorporation into the book of Genesis: thus sexuality comes to be entangled, in some mythically powerful but elusive way, with the problem of knowledge and the problem of the 'evil imagination'. Others were created and intensified by successive generations of commentators, eager to convert the myth into the basis of the ideology of marriage, the notion of a cataclysmic Fall, and the doctrines of Original Sin and Redemption, or to ratify their private fantasies. We have seen, too, that emotion and imagination, shifting terms denoting treacherous areas of the mind, could nevertheless be recognized as essential means of reaching beyond these textual and doctrinal difficulties, and realizing the happiness of primeval man and woman. Through them sin entered the world, but through them humanity may regain Paradise. As one who combined the

5. The Ethics of Confrontation

role of poet and exegete, Milton experienced these contradictions in a particularly urgent form.[1]

In Milton's own lifetime, moreover, we have seen that interpretations and applications of Genesis multiply at an astonishing rate. This is not simply a question of Reformation versus Counter-Reformation, but of different readings generated by neo-Platonism and secular libertinism, visionary theosophy, Christian Cabbalism, scepticism, and the various radical 'Adamite' or Antinomian sects that re-emerged during the English Revolution. Milton himself responded to this crisis of interpretation in ways that reflect the divisions within his own mind: he dissociated himself from its 'fanatick' and vulgar element—though this did not stop his conservative critics from denouncing him as a dangerous radical—but he welcomed the energetic polyphony of opinion and shared in several of these revisionist tendencies, sometimes directly, sometimes by a kind of osmosis or interior dialogue with them. His synthesis of the disintegrating Genesis-tradition shows a striking commitment to imaginative boldness and personal vision, within a framework of physical and emotional realism. Like Rembrandt, Milton is both a comprehensive figure of his age, responding to a great range of possibilities, and an isolated individual, 'extraordinary and singuiar', who converts all interpretations to his own private mythology. This is especially apparent in his very personal treatment, in the divorce tracts and other prose works of the revolutionary period as well as in *Paradise Lost*, of Genesis and sexual love.

Milton's responses to the problems of Genesis were intensified by his active participation in the political and religious crisis of his age. His 'mysterious' and lofty sense of his own poetic mission kept him in contemplative isolation for most of his younger years, but in the 1640s—impelled by reforming zeal and marital disaster—he committed his mind and his art to building a new social order and bringing about the restitution of all things. He was both poet and iconoclast, 'casting down imaginations' and destroying the false images of Royalism, while raising the regenerate imagination to new heights. This process is not suspended, but internalized and deepened, after his return to isolation in the 1660s; completing his

---

[1] For an interesting account of the vagaries of the term 'imagination', with some cautions about applying it to Milton, see John Guillory, *Poetic Authority* (NY, 1983), ch. 1 (I owe this ref. to Maureen Quilligan).

epic in an increasingly secular age is itself an act of defiance. Milton's revolutionary prose and his mature poetry are both dedicated, 'in some proportion', to the goal of radical regeneration first declared in the period of engagement—repairing the damage of the fall, leading his countrymen to the gates of Paradise, and overthrowing false images.

[*ii*]

The problem of reclaiming Paradise, whether through Biblical theology or by an act of the poetic imagination, had to be related to the larger epistemological and ethical inheritance of the fall. The problematic status of fallen consciousness, a gateway or an obstacle to redemption, was not an abstraction for Milton but a living issue, forced upon him by the crisis that produced the divorce tracts, *Of Education* and *Areopagitica*—the overwhelming sequence of social conflict and civil war, of marital failure and public denunciation of his attempts to set it right. He experienced the radical dilemma with especial urgency: whether to live by 'Paradisal' or 'fallen' standards, whether to dream of primitive righteousness in the state and Edenic happiness in the marriage-bed, whether to accept the *status quo* in a world at once collapsing and reborn. The great prose works cannot solve these intractable questions in any definitive way, but they set in motion a process of apprehension—characteristically dialectic, dynamic, and contradictory—that still works at the core of *Paradise Lost*. Before looking in detail at Paradisal marriage in the divorce tracts and the epic, then, we should briefly recall the famous texts in which Milton defines the capacities of mind and art in a fallen world.

Knowledge of the good, as he declares in *Of Education*, is essential if we are to 'repair the ruins of our first parents'—an astonishingly high claim for the powers of the human mind. *Areopagitica* wrestles with the question that underlies this claim: what kind of knowledge can bring us to this state? Since the fall, Milton explains, the knowledge of good is 'involv'd and interwoven with the knowledge of evil'; indeed, 'that doom which *Adam* fell into' is precisely that of having to know good *by* evil—'not to know good except through evil', as he later put it in the *De Doctrina*. Rather than lamenting this condition like the common expositors, however, Milton explores its moral implications with unusual vigour. Virtue is actually constituted by the knowledge of

5. The Ethics of Confrontation

evil: 'as the state of man now is, what wisdome can there be to choose, what continence to forbeare, without the knowledge of evill?' This knowledge, moreover, must be experiential and deep, not like the 'fugitive', 'cloister'd', and remotely 'Utopian' knowledge of conventional morality, which would keep us in 'perpetuall childhood'. Milton does not go as far as the Ranters, who pursue purity through 'acting sin as no sin', but his ethics still depend upon an activist, confrontational, quasi-physical grasp of evil. The 'warfaring Christian' cannot afford simply to know *of* things, to know in the abstract, but must know 'the utmost that vice promises to his followers'. We can only purge our inherited impurity by trial, 'and triall is by what is contrary'.[2]

The 'triall' of evil concerned Milton throughout his life, but he only arrived at his 'deep-experiential' epistemology in the political and domestic crisis of 1643-5. His model had been hitherto essentially Spenserian: in the imagery of his earlier poetry and prose, admirable characters refuse the charms of sorcerers and sorceresses, dash their cups to the ground, and enter the Bower of Bliss only to demolish it. In his pre-marital writings, however, Milton seems to adopt the external paraphenalia of Spenser without the sense of inwardness that Spenser sometimes captures. Sir Guyon's keenest temptation, for example, comes when he is surprised by sin, feeling intense desire for the bathing nymphs in Acrasia's earthly Paradise. The Ludlow *Mask*, on the other hand, shows us 'what vice promises to his followers', but without the Lady herself ever revealing an inner susceptibility to Comus's deliciously phrased appeals; she does not therefore know 'the utmost', and her working definition of innocence remains essentially the one that conventional commentators gave to Adam and Eve— a solely conceptual knowledge of evil, and a virginal purity untainted by experience.[3] But in *Areopagitica* Milton singles out that

[2] II. 366-7, 514-16, 526, VI. 352 (Col. edn. XV. 114); for the Ranters, see 2. 4. ii above. The notion that virtue depends on trial is standard (e.g. Arnold Williams, *The Common Expositor* (Chapel Hill, 1948), pp. 113-14), but M tends towards the more extreme position that virtue is greater when the danger is greater (e.g. *A Mask*, ll. 591-2), and applies it also to the unfallen state. M's vision is also more dialectical than his predecessors', in the sense that he welcomes emotional and conceptual interchange between hitherto 'sequestered' realities (though it is not dialectical in the Marxist sense).

[3] Cf. ch. 6 nn. 50 and 52 below; *FQ* II. xii. To a 20th-century reader the Lady's immobility (and even the 'gumms' on her seat) could suggest some inner complicity with Comus's seduction, but the agency is still external and magical, as befits the genre.

passionate episode in Spenser as a prime example of his teaching, and amplifies the point by developing other intimate and physical images for the inward knowledge of evil.

Forbidden heresies, sexual temptations, and even the rank pornography of Petronius and Aretino must be allowed to 'work' like homeopathic drugs; without their controlled absorption the soul cannot 'temper' good antidotes. The passions and pleasures themselves, both physical and mental, are God-given agents of temperance, the very constituents of virtue, essential for the 'growth and compleating' of every person; for this reason we are placed in an overwhelmingly abundant world, and given the capacity for infinite craving and infinite speculation. Knowledge itself is a passion in *Areopagitica*, and the encounter with new ideas is presented as a strong, vitalistic, and even erotic process, neither 'cloistered' like a celibate monk nor 'neutrall' like a eunuch.[4] This experiential and sensory theory of virtue became one of Milton's most rooted beliefs: it evidently filled him with the excitement of the challenge rather than with a Pascalian sense of the disorientation and misery of the fall. He even reiterates it in his last works; Christ in *Paradise Regain'd* considers his fast not to have been virtuous until he felt real hunger (II. 245-51), and the argument for tolerance in his final pamphlet—'by reading Controversies' the intelligent man will feel 'his Senses awakt, his Judgement sharpen'd, and the truth which he holds more firmly establish't' (VII. 437-8)—is founded on the same principles as *Areopagitica*.

At times, indeed, we may doubt whether Milton really believed that unfallen epistemology and ethics were any different from our own. Adam and Eve did not have to purge inherited impurity, of course, but in *Paradise Lost* their freedom and individuality must still be proved by 'trial with what is contrary'. Adam may rebuke Eve's excessive thirst for trial in Book IX, and perhaps Milton does reflect upon his own over-eagerness in *Areopagitica* here. But the fundamentals of knowledge are still the same; Adam himself explains that 'Evil into the mind of God or Man / May come and go' without blame, and assumes that unless it forms *sensory* images

---

[4] II. 516-18, 521, 527-8, 551. M recognized other models of medical operation (e.g. the corrosive) but the homeopathic is the most important because good and evil are 'twins'. Seminal and procreational images of writing abound in *Areopagitica* (e.g. II. 492-3, 505, 551-9 *passim*) and 'neutrall' clearly has a sense of 'neutered'. M's hint that reading Aretino could be useful may derive from Bruno; cf. *Lo spaccio della bestia trionfante*, ed. Antimo Negri (Milan, 1970), p. 98.

5. The Ethics of Confrontation

of evil the mind cannot exercise its choice of what to approve.[5] As Milton develops the same argument in *Areopagitica* he ranges freely between fallen and unfallen examples without pausing. After establishing the ethics of the present state—

> if every action which is good or evil in man at ripe years were to be under pittance, and prescription, and compulsion, what were vertue but a name, what praise could be then due to well-doing, what grammercy to be sober, just and continent?

he goes immediately to Adam in the state of innocence, created free to experience and choose in a world of 'provoking objects'. Even before the fall, Milton assumes, passion and emotive sensibility are the very constituents of humanity—the 'true *humanum*' that Karl Barth would later discover in the original creation of man and woman: 'he had been else a meer artificiall *Adam*, such an *Adam* as he is in the motions.' In the next breath Milton returns to the present state, and to the passional basis of ethics in supposedly fallen humanity: 'Wherefore did [God] create passions within us, pleasures round about us, but that these rightly temper'd are the very ingredients of vertu?'[6] At such moments Milton's passionate theory seems to take him beyond the confines of lapsarian thinking altogether.

In most Christian thought the fact of 'fallenness' is the supreme determinant of the human condition, and rules such as temperance and chastity are considered the moral equivalent of clothing, the arts of fallen necessity. But by endowing Adam and Eve with the same ethical and psychological situation as ourselves, and even making their freedom depend on strenuous experiential choice,

---

[5] *PL* IX. 364–6; V. 99–121 (and cf. VIII. 607–11). Contrast *Tetrachordon* (II. 601)—'the thickest arrows of temptation, under which we need not stand'—with *Areopagitica* (II. 521), where the argument from moral danger is dismissed in favour of the homeopathic model. M often seems uncertain about the active pursuit of 'fierce encounters' with evil (I. 769); in an earlier version of the *Mask*, for example, the Elder Brother is keen to challenge Comus and cleave him in twain, but in the later version he counsels caution (ll. 361–2, 408–9, and Carey's notes). In *PL* IX Adam argues from a fugitive and cloistered definition of virtue (even unsuccessful temptation is a defilement) and Eve counters with one of the Elder Brother's arguments (virtue can be assailed but never hurt, and is all the more glorious the more formidably it is tested).

[6] II. 527; cf. 342 ('Forc't vertu is as a bolt overshot, it goes neither forward nor backward, and does no good as it stands'—unusually witty for M) and *PR* II. 249–51: 'if Nature need not ... what praise is it to endure?' For Barth, see ch. 1 n. 2 above.

Milton effectively promotes the law of temperance over the fallen/unfallen division. The fall was a profoundly important historical event to him, of course—he did not go so far as those radicals and libertines who denied the fundamentalist reading completely or reduced it to allegory—but the dramatic re-enactment of its dilemma in the individual is even more important. When he came to write *Paradise Lost* he was at last able to combine the mythic and the personal. In later years Milton was not so keen to present the apple as a 'provoking' object, but he still based his justification of Providence on man's freedom to fall and strength to withstand genuine temptation; and he gave his Adam and Eve far more passion, and involved them far more deeply in experiential and moral conflicts, than any other author dared. Thereby he made them the opposite of the lifeless puppets—'such an *Adam* as he is in the motions'—that conventional exegesis had created, without falling into the heresy of those theosophists for whom passion, far from being a redemptive force, was the essence and motive of the fall.

[*iii*]

Milton's expansive and idiosyncratic interpretation of the law of temperance leads inevitably from ethics to poetics. Temperance, if it is to go beyond the 'pale and lean' caricature offered by Comus or the cloistered virtue denounced in *Areopagitica*, is meaningful only to the extent that the subject 'knows' in some more deep and living way than mere conceptual knowledge—knows evil so intensely that its rejection counts as virtue (without actually falling into its snares), and by the same process knows the excessive indulgence of passions and curiosities good in themselves. This apparently impossible combination of knowing and not knowing, a recent critic has argued, could be achieved by inventing something like the Freudian unconscious.[7] Milton himself suggests that it can be found in textuality, in books. Imaginative texts can both transcend and affirm the limits of fallen morality and epistemology. Man must know and not know, aspire and not aspire to 'be as Gods', welcome and yet not seek temptation; but in books, where contemplation and action are one, these 'trialls' can be pursued without restraint. It is clear, however, from Milton's own *Defence*

[7] Cf. William W. Kerrigan, *The Sacred Complex* (Cambridge, Mass., 1983), ch. 5 *passim*, esp. pp. 228-9.

5. The Ethics of Confrontation

of his earlier prose and by implication throughout *Areopagitica*, that he is only thinking of those books that rise *supra vulgus*, that attain 'autority which is the life of teaching' by their high level of vital energy, and thereby stimulate the activity of 'free philosophizing'.[8] Like all committed artists he detests inadequate art—the wooden image or 'artificiall Adam' is anathema to him. Milton assumes a *Phaedrus*-like distinction between dead texts and living texts, or in Christian terms the dead letter and 'the pretious life blood of a master spirit'. Books attain this 'living' and authoritative status not by moral correctness—the most scandalous authors may have it—but by emotive, imaginative, and aesthetic qualities.

For Milton 'philosophizing' and aesthetic activity merge together. The Younger Brother is not to be thought naïve when he exclaims

> How charming is divine philosophy!
> Not harsh and crabbed as dull fools suppose,
> But musical as is *Apollo*'s lute.

Exegesis likewise tends towards the aesthetic: Milton uses almost the same phrase as the Younger Brother to denounce Augustine's 'crabbed opinion' of Eve; in both cases doctrine is apprehended in terms of space, texture, and emotional impact—by what Pascal calls 'the heart'.[9] His ethics and his politics rest on a poet's epistemology, vitalistic, experiential, and even confrontational—hence the claim, in *Areopagitica*, that Spenser is a better teacher than Aquinas. Indeed, Milton may even have embraced this activist ethic because the alternative, the puppet-master's Adam, offended him by its aesthetic deadness.

Milton's own theory of poetry—which we may gather from those passages in the prose that proclaim its revolutionary power—is correspondingly emotional and vital. Poetry is essential to the education of new leaders for the 'noble and puissant Nation rousing herself like a strong man after sleep'; these cadres, enflamed with desire for that knowledge of God and the universe which alone can 'repair the ruins of our first parents', would finally extirpate the Frenchified culture of drunkenness, lust, and dishonesty that had dominated England under Royalism. Against the Cavaliers' 'libidinous' plays and 'Amorist' lyrics Milton set true poetry,

---

[8] II. 532-3; IV. i.624-5 (Col. edn. VIII. 130-2).

[9] *A Mask* ll. 475-7; ch. 3 n. 17 above. For an accurate account of what Pascal meant by 'le cœur', see Edward J. Kearns, *Ideas in Seventeenth-Century France* (Manchester, 1979), pp. 99-100.

grounded in firm intellectual discipline but more expansive than logic and 'more simple, sensuous and passionate' than rhetoric. The task of the new poet is not only to present a Sidneyan or Platonic golden world, but to make the whole range of experience available to sensuous apprehension, capturing the emotional essence of heaven and earth 'with a solid and treatable smoothnesse'. Thus poetry will 'delight', stir seeds of virtue in 'those especially of soft and delicious temper' who would not be moved by hard moralism, and 'set the affections in right tune'.[10]

But this remedial tempering of the emotions can only be effected by the living word. His own writings, Milton claims, satisfy both emotional and vitalistic criteria. Even in his juvenilia 'the stile by certain vital signes it had, was likely to live,' and he soon decides to devote himself to 'something so written to aftertimes, as they should not willingly let it die': the text must be 'alive' in two senses—by its own manifest vitality, and by the consensus of the readers. (When I speculate about the reader's response in *Paradise Lost*, it is less because of allegiance to a particular critical school than because Milton's own socialized poetics demand it.) Milton conceives his prose 'assertions' of the 1640s and his great poem in similarly vitalistic and procreational terms. In his divorce tracts he claims to ripen the ideas of the more timid commentators, who leave their own 'pregnant' ideas 'like the eggs of an Ostrich in the dust: I do but lay them in the sun.' And in *Paradise Lost*, with appropriately greater self-confidence, he implores the Holy Ghost to fertilize and incubate the epic just as in the creation of the world it had both hatched the abyss and made it pregnant.[11] Johnson may have been wrong to find no 'human interest' in the unfallen part of *Paradise Lost*, but he is certainly right to praise Milton's poetry for its 'energetick operation'. Furthermore, if writings at their best attain the status of a living person, a surrogate being, then a virtuous human life could conversely be described as a poem; as Milton says in his first autobiographical defence, the author 'ought him selfe to bee a true Poem', and should 'have in himselfe the experience and the practise of all that which is praise-worthy'

[10] II. 558 (and cf. I. 616); II. 366-7; I. 816-18, 820, II. 403.
[11] I. 809-10; II. 363; II. 598; *PL* I. 20-5. For the infertile 'wind-eggs' laid by M's incompetent opponents, see II. 726 and III. 467. For M and the 'living word' cf. John R. Knott, *The Sword of the Spirit* (1980), ch. 1 and pp. 111-12, 116, 120; Herman Rapaport, in contrast, sees M as an embalmer (*Milton and the Postmodern* (1983), pp. 15-16, 22).

(I. 890). The new epistemology of *Areopagitica* allows the poet, and the poem, to incorporate the 'experience' of evil without having to fall into the 'practise'.

The modern critic confronted with Milton's theory of 'vital signes' will probably welcome the semiotics but reject the vitalism, regarding it as sentimental and imprecise. If we are to construct a hermeneutic for Milton that builds on his own concepts and respects his own historical position, however, we should recognize its importance. Vitalism was the common ingredient in his ethics and his poetics, and appeared to offer a way out of the dilemma of being both a radical iconoclast and a conservative poet. If good and evil are 'twins' (as he called them in *Areopagitica*), then both present the same image to the world; some deeper form of apprehension is needed to tell them apart. Only the intuition of 'livingness' can breach the hypocritical façade and arrive at the essential distinction between the dead image (the idol, the puppet, the object of Protestant iconoclasm, the 'image of earth and phlegm' to which a hated marriage-partner is reduced), and the valid image, the 'life blood' of a good book, the 'lively Sculpture' that God Himself engraves in the heart, the object of regenerate poetry.[12] This is the unspoken argument that underlies Milton's attempt to weave his career as a poet into his social and political life.

Milton's poetics are not consistent and homogenous, of course. His descriptions of poetry, scattered throughout the prose and verse, reflect the struggles of the moment and the divisions within Milton's own temperament—between the practical reformer and the Utopian idealist, for example, or between pessimistic and optimistic conceptions of the fall. The same is true of the 'implied poetics' buried in the prose. The best critics will be attentive to how Milton describes exegesis, because here we can glimpse the poetic methods that later ripen into *Paradise Lost*. One of these, certainly, is the 'intangling' that Milton discovers in Christ's own teaching on divorce—the deliberate entrapment of the audience in fallen responses, the better to guide them towards regeneration.[13] But however brilliant the exposition of this theme, we should not

[12] *Prose* II. 514, 254 (original 'fleam', referring of course to the humour), 637; see also 6. 2. i and ch. 7 n. 3 below.

[13] The fullest exploration of this aspect of *PL* is Stanley E. Fish's *Surprised by Sin*; Fish does recognize other poetic functions, such as raising the imagination to angelic heights (pp. 201–2), musicality (p. 302), and pleasure—which his own thesis, he points out in a preface to the paperback edn., leads him to underemphasize.

see it as Milton's sole concern; he conceives his art in many different ways, and invests in multifarious and sometimes contradictory effects.

Several times in his prose and verse, for example, he presents poetry as a realm of neo-Platonic enlightenment, in which those whose 'ears are true' (as the Daemon says at the end of *Comus*) can grasp the kernel of truth in a mysterious narrative: Genesis is interpreted this way in the divorce tracts, and augmented by erotic myths of Milton's own invention. Poetic creation is also presented as a way of 'retaining the Promethean fire' or hearing the music of the spheres, or it may be itself a 'solemn music' that 'Dissolves us into extasies / And brings all Heav'n before our eyes.' The 'holy passion' of contemplation, in 'Il Penseroso', generates 'somthing like Prophetic strain'. Less esoterically, the 'sensuous and passionate' nature of art allows us not only to apprehend the workings of our own infected will, but also to transcend the limits of fallen epistemology at moments by imagining the good directly, with the immediacy of sense: 'Divine poetry' in the third Prolusion is a luxurious baptism in Paradisal nectar and perfume; the divine Urania visits the blind poet nightly, and allows him to see again. The interpreter as well as the poet shares in this higher sensuousness; Milton's new doctrine of divorce is a 'gentle stroking', a 'divine touch', better than wine and oil. Verse epic and prose commentary, in Milton's conception, both bring embryonic matter to life, both 'raise' the imagination, both 'assert' the original plan laid down in Genesis, and both attempt to regain 'as much as may be' the original happiness of Paradise; we shall see that he conceived his divorce tracts as a kind of liberating music, a 'charming pipe' that would lead his fellow-Englishmen back to the gates of Eden—even when he is persuading them not 'fondly to think within our strength all that lost Paradise relates'. It was from the prose tracts as well as from *Paradise Lost* that John Dennis gained his belief that poetry is 'a noble attempt of nature, by which it endeavors to exalt itself to its happy primitive state,' and that 'he who is entertain'd with the accomplish'd Poem, is for a time at least restor'd to Paradise.'[14]

But Milton must not be classed among those contemporaries whose mystic or restitutionist fervour led them to simplify the

[14] 'Ad Patrem', l. 20; 'Il Pens.', ll. 41, 165-6, 174; *PL* I. 25, VI. 297-301, VII. 28-9 (and cf. III. 21-55, IX. 21-4); *Prose* I. 243-4 (Col. edn. XII. 162), II. 240, 245, 333; Dennis, *Critical Works*, ed. J. N. Hooker (Baltimore, 1939), I. 330-6.

5. The Ethics of Confrontation

struggle for truth, to evade the contradiction of doctrine and imagination, and to return to the Adamic state 'carried away by their own libido'. The poetics of vital confrontation, regeneration, experience, emotion, and prophetic rapture is continually at odds, in Milton, with prudential rationalism and orthodox theodicy. However much he eroticizes Eden, he rejects the sanctified promiscuity of the Antinomians as he rejected the 'empty dream' of the pagan Muse and the bloodless fantasies of Utopianism. Knowledge and experiential temperance, guided by poetry, can certainly 'repair the ruins of our first parents', but only with the utmost difficulty. In the *Apology for Smectymnuus*, for example, Milton annihilates his opponent for too glibly claiming to have 'affections so equally temper'd' that he could see truth directly, 'which unlesse he only were exempted out of the corrupt masse of *Adam*, borne without sinne originall and living without actuall, is impossible.' Like the 'Adamites' and 'Perfectionists' mocked in contemporary satire, 'this man beyond a *Stoick apathy* sees truth as in a rapture'; he has miraculously circumvented 'the dim glasse of his affections which in this frail mansion of flesh are ever unequally temper'd, pushing forward to error and keeping back from truth oft times the best of men' (I. 909). Milton's sarcasm is realistic and well-placed. Yet paradoxically that very state of perfection, 'that *temper of [the] affections* which cannot any where be but in Paradise' (I. 910), is the goal and central achievement of the serious poet in Milton's own conception. And this claim to 'set the affections in right tune' was not just a product of temporary revolutionary enthusiasm; it was vividly expressed in the paradigmatic responses to the Lady's song in *Comus* (1634), and it is repeated in the preface to *Samson Agonistes*, published with *Paradise Regain'd* in 1671.

Poetic apprehension, then, is a problematic and strenuous vehicle of truth. Milton may never have resolved the paradoxes it forced on his attention; like his own Adam, he had to know and not know at the same time, to cast down and raise up 'imagination', to 'dream of other worlds' and to rest content with his own condition. But at its most intense, poetic apprehension allowed him to know and communicate evil in a 'solid and treatable' way, and to let his reader glimpse that good which would otherwise be beyond reach. The mind can thereby know the *extreme*, the 'utmost', when the law of temperance makes us inhabit the mean; and in Milton's dialectic morality the temperate centre is valueless unless we do know the extreme. God created 'passions within us, pleasures round about us' precisely because 'these rightly temper'd are the very ingredients of vertu'; this 'justifies the high providence of God, who though he command us temperance, justice, continence, yet pours out before us ev'n to a profuseness all desirable things, and gives us minds that can wander beyond all limit and satiety.' The poetic imagination allows us to appreciate the abundance of passion and the infinite trajectory of the mind in pursuit of it. Milton's supreme confidence in his own creativity is hard won, of course; he struggled with the 'feare to faile' that inhibited du Bartas, and the sense of fallenness and alienation that bewildered Pascal. But for Milton 'the mind', in a memorable phrase, can still be 'at home in the spacious circuits of her musing'; it is this capacity of the imagination to 'wander beyond all limit' that allows him to conceive and imitate the 'enormous bliss' of Paradise and the intimate rapture of 'such a love as Adam exprest to Eve'.[15]

The confluence of 'passionate' imagination, redemptive poetics, and an erotic conception of unfallen life gives *Paradise Lost* its special power, and appears already, less coherently, in the revolutionary divorce tracts. How does this 'sensuous' vision fit with the didactic or ideological function of his writing, expressed most severely in his pronouncements on the sexes? Virginia Woolf set out the problem with her usual acuity: on the one hand Milton is 'the first of the masculinists', scattering 'peevish personalities about the woman's duties' through the epic as if it were a domestic quarrel, but on the other hand 'how smooth, strong and elaborate it all is! What poetry!'[16]

The poetic process in fact allowed Milton an alternative to the narrow 'masculinism' that disfigures his divorce tracts and sometimes troubles *Paradise Lost*, and a model of reading that does not exclude the 'female'. This might seem surprising in view of Milton's notorious reputation as a patriarchalist, but the seeds of a redemptive and inspirational revaluation of the 'female' may be found throughout his poetry. *Paradise Lost* itself is fostered by a partly-female Holy Ghost and dictated by a 'celestial patroness',

[15] II. 446, 527–8; I. 812–13; cf. *PL* V. 297.
[16] *Diary*, 10 Sept. 1918. Woolf's pronouncements form the basis of Sandra M. Gilbert, 'Patriarchal Poetry and Women Readers: Reflections on Milton's Bogey', *PMLA* XCIII (1978), pp. 368–82.

and the creative process is analogous, not only to the workings of grace upon the heart, but to the rapture inspired by a female singer. The infamous separation of the functions of Adam and Eve, into 'contemplation and action' for him and 'sweet attractive grace' for her, is confounded in the course of the poem as both partners reveal a mixture of these qualities, and after the fall the 'female' virtues become essential to a new definition of heroism. The mind itself, 'at home in the spacious circuits of her musing,' bears a feminine pronoun. (I am referring of course to features conventionally marked as 'female' in Milton's own culture, rather than to essential or innate qualities.) Most of the special sensibilities that Milton ascribes to the poet were universally construed as 'female' in his day; the Lady of Christ's even claims a specifically feminine 'simplex munditiis' for his own verse. Similarly a 'soft delicious temper' is assumed in the reader, despite the intensely male preoccupations of the divorce tracts and parts of *Paradise Lost*. Indeed, when in the *De Doctrina* he defined the redemptive operation of grace, a paradigm for reader and poet alike, Milton chose as his example the 'opening of the heart' of a female believer.[17]

[17] *PL* I. 20-2, IX. 21, IV. 297-8 (and cf. 7. 1. ii below); 'Ad Leonoram', ll. 9-10; 'Ad Joannem Rousium', ll. 1-3 (transferring Horace's phrase (Ode I. v) from female hair to his own poetry); *Prose* VI. 189.

6
The Intelligible Flame

PARADISAL EROS AND OLD TESTAMENT DIVORCE IN MILTON'S PROSE

> They ... live as they were dead, or live as they were deadly enemies in a cage together; tis all one, they can couple, they shall not divorce till death, no though this sentence be their death. What is this, besides tyranny, but to turn nature upside down, to make both religion and the minde of man wait upon the slavish errands of the body, and not the body to follow either the sanctity or the sovranty of the mind unspeakably wrong'd?
> (*Tetrachordon*)

In his five divorce tracts—written after his own marriage had 'burst like a rotten thread' in the first month, and before his wife's return from a three-year estrangement—Milton gives central importance to the dynamic and dialectic nature of the response to Genesis. The Word 'offers itself' to the reforming nation. Christ 'recalls us to the beginning' by quoting the original 'one flesh' in Matthew 19:4-6, rather than 'recalling' the text to us. But that journey to the source, inspired by 'all that lost Paradise relates', is prevented by 'the sword that guards it'. The unhappy husband finds himself in an intolerable impasse, yearning for the Paradisal ideal inscribed within him, but apparently imprisoned by the very words of the original ordinance. Milton undertakes to solve at once the marital and the hermeneutic problem, by restoring the activity and vitality of the interpretative process. Led out of false consciousness by his new reading, Milton claims, liberated Englishmen—though not Englishwomen, as we shall see—will begin 'venturing to pierce with our free thoughts into the full latitude of nature and religion' and 'setting a foot forward with manly confidence', rather than 'suffering those ordinances which were allotted to our solace and reviving to trample over us, and hale us into a multitude of sorrows'. Milton will provide a thread to lead out of the labyrinth, a 'charming pipe' for the godly people to follow; he is literally an *exegete*—a 'leader out' from perplexity or bondage.[1]

Milton's new idea is this: the legislature of England, regenerated by its struggles against Royalism, should restore the wise and pious law of Deuteronomy that allowed the husband, if he is genuinely convinced of his wife's 'uncleanness', to declare a divorce and dismiss her from his household. Uncleanness must be interpreted in a strikingly new way, however. It does not mean fornication, the one exception that Christ had allowed in his general abolition of Old Testament divorce—in fact it does not refer to a physical condition at all. We must interpret both Old Testament legislation and New Testament abolition in the light of the Edenic ideal; Christ himself intended his apparent prohibition as an 'intangling' that would lead back to Paradise. 'Uncleanness' must therefore mean permanent psychological and spiritual incompatibility, the inability or unwillingness to be a 'meet help' as Eve was to Adam. Thus Milton would restore the true, dualistic, spiritual interpretation that God Himself intended.

The results of this interpretative breakthrough are not merely intellectual and doctrinal, moreover, but practical, emotional, and existential, felt in 'the very foundations of [the husband's] inmost being'. False interpretations are likewise measured in terms that combine the emotional and the intellectual; they 'ought not to satisfie a Christian mind' and 'cannot give quiet to the breast of any intelligent man'. The old reading of Genesis, which uses it to banish the idea of divorce, 'mangles' and 'gashes' the human spirit; the new interpretation 'like a divine touch in one moment heals all, and, like the word of God, in one instant hushes outrageous tempests into a sudden stilnesse and peacefull calm' (II. 259, 297-8, 333). The tracts themselves, however, shot through with the 'fits and workings of a high impatience' (Milton's term for marital

---

[1] II. 631, 232, 309, 316, 319, 343, 240-1. M's five tracts are *DDD* (1643), a 2nd edn. of this, greatly expanded and divided into chapters and books (1644), an edited tr. of the 16th-century Protestant Martin Bucer's opinions on divorce (1644), and two further tracts published simultaneously in 1645—*Tetrachordon*, a detailed commentary on the four main passages in Scripture that define marriage and divorce, and *Colasterion*, a satirical reply to an anonymous critic. Useful studies include the introductions in *Prose* II, and Arthur E. Barker, *Milton and the Puritan Dilemma, 1641-1660* (Toronto, 1941), Part II; Halkett, *passim*; V. Norskov Olsen, *The New Testament Logia on Divorce* (Tübingen, 1971); Aers and Hodge (ch.7 n. 1 below). Gladys Willis, *The Penalty of Eve: John Milton and Divorce* (1985) appeared too late for me to take it into account.

frustration), tend to counteract their own pacific intention. At times they treat the question of divorce not in a detached, rational manner but with 'almost fanatical courage', with 'headlong confidence', and with an energy and comprehensiveness that would be called 'epic' if the term were not dwarfed by Milton's later achievement; William Warburton would later find in the prose works 'a prodigious spirit of poetical enthusiasm' and 'strains as sublime, or if possible more so, than any in his higher Poetry'.[2] But the raw emotional vehemence of the divorce tracts is difficult to reconcile with the ideal of temperance that sustains *Areopagitica*. Milton devours Scripture with an almost indecent hunger for those truths which will confirm his passions, release him from bondage, and assuage his sense of having been 'unspeakably wrong'd'.

1. Patterning from the beginning: exegesis and the vision of perfect marriage

Milton approached the question of divorce with a strange combination of harsh practicality and exalted idealism. Though he despised 'empty dreams' and 'Utopian politics', his proposals are matched not in the tentative and circumscribed suggestions of his Protestant forebear Bucer, but in the Paradisal fantasies of the Spiritual Libertines and the divorce laws of More's Utopia. He bases his doctrine on fallen weakness and the impossibility of gaining 'lost Paradise', and yet he insists that unless a marriage recaptures the Paradisal bliss 'in some proportion' it is not a marriage at all but 'a daring phantasm, a meer toy of terror'—and should be immediately annulled.[3] Milton remains profoundly divided between two models of marital perfection: Old Testament patriarchy, and the inspiring but elusive ideal gained from immersion in the first chapters of Genesis.

Though Milton's proposals were denounced as the work of a scandalous libertine, their declared intention is to restore the institution of marriage by reclaiming its original essence as defined by Genesis—a process initiated by Christ himself. *Tetrachordon*,

---

[2] Quot. in *Milton, 1732-1801: The Critical Heritage*, ed. John T. Shawcross (1972), p. 92; cf. W. R. Parker, *Milton: A Biography* (Oxford, 1968), I. 240; William and Malleville Haller, 'The Puritan Art of Love', *HLQ* V (1942), 271.

[3] *PL* VII. 39; *Prose* II. 253, 316, 526, 667; cf. 2. 4. ii above and *Utopia* II, where the Utopians provide divorce for incompatibility, by mutual consent and after serious deliberation (though only when both partners have found alternative spouses, as Stephen Fallon points out in a private communication).

6. The Intelligible Flame

for example, begins by explicitly relating his own method to Christ's quotation of Genesis in Matthew 19:6: 'it will undoubtedly be safest, fairest, and most with our obedience, to enquire, as our Saviours direction is, how it was in the beginning.' To clarify the original state of creation will restore, to a degenerate age, a sense of 'the true dignity of man ... especially in this prime institution of Matrimony, wherein his native pre-eminence ought most to shine' (II. 586-7). Returning to the beginning thus provides not only the first principles of historical interpretation and Scriptural exegesis, but also a sense of primacy and loftiness suitable for the opening of a treatise on what is here defined as the highest form of human life. Milton claims the supreme authority of 'our Saviours direction' because Christ too, confronted with a marital problem by the Pharisees, had solved it by turning to the 'first institution' of marriage in Genesis; Deuteronomy may be an important support of the edifice of divorce law, but Genesis is its main pillar. Nevertheless *The Doctrine and Discipline of Divorce* and *Tetrachordon* aim to demolish the law of indissoluble marriage that took its authority from the very words that Christ spoke to the Pharisees on that occasion—'they are no more twain, but one flesh; what therefore God hath joined together, let no man put asunder.'

Milton recognizes that 'the first institution will be objected to have ordain'd marriage inseparable' (II. 244), but he answers not by abandoning the scrutiny of Genesis but by redefining that original institution more stringently—by seizing upon its first principle ('it is not good that man should be alone') and subordinating all subsequent purposes to that one. (Luther used a similar method, as we have seen, but he chose the procreative 'increase and multiply' as his master-verse.) Thus Milton will maintain 'that marriage, if we pattern from the beginning as our Saviour bids, was not properly the remedy of lust, but the fulfilling of conjugall love and helpfulness' (II. 250); he will uphold Christ's method of 'patterning after the beginning' even if it means wresting Christ's own words into a contrary meaning.

Milton begins this apparently impossible reversal by co-opting the Saviour into his own dynamic and emotive vision. Christ and the 'adventuring' exegete are presented in identical terms, as liberators and healers, agents of warmth and life: Christ's words have been 'congeal'd into a stony rigor'; Milton's new reading will 'soften and dispell rooted and knotty sorrowes', and so enable his countrymen, unlike the stubborn Jews, 'to follow freely the charming pipe of him who sounded and proclaim'd liberty and reliefe to all distresses'. The heroic pamphleteer will 'ease and set free' the minds of men from the 'needlesse thraldome' of a bad marriage, and 'lend us the clue that windes out of this labyrinth of servitude' (II. 237-41). He even claims that his legislation for divorce could lead the way back to Paradise, or establish contemporary marriage as the Paradise within: it would 'restore the much wrong'd and over-sorrow'd state of matrimony, not onely to those mercifull and life-giving remedies of *Moses*, but, as much as may be, to that serene and blisfull condition it was in at the beginning' (II. 240). The crucial phrase, however, is 'as much as may be'.

Milton's interpretation of Genesis hesitates between optimism and pessimism. The story of the fall provides not only an authoritative (though cryptic) definition of human nature, but a 'way to perfection'; in our efforts to retrace that arduous route, however, we also discover the limits of human potential. Analysing Genesis will reveal the relative depth and strength of our most powerful constitutive drives, and this in turn will teach us how far we can expect to fulfil them. So the chronological order of God's words (as Milton reconstructs it) proves that the soul's longing for companionship is 'more deeply rooted' in human nature than is sexual desire, 'even in the faultless innocence', and must likewise take precedence in our marriage-laws; Milton's whole argument, that mental incompatibility should be grounds for divorce, is based on the primacy of this 'intelligible flame, not in Paradise to be resisted ... which if it were so needful before the fall, when man was much more perfect in himself, how much more is it needful now against all the sorrows and casualties of life' (II. 251-2). But this comparison of the fallen and the unfallen state may also teach us our weakness, and we might therefore conclude that we should *not* try to conform to the 'first institutions' of Paradise: 'while man and woman were both perfet each to other, there needed no divorce,' but after the fall it was an act of mercy to establish divorce in the Mosaic law—and can the New Testament law of charity be less merciful than the Old? 'The Gospel, indeed, tending ever to that which is perfetest, aim'd at the restorement of all things as they were in the beginning'; but 'if ... marriage must be as in the beginning, the persons that marry must be such as then were' (II. 665-6). Using Genesis to solve the problem of divorce brings out a flaw in the scheme of redemption, for the impossibly high demands of the 'way to perfection' contradict the mildness and mercy of the Redeemer.

Milton solves this dilemma by making a crucial distinction, a dichotomy that reflects the tension in his own mind between the hard realist and the Utopian idealist, the agitator and the poet. 'In our intentions and desires' we must pursue the full Edenic ideal, but 'in execution' we must fight for such regulations 'as reason and present nature can bear' (II. 666). In the inner realm we can still try to be 'persons such as then were', but in practice we must recover and obey the true spirit of the Mosaic law, to save us from the rage and exhaustion of the failed idealist. If God had meant us to imitate the life-long marital commitment of Adam and Eve, Milton argues, He would have said so in the books of law; instead the description of Paradisal marriage is 'set ... out of place in another world at such a distance from the whole Law, and not once mention'd there,' and cannot be interpreted as a command. The story of the fall—hitherto assumed to provide the most intimate and authoritative definition of human nature—is now described as remote and other-worldly. In the case of a bad marriage we should not try to live up to the Edenic ideal: it is more humanly realistic 'to follow rather what moral *Sinai* prescribes equal to our strength, than fondly to think within our strength all that lost Paradise relates' (II. 316). 'Strength', which elsewhere in the divorce tracts refers to the passive endurance of an irritating marriage, here describes the ability to live up to an imaginative response to the original text—an attempt which must inevitably crash against the practical limitations of fallen humanity.

But by recommending a pragmatic renunciation of the Paradise within, Milton does not abandon the idealism he derives from Genesis. By restoring the Mosaic divorce for hatred, which allowed for post-lapsarian imperfections, English legislators would paradoxically revive God's original conception of marriage, since spiritual compatibility would then be once again the primary factor. Moses may have enshrined fallen weakness in his written law, while letting the 'supernatural law' of lifelong fidelity 'vanish in silence ... ev'n as the reason of it vanisht with Paradise', but he did this precisely *because* the bond of love is 'ancienter, and deeper engrav'n in blameless nature' (II. 330). The text of 'lost Paradise' is thus both 'vanisht' and ever-present. Moses's legislation, and Milton's heroic endeavours to restore it, rest on a central contradiction: they will lead us back to the Paradisal happiness by pushing to its logical conclusion the fact that it is beyond our strength ever to return there.

2. Love, sexuality, and hatred

Milton's exegetic method, then, is to define marriage exclusively in terms of God's remark before creating Eve—'it is not good that the man should be alone; I will make a help meet for him'—and to dismiss all other clues to the significance of gender ('male and female created he them', 'increase and multiply', 'they shall be as one flesh') except in so far as they conform to the central concept of spiritual compatibility. Simultaneously, however, he demotes the relevance of Paradisal standards, and insists that ordinary fallible 'nature' be the criterion of marriage. This dichotomy in Milton's hermeneutic reflects, and perhaps determines, his strangely polarized attitude towards sexuality. Compared to the normal exponents of Protestant marriage-doctrine, with their praise of moderate 'due benevolence', Milton seems both an unbridled amorist and an embittered ascetic. He floods his text with Eros, but he feels so 'unspeakably wrong'd' by the emphasis on physical sexuality in current divorce law that he veers towards the opposite extreme; he seems almost to indict the existence of sexuality itself, and to reintroduce precisely the Old Testament sense of 'uncleanness' that he had tried to eliminate.

Milton's thesis—'that marriage, if we pattern from the beginning as our Saviour bids, was not properly the remedy of lust, but the fulfilling of conjugall love and helpfulness'—seems reasonable enough, but it is in fact phrased so as to beg the question. Sexuality provided not one but two of the 'ends of marriage' normally listed by commentators: the remedy of lust, which all agree to be a post-lapsarian necessity, and the blessing of 'increase and multiply' in God's original creation. 'Lust', when it is used by scrupulous thinkers, refers not to sexual desire *per se* but to its corrupt and uncontrollable form. We have seen that Aquinas ascribed intense erotic pleasure to the pre-lapsarian state (where continence was not a virtue because it was unnecessary), and the Protestant reformers in their polemic against celibacy also celebrate the innocence of procreation, and describe the 'remedy of lust' as a benefit of marriage 'that before Man's fall was not, because there was no need for it'.[4] Even Donne, who called the marriage of Adam and Eve 'our funerall', and equated the 'excrementall jelly' of semen with 'that jelly which thy body dissolves to at last', still assures the married couple that God 'imprinted in man ... a *naturall* desire to conserve and propagate their kinde by way of *Generation*' — indeed, until this infusion of sexual desire 'there is no mention of any blessing in the creation'.[5] But Milton makes the post-lapsarian 'remedy for lust' stand for the whole phenomenon of human sexual desire from the beginning, insists that 'male and female created he them' refers to companionship and not to sexual 'solace', and treats 'increase and multiply' at best with laconic condescension and at worst with indignant contempt.

Many Protestant commentators, dissatisfied with the argument that Eve was created solely for procreation, stress that social comfort and mutual piety are equally important, and some even offer to arrange these 'ends of marriage' in order of priority with reproduction in a secondary position.[6] But secondary does not mean subordinate, negligible, less 'ancient', and less 'deeply ingraven' in human nature, as Milton repeatedly asserts. His case for divorce does not even depend on the subordination of physical to mental criteria: he could have rested content with the undisputed fact that 'hearts must be united as well as bodies',[7] and proved that spiritual compatibility was as much a *sine qua non* as sexual capacity. But instead he plunges belligerently into the question of precedence. 'He who affirms adultery to be the highest breach, affirms the bed to be the highest of marriage, which is in truth a grosse and borish

[4] 2. 2. ii above; Thomas Gataker, *A Wife in Deed*, p. 27, in *A Good Wife Gods Gift, and A Wife in Deed: Two Mariage Sermons* (1623). Laurence Lerner finds this passage puzzling (*Love and Marriage* (1979), p. 112), but Gataker is repeating the standard opinion (e.g. Luther I. 116).

[5] *First Anniversarie*, ll. 105-10; *Sermons*, III. 105 and II. 335. Donne contradicts himself on the question of whether the 'remedy of lust' was in God's mind when he first established marriage (contrast *Sermons* II. 339 and III. 244). On Donne's bracing morbidities see also John Carey, *John Donne: Life, Mind and Art* (1981), ch. 5.

[6] e.g. Halkett, ch. 1 *passim*; cf. *Prose* II. 246 and n. 4, 599. M's argument is weak in any case: Jeremy Taylor pointed out (quot. Halkett, p. 16) that temporal order in Genesis is no indication of essential priority; he could have added that temporal order is in any case impossible to determine, since the two accounts are incompatible. Cornelius Agrippa (3. 2. ii above) made Eve's late creation a sign of her superiority.

[7] William Whately, *A Bride-Bush* (1619 edn.), quot. in Haller and Haller, p. 268; cf. Grotius in Halkett, p. 62. M sometimes did claim that his criteria should be merely *equal* to the physical ones (e.g. II. 239-40).

opinion.' (Far from being the gravest of disasters, Milton believes, adultery need not diminish and may even stimulate the love that preserves a marriage.) God did not create male and female for the sexual 'work of male and female', but for spiritual companionship. To invert the hierarchy of marriage-purposes is to enslave the soul to the body, 'to turn nature upside down', 'to abuse the sacred and misterious bed of marriage to be the compulsive stie of an ingratefull and malignant lust, stirr'd up only from a carnall acrimony, without either love or peace, or regard to any other thing holy or human.' To take this 'prone and savage necessity' seriously is to be oneself a 'Pork', a 'Boar', a 'snout', offensive to all 'gentle breeding'.[8]

This scorn of sexuality leads Milton to a remarkable interpretation of Scripture: the desire which made Adam yearn for a mate is the same desire that St. Paul described as burning ('it is better to marry than to burn'); this does not refer, however, to sexual longing, as all the commentators assume, but to the need for a spiritual companion. The central emotion of marriage is 'certainly not the meer motion of carnall lust, the meer goad of a sensitive desire; God does not principally take care for such cattell.'

Sexual desire is a pathological by-product of bodily imbalance, 'the venom of a lusty and over-abounding concoction', contemptibly easy to eliminate by diet and exercise, and for that reason not to be counted as a real part of human nature.[9] Love is something utterly different—an intelligible flame, 'a more human burning ... than that of copulation'. 'The dignity and blessing of marriage'— that is to say, the intention of the original 'blessing' of Genesis 1: 28—'is plac't rather in the mutual enjoyment of that which the wanting soul needfully seeks, than of that which the plenteous body would jollily give away.'[10] There is no room in these phrases for a pre-lapsarian sharing or mingling of sexual and spiritual love, and no sense that sexuality belongs among the God-given 'passions' and 'pleasures' that constitute the true *humanum*.

[8] II. 269, 674, 240, 600, 733, 739, 747. The pig imagery is particularly directed at the unidentified critic answered in *Colasterion*, whom M from his lofty social position accuses of being an ex-servant and lower-class lawyer: 'all persons of gentle breeding (I say gentle, though this Barrow grunt at the word)' will agree with him (II. 747 and cf. 741). M may be imitating Christ's tactic of 'arguing extremes' with the Pharisees (I owe this suggestion to Stephen Fallon).

[9] II. 251; cf. *Colasterion* (II. 737–8) for a coarse satirical attack on the notion that incompatibility of mind can be improved by medical treatment.

[10] II. 252; M often uses 'jolly' to mean 'sexual', with no associations of benign merriment.

6. The Intelligible Flame

Milton's general argument, of course, is that sex must not be abstracted from spiritual considerations and promoted to the supreme determinant of marriage—as the canon law had done, *de facto*, by recognizing adultery and impotence as causes of annulment but refusing to grant that privilege to incompatibility. Milton's polemic aims not to level these priorities but to overturn them. His disgust is therefore directed at sex in isolation, at body in opposition to spirit, and he accepts erotic delight, as we shall see, if it can somehow be integrated with 'the cheerful society of wedlock' (II. 251). Indeed, Milton assumed that contemporaries would find his *Doctrine* daringly hedonistic—the sons of Belial will probably use it to support their 'debausheries', and 'our severe *Gnostics*' will find it 'new and dangerous' (II. 225, 579). Milton does not feel that sexual arousal automatically pits the soul against the senses, as Augustine had done, and to this extent he believes that marriage can lead to pre-lapsarian happiness. But there remains a striking imbalance in his treatment of the subject.

Both before and after the divorce tracts Milton insisted, with the Epistle to the Hebrews, that 'marriage must not be call'd a defilement' (I. 893, VI. 366, 370). But what constitutes marriage? In his zeal to overthrow the habit of defining it by sex alone, he strays into the opposite heresy; like the Gnostics he despises, he brings his contempt for sexuality even into the 'first institution', the pre-lapsarian creation of male and female. Milton's farmyard vocabulary—brute, goad, cattle, compulsive sty, provender burning—is used even to describe God's own attitude to His creation: 'God does not principally take care for such cattell.'[11] By calling sex 'the *prescribed* satisfaction of an irrational heat' he seems to lash not only St. Paul's law of 'due benevolence' but the original divine injunction to increase and multiply (II. 249, my emphasis). And his explanation of God's ordinance to 'be one flesh' is equally grudging: God said these words 'only to make legitimate and good the carnal act, which els might seem to have somthing of pollution in it.'[12] Calvin, as we have seen in chapter 2, calls sexual intercourse

---

[11] II. 251; cf. also 259, 269, 275, 739. M here imitates St. Paul's rhetorical question in 1 Cor. 9:9—'Doth God take care for oxen?'—which suggests that cattle, unlike sparrows and lilies of the field, were considered beneath the care of the Deity.

[12] II. 326. The same point is made more evasively in *Tetrachordon*: God encourages the lovers to '*bee as one flesh*, to justify and make legitimat the rites of the Mariage bed; which was not unneedfull, if for all this warrant, they were

a *res per se pudenda* and praises God for having helped Adam not to recoil from the horror of copulation. But these remarks apply only after the fall, when *foeditas* was visited on the sexual process; Milton's comment is directed at the original establishment of marriage. He assumes that the sense of pollution was built into man in the state of innocence, and was even in God's mind when He made provision for it.

Lovers, then, are 'one flesh' only in the sense that 'the fit union of their souls be such as may even incorporate them to love and amity': the pun on *incorporate* presents, not a monist fusion of body and soul, but a sharp reminder of their separation. Without this mental union, 'instead of beeing one flesh, they will be rather two carkasses chain'd unnaturally together; or as it may happ'n, a living soule bound to a dead corps, a punishment too like that inflicted by the tyrant *Mezentius*' (II. 326-7 and cf. 595, 677). William Whately had used a similar image to prove the necessity of love: 'Love is the life and soule of marriage, without which it differs as much from it selfe, as a rotten apple from a sound, and as a carcasse from a living body.'[13] But whereas Whately's image refers diffusedly to the general comfort of the household, Milton's focuses explicitly on 'the carnall act', and seems to well up from a concrete experience of horror. He intends us to recall Virgil's description of Mezentius's torture (*Aeneid* VIII. 485-8), in which the victim is bound face to face with a corpse, 'sanie taboque fluentis / complexu in misero (flowing with blood and pus in a wretched embrace)'. Milton has reliteralized Virgil's metaphor of the embrace, and substituted human carrion for the ecstatic union of 'one flesh'.

Many of Milton's attempts to convey the misery of bad marriage show a similar physical particularity. His 'quintessence of an excrement', like Donne's 'excrementall jelly', refers with medical precision to the fluids of reproduction, which some physiologists saw as the 'venom' cast off by an unbalanced body. So do 'carnall acrimony' and 'the promiscuous draining of a carnal rage'.[14] 'Weapon'd to the least carnall enjoyment', 'an impetuous nerve

suspected of pollution by some sects of Philosophy and Religions of old, and latelier among the Papists, and other heretics older than they' (606-7 and cf. 613). The reader is tempted to reply in M's own words: does God take care of such cattle?

[13] Quot. in Haller and Haller, p. 268.

[14] II. 248-9, 600, 355. 'Excrement' refers technically to anything that grows from the body, but M's usage, like Donne's (n. 5 above) is clearly pejorative.

[*from Latin* nerva, *penis*]', 'the vessel of voluptuous enjoyment', 'the veins of sensuality', 'the channell of concupiscence', 'the furrow of mans nativitie'—these phrases allude unmistakably to the genitals, and in such a context to call the hated wife 'an image of earth and phlegm' seems almost equally specific (II. 236, 248-9, 254). Milton's divorce tracts provide a sort of reversal of *Aretino's Postures*, a series of portraits of copulation in which its fluids turn to repulsive excreta, its passionate movements are reduced to the 'grinding' of an animal or blinded giant in the mill (II. 258), and its tight embraces become the cords that bind a living man to an effigy or a corpse. And all this does not refer to a perverted or reified form of sexuality, but to normal physical copulation, 'due benevolence'. The attentive reader will not emerge with the impression that 'what links the divorce tracts with *Paradise Lost* is the conviction that sexual appetite in itself is good'.[15]

[*ii*]

We have seen, then, that Milton treats sexual arousal and emission in pathological terms, as inflammations from an 'acrid humour' and as the waste product of a distempered and overheated body, and that he rigidly separates this physical burning from the 'rational burning', the 'intelligible flame' of true love. The human is defined in such a way as to exclude the physiological completely, and physiology is associated almost entirely with animality or disease. Growth, fertility, reproduction, and nurture are barely mentioned— a strange contrast to the ethics of *Areopagitica*, where growth and vitality are all-important. Milton's remarkable indifference to the question of children, whether as a goal of marriage or as a problem for divorcees, seems to correspond to this noxious-excremental vision of the human seed.[16] But here and there we glimpse a different attitude, which not only anticipates the 'spiritual monism' of *Paradise Lost*, but also helps to explain the strength of Milton's disgust and misery. The passages so far studied imply that, in the

---

[15] Hill[2], p. 261. For another generous estimation of the divorce tracts, which takes fuller account of M's polemic against lust, see Hagstrum, esp. p. 49. Though I differ in emphasis here, I have greatly benefited from Prof. Hagstrum's comments on an earlier version of this book.

[16] M actually doctors the texts he quotes in order to eliminate references to children: cf. II. 465 and n. 8; 609 and n. 55; Edward Le Comte, *Milton and Sex* (1978), pp. 29-30. When M does treat the question of children in *Colasterion*, he adopts a tone of contemptuous bawdry (II. 734-5); cf. Aers, p. 132).

God-given order of things, mental states are utterly distinct from physical phenomena, and that to deduce one from the other is outrageous and even blasphemous. But though as a moralist Milton reinforced this separation, as a natural philosopher he seems to have entertained a more unified vision of mind and body, and even to have hazarded a physiological explanation of hatred. The incompatible couple are driven apart by a powerful and potentially fatal antipathy, 'not morall but naturall', built into the very structure of their bodies. Semen becomes the quintessence, not of an 'excrement', but of a 'disposition', and the sexual 'due benevolence' commanded by St. Paul becomes a kind of stealthy robbery or vampiric depletion—'the most injurious and unnaturall tribute that can be extorted from a person endew'd with reason, to be made pay out the best substance of his body, *and of his soul too* as some think' (II. 271, my emphasis). In this more monist view, the sexual intercourse of an incompatible couple is not merely irrelevant but ominous and obscene, since mind and body are so closely interfused that the buried malignancy of the couple may issue equally as an attitude or a disease.[17]

Milton is here torn between materialist monism and hierarchic dualism. Mind and body are so intimately linked that quarrelling may prevent conception and ejaculation may suck away the 'best' part of the soul, and correspondingly a 'naturall' sympathy can convert bestial coupling into an act of benevolence; but the two substances are still distinct enough for one to dominate the other, and the subordinate flesh is still a source of anxiety and disgust—all the more so, paradoxically, when it is imagined instinct with soul. In *De Doctrina Christiana* Milton seems to accept, almost to celebrate, the immanence implied by generation—whether influenced by the experience of fatherhood, or the greater proximity of his theme to Eden, is impossible to determine: 'how can the human seed, that intimate and most noble part of the body, be

---

[17] II. 270-1, 739 and n. 73; note that M's scientific speculation increases in the 2nd edn. of *DDD*, and that on p. 274 he even accuses the bad wife of attempted murder (she prevents the husband's 'vigor and spiritfull exercise'). In his commonplace book (I. 414) M had copied from J. B. Sinibaldus a sentence describing sex without love as *infertile* as well as harmful, bestial, and disgusting, which may have explained to him why Mary had not conceived after a month's grinding in the mill of copulation; cf. *Geneanthropeiae* (Rome, 1642), cols. 15 and 750, for a 'more human' view of sex (*not* transcribed by M) and for other psychosomatic causes of infertility (e.g. rage and gloom).

imagined destitute and devoid of the soul of the parents, or at least of the father?' (VI. 321-2, Col. edn. XV. 48) And *Paradise Lost* evolves a form of hierarchical monism: the universe is conceived as 'one first matter' growing up towards God in lighter and lighter flowerings, only falling into the dualistic conflict of gross matter and estranged spirit when it falls away from divinity (V. 469-93). But in 1643 it was all too easy for Milton to imagine the human seed devoid of soul, and the alternative (what 'some think') filled him with more dread than delight.

Despite this anxiety, Milton does move from a 'morall' to a 'naturall' explanation of *one flesh*: he speaks in deliberately 'mysterious' terms of the 'reverend secret of nature' that must not be violated by bad marriage (II. 270, 751). This higher physiology allows him to connect the attraction and repulsion of the sexes to larger cosmic forces, and so to weave in the first as well as the second chapter of Genesis: 'God and nature' both insist on the importance of compatibility, 'not only by those recited decrees, but ev'n by the first and last of all his visible works; when by his divorcing command the world first rose out of chaos, nor can be renew'd again out of confusion but by the separating of unmeet consorts' (II. 273). Milton's philosophy of genesis thus assigns a primordial creative power not to love but to divorce. Indeed, the idea of physical abomination provides the missing link between Christ's prohibition of divorce and Milton's own argument for the opposite: 'if it be unlawful for man to put assunder that which God hath joyn'd, let man take heede it be not detestable to joyne that by compulsion which God hath put assunder' (II. 651). In the course of these speculations, Milton was able to restore some common ground between the two central concepts of Genesis, 'meet help' and 'one flesh'. He begins with a dualism that defines the lovers' bond in exclusively mental terms and dismisses physical sexuality with a loathing sometimes reminiscent of the Desert Fathers; but he gradually evolves a different model—for true spiritual lovers, the flesh may be transformed into a 'reverend secret of nature', something integrated with and generated by the mind. The connection of flesh and spirit becomes, in a favourite word, more 'intimate', and the interpretation of *one flesh* and *help meet* becomes less dualistic as it becomes more 'mysterious'. The true 'union of the flesh', Milton insists, '*proceeds from* the union of a fit help and solace' (II. 606, my emphasis).

Once this emanational hierarchy is established, the sexual act itself may become 'legitimate' and receive 'a human qualification'. Physical consummation is thus admitted among the ends of marriage, albeit grudgingly, when it is 'an effect of conjugal love ... proceeding as it ought from intellective principles'.[18] If the sexual act is initiated by bodily passion or 'sensitive force' it is 'at best but an animal excretion, but more truly worse and more ignoble than that mute kindlynes among the herds and flocks.' But Milton is prepared to imagine a truly 'human' form of sexuality, 'holy' and 'pure', in which the delights of mental compatibility blend or flow over into the physical act of love—'which act being kindly and voluntarie, as it ought, the Apostle ... call'd ... *Benevolence*, intimating the original thereof to be in the understanding and the will' (II. 609, 270). Animal physicality can thereby be subsumed into the voluntary realm—an ideal that Augustine, and mainstream commentators after him, could only embody in fantastic speculations about the intercourse that Adam and Eve might have enjoyed if they had not fallen before their wedding night. Here it is the common expositors who locate Edenic sexuality 'in another world', and Milton who insists on establishing it in the present. But in the divorce tracts these tributes always come backhandedly, in concessional or contrastive clauses whose main target is the infamy of 'despis'd' copulation, compulsory 'benevolence' with a hated spouse.

Even in these rejections, however, Milton will assume an intimate and deterministic relation between mind and body: 'how unpleasing and discontenting the society of body *must needs be* between those whose mindes cannot bee sociable' (II. 741; my emphasis). The sexual experience of the man who hates his wife, Milton tells us, is not indifference or animal 'mute kindlynes' (as one might expect if the hating mind were quite distinct from the copulating body) but rather a horror equal to the delight of the true 'act of love', and generated by the same intimacy of spirit and flesh. St. Paul may have called it 'benevolence', but without mental union 'surely there is nothing which might more properly be call'd a malevolence rather'—a malevolence, moreover, which not only darkens the mood but sucks away the vital essences of body, and 'some think'

---

[18] II. 606, 609; cf. *De Doctrina* VI. 355 (Col. edn. XV. 122): pre-lapsarian sexuality was 'an effect or natural consequence of that very intimate relationship which would have existed between Adam and Eve in man's unfallen state'.

6. The Intelligible Flame

soul (II. 270-1). Thus the 'sacred and misterious bed of mariage' becomes 'an old haunt of lust and malice mixt together', an 'intimat evil', perhaps the very 'mystery of iniquity' mentioned by St. Paul.[19] In this act of 'pollution' the self is inescapably bound to 'something beneath', a sort of succubus human in flesh but not in spirit (II. 609); the living being is tyrannically chained to the dead, as Virgil put it, in a putrid embrace. Milton's indignant separation of 'humanity' from sexuality is thus all the more extreme because he felt them to be close. He is in effect the victim of his own drift from 'morall' to 'naturall' explanation: as a moralist he asserts in *Areopagitica* that 'those actions that enter into a man ... defile not'; but sexual pollution breaches this comforting distinction of outer and inner. Nevertheless, Milton's vision of perfection also derives from a fusion of mind and body: he imagines the married state—'this prime institution of matrimony, wherein [man's] native pre-eminence ought most to shine,' and for which we yearn with all our 'intentions and desires'—as an 'intimate conversation' in which the spiritual and the sexual are combined, and where Logos and Eros are friends.[20] The failure to realize this impossibly lofty ideal left him 'unspeakably wrong'd', and he took his revenge by creating an equal but opposite picture of loathing and separation.

[*iii*]

It is ironic, given their vivid evocations of sexual disgust, that Milton's divorce tracts should have been so widely denounced as the work of a 'Libertine', a second Aretino, a devotee of 'divorce at pleasure'.[21] But his own many-layered conception of sexuality may be partly responsible. Milton recognizes four kinds of sexual experience. Two of these—the 'mute kindlynes' of sheer animality and its opposite, ascetic renunciation—depend upon the complete

[19] II. 600, 665, 607 (referring to 2 Thess. 2:7).
[20] II. 513 (cf. Matt. 15:17-20 and 2. 4. iii above), 587, 666, 609.
[21] Le Comte, p. 24; Hill[2], pp. 109, 130-2, 315, 323, 451-3. M seems at times to provoke such criticisms: Sonnet XII ('I did but prompt the age to quit their clogs') adopts the same contemptuous vocabulary towards marriage as the libertine Francis Osborne ('a Clogge fastened to the neck of Liberty', *Advice to a Son* (Oxford, 1656), p. 52), and the Restoration lampoon 'The clog of all Pleasure, the luggage of Life' (Roger Thompson, *Unfit for Modest Ears* (1979), p. 120). M's main defence against the charge that he is in fact calling for '*Divorce at pleasure*' (II. 723) is that found in *Tetrachordon*, where he interprets Christ's words as an attack on those who, like the Pharisees, abuse the OT powers of divorce by dismissing a wife on impulse or on trivial grounds; the true Christian is more responsible (II. 667-78).

separation of mind and body, sexuality and humanity. Two, however, involve a less 'mute' and more complex interpenetration of erotic drives and 'intellective principles': the 'voluntarie' sexuality of true married love (turned to horror in a false marriage), and the perverse state—the ideal of libertinism—in which physical desire is enhanced and promulgated by intellectual practice. The former of these is of course the *summum bonum*, and the latter entirely evil, worse than animal. In the simpler moral universe of 'Puritan' marriage-theory, any use of the mind to provoke or prolong desire is condemned as 'Lust' and banished from the home.[22] But Milton dallies with a more complicated and controversial model. The crime of placing the intellect at the service of lust is not only committed by libertines and Sons of Belial, like those who will use the divorce tracts as if they were the 'choicest delights and criticisms of sin' discussed in *Areopagitica* (II. 518); it also underlies the 'gross and borish opinions' of the existing canon law and its Protestant defenders. But the contrary virtue, the interfusion of will and desire in true married love, is itself conceived in terms that border on the libertine ideal.

The characteristic movement of the divorce tracts is one of oscillation: Milton ventures hesitantly into the complex implications of voluntary sexuality, only to take frequent refuge in the simplicities of dualism and ascetic denunciation of the flesh. Thus he sometimes assumes a wide gulf between sex and 'conversation', the social intercourse of properly compatible lovers, but in the next breath will bring them closer again: 'why then shall divorce be granted for want of bodily performance, and not for want of fitnes to intimate conversation, when as corporal benevolence cannot in any human fashion bee without this?' (II. 609). Occasionally he goes even further: when he complains that the inexperienced suitor 'may easily chance to meet, if not with a body impenetrable, yet often with a minde to all other due conversation inaccessible' (II. 250), he is assuming that sex is itself a form of conversation, and when he upholds the true love of male and female against the claims of male friendship made by the 'crabbed' and 'rustic' Augustine, he even suggests that the 'conversation' of the ideal couple will rekindle their sexual ardour: 'there is one society of grave friendship, and another amiable and attractive society of conjugal love, besides the deed of procreation, which of it self soon cloies, and is despis'd,

---

[22] e.g. William Whately, pp. 19–20.

unless it bee *cherisht and re-incited* with a pleasing conversation.' He even claims that the wife's adultery could make her a better companion.[23] At such moments we glimpse, however tantalizingly, a Milton who prides himself on his expansiveness and urbanity (neither 'crabbed' nor 'rustic'), and who projects into marriage an almost libertine fusion of erotic excitement and mental life.

The context for this attack on Augustine shows how vulnerable and defensive Milton was in this area. The coarse 'narrow-Augustinian' opinion had been used in the anonymous *Answer to ... the Doctrine and Discipline of Divorce* (1644) to challenge Milton's ideal of 'conversation'. We should recall that 'conversation' was not only a general term for social intercourse but also a legal and colloquial term for copulation; the Answerer tries to trap Milton between these two meanings. On the one hand he snickers lewdly at Milton's claim—admittedly an astonishing one—that the experienced libertine is better than the sober man at finding out whether a bashful fiancée is really 'fit for conversation'; on the other hand he reiterates Augustine's denigration of female companionship—marriage cannot have been constituted in Genesis by 'the solace and content in the gifts of the minde of one another only', for then God would have made a male friend out of the rib. The bond of marriage is not 'delectableness of converse', which women cannot so much provide, much less to 'speak Hebrew, Greek, Latine, and French, and dispute against the Canon law as well as you'; it is rather 'a pleasant conversation' in the purely sexual sense.[24]

It is thus Milton's fury at the devaluation of woman that drives him to define 'conversation' in such exalted terms—without, however, repudiating any of the eroticism that provoked the original attacks. To humble his opponent and protect himself still further, he claims the authority of a Protestant consensus: 'our Writers deservedly reject this crabbed opinion' (II. 596). But we have seen in chapter 3 that Protestant doctrines, and Milton's relation to

---

[23] II. 740 (my emphasis), 674; cf. Vives (quot. in Halkett, pp. 64-5), who asserts that 'every bodye dispiseth' the act of love, without allowing for the possibility of redemption or cherishing reincitement.

[24] *An Answer*, pp. 12-16 (facsimile in W. R. Parker, *Milton's Contemporary Reputation* (1940)); see *OED* 'conversation' 3, and Halkett, ch. 3 *passim*, esp. p. 61 and n. 24. In *Colasterion* M replies that, whatever 'conversation' means, it is something only available to the gentry, and not to cast serving-men such as he supposes the Answerer to be (II. 742).

them, are far from straightforward. Luther and Donne, for example, still adhere to the narrow-Augustinian view, and those who reject it do not necessarily share Milton's reading of Genesis. Traditional marriage-treatises had certainly emphasized physical 'due benevolence'—too much, in Milton's view—and had applied the Solomonic rapture to the love that binds husband and wife; but they determine the essence of marriage, and its conformity to the 'ordinance' of Genesis, by more sober criteria. Thomas Gataker, for example, insists that the wife is given to the husband 'not to be *a play-fellow*, or *a bed fellow*, or *a table mate* ... (and yet to be all these too) but to be *a yoake-fellow*.'[25] In Milton, however, these kinds of fellowship are recombined and reordered. The bond of labour appears only as a grotesque image for the fellowship of the bed: the poor husband must 'grind in the mill of an undelighted and servil copulation ... oft times with such a yokefellow, from whom both love and peace, both nature and Religion [yearn] to be separated' (II. 258). And the subordinate function of play, the erotic 'rejoicing' encouraged by Solomon, now subsumes every other purpose; the 'help meet' of Genesis is redefined as a relaxing amorous playfellow.

The constituent passion of marriage, the 'desire which God put into *Adam* in Paradise' and in which God saw 'it was not good that man should be left alone to burn', is defined by Milton as a longing for 'cheerfull society', 'due conversation', the 'dearest and most peacable estate of household society' (II. 250-1, 242). This might sound like a cool, asexual impulse, especially since it is so vehemently dissociated from the 'burning' of copulation. But in fact Milton describes it in intensely passionate language. This 'rationall burning' is the love celebrated in the Song of Songs, stronger than death, and unquenchable by many waters; no man 'hath the power to struggle with an intelligible flame, not in Paradise to be resisted, become now more ardent by being fail'd of what in reason it lookt for.' This desire, though it must not be *equated* with the sexual urge, is nevertheless so intimately *connected* to sexuality that it reaches its greatest intensity in the post-coital moment: it is 'even then most unquencht, when the importunity of a provender burning is well enough appeas'd, and yet the soul hath obtain'd nothing of what it justly desires' (II. 251-2). The soul had evidently expected to find what it wanted in the sexual act itself.

[25] *A Marriage-Prayer* (1624), quot. in Halkett, p. 40.

Milton's ideal of married love should not therefore be thought of as a social drive or as a higher form of friendship, but as a private bonding of male and female suffused with erotic energy.[26] (Even when he does link marriage to the public sphere, he does so in terms of personal mood and energy rather than social utility.) Milton would certainly not have agreed with John Heydon, that a good wife is female only in body, and masculine in companionship: heterosexual union alone can generate the 'peculiar comfort in the married state besides the genial bed, which no other society affords' (II. 596 and cf. ch. 3 n. 34 above). It would be misleading to assert that 'besides the genial bed', or 'besides the deed of procreation', refer to an alternative to sexuality or to an asexual area within marriage; as Milton proceeds to explain, he has in mind a special kind of voluptuousness into which the man can escape from the pressures of contemplation and action in the outside world. 'We cannot ... alwayes be contemplative, or pragmaticall abroad, but have need of som delightfull intermissions,' and the company of the 'different sexe', with its 'most resembling unlikenes, and most unlike resemblance,' provides the most delightful vacation for the soul.[27] The same gender-based division of the three modes of life, Contemplative, Active ('pragmaticall'), and Voluptuous, persists in *Paradise Lost*—'For contemplation hee and valour formd, / For softness shee and sweet attractive Grace' (IV. 297-8). This 'slackning the cords' is achieved through a kind of erotic play, contingent with but not identical to the sexual act itself.

Milton defends this hedonistic definition of Edenic marriage with vehement conviction. Prudes and Gnostics may find it 'overfrolick', and the Sons of Belial may use it to justify their debaucheries, but God Himself encourages erotic play through the words of Solomon. Wisdom in Proverbs 8:30 reveals herself *'playing alwayes'* with God—Milton's translation is close to the Hebrew original, which

---

[26] Hagstrum's definition of the Miltonic ideal as 'heterosexual friendship' (ch. 2 and *passim*) should be qualified, since M himself distinguished and contrasted the 'amiable' bond of lovers and the 'grave' bond of friendship. Halkett (e.g. pp. 26-7) shows how M differs from all his contemporaries in not stressing the social aspect of marriage.

[27] II. 596-7; ideal matrimony combines the comforts of 'home' and the pleasures of 'wandring vacancy', and thus redeems the association of 'wandering' and fallen sexuality discussed in ch. 7 n. 86 below. Cf. also *A Mask*, ll. 684-6 and William Heale, *An Apologie for Women* (Oxford, 1609) p. 58, where the places of masculine trouble are listed in order to make the reader appreciate the domestic comforts provided by the wife.

has erotic connotations—and in 5:18-19 exhorts the young man to 'rejoice with the wife of thy youth ... let her breasts satisfy thee at all times, and be thou ravished always with her love.' Passages such as these, and the 'thousand raptures' of the Song of Songs, should be interpreted as God's *ars amatoria*, instructing the inexperienced and strengthening their spirits against harsh and ascetic denials of the flesh. Solomon understood that virginal young men might be 'too timorous' of female company, and that they could be intimidated by the kind of austere 'Hypocrites' later denounced in the hymn to Wedded Love in *Paradise Lost*; he therefore 'among his gravest Proverbs countenances a kinde of ravishment and erring fondness in the entertainment of wedded leisures' (II. 597 and cf. n. 256). Milton was presumably aware that, as we have seen in our discussion of the 'Puritan Art of Love', the Hebrew phrase translated as 'be thou ravished' actually means 'err thou' (ch. 2 n. 60 above); he typically 'hatches' a latent possibility in the Protestant tradition. Just as in *Paradise Lost* 'mazy error' or 'liquid lapse' can be used with a conspicuous absence of pejorative meaning (IV. 239, VIII. 236), so in the earthly Paradise of marital dalliance, Milton fondly dreams, the husband can lose himself without fear of transgression in 'a kinde of ravishment and erring fondness'.

Thus the defence of virtue generates in Milton a vision of delight, ostensibly in agreement with Protestant conceptions of holy matrimony, but paradoxically more ascetic and more erotic. The vehemence of his response to criticism, and the 'sensuous and passionate' vision that confirmed his reputation as a libertine, both match the combative morality of *Areopagitica*, written in the thick of the divorce controversy. Even before this, however, Milton had been accused of sexual debauchery, and had replied by proclaiming a loftier theory and practice of sexuality—in the *Apology for Smectymnuus*. In this earlier episode, as in the divorce battle, the hostile reader had deduced from Milton's own writing a deep personal knowledge and experience of illicit sex. Here too Milton responded by claiming the respectability of traditional thought, but redefining it in the process. In the *Apology*, as later in the *Doctrine and Discipline of Divorce*, this protective colouring is provided by the Platonic doctrine of Eros.

To defend himself against the charge of brothel-going, Milton provides an autobiographical account of his own erotic initiation.

As we might expect from *Areopagitica*, this took place in books rather than in action, since the governing principle was a 'sage and serious doctrine of virginity' derived from Socrates, St. Paul, and Revelation. He steeped himself not in Puritan marriage-manuals but in secular erotic poetry, first of an Ovidian and then of a Petrarchan flavour. Even from texts that would be lascivious and corrupting to a weaker man he was able to extract a devotion to male chastity: he learnt to dream of an ideal mistress in whom 'good and faire meet'—'such a reward as the noblest dispositions above other things in his life have sometimes preferred'—and who would be his Beatrice and Laura, though in a real marriage. From here the amorous Quixote progressed through chivalrous romances to the erotic philosophies of Plato and Xenophon, and these in turn blended with the 'chaste and high mysteries' of St. Paul.[28] Thus in the *Apology* he recounts the stages of his initiation into philosophical Eros, just as Socrates had told of his own initiation by Diotima, and in the *Doctrine and Discipline* he presents the fruits of this wisdom, first revealing the true meaning of Genesis and 1 Corinthians by assimilating them to the teaching of Plato, and then developing his own myth of Eros dictated by 'my author'— Milton's own poetic genius—as Socrates's was dictated by Diotima.

The divorce tracts are heavy with the accumulated longing of this quest for a perfect mistress, and suffused with a vision of Eros that is both neo-Platonic and intensely practical. Plato's myth of Poros and Penia, St. Paul's 'burning', and Adam's loneliness are all harnessed to the same point: that the yearning for a mate is divinely implanted, and that if a marriage does not re-enact the primal love-scene in the garden, and cannot engender the true Eros described by Diotima 'at least in some proportion', then it must be annulled (II. 252-6). Every proposal in these tracts is weighed by the standard of love, and every complaint issues from a wounded expectation of love. (This seemed extravagantly romantic to one early reader of Milton's tract, who remarked that in marriage 'what we extravagantly hope for usually answers not the richness of our fancy.')[29] 'Love' in the context of Scriptural interpretation may mean 'the rule of charity', the *agapē* of Christ, but far more often

---

[28] I. 889-92 and cf. 588-9; for M's cult of virginity cf. 'At a Vacation Exercise', 'Elegia Sexta', lines appended to the Elegies, and *A Mask* ll. 455-74, 784-5, 915-16, 1002-4; 'Epitaphium Damonis', ll. 191-219; Le Comte, pp. 1-2.

[29] Antony Ascham, quot. in Le Comte, p. 32.

it refers to interpersonal Eros, the 'acts of love and peace' generated by the conjunction of male and female.[30]

Milton's vivid evocation of amorous play translates into 'sensuous and passionate' terms this intuited 'proportion' between ideal Eros and potentially real marriage. Such a 'liberty' may risk being taken for sexual 'license', but according to *Areopagitica* this can only confirm the authenticity and vitality of the vision. How else could the intended reader and beneficiary, the chaste youth who has 'layd up his chiefest earthly comforts in the enjoyment of a contented marriage' (II. 254), gain the experience necessary to make a wise choice? This preoccupation with 'raptures on the hither side of carnall enjoyment' also addresses a contradiction within Milton himself, however. His 'chast hopes' (I. 588), fed by an imagination trained on the *Symposium* and the Song of Songs, did not encourage him to drain erotic energy from any aspect of marriage, but his sense of pollution would not let him celebrate copulation as a good in its own right. He was too gallant to reduce woman to the biological function of procreation, but he could not conceive of her except as an erotic presence, suffusing everything with what Adam would later call 'the spirit of love and amorous delight'. He thus develops a theory and practice of Eros which bridges these two extremes, which depreciates the central act of sexuality while extending its peripheral delights into every corner of the relationship. Milton almost embraces the system of Rochester's 'Platonic Lady', who despises 'the feat' of copulation only because all the other gestures of love-making are more exquisitely pleasurable.[31]

[iv]

Milton's revision of Platonism and his quasi-libertine celebration of Solomonic rapture help him to articulate the Paradisal ideal, but they also have an important practical function, as a means of dealing with the bitter side of erotic experience. The divorce tracts are concerned not only with the male reader living in 'chaste hopes', but with the one already trapped in a hasty and miserable

---

[30] e.g. II. 587-8. Theodore L. Huguelet, 'The Rule of Charity in Milton's Divorce Tracts', *MS* VI (1974), 199-214, only deals with love in one tantalizing footnote (15), and Halkett likewise underestimates the erotic when he asserts that M judged the wife's fitness in purely spiritual terms, and 'not in the sense that she was a female' (p. 62).

[31] *Poems*, ed. Keith Walker (Oxford, 1984), pp. 23-4; attribution doubtful. For M's borrowings from the Cavalier 'fruition' debate, see 7. 1. iii below.

marriage—a frequent occurrence, Milton points out (attempting to veil the autobiographical reference).[32] In Areopagitican terms, Milton's text—vivid with the life-blood of a master spirit—will provide a surrogate 'experience' of marriage both good and bad, so that the reader will not have to rely on the 'practise' of fornication or worse: he freely admits that 'they who have liv'd most loosely by reason of their bold accustoming prove most successful in their matches, because their wild affections unsetling at will have been as so many divorces to teach them experience' (II. 249-50). This strangely moving tribute to the libertine enemy points to a contradiction in Milton's understanding of experience. In *Areopagitica* it is welcomed as a 'triall' even in the moral economy of Paradise; but the complexities of marital discord, which could have been avoided by the experienced man, carry Milton beyond the confines of discourse, into areas which are 'lesse paine to conjecture than to have experience' (II. 250). The divorce tracts are sustained by a vision of 'love and peace', but this goal can only be reached by learning how to articulate the 'paine' that comes from the collapse of love.

Milton's distinctive contribution to the cross-pollenation of Genesis and Plato is to bring hatred into the orbit of Eros. When Loneliness and its partner have failed to engender Love in the primal garden, 'then enters *Hate*'; but Hate is not the equivalent of the serpent in this parallel to Eden, but rather a righteous anger, 'not that Hate that sins, but that which onely is naturall dissatisfaction'. Love and hatred are negative and positive poles of the same energy, and both are purely natural: 'both the hate which now diverts [the unhappy husband], and the lonelines which leads him still powerfully to seek a fit help, hath not the least grain of a sin in it.'[33]

Milton's monistic, physiological description of Love and Hate, in which the 'mysterious' natural philosophy of erotic sympathy and antipathy combines with the unwholesome stoppages and

[32] e.g. II. 249 (M's immediate audience is the legislature, but he obviously addresses individual readers too). For the general issue of 'experience' in radical Puritanism, see Hill[1], pp. 298-9; for an extreme version of the biographical approach, see Swift, *Prose*, ed. Herbert Davis, II (Oxford, 1957), 67 (and cf. 97): 'when *Milton* writ his Book of Divorces, it was presently rejected as an occasional Treatise, because every Body knew he had a Shrew for his Wife.'

[33] II. 253; cf. the correct, and Vulgate, version of Ps. 4:4 ('be angry, and sin not'), and II. 257, where M stubbornly defends a reading of Mal. 2:16 that has 'hate' refer not to God's hatred of divorce but to a man's hatred of his wife.

beneficial releases of humoral theory, sometimes seems to anticipate later notions of repression and sexual health. It is foolish 'to stop every vent and cranny of permissive liberty, lest nature wanting those needful pores and breathing spaces ... either suddenly break out into some wide rupture of open vice and frantick heresy, or els inwardly fester with repining and blasphemous thoughts.' Sectarian extremism and open libertinism stem from the same blockage, he argues: the *'fanatick* dreams' of Antinomians and Familists are mostly caused by 'the restraint of some lawfull liberty, which ought to be given men, and is deny'd them, as in Physick we learn in menstruous bodies, where natures current hath been stopt.' But the same restraint or 'suffocation' makes less religiously-inclined people 'give themselves much the more to whoredom and adulteries', and 'turn aside, oft-times unwillingly, to all dissolute uncleannesse'—until they sink down exhausted by 'the incredible frequency of trading lust'. If these outlets are refused, as on moral grounds of course they should be, frustration burrows inward, and even 'almost the strongest Christian ... will be ready to dispair in vertue, and mutin against divine providence.' Milton can be most perceptive in his analysis of the unconscious effects of thwarted desire: 'this doubtles is the reason of those lapses and that melancholy despair which we see in many wedded persons, though they understand it not.' In one significant respect, however, Milton's theory of baneful repression differs from Renaissance pathology and from twentieth-century psychiatry alike: the fundamental act of relief, the necessary freedom, the flow of 'nature's current'—all these refer not to healthy sexuality but to healthy divorce.[34]

The central passion that seeks satisfaction in marriage, itself a product of 'the issues of love and hatred distinctly flowing through the whole masse of created things' (II. 272), may thus be deflected by frustration into various channels—religious insanity, withering private fury against divine providence, and sexual adventures in other beds. Again, the intelligible flame, not sexual in itself, turns out to be intimately connected to sexuality. Significantly enough these prostitutions and adulteries are not motivated by mere lust

---

[34] II. 354, 278-9, 341, 254, and cf. 2. 4. iii above. Augustine (2. 2. i above) could conceive psychic health only as a Paradisal possibility forfeited by the Fall—repression (*refrenendum et cohibendum*) is a necessity of the fallen state; here again M's idiosyncratic interpretation of Scripture has transferred an aspect of Paradise from the irrecoverable past to the possible present.

(the unhappy husband is always assumed to be physically 'appeas'd' at home) but by the same yearning of the soul that made him marry in the first place: frustration 'drives many to transgresse the conjugall bed, while the soule wanders after that satisfaction which it had hope to find at home, but hath mis't; or els it sits repining even to Atheism' (II. 269). Sexual and spiritual rebellions are contingent, and in the paroxysm of hatred, as in the ecstasy of love, flesh and spirit tend toward deterministic fusion: unfitness 'induces hatred, which is the greatest dissolver, both of spiritual and corporeal union, turning the minde *and consequently the body* to other objects' (II. 733, my emphasis). This apparently necessary turn towards adultery occurs, as we saw, 'oft-times unwillingly'. The anonymous critic of Milton's *Doctrine and Discipline* could not understand why mental incompatibility should increase the danger of adultery: married partners frustrated by physical impotence 'are in a great measure as likely to burne in lust towards others as unmaried persons are; which such as have only a contrarietie of minde and disposition ... are not likely so subject to' (*Answer* p. 13). This crudely dualist assumption allows us to see by contrast how deeply, in Milton's vision of ideal marriage, mind, body, and sexuality are interfused.

What outlet, then, could the tragic husband obtain? Milton's own Platonic and Christian love-philosophy would not allow him to escape into the adultery he so feelingly describes, and he was repelled, though fascinated, by popular 'fanaticism'. Two possibilities thus remained: to suffer in private 'the fits and workings of a high impatience (II. 343)', raging against providence like Samson in his chains; or to launch an adventurous campaign for divorce-laws that would free both himself and his countrymen, and restore marriage 'to that serene and blisfull condition it was in at the beginning'. Indeed divorce itself is a 'manly' and heroic act, an acceptable sublimation of that passion which would otherwise corrode inwardly or boil over into frantic sexual athletics. 'The agrieved person shall doe more manly to be extraordinary and singular in claiming the due right whereof he is frustrated', Milton insisted, 'than to piece up his lost contentment by visiting the Stews, or stepping to his neighbours bed, which is the common shift in this misfortune, or els by suffering his usefull life to wast away and be lost under a secret affliction of an unconscionable size to humane strength' (II. 247).

The husband's dilemma is also the author's. In Milton's own terms, we may ask how far he contributes to the 'high enterprise' of reform, the promulgation of 'love and peace', and how far he merely expresses impotent rage. The divorce tracts attempt to be Milton's own restorative, a test of strength in which he seeks to 'piece up his lost contentment' and cure his 'secret affliction' by subsuming it into a public cause. They constitute not only a discussion of divorce but an act, a verbal dismissal of the bad wife in the patriarchal manner of Deuteronomy. But it is an act doomed to frustration. The divorce tracts produced no practical results, and their moral and literary success—according to the criterion of temperance—is qualified by the very energy that makes them outstanding; Milton's commitment to hatred produces a petulant violence that threatens the author's control of his own text.

The comparison to *Samson Agonistes* is irresistible, since the central character is similar in both—the gifted Nazarite who struggles with the temptation to mutiny against Providence, so terrible are the consequences of a foolish marriage. But in the tragedy 'the fits and workings of a high impatience' are shaped into a cathartic pattern, whereas in the pamphlets, where the generic vehicle encourages piecemeal exposition rather than aesthetic unity, sexual fury struggles for expression and often intrudes the rhetoric of passion into a text which nominally appeals to charity and reason. Milton's prose surges when he touches on marital hatred; wounded pride and self-pity burst through the cool restraint of the argument:

What therefore God hath joyned, let no man put asunder. But here the Christian prudence lies to consider what God hath joyn'd; shall we say that God hath joyn'd error, fraud, unfitnesse, wrath, contention, perpetuall loneliness, perpetuall discord? (II. 650)

(This sequence of outrages chronicles in miniature the progress of the wise man who chooses too hastily.) Or again,

Cleav to a Wife, but let her bee a wife, let her be a meet help, a solace, not a nothing, not an adversary, not a desertrice; can any law or command be so unreasonable to make men cleav to calamity, to ruin, to perdition? (II. 605)

Appeals to Christian patience did not mitigate this fury. When the *Answer* pointed out that 'one Christian ought to bear the infirmities of another, but chiefly of his Wife,' Milton rejoined 'I grant, infirmities, but not outrages, not perpetuall defraudments of truest conjugal society, nor injuries and vexations as importunate as fire.'[35] Milton's rage, he feels, is 'not that Hate that sins', nor is it a passion to be spent in catharsis, but a weapon to reinforce his 'extraordinary and singular' claim. At this tumultuous stage of his life he would not have sympathized with Yeats's realization, in 'A Prayer for my Daughter', that only with 'all hatred driven thence' can the soul 'recover radical innocence'.

3. Female usurpation: the act of bondage

Milton's doctrine and discipline of divorce may be summarized as follows: marriage must retain its pre-lapsarian bliss 'in some proportion', and to do this it must not be grounded in mere procreation—whereby woman becomes a department of the domestic economy, a kind of brood mare—but in 'a mutual fitnes to the final causes of wedlock, help and society,' in a 'due conversation' suffused with erotic gestures of the sort that pass between the lovers in the Song of Songs. (The husband should lie between the breasts of his wife, comfort her with apples, and drink of the juice of her pomegranate, while the wife, if 'mutual fitness' has any meaning, will rejoice in the kisses of his mouth, and perfumes will blow from her garden.) Without this 'cheerful society of wedlock' man is incomplete—she is 'another self, a second self, a very self itself'; within it every facet of life, even the bestial genitals, receives 'a human qualification' (II. 251, 600, 606).

It seems, then, that *humanitas* is only properly forged in the reciprocal delight of compatible lovers. When this ideal relationship breaks down or proves illusory, however, the 'manly' course— far manlier than private despair and manlier even than sexual adventurism—is to fight for divorce, to expel the female in a heroic gesture of separation that at one point is even compared to the primal act of Creation itself. We should therefore enquire how Milton reconciles the obligations of mutuality and manliness, and how he conceives the reciprocal relation of the sexes—the 'most resembling unlikenes and most unlike resemblance' that alone can generate true marital delight.

---

[35] II. 731. *De Doctrina*'s description of a bad marriage as 'importunus atque intestinus' (VI. 372) seems to combine this passage and *SA* 1037-8 ('a thorn / Intestin'). For other violent accusations in *Colasterion*, see 744 (and cf. n. 98), 748, 756.

It is essential to recall at this point that the early Christian teaching on male-female relations is paradoxical, and left a divided heritage. St. Paul provides several clear declarations of male supremacy, neatly summarized by Milton:

The head of the woman, saith he, I *Cor.* 11 *is the man*: *he the image and glory of God, she the glory of the man*: *he not for her, but she for him.* Therefore his precept is, *Wives be subject to your husbands as is fit in the Lord, Coloss.* 3.18. *In every thing, Eph.* 5.24. (II. 589)

But side by side with these bold sentences are others which suggest that subordination is only a temporary arrangement during persecution (1 Cor. 7:26-9), and others again which explicitly identify areas of equal obligation: in the words of one of the most reckless seventeenth-century suprematists, the Pauline rule of 'due benevolence' (1 Cor. 7:3-4) means that 'the Lord hath granted as great power to the woman over the man, as he hath granted to the man over the woman ... in the mutuall use of their bodies; and in this case he is as well subject to his wife, as he is her Lord.'[36] And some of Paul's clearest and hardest statements, when he derives subordination from the original creation and not from the fall, are immediately qualified (1 Cor. 11:8-9, 11-12). However subordinate in the community, woman is an equal partner in two areas—'in the Lord', and in the marriage-bed. Not only that, but the unequal, submissive behaviour demanded of the wife is of a special kind: *all* Christians, Paul insists, must 'submit themselves one to another in the fear of God', and the headship of the husband involves not God-like dominion but Christ-like humility—he must give himself for her, nourish and cherish her flesh as if it were his own (Eph. 5:21, 25-9).

Even within the Christian community, it is not clear that social relations should be hierarchic. As Milton himself pointed out in *Tetrachordon*, the early church re-established the primal state of man in which there was no private property and no relation of master and servant: 'prime Nature made us all equall.' As we have seen in chapter 3, the 'pre-subordinationist' reading of Genesis, which assumes (without basis in the text) that Eve was created inferior to Adam and under his command, was by no means universal, and had been memorably challenged in Lutheran commentary. Since 'the Gospel ... tending ever to that which is

---

[36] John Weemse, *The Portraiture of the Image of God in Man* (1638), p. 266.

perfetest, aim'd at the restorement of all things as they were in the beginning', should not the Christian couple strive for the greatest possible mutuality and equality in their relationship, or at least interpret subordination not according to the flesh but according to the paradoxical humility of Christian *agapē*?[37]

Milton was obviously very moved by the ideal of equality. In *Tetrachordon* 'prime Nature made us all equall', in *The Tenure of Kings and Magistrates* 'all men naturally were born free, being the image and resemblance of God himself, and were by privilege above all the creatures born to command, and not to obey' (III. 198), and in *Paradise Lost* Adam demands a companion of the same species—for no 'societie ... harmonie or true delight' can exist between 'unequals' (VIII. 383-4). In his earlier writings, however, Milton seems uncertain whether to include females in the species 'man'. He embraces the harsh Pauline interpretation of Genesis ('he not for her, but she for him') without the subsequent qualification, that man is 'by' woman and does not exist without her. He seizes upon one aspect of a complex, braided text—male supremacy—and forces every other strand into compliance with the single principle he has promoted.

Every mention of 'man' or 'him' in Scripture is thus interpreted by Milton as referring not to *homo*, the human being, but to *vir*, the male as opposed to the female. This gives a querulous, tight-lipped tone to his exposition—the 'peevishness' that Virginia Woolf detected, less justly, in *Paradise Lost*. The first chapter of Genesis, as we have seen, uses the plural to describe the creation of man in God's image except for one rhetorical variant with 'him', but Milton supplies, as it were, italics for this solitary pronoun—*he* was created in God's image, and *she* was not (II. 589). Consequently marriage must be defined as 'the apt and cheerful conversation of man with woman, to comfort and refresh *him* against the evil of solitary life'.[38] Milton is frequently praised for having admitted an exception to the rule of male supremacy if the

---

[37] II. 661, 665-6. Elaine Pagels points out that St. Paul recognized female apostles and spoke of one, Junia, as senior to himself (*The Gnostic Gospels* (NY, 1979), pp. 61 and 165 n. 64; cp Rom. 16:7, where the RSV has a male 'Junias').

[38] II. 235 (emphasis by Hagstrum, p. 35); cf. Woolf, ch. 5 n. 16 above. Mary Astell mentions M among those who cry up liberty in their political writings even though they would deny it to 'poor *Female Slaves*' (*Some Reflections on Marriage*, 4th edn. (1731; repr. NY, 1970), pp. 34-5); but she does not appear to know the divorce tracts.

wife 'exceed the husband in prudence and dexterity, and he contentedly yeeld,' for 'the wiser should govern the lesse wise, whether male or female.' But he strikes down this hypothesis in the next sentence. Genesis itself, 'the breath of this divine utterance', demolishes such an idea for Milton; man, 'the portraiture of God', must never become the 'thrall' of an absolutely 'inferiour', 'occasionall', and subordinate sex. The assertion of masculine pre-eminence by divorce is thus a reclamation of man's 'naturall birthright, and that indeleble character of priority which God crown'd him with'. In this context, it is clear that Milton has conflated male supremacy with the 'image of God' itself. The objection immediately occurs that 'sin hath lost him this', and indeed Michael explains to Adam in *Paradise Lost* that the image of God was lost at the moment of 'the sin of *Eve*', though some obscure 'similitude' survives in diminished form. In the *De Doctrina* Milton asserts that some traces of the image of God can still be found in man's ability to quell animals: the 'rule' over other species given in Genesis 1:28 is an integral part of this image. But in the grip of his passion for divorce, Milton extends this species-rule to woman, and assumes that the vanished or obliterated image is 'indelible'.[39] It becomes apparent that the noble words which begin *Tetrachordon*—'nothing now adayes is more degenerately forgotten, than the true dignity of man . . . especially in this prime institution of matrimony, wherein his native pre-eminence ought most to shine'—open the way not to human greatness but to the triumph of masculinity.

Mutuality can of course coexist with inequality. The relationship of husband and wife, like that of prince and subject, was normally interpreted as a harmonious balance of obligations—wives, submit to your husbands (lovingly and cheerfully), husbands, love your wives (sacrificially, considerately, protectively). The husband must be meet help to the wife, one popular sermon declared, as well as the wife to the husband. Some critics find this harmony in Milton's marital writings.[40]

[39] II. 589 (and cf. 587), VI. 396 (Col. edn. XV. 209), *PL* XI. 509-19; cf. Aers and Hodge, p. 130; Le Comte, p. 59; Mary A. Radzinowicz, *Towards Samson Agonistes* (Princeton, 1978), p. 48 n. 35. M appears to offer alternatives here, but then sweeps them away; as Stanley Fish says of a passage in *Reason of Church Government*, 'the choice is . . . no choice at all' (*Self-consuming Artifacts* (Berkeley, 1972), p. 302).

[40] Eph. 5:22, 25, Col. 3:18-19; William Secker, *A Wedding Ring* (1658), p. 23; Hagstrum, p. 28; Radzinowicz, pp. 42-8; McColley, pp. 30, 47, 180.

It is possible to glean phrases from the divorce tracts that recognize the needs and desires of both partners in marriage: before the fall 'man and woman were both perfet each to other' and united by yearning 'towards each other'; their conversation should minister to 'the solace and love of each other' otherwise they will become 'an intolerable evil each to other' (II. 665, 252, 328). It is also true that the *Doctrine and Discipline* is subtitled 'to the Good of Both Sexes', that 'mutuall consent' (II. 242) is preferable though not essential in divorce, and that Milton several times argues that divorce is easier on the feelings of a rejected wife than perpetual marriage to a husband 'disinabl'd to return that duty which is his, with a clear and hearty countenance, [who] thus continues to grieve whom he would not' (II. 258). The divorcer is described, in convoluted prose, as a rational and considerate man 'who after sober and coole experience, and long debate within himselfe, puts away whom though he cannot love or suffer as a wife with that sincere affection that marriage requires, yet loves at least with that civility and goodnesse, as not to keepe her under a neglected and unwelcom residence, where nothing can be hearty' (II. 669). And the dismissal itself should be 'beneficient and peacefull' (II. 732), according to the rule of charity.

These moments of concern for the divorced wife's feelings should be recognized, but their presence throws into greater relief a far more important absence. We look in vain in Milton's treatises for any meditation on 'Husbands, love your wives,' any cherishing or giving from the husband to the wife within marriage, or any more than a brief mention of his emotional duties. We find none of the 'strange *Metamorphosis*' of male into female that delighted Heale in the creation of Eve, and none of the *amor complacentiae*, the satisfaction in the enjoyment felt by the other partner, that Milton's contemporary Nathaniel Hardy praised as the chief bond of husband and wife, and which Montaigne valued most highly even in his adulterous affairs.[41] Milton treats wifely failings, as we have seen, in a tone not 'beneficient and peacefull' but tumultuous and aggrieved—not only in the *Doctrine and Discipline*, where the memory of desertion was still fresh, but in the more stately and controlled *Tetrachordon*. Despite his theories of 'naturall' antipathy, he does not recognize that marital conflicts grow from a mutual

---

[41] Heale, p. 52 (cf. Introd. i above); Hardy, *Love and Fear the Inseparable Twins of a Blest Matrimony* (1653), p. 8; Montaigne, *Essais*, III. v.

entangling that can never be solved by unilateral blame—a point made shrewdly by the anonymous Answerer, challenging Milton's equation of wifely recalcitrance and attempted murder:

it will not follow in your case, that because a man may seek divorce from her who seeks his life ... therefore for disagreement of disposition, causing sadnesse, and wherein they are both actors, if not equals, there the Husband may will-she nill-she put her away; this is just a taking advantage of our own faults and corruptions, to release us from our duties (p. 42).

Above all, we find in Milton's tracts no admission, except in a few impracticable cases borrowed from Roman law, that the wife has any right to divorce her husband, and an absolute denial that mental 'fitness', the supreme criterion of marriage, can ever be applied by the woman to the man.[42]

The suggestion that women (rather than men) should be free to divorce, which Milton mistakenly attributed to Beza and Paraeus, fills him with an indignation so strong that it overthrows not only the rule of charity but the laws of sentence-structure: 'Palpably uxorious! Who can be ignorant that woman was created for man, and not man for woman' (II. 324). The attitude of the *De Doctrina* is more mature and sympathetic: 'the husband is not allowed to divorce his wife merely because of his hard heart, but ... the wife is allowed to leave the husband if he is harsh and inhuman, which is a very just reason indeed'; the Mosaic law was established 'not in order to make any concessions to the hard-heartedness of husbands, but to rescue the wretched wives from any hard-heartedness which might occur' (VI. 374-5). In the earlier tracts, however, 'hardness of heart'—the post-lapsarian infirmity which Christ used to explain the necessity of the old Mosaic law in Matthew 19:8—is turned into another accusation against the failing wife. After 'hardnesse of heart came in', God allowed divorce (with other mitigations of 'our imperfet and degenerat condition') as 'a remedy against intolerable wrong and servitude above all the patience of man to bear'. The true reason for God's indulgence was to protect the tender male against the depredations of the female, and to ensure that 'the hardnes of anothers heart might

---

[42] II. 324, 327, 627; Halkett, pp. 51, 89-90. M's Roman Law examples of the wife's right to divorce come mostly from his tr. of Bucer (II. 448-9, 458, 462-3), and even here he doctors the original when it refers to women's divorce (cf. 461 and n. 1). In one passage of *Tetrachordon*, however, he does refer to 'helpe' as something the man must also provide (II. 691).

not inflict all things upon an innocent person, whom far other ends brought into a league of love and not of bondage and indignity' (II. 661-2).

The principle of mutuality is thus strained on the rack of Milton's divergent attitudes. He accepts the need for a sweet interchange of hearty affection, and recognizes, though in a cursory fashion, the obligations of the husband in this partnership. He admits that 'the law is to tender the liberty and human dignity of them that live under the law, whether it bee the mans right above the woman, or the womans just appeal against wrong and servitude' (II. 625). But immediately after this sentence, and generally throughout the divorce tracts, he reverts to a fearsomely unilateral form of accusation:

the duties of mariage contain in them a duty of benevolence, which to doe by compulsion against the Soul, where ther can bee neither peace, nor joy, nor love, but an enthrallment to one who either cannot, or will not bee mutual in the godliest and the civilest ends of that society, is the ignoblest and lowest slavery that a human shape can bee put to (II. 625-6).

In the context of Milton's refusal to let women divorce for incompatibility, or even enter into the 'long debate' that decides the breakdown of a marriage, these strictures against the unfit wife take on the quality of an oxymoron: only the woman is obliged to be mutual.

[*ii*]

For Milton the crux of the marriage-problem was evidently the unselfish 'benevolence' commanded by St. Paul: the sexual act took away, on unimpeachable authority, not only the subordination of the female but the power of self-determination—'the husband hath not power of his own body, but the wife.' The divorce tracts try to reinvent what Adam possessed before the fall, a form of *voluntary* sexuality; in this happy state, that Augustine had also attempted to imagine, the flesh proceeds from and therefore obeys the spirit, and no shadow falls between desire, will, and performance. But when this fails, all that remains is 'the compulsive stie of an ungratefull and malignant lust'—'compulsive' not in its modern psychological meaning, but in the sense of *compulsory*. Such enforced copulation is for Milton the most ignominious 'slavery', 'tyranny', 'bondage', and 'enthrallment'. The toiling male is filled, not with a Christ-like sacrificial love of the inferior, but with indignation at the loss of manhood: 'the Law therefore justly and piously provides against such an unmanly task of bondage as this.' He finds there nothing but the polluting touch of 'something below'—certainly not the beauty that Luther, as we saw in chapter 2, found in the sexual bond because it shadows forth the Incarnation. Milton's attitude here comes closer to the one he later gave Satan, contemplating his own anti-christian incarnation in the serpent: 'O foul descent!'[43]

Milton is divided between two conceptions of subordination. He recognizes, with contemporary marriage-theorists, that the relation of man and wife is an inequality 'tempered with equality': 'man is not to hold her as a servant, but receives her into a part of that empire which God proclaims him to, though not equally, yet largely, as his own image and glory; for it is no small glory to him, that a creature so like him, should be made subject to him.'[44] This is consistent with his approval of 'the woman's just appeal against wrong and servitude' in Roman law. Elsewhere, however, we hear nothing of this temperate and accountable authority: any derogation of masculine power, any lapse of female duty, which for Milton consists in the constant voluptuous manifestation of her own subordination, is denounced in the harsh language of extremism. Marriage to a less than perfect wife, as we have seen, is an 'intolerable wrong and servitude above the patience of man to bear', 'a league [not] of love [but] of bondage and indignity', 'an enthrallment to one who either cannot, or will not bee mutual'. Man must therefore 'acquitt himself to freedom' by divorce, for 'all men naturally were born free ... to command and not to obey'; woman apparently was born to the reverse. It is not clear what distinguishes this from 'servitude', from which the wife is supposedly exempt.

Milton's trouble with subordination should be related to the neurotic fear of sexual pollution, thraldom, and emasculation expressed not only in the virginal philosophy of *Comus*,[45] and in

[43] *Prose* II. 626, *PL* IX. 163; cf. ch. 2 n. 30 above, and *SA* 944-6: 'How wouldst thou insult / When I must live uxorious to thy will / In perfect thraldom?'

[44] II. 589; cf. Halkett, p. 84.

[45] The Elder Brother avers that the 'lewd and lavish act of sin / Lets in defilement to the inward parts', and the soul thereby 'grows clotted by contagion, / Imbodies, and imbrutes' (ll. 465-8); cf. the 'gumms of glutenous heat' (l. 917) and Le Comte's interpretation (pp. 1-2).

his dramatizations of marital failure, but in his attacks on political enemies. In *Of Reformation* (1641), for example, he accuses the bishops of sexually corrupting the youth of England; true Liberty 'consists in manly and honest labours, in sobriety and rigorous honour to the Marriage Bed, which in both Sexes should be bred up from chast hopes to loyal Enjoyments,' but the bishops concentrate their designs on boys, conspiring to 'effeminate us' and to 'despoile us both of *manhood* and *grace*'.[46] In the works of the later 1640s and 1650s, the dangers of effeminacy are discovered not just in the narrow area of illicit sexuality but in the household and the state. Those books of the *History of Britain* written during his first marriage, as Edward Le Comte has shown, quiver with a coarse dismissive disdain of female rule that sometimes leads Milton to contradict his own sources.[47] In his anti-monarchist tracts he mocks Charles I's attempts to perform 'masculin coition' upon Parliament, and sneers at him for praising Henrietta Maria 'in straines that come almost to Sonnetting': this shows 'how great mischeif and dishonour hath befall'n to Nations under the Government of effeminate and Uxorious Magistrates, who being themselves govern'd and overswaid at home under a Feminine usurpation, cannot be farr short of spirit and authority without dores, to govern a whole Nation.' Woman's task is evidently to infuse 'spirit and authority' into her husband by her amorous submissiveness, so that he can function in the world of men. In the *Defences*, again, he attacks Salmasius (and later More) as a submissive husband, a grovelling swine, a eunuch, and a hermaphrodite—apparently interchangeable terms. In contrast he points explicitly to his own manly efforts, in the divorce tracts and elsewhere, to restore liberty both political and domestic: 'in vain does he prattle about liberty in assembly and marketplace who at home endures the slavery most unworthy of man, slavery to an inferior.' The loathing that pervades Milton's battles over status and territory confirm the anthropologist's insight, that 'pollution ideas' are necessarily related to 'a total structure of thought whose

---

[46] I. 588-9, and cf. n. 56: M draws a parallel from Herodotus's account of the destruction of the Lydians, undefeated in battle, who were nevertheless made to 'slacken, and fall to loosenes' by the spread of dancing, feasting, and dicing—to which M significantly adds '*Stews*'.

[47] pp. 53-8. M assumes that their praise of Boadicea is in fact a secret insult ('as if in Britain women were men, and men women'), and later blames the Normans for bringing in 'Vices which effeminate mens minds' (V. 402).

key-stone, boundaries, margins and internal lines are held in relation by rituals of separation'.[48]

Milton may have steeped himself in chivalrous romance, as he claims in the *Apology*, but neither in the divorce tracts nor in the political tirades do we hear anything of the gentle sway of beauty, the courtly pretence that the realms of male and female power are absolute and complementary. He appears to share the fear of a later knight errant, that *la belle dame sans merci* might have him in thrall. The only power a woman can exercise, in Milton's view, is tyranny; and the sexual act, far from being the one area this side of heaven exempt from power-relations, as St. Paul would have it, is the very factory of female usurpation. Milton allows the husband no gracious surrender, no 'condescension' in its old non-pejorative sense; in bed he must redouble his efforts not to fall into the opposite of manliness, into thraldom, effeminacy and palpable uxoriousness. Indeed, marriage becomes the realm of Lilith, a sinister and magical power. Throughout the political pamphlets, the divorce tracts, and *Samson Agonistes*, the female is endowed with associations of deceit and sorcery which confuse the boundaries of the whore, the wife, and the witch.

The *Apology* describes the Reformation as an Old Testament divorce subverted by the 'whoorish cunning' of the 'crafty adulteresse', who 'like a witch' leaves sentimental mementos and 'inticing words' behind her so that she can still exercise her power: 'thus did those tender hearted reformers dotingly suffer themselves to be overcome with harlots language' (I. 942). *Eikonoklastes* denounces the followers of an uxorious king as 'men enchanted with the *Circaean* cup of servitude' (III. 488). The divorce tracts address the case of the wise but inexperienced man, whose bad marriage-choice is sometimes described as an error in his own judgement but sometimes as a sinister beguilement—'wisest men' have often been 'drawn ... by suttle allurement within the train of an unhappy matrimony' (II. 603); likewise the Chorus advises Samson to 'tax not divine disposal' (a temptation also for the unhappy husband, we recall) because 'wisest Men / Have err'd, and by bad Women

---

[48] IV. i. 309, 312, 476, 518, 625 (Col. edn. VII. 14, 20, 400, 510, VIII. 132); III. 420-1, 467; cf. III. 195 ('the unmaskuline (*sic*) Rhetorick of any puling Priest or Chaplain'), *SA* 1059-60 ('not sway'd / By female usurpation'), and ch. 5 n. 17 above (for a feminine aspect of M's own poetry). Regina Schwartz and David Loewenstein both suggested the connection with Mary Douglas, *Purity and Danger* (1966), p. 41.

been deceiv'd' (210-11). Samson himself in his tirade against Dalila denounces the 'arts of every woman false like thee', which have 'beguil'd' and even killed the 'Wisest and best men';[49] accusations of hastening death, which had also been made in the *Doctrine and Discipline*, are repeated throughout the interview with Dalila, and form Samson's last words on the subject (1009). The 'arts' of this 'sorceress' are clearly those of a Circe or a female Comus; she has tried to ensnare him with 'trains', 'ginns and toyls', a 'fair enchanted cup', and 'warbling charms'.[50] Anti-marital bitterness led Milton to apply the fate of Samson to the unhappy husband, grinding in the mill of an undelighted and servile copulation, and later to change Dalila from a strumpet to a wife in *Samson Agonistes*— though in the heat of fury Samson ceases to distinguish between the wife and the 'Concubine' or between sexual attraction and the 'venereal trains' of sorcery; he even suggests that it is post-coital sleep, rather than telling his secret, which has shorn him of his strength and 'Softened' him 'with pleasure and voluptuous life' (532-8). It is ironic that 'voluptuous life', as distinguished from contemplative or active, is precisely the area consigned to the wife in Milton's vision of ideal marriage, and relaxation is precisely the service she provides. And the liberation offered by divorce is itself described as a softening and a charm. The corruption of marriage, vividly portrayed in this central scene of *Samson Agonistes*, thus disturbingly retains features of its happiest state.

Milton's divorce writings share with many of his contemporaries a disturbing sense of sexuality as a metamorphosis, a change of state into 'something beneath man', a slackening or softening into effeminacy. Donne believed, as we have seen, that Eve was created from a rib in order to show how much she weakens man, and he warns the husband not to be so '*uxorious*' as to love his wife 'like

[49] 749, 759, 762-4; cf. M's treatment of Solomon, 'that uxorious king, whose heart though large, / Beguiled by fair idolatresses, fell / To idols foul (*PL* I. 444-6)', on whom he proposed to write the tragedy *Salomon Gynaecratumenus* (*Prose* VIII. 556). Though W. R. Parker's arguments for the early date of *SA* are often weak, his collection of echoes from the divorce tracts remains impressive (*Biography*, pp. 911-16); the tone and ethos of the Dalila scenes, closely juxtaposed to scenes in which the protagonist mutinies against Divine Providence and wrestles with despair, is not otherwise found in M except in the period of marital difficulty, i.e. from the first edn. of *DDD* to the letter to Dati of April 1647 (II. 762-3).

[50] 819, 932-5; cf. 427, on the 'over potent charms' of Samson's first wife, and Leonora L. Brodwin, 'Milton and the Renaissance Circe', *MS* VI (1974), 21-83, a useful article marred by excessive claims for the importance of its subject.

a Mistresse ... lest otherwise she prove *in Ruinam*, who was given *in Adjutorium*, and he be put to the first mans plea, *Mulier quam dedisti*, The *woman whom thou gavest me, gave me my death*'; here, as in the *First Anniversary*, the fall is equated with the death hastened by loss of sperm. And in the folklore of popular misogyny, women are dangerous because 'in the night they will work a man like Wax'.[51] We are again reminded of the connection between pollution and the maintenance of structures and boundaries—in Milton's case particularly the vertical boundaries, fragile in a time of revolution, that guaranteed his status as an author 'above the crowd' and as a husband above the woman.

In some part of his mind, Milton seems to think of male and female not as two individuals of the same species but as two substances, an upper and a lower, that must never be emulsified. Consequently the sexual mingling of bodies (what D. H. Lawrence would later call a 'communion of the two blood-streams' and a 'touching on one another of the two rivers where Paradise was, or the Park of Eden, where man had his beginning') becomes the torture of a slave or tyrant's victim, an 'unmanly task of bondage', an enforced embrace with a deliquescent corpse or 'image of earth and phlegm', a 'thick intoxicating potion' offered by a 'Sorceresse'.[52] Femaleness is conceived not as an alternative and complementary mode of humanity but as a lower form of existence—*voluptas* rather than *contemplatio*, sense rather than reason, softness and dissolution rather than firm structure and definition. If so, then man includes the female as a lower nature, and male identity must be preserved all the more vigilantly because it could easily deliquesce into the female, the 'effeminate'. For Milton all relations between the sexes that are not strictly hierarchic, and all sexual embraces that are not irradiated by an almost unattainable union of souls in Edenic marriage, involve a contagious metamorphosis into female substance.

---

[51] *Sermons* II. 345-6 (cf. n. 5 above); G. Thorowgood, *Pray Be Not Angry* (1656), quot. Halkett, p. 74.

[52] Lawrence, 'A Propos of "Lady Chatterley's Lover" ', in *Phoenix II*, ed. Warren Roberts and Harry T. Moore (1968), p. 506 (quot. in Lerner, p. 160); Milton, *Prose* II. 626, 327, 254, and I. 891-2—the 'potion' comes from M's Platonic initiation in the *Apology*, where it is opposed to the 'charming cup' of true Eros.

6. The Intelligible Flame

[*iii*]

In Milton's earlier writings, and in his dramatization of disastrous marriage, the roads of love lead to the palace of divorce. In the *Apology*, alongside the intensely romantic devotion to ideal Eros, and some time before he had faced the problems of marriage on a practical level, we find Milton's imagination kindled by the idea of Old Testament divorce, producing a detailed and dramatic scene of masculine dismissal and feminine blandishment (I. 942). (The 'whoorish cunning' of the wife [Popery] has plunged England 'deepe in dotage' and 'uncleane wallowings'—suggesting the swine of Circe, or Comus's followers rolling in their 'sensual stie', or the 'compulsive stie' of the unhappy marriage-bed.) In the *Doctrine and Discipline of Divorce*, as we have seen, the expulsion of the female is compared to the divine command that brought order out of the unwholesome minglings of chaos. In *Tetrachordon* divorce is radical surgery which will 'sever us from an intimat evil (II. 665)', restoring life to the suffering individual and primal happiness to 'the much wrong'd and over-sorrow'd state of matrimony'. The man who re-establishes divorce 'shall deserve to be reckon'd among the publick benefactors of civill and humane life, above the inventors of wine and oyle; for this is a far dearer, far nobler, and more desirable cherishing to mans life' (II. 240). The old law, Christ maintained, had introduced divorce as a concession to callousness and infirmity; Milton, however, makes his own 'extraordinary and singular' claim that it is divorce, rather than perpetual marriage, which comes closest to the spirit of 'peace and love', to 'the rule of perfection', and so to Christ's own 'rule of charity'. Indeed, *not* to dare divorce is the real infirmity, and reveals a lack of faith and a 'timorous and low conceit of charity'. By putting his bold programme into law, the rulers of England will be obeying 'the greatest, the perfetest, the highest commandment' (II. 666-7).

The overwhelming impression of the divorce tracts, however, like that of the Dalila-episode in *Samson Agonistes*, is one of violence. We can certainly detect in both cases the bruised remains of an ideal vision of Paradisal happiness and love.[53] But when Samson

[53] Cf. *SA* 836-9 ('But *Love constrain'd thee*; call it furious rage / To satisfie thy lust: Love seeks to have Love; / My love how couldst thou hope, who tookest the way / To raise in me inexpiable hate?'), and 1008-9 ('Love-quarrels oft in pleasing concord end, / Not wedlock-trechery endangering life').

expels Dalila we do not witness the 'beneficient and peacefull' dismissal required by the rule of charity, nor do we feel, as one critic has claimed, that we are in the presence of a man who has suddenly regained a vision of marriage as 'an image of a well-tempered human Soul'; we see an act of fundamental savagery, quite unlike the calm to which he is led at the end of his crisis of confidence in the Lord.[54] The rage of the divorce tracts likewise undermines their professed devotion to 'love and peace', and disrupts the calm and rational procedure of exegesis. In the closing books of *Paradise Lost* we follow the painstaking reconstruction of trust, forbearance, and mutual loyalty in the face of unprecedentedly destructive emotions, and we see two individuals struggling with but resisting the very desire that Milton so richly indulges in his other marital writings—the temptation to expel and annihilate the other. The divorce tracts and *Samson Agonistes*, on the other hand, seek the restitution of order in a great sundering, a solitary and destructive cataclysm.

The major problem of bad marriage, Milton believed, is that it forces the godly and sensitive young man to 'live a contentious and unchristian life'. The main problem of the divorce tracts, in turn, is this: how far can a contentious and unchristian book rectify this intolerable wrong? The radical in Milton of course believed that he was overthrowing Dagon, imitating the violence of God Himself when He takes reformation in hand;[55] and the artist in him also would recognize the need for an intensified mimesis or surrogate experience. But Milton's almost fascistic enthusiasm for violence surely clashes with the principle of temperance, which involves managing and shaping, rather than surrendering to, the forces of 'passion', 'paine', and 'experience'. This judgement of failure may seem to be inappropriately moralistic, but we should not forget that *Areopagitica* itself, and the activist poetics proclaimed throughout Milton's prose, forges a vital link between ethics, aesthetics, and the reader's response.

We conclude, then, that though they are suffused with theoretical

[54] *Prose* II. 732; Radzinowicz, p. 37; cf. Samson's response to Dalila's request to 'approach at least, and touch thy hand': 'Not for thy life, lest fierce remembrance wake / My sudden rage to tear thee joint by joint. / At distance I forgive thee, go with that' (951-4).

[55] II. 666-7; M's apocalyptic violence is explored in David A. Loewenstein, 'Milton and the Drama of History: From the Revolutionary Prose to the Major Poems' (Ph.D. diss., University of Virginia, 1985).

eroticism and Utopian dreaming, and illuminated by moments of 'poetical enthusiasm', at the core the divorce tracts are authentically ugly. They lack the fair-mindedness of Milton's later summary of the divorce question in *De Doctrina Christiana*, and their Old Testament sense of pollution is not redeemed by the miraculous presence of real love, as it is in the sonnet 'Methought I saw my late espoused saint'. These tracts claim to bring 'love and peace', a 'divine touch' that 'in one instant hushes outrageous tempests into a sudden stilnesse and peacefull calm'; but they are distorted by rage, petulant accusation, and violent disdain. Theirs is not the ugliness of Rembrandt's Adam and Eve, shot through with an almost Kierkegaardian compassion,[56] nor the lyric grief over human failure that runs through *Paradise Lost*, but the shapeless and incoherent vehemence of a man who considered himself 'unspeakably wrong'd'. If the bond or 'conversation' between reader and text were regarded as a marriage and subjected to the criteria of these tracts, Milton himself would be expelled.

The divorce tracts are still a necessary stage in the dialectic of Milton's development, however; they belong to his 'growth', if not his 'compleating'. In the terms of *Areopagitica*, conflict is a mark of authenticity. A rational and coherent text would not have been true to Milton's ideology of sex and gender, nor would it have been an adequate vehicle for his fractured response to the Paradisal ideal. He refuses to abandon 'experience', but he also refuses to lose hold of the idea that 'some proportion' must obtain between squalid reality and the myth of perfection. In these tracts his sense of proportion is uncertain, often submerged in the struggles of the moment or pulled apart by contradictory responses to the fall; but it is precisely these tensions that propel him towards *Paradise Lost*.

[56] Cf. Kierkegaard, *Works of Love*, tr. Howard and Edna Hong (1962), pp. 342–3: 'and what is *the ugly*? It is *the neighbour*, whom one SHALL love.' For Rembrandt see frontispiece and 4. 1. iv above.

7
Love Made in the First Age

EDENIC SEXUALITY IN *PARADISE LOST* AND ITS ANALOGUES

> Human passions did not enter the world before the Fall....
> The reader feels no transaction in which he can be engaged,
> beholds no condition in which he can by any effort of the
> imagination place himself; he has, therefore, little natural
> curiosity or sympathy. (Samuel Johnson, *Life of Milton*)

> Whoever considers the few radical positions which the Scripture afforded him, will wonder by what energetick operation he expanded them to such extent, and ramified them to so much variety, restrained as he was by religious reverence from licentiousness of fiction.... An accumulation of knowledge impregnated his mind, fermented by study, and exalted by imagination. (Ibid.)

The words of William Heale apply equally to the critic who approaches Milton's Eden: 'now here towards the evening of the day and end of my journey I sit me downe in the bloomy shade of *Paradise*, and contemplate the monuments both of womans first creation, and first institution of her marriage.' We are so much 'at home' with the erotic Milton[1] that Johnson's famous strictures, quoted here as an epigraph, still come as a shock. He is deeply

---

[1] The volume of critical work on M is so vast that any new study must be content to rearrange the exhibits. Most studies of *PL* include a section on the marriage of Adam and Eve; separate studies of M and sexuality include: Halkett, *passim*; Purvis Boyette, 'Milton and the Sacred Fire', *Literary Monographs*, V (1973), 63–138; Peter Lindenbaum, 'Love-making in Milton's Paradise', *MS* IV (1974), 277–306; Edward Le Comte, *Milton and Sex* (1978); Hagstrum, ch. 2; David Aers and Bob Hodge, ' "Rational Burning": Milton on Sex and Marriage', *MS* XIII (1979), repr. in Aers *et al.*, *Literature, Language, and Society in England, 1580–1680* (Dublin, 1981), ch. 6; McColley, *passim*; John Bayley, 'The Epic Theme of Love', in *Aspects of the Epic*, ed. Tom Winnifrith *et al.* (1983), pp. 64–79. (Two forthcoming articles came to my notice after this book was complete, 'Milton's Coy Eve: *Paradise Lost* and Renaissance Love Poetry' by William Kerrigan and Gordon Braden, and 'The History of Sexuality in *Paradise Lost*' by Nancy Armstrong and Leonard Tennenhouse, the latter kindly sent in draft form by Prof. Armstrong).

7. Love Made in the First Age

appreciative of Milton's 'fervid and active' imagination and 'pregnancy of mind', and yet he is strangely inattentive to the poem's intense and troubled eroticism, the core of its 'human interest': Johnson asserts of Milton's Adam and Eve that 'fruition left them nothing to ask', but they have no fruition and a great many questions; he claims that 'passion did not enter the world', but Adam confesses 'passion' and 'commotion' from the very first encounter with Eve. Indeed, it is precisely the centrality of passion, joined with the 'licentiousness of fiction', that guarantees the 'energetick operation' of the poem.

This chapter will explore the areas where Milton's erotics meet other essential concerns that arise from the confrontation with Genesis. Sexuality is linked to perception and interpretation, as it was in Milton's own myth of Eros, half-blind in this world but fully-sighted in the next. It is linked to the politics of gender; in Woolf's terms, we will ask whether his 'masculinism' is compromised, reinforced, or redeemed by his 'poetry'.[2] And it is linked to the central struggle between the poetic and the iconoclastic: we will see how Milton defines and expels the false 'image' of corrupted sexuality—the efforts of his contemporaries to create what Johnson called 'sentiments for the state of innocence' will help to clarify the problem—and how he develops an almost Pygmalion-like affection for his living image of Eve. He may sum up a tradition of speculation that goes back to Augustine, but he also looks forward to the narrator of *A la recherche du temps perdu*, who describes— at the very beginning or 'Ouverture' of the work—his pursuit of an imaginary sexual partner, born from his own thighs in an erotic dream 'as Eve was created from a rib of Adam'.

Milton himself would dismiss this secular Genesis as an 'empty dream', a mockery of the true inspiration that comes with the nightly visitations of Urania. My approach effectively reverses this relation. Milton's imaginative encounters with higher beings reflect his own creativity, and may be translated into models of the reader's

---

[2] Ch. 5 n. 16 above. The critical commentary on M's attitude to women is immense; cf., among many others, Marcia Landy, 'Kinship and the Role of Women in *Paradise Lost*', *MS* IV (1972), 3-18; Barbara K. Lewalski, 'Milton on Women— Yet Once More', *MS* VI (1974), 3-20; F. Peczenik, 'Fit Help: The Egalitarian Marriage in *Paradise Lost*', *Mosaic* XVII. i (Winter, 1984), 29-48; Jim Swan, 'Difference and Silence: John Milton and the Question of Gender', (forthcoming article kindly communicated by Prof. Swan). Stevie Davies, *The Feminine Reclaimed* (Louisville, 1986) appeared too late for me to take it into account.

response to his own work. In the divorce tracts, for example, God actively 'writes' or 'engraves' the original ordinance of Paradisal marriage on the human heart, making it 'a lively Sculpture'—a work of art that would satisfy Milton's own vitalistic criteria (II. 588, 621, 637). The 'fit audience' of *Paradise Lost* may likewise expect their darkness to be illumined, their imagination raised to a height, their 'sense and passion' engaged, their 'growth and compleating' stimulated;[3] the twentieth-century preoccupation with emotional intensity and psychological realism comes to seem less anachronistic. The premises of this study, and the working assumptions of the close readings that follow, are naturally quite different from those of the seventeenth-century Christian: Milton would have been horrified by the privilege here granted to sexuality, egalitarianism, the play of the fictive imagination, and the spirit of contradiction. But these potentially revolutionary values are included in his own vision of the Word, and his poem gives them a body and a life.

1. Love and poetry in the state of innocence

Paradise Lost represents the climax of Milton's lifelong struggle to create a vision of Eros based on his reading of Genesis. As a truly comprehensive epic it must be a theology, an encyclopaedia, and a history, but it is also an erotology, a *Symposium*, a Carte du Tendre. In the *Apology*, as we have seen, he brings his own reading and writing of secular love-poetry into this quest for an ideal Christian-Platonic love; but his own earlier verse, dedicated first to Ovidian *amores* and then to virginity, nowhere tackles the theme of married love. The divorce tracts erected a theory of perfect wedlock on the basis of Genesis and Plato, and battled valiantly with the contradictions of applying this to a real marriage; but there, enmeshed in his own problems, Milton could not incorporate sexuality into the ideal without tension, violence, and open disgust. His reconstruction of the love of Adam and Eve may thus be seen as an imaginary reversal of the incompatibility and hatred depicted in the earlier prose, an attempt to 'revisit safe' the realm of light in which Eros can see again.

[3] *PL* VII. 28–39, I. 22–3 ('what in me is dark / Illumine, what is low, raise and support'), and VI. 297–301 ('who [can] lift / Human imagination to such highth / Of Godlike Power?'); this question is asked by Raphael with the implication that it cannot be done, but Raphael's own narration, and indeed the whole of *PL*, shows that it can.

In both *Paradise Lost* and the divorce tracts sexuality is the 'sole proprietie / In Paradise of all things common else'—the term connotes privacy, closeness, and exclusive mystery as well as ownership—but in the prose this served only to explain what an 'intimate evil' it becomes when the marriage turns sour. Now this intimacy is a source of delight rather than horror; it is this, rather than any Hobbesian need for defence or post-lapsarian shame of nakedness, that makes Adam and Eve retire to their inner recess. In the unhappy marriage described by the divorce tracts Love's 'arrows loose their golden heads and shed their purple feathers, his silk'n breades untwine and slip their knots, and that original and firie vertue given him by Fate all on a sudden goes out'; but in Paradise, where he has found his true Anteros,

> Love his golden shafts imploies, here lights
> His constant Lamp, and waves his purple wings,
> Reigns here and revels.[4]

This refers specifically to the nuptial bower, but throughout the pre-lapsarian books of *Paradise Lost* the gestures of the lovers—'youthful dalliance as beseems fair couple'—illustrate and fulfil what the divorce tracts glimpsed as the 'peculiar comfort in the married state besides the genial bed', the 'thousand raptures' of the Song of Songs, or the 'ravishment and erring fondness in the entertainment of wedded leisures' recommended in Proverbs. Indeed, the poem may actually take over the function that the divorce tracts had ascribed to the Solomonic scriptures themselves—to encourage the godly but timid reader in these enjoyments.

Thus when Adam hangs 'enamour'd' over the sleeping Eve and whispers

> Awake, the morning shines, and the fresh field
> Calls us, we lose the prime, to mark how spring
> Our tended Plants, how blows the Citron Grove,

he echoes (Milton would say anticipates) the morning invitation of the Song of Songs, and thereby unwittingly dispels the nocturnal parody of a similar passage that Satan had put into Eve's dream. Or when he smiles at the pressure of Eve's 'swelling Breast' and

---

[4] *PL* IV. 751-2, 763-5, *Prose* II. 255, 665. Maureen Quilligan interprets 'sole proprietie' to mean the property-rights of the husband over the wife, but it is clear that M is thinking of the *mutual* rights of Pauline 'due benevolence' (*Milton's Spenser* (1983), p. 236).

showers 'her Matron lip / With kisses pure'—filling Satan with jealousy and 'fierce desire'—we hear *Rejoice with the wife of thy youth . . . let her breasts satisfy thee at all times, and be thou ravished always with her love* and *let him kiss me with the kisses of his mouth, for thy love is better than wine*.[5] But whereas in the earlier writings the woman was to provide only 'delightfull intermissions' from the strains of school or office (II. 597), here for the most part labour and discussion are shared and thereby also 'mixt with Love', brought into the orbit of Venus. When Eve proposes to spend the morning working apart, Adam feels a lover's rather than a manager's chagrin; their work has always included the refreshment of body, mind, and heart, the 'sweet intercourse / Of looks and smiles' that is the food of Love, interwoven with conversation that feeds the mind (IX. 237-41). And when Eve slips out to the garden for the more abstruse part of the dialogue with Raphael, it is not (Milton insists) because she is bored or intellectually out of her depth, but rather because she prefers to share mingled conversation and kisses with her lover. Her departure is itself an erotic moment, for it is here that 'a pomp of winning Graces' shoot 'Darts of desire / Into all Eyes to wish her still in sight' (VIII. 48-62).

Milton's symphony of erotic gestures derives partly from Scripture and partly from private reserves of sensuousness. The reconciliation of Eve and Adam after her dream, for example, has a peculiar intimacy found in no other treatment of Genesis:

> [Eve] silently a silent tear let fall
> From either eye, and wiped them with her hair;
> Two other precious drops that ready stood,
> Each in thir chrystal sluce, hee ere they fell
> Kiss'd as the gracious signs of sweet remorse.   (V. 130-4)

Adam certainly anticipates Christ's comforting of his female disciples here (though Milton's 'wanton' and 'dissheveld' Eve is closer to Titian's Magdalene than to St. Luke's); but no other poet or painter, not even Spenser in his scenes of intimate temptation, has captured the moment of kissing tears—the sound of the word 'sluce' even suggests drinking. Eve's hair, for Milton, is simultaneously the object of sensuous dreaming and the badge of subjection that St. Paul demanded. Many divines had echoed the

---

[5] *PL* V. 13, 20-2, IV. 494-502; Prov. 5:18-19; S. of S. 7:11-12, 1:2. This section frequently alludes to points made in ch. 6 above; I have not given cross-references in every case.

Pauline command (frequently blurring the distinction between the natural and the fallen state as they did so), but none had invested it with erotic significance. Nor does 'coy submission' play much part in the amorous writings of Solomon. But it is the conjunction of Eros and submission that seems to inspire the sharpest authorial excitement in *Paradise Lost*, and to give its heroine the quality of a Proustian Eve, born from an erotic dream. When Adam feels the touch of Eve's breast through her hair and 'in delight / Both of her Beauty and submissive Charms / Smil'd with superior Love (IV. 497-9)', we feel perhaps uncomfortably aware of Milton's predeliction; and our discomfort may increase when we recall that, in Genesis, the submission of woman to man is only established as a punishment for the fall.

The prose tracts had rather nervously described these Solomonic and recreational delights as 'farre on the hither side of carnal enjoyment' (II. 597); here love is integrated with sexuality. Offspring, an aspect of marriage ignored or demoted in the earlier writings, are now anticipated in every speech, announced emphatically in the first words of God to each person, and evoked again in the evening hymn of Adam and Eve on the threshhold of their bower (IV. 732-4). Their spontaneous feelings accord with the ends of marriage as defined by doctrine: they are 'happie in our mutuall help / And mutual love', as the divorce tracts demanded in theory but undermined in practice; and they are also filled with what Augustine said the joy of procreation should be—the desire to produce children for God, up to the pre-ordained number of the elect. An exclusive emphasis on worship and dutiful procreation might in itself seem rather bloodless, however. Milton must ensure that his primal lovers satisfy strict Augustinian criteria, when he describes the side of their sexual love they present to God, but he also wishes to give them the richest possible emotional life, thus proving what Aquinas had conjectured about their capacity to feel, and establishing in unforgettably 'solid' and 'sensuous' terms what the divorce tracts called 'the internal Form and the soul of this relation'.

When Adam discusses his own sexual passion with the archangel Raphael, he is driven by the desire 'to say all' (VIII. 505); the same impulse leads Milton into the secret recesses of the nuptial bower. Two other poets, both Dutch, had also contravened the exegetes and dated consummation before the fall: the nineteen-year-old

Hugo Grotius gave Adam and Eve lushly erotic declarations of love which refer vaguely to the marriage-bed, and Jacob Cats had actually created a scene of cheerful domestic coarseness 'when Eve was deflowered (*beslapen*)'—the woods rejoice that 'the first couple had just made a third', and the animals come to congratulate the husband.[6] Neither poet reflects on the consequences of his unorthodox assumption, though Cats does append an unwieldy prose dialogue proving his case by misapplication of Augustine, Paraeus, and Rivet.[7] But Milton is not content to take Paradisal sexuality for granted like Grotius, or offer a spurious defence in a divided text, like Cats. He integrates his considered opinion into the poetic narrative:

> nor turnd I ween
> *Adam* from his fair Spouse, nor *Eve* the Rites
> Mysterious of connubial Love refus'd.   (IV. 741–3)

In this delicate but surprisingly precise description Milton embodies the mutuality of 'due benevolence'. The couple 'Straight side by side were laid': Adam does not assume a dominant posture, and Eve exhibits none of the 'sweet reluctant amorous delay' announced on her first appearance ('straight' indicates time as well as space); the negative construction shows that each is capable of 'turning' or 'refusing', but chooses not to do so.

Luther had suggested that unfallen love-making would have been a form of worship (2. 2. iii above), and Milton here realizes Luther's wistful conjecture. The same word describes their spontaneous declaration of happiness at evening ('other Rites / Observing none') and their actual coupling. Intercourse is a 'rite' in the earlier prose— in a happy couple 'the rites of the Mariage bed' can be legitimate despite their intrinsic pollution, whereas the mismatched pair are 'coupl'd in the rites of nature by the meer compulsion of lust'—

---

[6] Kirkconnell, pp. 136–8, 180, 200; Cats, *Gront-Houwelick*, in *t'Samen-sprake van Philogamus . . . met Sophroniscus*, pp. 5–8 (*Alle de Wercken* (Amsterdam, 1658), separate pagination). Cats effectively bypasses Christianity and returns to the Rabbinical idea that 'in the eighth hour Adam and Eve ascended to bed as two and descended as four'.

[7] *t'Samen-sprake*, pp. 13–14; Cats attempts to prove that Adam and Eve were 'created in all the strength of youth, full of haste and inclination (*snellende en hellende*) for procreation,' and would therefore not have refused the divine command to increase and multiply; but the authorities he cites actually say something quite different—that the first couple *would have* had innocent sexual reproduction (in a controlled and orderly manner) if the fall had not come so soon.

and in *Paradise Lost* we encounter, before we arrive in Eden, the 'wanton rites' and 'lustful Orgies' of Peor. But here sexual worship is rescued from the dusky margins and installed in 'holiest place', which means not only the most 'sacred and sequesterd' space in Eden, but also the most central and private moment of the description, fiercely guarded against Hypocrites on one side and Courtly Amorists on the other. Here Eros becomes numinous and 'strange'. The physical act itself, of course, cannot be described: as Augustine says, it longs to be known but blushes to be seen. But in his eulogy of Wedded Love, not so much a digression as an *obbligato* to unfallen love-making, Milton allows us to glimpse its general character through the veil of imagery: it is a 'Perpetual Fountain of Domestic sweets', where Eros spreads his wings and fires his golden shafts, and at the point where Milton can resume direct description it sinks into the roseate sleep of what would later be called 'afterglow'—

> These lulld by Nightingales imbracing slept,
> And on their naked limbs the flowrie roof
> Showrd Roses.[8]

Such is the transformation of what the divorce tracts were pleased to call an animal excretion.

[ii]

Sexuality in the Paradisal state is not a specialized area or subcategory of experience, as it is in 'Court Amours', but a transformation of the whole way of perceiving and being. Eve's response to her surroundings, beautifully enumerated in her aria 'With thee conversing I forget all time', is entirely subsumed into her love for Adam. Nor is this love-centredness confined to the female, as one might expect in an author so eager to prove that 'she is for him, not he for her'. Milton broadens and diffuses the usual division of faculties into 'male' and 'female'; his Eve is more logocentric and intelligent than the conventional treatment, and his Adam, even in his prime, is more emotionally susceptible. We may see this in those episodes when Eve and then Adam narrate their own first encounter with each other.

---

[8] *PL* I. 414–15, IV. 736–73; *Prose* II. 606, 739. For Peor, the original of 'Priapus', see also 'Nativity Ode' l. 197 and *Prose* I. 589.

In their first moments of consciousness each relates to the world according to the divisive formula laid down in Milton's original description: Adam strides about full of 'contemplation' and 'valour', examining the landscape for evidence of monotheism; Eve (made for 'softness' and 'sweet attractive grace') falls in love with her own image in a lake. Stated baldly, this might seem to justify the eighteenth-century sneer 'that the first woman immediately after her creation ran to a looking-glass, and became so enamour'd of her own face, that she had never removed to view any of the other works of nature, had not she been led off to a man.'[9] The actual effect of the episode is more generous, however. Contemplation, Action, and Eros are not oppugnant but interlaced. Adam exerts his knowledge of the world—in a daring argument with God that is both thought and action, as his subsequent exhaustion shows— to demand an object for Love; Eve expresses her love actively and intelligently, driven by the urge to discover 'where / And what I was'. She moves to embrace the object she finds most lovable, and turns away from what does not meet her standards. First God, and then Adam, must woo her reason to approve the nuptial arrangement. It is perverse to accuse her of vanity on the basis of this mirror-scene, as Dryden does in his adaptation ('I myself am proud of me') or as some of the more fatherly critics do ('her state of mind is not pride but the kind of vanity that we find amusing and disarming, and so innocent').[10] Eve herself provides a truer and franker explanation when she expresses amused relief at her escape from fleshless unreciprocated 'desire', from a state of pining that tortures Satan himself, only a few lines later, as he watches the embrace.

Milton's Eve is closer to Desdemona than to Millamant. The voice of God leads her because it promises to 'bring thee where no shadow staies / Thy coming, and thy soft imbraces' (IV. 469-71), and her initial aversion from Adam shows that it takes his heartfelt wooing and tender yet violent gesture ('thy gentle hand / Seis'd

[9] *PL* IV. 297-8, 449-65, VIII. 257-82; cf. Thomas Newton's parody of Addison, quot. in Fish, pp. 219-20. For an interesting Rabbinical perspective on the mirror-image in this scene, see Kitty Cohen, *The Throne and the Chariot* (The Hague, 1971), pp. 112-15; for its 'suspended', 'twilight' effect, see Patricia Parker, *Inescapable Romance* (Princeton, 1979), pp. 114-23, 151.

[10] *PL* IV. 451-2; *The State of Innocence*, in *Dramatic Works*, ed. Montague Summers, III (1932), p. 435; Northrop Frye, *The Return of Eden* (Toronto, 1965), p. 77. and cf. Boyette, p. 110. Dryden's Eve is already in the narcissistic state that Satan tries to lead her to in his dream and in his first speech as a serpent.

mine') to convince her that his rougher body really will give her the fullest return of love. When she explains how

> I yeilded, and from that time see
> How beauty is excelld by manly grace
> And wisdom, which alone is truly fair,   (IV. 489-91)

and then leans her whole body against his, she is delicately but pointedly expressing what Adam himself puts more rapturously in his conversation with Raphael—that it was the joys of the wedding-night, the very moment alluded to by Eve's gesture, that fulfilled his whole being and 'brought / My Storie to the sum of earthly bliss' (VIII. 521-2). Though Milton would vehemently deny this implication, it is clear that *Paradise Lost* brings into being an erotic ontology that defines and subsumes both male and female, qualifying the original attempt to limit the zone of Eros to Eve alone. The 'prae-eminence' or higher 'excellence' that Eve discovers in Adam need not refer exclusively to gender; it is rooted in the erotic superiority of substance to shadow, of act to dream.

Even before the creation of Eve, Adam discovers that erotic love includes and surpasses every other response to the world. His first pleasure in landscape, even before he is aware of his lack of a partner, is already potentially a love-encounter: 'all things smiled', and in response 'with fragrance and with joy my heart oreflow'd' (VIII. 265-6). This promise is fulfilled when God provides him with Eve. As his rib is being removed, he is shown a being so beautiful that all his responses to nature seemed now

> Mean, or in her summ'd up, in her contain'd
> And in her looks, which from that time infus'd
> Sweetness into my heart, unfelt before,
> And into all things from her Air inspir'd
> The spirit of love and amorous delight.   (VIII. 473-7)

In Adam's first dream he was shown the fruit-trees of Eden, which 'Tempting, stirr'd in me sudden appetite / To pluck and eat', and then waked to find his Keatsian dream translated into Miltonic reality; in this second dream he is again stirred with sudden love— for a being in whom these earlier pleasures are 'summ'd up'—and again he 'wak'd / To find her, or for ever to deplore / Her loss, and other pleasures all abjure.' The response to Eve thus involves a great range of emotions, the deepest being the social and amorous communion whose loss is lamented in the meditations on his blindness and in the sonnet 'Me thought I saw my late espoused saint'.[11] But wedded love includes all the pleasures that can be derived from the landscape, and these in turn are suffused with nuptial and amorous significance.

These correspondences between erotic response and natural process go deeper than conventional metaphor. Human emotion and physical exhalation are interchangeable here, not as a metaphysical conceit, but as a natural outcome of the structure of matter explained by Raphael. The biological urge for growth is a kind of aspiration towards deity:

> so from the root
> Springs lighter the green stalk, from thence the leaves
> More aerie, last the bright consummate flowr
> Spirits odorous breathes.

The flowers and fruits pass upward in this 'gradual scale' by feeding man (fragrance is a kind of nourishment for Milton), and thus

> To vital Spirits aspire, to animal,
> To intellectual, give both life and sense,
> Fansie and understanding, whence the Soul
> Reason receives. (V. 479-87)

'Spirits odorous', in this dazzling monistic system, actually produce the states of mind they resemble. Fragrance and joy both well up and overflow because both for Milton are spirituous 'liquids' or vapours; the air of Eve 'infuses' sweetness into Adam's heart and 'inspires' the spirit of love into all things, just as she crowned the flowing cups of Raphael and Adam, causing the hearts of the Sons of God to brim, if not overflow, with amorous enthusiasm (VIII. 474-7, V. 443-8).

The fruits, the flowers, the liquid 'sweets', and above all the fragrances of Eden thus provide an exact counterpart to the movement of the spirits in love, and may even help to satisfy our curiosity about those 'mysterious' aspects of Eros that long to be known but blush to be seen. The association of scent, vernal air, and sexual awakening produces some of the most sensuous passages

---

[11] *PL* VIII. 308-10, 478-80; cf. the climactic placing of 'human face divine' (*PL* III. 44) and 'woman' (Sonnet 22, l. 6) in the catalogue of what he misses in his blindness. Keats used Adam's dream as a paradigm of the creative imagination (letter to Bailey, 22 Nov. 1817).

in Milton's own early secular poetry,[12] and in *Paradise Lost* he reappropriates and intensifies the effect. The first distant perfume of Eden was powerfully associated with marital love by cross-references to the story of Tobit, and its foul opposite is remembered as the 'fishie fume' that repelled Asmodeus. In Adam's description of his wedding night, the features of the landscape are transformed into participants in the ceremony, and when the 'gentle Aires ... Flung Rose, flung Odours from the spicie Shrub' they anticipate the rhythmic excitement of the bride and groom. When Raphael arrives at noon the sun 'Shot down direct his fervid Raies to warm / Earths inmost womb', and Nature—like Eve herself both wanton and virgin—pours forth an almost frantic abundance of the spices that in the Song of Songs refer most directly to human sexual arousal. The light of the solar system is 'male and female', the sun mounts the earth, and the ocean

> with warm
> Prolific humour soft'ning all the Globe,
> Fermented the great Mother to conceave,
> Satiate with genial moisture.[13]

Correspondingly, the smiles of the human lovers are compared to the fertilizing radiance that beams onto 'Clouds / That shed *May Flowers*' (IV. 500-1). This reciprocity of tenor and vehicle has the effect of extending human sexuality rather than contracting it to a conceit; the reader, too, begins to participate in an eroticized universe, satiate with genial moisture.

Milton's depictions of vegetable nature resemble the great panegyrics to natural fertility in *De Rerum Natura* and the *Georgics*, but he does not share the classical vision of man swept helplessly away by the torrents of Venus, and he therefore does not emphasize animal sexuality, which Lucretius and Virgil had made their paradigm. He is concerned to show innocent human Eros at the centre, with its paradoxical combination of luxuriance and restraint, virginity and wantonness; his analogies link the human body to the plants rather than to the beasts, and he even omits the animal perfumes like musk and civet, which might suggest rutting. (The theosophical desire to propagate like plants is here rescued and

---

[12] e.g. 'Carmina Elegiaca', ll. 9-12, 'Elegia Quinta', *passim*, 'Song, On May Morning', l. 5.
[13] *PL* IV. 156-71; VIII. 515-17; V. 292-302; VIII. 150; VII. 279-82; IV. 499-501. Cf. S. of S. 1:12, 4:6, 5:5, Ps. 45:8.

translated into erotic realism.) These analogies are diffused throughout the landscape, but they are concentrated in those places where the most crucial scenes take place: in Eve's private rose-garden, in the approaches to the Tree itself—a Satanic parody—and in the archetypal nuptial bower. What Joseph Rykwert says of the Old Testament *huppah*, the wedding-canopy in which he traces the mythic genesis of all architecture, applies particularly well to the bower in *Paradise Lost*:

> Its floor was the earth, its supports were living beings, its trellised roof was like a tiny sky of leaves and flowers: to the couple sheltering within it, it was both an image of their joined bodies and a pledge of the world's consent to their union. It was more; it provided them—at a critical moment—with a mediation between the intimate sensations of their own bodies and the sense of the great unexplored world around.[14]

In these places Eve exercises her greatest freedom of self-expression, both for good and for evil; they are the places of her temptation, but they are also where she develops her own distinctive arts—arts that foreshadow not only the redemptive 'offices of Love' that she initiates after the fall, but also the 'sensuousness' and 'passion' of poetry itself.

When she cultivates and names the plants, or decorates the bower, or creates a meal, Eve is also investing the produce of the earth with connubial significance. When she 'strews the ground / With Rose and Odours from the shrub unfum'd' (V. 348-9) she reconstructs, in a more muted rhythm, the 'flung Rose, flung Odours' of the wedding night. (We encounter these episodes in reverse order, of course; the allusion is offered first in private, and only later to the reading public.) And when she deliberates

> What choice to chuse for delicacie best,
> What order, so contriv'd as not to mix
> Tastes, not well joyn'd, inelegant, but bring
> Taste after taste upheld with kindliest change,   (V. 333-6)

she creates an art of sensuous choice and controlled exuberance that we can apply by analogy, not only to Milton's art of description, but to the more secret arts of the bed. The association of food and sexuality, suggested throughout the poem and parodied in the aphrodisiac effect of the forbidden fruit, is made explicit when Raphael, setting eyes at once on Eve and on her meal, hails her

[14] *On Adam's House in Paradise* (New York, 1972), p. 188.

'fruitful Womb' and draws a parallel between abundant progeny and the heaped-up fruit (V. 388-91). This association extends not only to the content but to the mental processes of Eve's art. God Himself characterizes Adam's conception of wedded love in similar terms:

> A nice and suttle happiness I see
> Thou to thy self proposest, in the choice
> Of thy Associates, *Adam*, and wilt taste
> No pleasure, though in pleasure, solitarie.[15]

(Though God is testing Adam by pretending to rebuke his demand for a love-partner, we clearly sense His avuncular approval.) In both passages, 'taste' and 'choice' contribute to the perpetual sustaining of domestic sweets, and the similarity is increased when we remember that 'elegance', in Milton's etymological mind, does not refer to a superficial social accomplishment but to the act of choice—and 'reason is but choosing'.

Eve's arrangement of the meal, then, is an emblem of the transfiguration of physical pleasure in the ideal marriage. Dryden's Eve remarks, with jaded expertise, that 'touching is a remoter taste in love'; Milton's Eve practises something like the reverse. The potential danger of such connoisseurship broods heavily over the fall, however. The fruit simultaneously enhances the sense of taste and increases the sexual urge, and Adam's first speech of fallen seduction—

> Eve, now I see thou art exact of taste,
> And elegant, of Sapience no small part,
> Since to each meaning savour we apply,
> And Palate call judicious—

echoes the terms of the art through which Eve transforms eating into an act of love.[16]

In these central idyllic books of *Paradise Lost* the voice, too, becomes an instrument of love. The synaesthesia of natural imagery mingles together the exhalation of scent, the tones of music, and the human voice. Each morning in Eden 'all things that breathe /

---

[15] *PL* VIII. 399-402 (God puns on the etymology of Eden/Hedone); cf. *Prose* II. 527. The objection that M gives Eve trivial and domestic 'arts' overlooks the fact that in the primitive state these are the *only* arts.

[16] *State of Innocence*, p. 449; *PL* IX. 1017-20. For an earlier association of 'elegant' with sophisticated sexuality, cf. *Areopagitica*: 'the Bible it selfe ... describes the carnall sense of wicked men not unelegantly' (II. 517).

From th'Earths great Altar send up silent praise / To the Creator', and Adam and Eve join their 'vocal Worship' to 'the Quire / Of Creatures wanting voice' (IX. 194-9). At our first arrival in Paradise 'aires, vernal aires, / Breathing the smell of field and grove,' are unabashedly equated with the musical 'airs' of the feathered choir and the dance of Pan (IV. 264-8). It is Eve's 'Air', in another sense, that breathes the amorous spirit into all things. When the 'enamour'd' Adam wakes the sleeping Eve his voice is 'Mild, as when *Zephyrus* on Flora breathes,' and when he invites her to come and watch 'how the Bee / Sits on the Bloom extracting liquid sweet', he provides a correlative to his own soothing tone as well as to his comforting interpretation of Eve's Satanic dream (V. 16-25).

These idealized erotic conversations, in which 'amorous power' is linked to a special quality of voice, serve as a model for the artist as well as the lover. A paradigm is provided by the nightingale, a constant presence in these nuptial books and a lifelong emblem of Milton's artistic aspirations. Even in his first sonnet he implores the nightingale to bring him poetic or amatory success, 'if Jove's will / Have linkt that amorous power to thy soft lay'. The Lady singing alone in the dark, warding off the 'barbarous dissonance' of Comus's gang, is compared twice to the nightingale, and in the invocations of *Paradise Lost* the same image describes Milton's own vocal art: he writes in the midst of personal darkness 'as the wakeful Bird / Sings darkling', and he trusts his heavenly Muse to quell the 'barbarous dissonance' of hostile rioters. The song of the nightingale, in synaesthetic combination with flowers and scents, defines the most intimate moments of married love: on the wedding night, immediately after the airs flung rose and odours, 'the amorous Bird of Night / Sung Spousal', and after the first love-making described in the poem the happy couple 'lulld by Nightingales imbracing slept'. Milton's liquid and sustained tonality is clearly intended to emulate the 'amorous descant' of the nightingale itself, and thus to re-enact, in the actual texture of his verse, the return of Eros and creativity to their common Paradisal source.[17]

[17] Sonnet 1, ll. 7-8 (contrasted to the threatening 'rude Bird of Hate' in l. 9); *A Mask*, ll. 232-4, 550 and 566; *PL* III. 38-9, IV. 771-3, 603, VII. 32-5, VIII. 518-20. The obvious link between 'the barbarous dissonance / Of *Bacchus* and his revellers' and drunken Royalist street gangs—the *race* of the Bacchantes, but not actually maenads—undermines Quilligan's argument that M's chief fear was of female violence (pp. 219-21).

7. Love Made in the First Age

Milton had often presented vocal art in synaesthetic images that anticipate, in miniature, the Paradisal environment. The third Prolusion, as we have seen, shows Divina Poesis breathing nectar into the soul, flooding it with ambrosia, instilling it with beatitude and 'whispering immortal joy into it'. (In the heaven of *Paradise Lost*, conversely, the emission of perfume is a kind of applause that follows the Father's speeches.) The association of breath, musical solemnity, perfume, and vocal enchantment is even closer in the lines that describe the Lady's singing in *Comus*:

> a soft and solemn breathing sound
> Rose like a steam of rich distill'd perfumes
> And stole upon the air.

Milton's working draft shows that time was also to be included in the synaesthesia, since 'slow' was originally written instead of 'rich'. In the early writings these effects perhaps describe the aspiration rather than the achievement of the artist, but in *Paradise Lost* they are more fully manifested, both when the narrator emulates the 'vernal airs' of Eden and when Adam and Eve themselves raise their voices in praise. Milton's poetic practice again hatches what Luther conceives only as a vanished possibility, raised during a meditation on fragrance and worship in Genesis 8:21—that unfallen man could have outsung the Psalms themselves, and that divine inspiration could cure the 'evil imagination' that comes with original sin.[18]

Eve creates a special poetry of redeemed sensuousness and amorous voice, not only in the psalms she raises jointly with Adam, but in her own expressions of love for him, and especially in the magnificent 'With thee conversing I forget all time' (IV. 639-52). Here St. Augustine's meditation on the love of God as a redemptive transposition of earthly love (2. 1. i above), is converted into poetic form—eighteen lines of blank verse with the grace and recapitulative pattern of an Elizabethan sonnet, and the rich solemnity of the Lady's singing in *Comus*. This passage may well be described as an aria, not only because it is stately, melodious, and organized around an internal *da capo*, but because it stands out in contrast from the flat unmelodious lines on either side. Before this Milton

---

[18] Ch. 5 n. 14 above; *PL* III. 135-6; *A Mask*, ll. 554-6 and Carey's note; ch. 1 n. 36 above. M evokes the sweetness of speech in what was perhaps the last line he ever wrote, *PL* XII. 5 (added to the 1674 edition).

gives her four woodenly didactic lines, presumably intended as 'submissive Charms', that refuse to assimilate into the poetic texture—

> My Author and Disposer, what thou bidst
> Unargu'd I obey; so God ordains,
> God is thy Law, thou mine: to know no more
> Is womans happiest knowledge and her praise—

and afterward her abrupt question about the stars seems to press too close to fallen curiosity. This didactic Eve is indeed 'an image of earth and phlegm', contrary to Milton's intentions; but the singer of the intervening lines is a living voice, an autonomous poetic authority. Her 'Air' captures what the whole description of unfallen Eden suggests—the hypnotic strangeness of being in love, the mood of intense subjectivity in which time itself is almost suspended, becoming sweet and thick with 'amorous delay'.

[*iii*]

Many of Milton's literary predecessors had attempted to imagine the erotic life of Paradise, though never so comprehensively. They were encouraged by Adam's recognition of 'one flesh' and by God's blessing of 'increase and multiply', and followed the exegetes' notion that by bringing Eve to Adam God had initiated the first wedding service and the 'prime institution' of marriage. Thus Grotius's Adam is 'dissolved by a new flame and fire of love', while his Eve feels a *dulcior voluptas* and an *ardor* which she prays for God to continue; in Cats Adam becomes a quite different being, shot through with 'a fever without pain, a heat without burning', and Eve, like a primitive Miranda,

> I knew not what she saw, but saw with pleasure....
> She feels her tender mind moved to its depths
> And she is drawn to what she does not know.

This recalls a moment in Milton, not in *Paradise Lost* but in his Ovidian 'Elegia Prima', where he reads of a girl, 'astonished by new warmth of feeling', falling in love even though she 'knows not what love is'.[19]

---

[19] Kirkconnell, pp. 136-8; *t'Samen-sprake* pp. 5-6; 'Elegia Prima', ll. 35-6; Ovid, *Metam.* IV. 330. Cf. Geoffrey Bullough, 'Milton and Cats', in *Essays in English Literature*, ed. Millar Maclure and F. W. Watt (Toronto, 1964), pp. 103-24.

7. Love Made in the First Age

Many earlier versions of Genesis—from Avitus in the sixth century to Cats and Vondel in the seventeenth—expand its erotic and nuptial implications into elaborate scenes of courtship, leading to a full wedding ceremony. When it is constrained by the orthodox teaching—that the fall happened before consummation, and thus with incredible rapidity—these nuptial preparations make the catastrophe itself more gratuitously abrupt, encouraging bizarrely ironic effects in authors of a Baroque temperament. The notion that 'our first wedding was our funeral' caught the imagination of Donne, and provided a grim conceit in da Salandra's *Adamo Caduto*: Eve sees the trees of Eden, ignited by the cherub's flaming sword, as hymeneal torches that light her to her marriage-bed. The whole of Vondel's tragedy *Adam in Ballingschap* takes place on the wedding-day, and the narrations and mutual declarations of love are comprised in musical odes as part of the ceremony (as the devils plot they hear snatches of bridal music); the chorus changes to a dirge after Belial, disguised as a wedding-guest, seduces the bride at her own reception.[20] Milton himself encountered a different sort of irony when he first approached the subject: he planned to devote the second act of his tragedy 'Paradise Lost' to the wedding, but found that he could not include the bridal pair themselves— Moses was to have explained to the earthly audience that they could not see Adam and Eve at all, because of sin.[21] The tragedy remained unwritten, of course. This crisis of representation, a sophisticated form of the 'feare to fail' that inhibited du Bartas, is suspended in *Paradise Lost*, where images from the wedding-ceremony are diffused throughout the idyllic books, extending rather than harshly truncating the sense of consummated happiness. Figures that in the tragedy would have recounted the wedding of the absent couple ('Evening Star', for example) now contribute to their erotic presence. In Book IV the music of the nightingale, the lamp of Hesperus, the 'Hymenaean' choir, the evening prayer which defines the ends of marriage, and the shower of roses which blesses the 'Nuptial Bed', all belong to this coherent metaphor: when Adam finally describes his wedding night to Raphael in Book VIII,

---

[20] Donne, *First Anniversary*, l. 105; Kirkconnell, pp. 503, 618, 218, 434–79; Joost van den Vondel, *Adam in Ballingschap* (Amsterdam, 1664); cf. J. M. Evans, *Paradise Lost and the Genesis Tradition* (Oxford, 1968), p. 265. Lindenbaum is wrong to say that Vondel, like Grotius, assumes pre-lapsarian intercourse (p. 279); his error may stem from Kirkconnell's mistranslation of *bruiloftsschaer* as 'nuptial joys' (p. 457).

[21] For M's drafts of a tragedy on the fall cf. Fowler, introd.

we recognize it as the source from which these echoes have been resounding.

When Milton implores 'celestial Light' to 'purge' his inward eye, 'that I may see and tell / Of things invisible to mortal sight' (III. 51-5), he identifies both his new artistic aspiration and the problem that crippled his earlier attempt, and that led less conscientious artists into grotesque irony. Edenic sexuality and the dialogue in heaven are equally invisible to sinful sight, and both are strictly impossible to represent; but a vision 'purged' of lapsarian impurity will enable him not only to *see* but to *tell*, and proper telling will in turn permit his fit audience to see, 'at least in some proportion'. Milton's theory of purgation through 'triall with what is contrary' makes him incorporate, rather than evade, the sinful response. Hence in the hymn to wedded love, and throughout the erotic idyll, he defines his ideal by attacking its two main enemies—austere 'Hypocrites' who deny the existence of innocent sexuality, and fashionable libertines who debase sexual freedom into the 'casual fruition' of 'Court Amours'. Precisely these enemies of true marriage had been attacked in the divorce tracts—the 'sages' and 'Gnostics' who repress the Solomonic rapture, and the Sons of Belial who use it to confirm their own debaucheries. Just as Milton had attempted to rescue Old Testament divorce (and thereby 'in some proportion' Paradisal marriage) from both forms of extremism, so now he attempts to redeem marital sexuality from repression and libertinism. The chief obstacle to true vision is disordered passion, as Milton explains when he attacks false claims to Edenic enlightenment (5. iii above); but passion is essential to virtue, and deeply 'engraven' in the Paradisal state. The process of redemption must therefore involve not only rejection, but expropriation.

Milton's poetry gains much of its power from repossessing those 'sensuous and passionate' effects that had fallen into the hands of the ungodly. In the prose of the 1640s he showed how to extract virtue from the act of reading amorous poetry; now he translates this process into the 'solid and treatable smoothness' of writing. In early reading and late writing alike, this redemption extends to those delights that secular poets had placed in the Earthly Paradise or Golden Age, the libertine equivalents of Eden. Poets from Aretino to Rochester, conscious of the charms of blasphemy, had borrowed elements of Genesis and the Genesis-tradition for their own vision of primeval sexual liberty. Milton now returns the debt,

7. Love Made in the First Age

and thus puts into practice the suggestion made in *Areopagitica*, that a wise man can 'temper useful drugs' from scandalous and licentious texts, and even from Aretino.

The most striking example of this reappropriation is perhaps the echo, in Milton's first description of Adam and Eve, of Tasso's ode to the *bella età del'oro* when 'honor dishonorable' placed no restraint on sexuality. The fullest 'Cavalier' expansion of this paradox, Thomas Carew's *A Rapture*, anticipates some of the bolder effects of Milton's Paradise—a *locus amoenus* set aside for copulation on beds of flowers, a landscape that mirrors the amorous union of its destined couple, a 'Paradise' and a 'bower of bliss' that are summed up in the person of the heroine, moist kisses that turn to balm and incense, love-making described as 'rites', desire renewed after slumber. But 'Love's Elysium' turns out to be strangely limited; Carew's rapture is not so much a free flight of erotic imagination as a strict inversion of strict morality. The vocabulary of condemnation ('lust', 'shame', 'whore') and the 'panic fear' of transgression resonate with increasing force in a poem that has ostensibly abandoned them. This injects a self-consciousness into the poem that is enough to collapse the sensuous vision into its opposite. Carew's pornographic Elysium is self-consumptive in a way that Milton's description of Paradisal marriage is not, however much Milton may use it as an object-lesson in fallen inadequacy. By creating in *Paradise Lost* IV-IX a sustained and delicious eroticism integrated with the natural landscape, Milton has outdone the Courtly Amorist Carew, Gentleman of the Privy Chamber to Charles I, at his own game.[22]

In Richard Lovelace's 'Love made in the First Age', again, the edible and the erotic fruits of the golden age are mingled together, the primal lovers dine on banks of strawberries that are at once their 'Table, Table-cloth and Fare', and couple in beds 'softer than the Cignets Down'. They woo 'in direct *Hebrew*', walk 'naked as their own innocence', are bound for life by natural trust and affinity, and enjoy almost the same pleasures as the angels. Only Milton, among all the literary adaptors of Genesis, gives this range of delights to Adam and Eve. Lovelace's description, like Carew's, is intended as an expostulation to his fictitious mistress—a dramatic

[22] Carew, *Poems*, ed. Rhodes Dunlap (1949), pp. 49–53; cf. Pietro Aretino, *Sonnetti lussuriosi* 9 ('Fottianci vita mia, fottianci presto') and Rochester, 'The Fall'. Carew's *Coelum Brittanicum* (sic) was likewise a predecessor and rival to M's masque.

context that reduces, rather than enlarges, their Paradisal vision. But whereas Carew's poem begins as a 'persuasion to love' (though one effectively abandoned by the end of the poem), Lovelace's is set in the petulant aftermath of failed persuasion. His concluding stanza undermines the narrator and reveals him to be solipsistic and autoerotic: Chloris is invited to beg in vain for the bliss she rejected before,

> Whilst ravish'd with these Noble Dreams,
> And crowned with mine own soft Beams,
> Injoying of my self I lye.

Lovelace cleverly switches sides in the traditional poetic debate 'for' and 'against fruition', and gives his allegiance—as Marcel does in Proust's 'Ouverture'—to the dream state in which an ideal mistress is born out of erotic frustration 'as Eve was created from a rib of Adam'. In Comus's terms, his disappointed urge for 'mutual and partaken bliss' leads him to an 'unsavoury' alternative, 'th'injoyment of [him] self'. But for Milton the whole dichotomy would merely show the polarity of Hypocrites and Courtly Amorists, since it omits the tempered eroticism of marriage.[23] The false Edens of the Cavaliers are thus fragile, deliberately self-referential and preposterous, and bound to the tracks of the narrow morality they profess to scorn. Lovelace's solipsistic commitment to the dream world cuts him off from the traditions he playfully combines: he is neither a good Christian nor a good libertine. Schiller would later observe that 'all peoples that have a history have a paradise, a state of innocence, a golden age; moreover, every single man has his paradise, his golden age, which he recollects with more or less rapture according to his more or less poetic nature.'[24] In Lovelace's poem the personal and poetic vision of the 'single man' is articulated in contradistinction, or even in scandalous opposition, to the historic beliefs of his culture. Milton on the other hand tried to reconcile the two, and so by 'extraordinary and singular' projects to forge a marital Elysium for his people—for regenerate England in the 1640s and for the 'fit audience though few' in the 1660s. He was prepared to expose his most profound emotions (his dreams

---

[23] Cf. 4. 3. iii above, and *A Mask*, ll. 741-2. Lovelace's almost Marvellian conceit—that Hebrew (proverbially known to be written backwards) should stand for straightforwardness—adds to the sense of deliberate preposterousness.

[24] Quot. in Harry Levin, *The Myth of the Golden Age in the Renaissance* (Bloomington, 1969), p. xv.

of an ideal mistress, his yearning for divorce, his susceptibility to the innocent Eve) and even to reveal a shadowy affinity with the libertine opposition that his enemies were quick to amplify into open sensuality.[25] According to the experiential ethics of *Areopagitica*, it is precisely these moments of sensibility that prove the homeopathic extract to be 'working'.

These secular manipulations of the Paradise-myth, like Donne's 'Twickenham Garden', raise the possibility that there is a self-destructive, self-cancelling component in the very act of depicting innocence, that 'bare words' and fallen 'arts' can only authenticate Eden by bringing in the serpent. The impression is confirmed when we compare *Paradise Lost* to other literary versions of Genesis, where fallen attitudes will often unwittingly intrude. The problem is particularly felt in the 'artificiality' of literary language—the quality that distinguishes the puppet from the authentic and passionate Adam in *Areopagitica*. We may see this conflict between intention and expression in two versions close to Milton in time and occasionally in expression, the Italian prose *Life of Adam* by Giovanni Francesco Loredano (1640), and Canto VI of the allegorical epic *Psyche* (1648, revised 1702) by Joseph Beaumont, whom we have already encountered as a lyric poet. Both of these claim an orthodox religious-didactic purpose, and seek to arrest and transform the reader with sobering truths about human sinfulness. Their rhetoric thus aims to match the original intention that some commentators had discovered in the style of Genesis— to admonish us and persuade us to desire a better state.[26] But the poet must persuade by moving the passions, and the existing stock of persuasive techniques is premissed on the passions of a fallen audience. The presence of Eve intensifies this problem for Loredano and Beaumont, since they seem unable to praise her without the conventional contemporary rhetoric of romantic interest. Their treatment of the first couple thus oscillates between harsh moralizing

[25] The chief points in which M's 'liberty' resembled sexual 'license' (*Prose* II. 225), as we saw in ch. 6, are: the call for 'reincitement' of desire by 'conversation'; the stress on Solomonic rapture (Prynne referred to M's doctrine as 'divorce at pleasure'); the recognition that the Sons of Belial will use his argument to justify their debaucheries; admiration of the good marriages made by those experienced in extra-marital affairs; treatment of the wife's adultery as a trivial offence or even as a source of marital happiness.

[26] Loredano, *L'Adamo*, tr. as *The Life of Adam* by J. S. (1659), p. 21 (subsequent refs. will be to this tr. unless otherwise indicated); Beaumont, *Psyche*, 2nd edn. (Cambridge, 1702), VI. 334; cf. Calvin 1:27.

and the ornate rhetoric of high-Renaissance love-poetry, with its attendant cult of all-conquering Amor. Form and content begin to disintegrate, and each peels off towards the respective extremes of monkish austerity and worldly gallantry.

Loredano's Adam inhabits an ascetic and clear-cut moral universe: he is created to be a perpetual virgin, and he is entirely 'free from those passions of the mind which proceed from the sensitive appetite'. For his friend and critic Nicolo Crasso, Loredano succeeds in matching this austerity with a suitably plain and dignified style: 'a History extracted out of holy Writt, is not to be trimmed like Playes and Romances'—or 'Pieces of Wit and Gallantry' as an eighteenth-century translator put it. (Thanks to Loredano's genius, Adam is now 'revived, sanctifyed and immortall'.)[27] The reader is therefore surprised to find that Eve appears, not in simple beauty, but in a blaze of Petrarchist conceits. Adam is 'stupified' by such features as 'two Sunns under one pair of eybrows' and tresses so like gold 'that they pleaded *Adams* excuse, if he did not refuse so honourable a prison'. The desire to dramatize the beauty of his heroine, understandable in 'Playes and Romances', brings with it certain stock attitudes that compromise the state of innocence: Adam feels his 'Reason' temporarily succumb to 'Sense', and he is tempted to adore Eve 'as a Goddesse', which would have been 'the first of his sins'. God intervenes to save Adam here (by letting him know that Eve is part of himself) but it is not clear why, in an entirely non-sensuous and non-reproductive Paradise, He should confront the man with 'everything proper for a woman in reference to Procreation and Love' (pp. 18–20). Loredano and Milton both introduce moral danger into the erotic life of Eden; but for Loredano it is entirely inexplicable, whereas for Milton it is the essence of freedom. And the elegant insincerity of High Renaissance love-rhetoric, in Milton's version, is transferred from the narrator to the serpent.

Beaumont's problems are similar to Loredano's, but here the contrast with Milton is more telling because the poets share certain goals and methods. *Psyche* and *Paradise Lost* are both religious epics with a debt to Spenser, they both mix allegory and narrative, and both lead the soul through a series of 'Stations' that are at once moral crises and episodes of sacred history. Both poets are

[27] (1659) f. A3^{r-v}, pp. 9–10, 58; (1720?), p. ii. The original preface ('8th impression' (Venice, 1666)) refers to 'Scherzi' and 'Romanzi'.

concerned to make Genesis 'walk' within the reader (the term is Beaumont's), and both develop a consecrated version of Classical rhetoric and ornament, eschewing the plain style for one more figured and allusive, thronging their narrative with antique spirits and moral personifications. Eve inspires both with amorous conceits—in Beaumont her 'waist itself did gird / With its own graceful Slenderness', in Milton she is 'undeckt, save with her self'—and both equip her with 'winning Graces' that shoot 'Darts of desire'.[28] The purpose of these figures may sometimes be to force pagan or fallen attitudes on the reader, but they may equally represent the attempt to 'see' and 'tell' directly the sensuous delights of Paradise.

The formal introduction of Eve in *Psyche* is heightened by the responses not of Adam (as in most literary versions of Genesis) nor of Satan (as in Milton's brilliant variation), but of allegorical figures and personified features of the landscape—disembodied subjectivities who focus the reader's own response. First the nymphs of the garden, and then the attendant graces of Eve (who sums up all of Eden, as in Milton), personify the oxymoronic combination of attractiveness and asexuality that Beaumont conceives as the height of unfallen bliss: on the 'precious Cushonets' of her cheeks, for example, he discovers 'Chaste *Blandishments*, and modest cooling *Heats*, / Harmless *temptations*, and honest *Guiles*', while her mouth is guarded by a retinue of 'Inamoring *Neatness*, *Softness*, *Pleasure*' (1702, VI. 200, 228-9, 165-6). Beaumont's allegory transforms every feature into a device for provoking an erotic response, a theatrical turn for the amorous spectator. Eve's arms were 'chains of Love'; her temples 'lie / In dainty ambush, and peep through' her hair; her voice and breath please 'Nicest Criticks' (or 'thou' in the first version); her eyes 'Shoot deaths of love into Spectators' hearts'.[29] Personification is sometimes no more than a high-sounding way of describing a sensuous response to the female body: Eve's 'luxuriant Hair', for example, 'Pour'd down itself upon her ivory back', forming a 'soft flood' in which 'ten thousand *Graces*' played, and her hands were 'so leggiadrous... that *Pleasure* mov'd as any finger stirr'd'. This movement stirring within the observer may even be transferred to the flesh observed:

[28] *Psyche* (1702), VI. 233; *PL* V. 380, VII. 61-2. Subsequent refs. to Beaumont will be to Canto and stanza of *Psyche*, specifying the 1st edn. (1648) or the posthumous rev. edn. (1702).

[29] (1648), VI. 202; (1702), VI. 222, 224-6, 230, 233-4.

> Her blessed Bosom moderately rose
> With two soft Mounts of Lilies; whose fair top
> A pair of pritty sister Cherrys chose,
> And there their living Crimson lifted up.

Far from persuading us of the innocence of pre-lapsarian sexuality, this conceit reproduces the conspicuous focus on the erogenous zones that Augustine identified as the very moment of man's fall. And far from mortifying our pride—the declared purpose of the episode—Beaumont's description seems to exult in its own powers of evocative portraiture.[30]

Beaumont is quite aware of his manipulations of the reader's response, both here, in the description of Eve that accompanies Adam's sleep, and in his account of the perfect love that follows Adam's awakening. His interpretations are openly didactic, and his paradoxes are directed point-blank at the reader—the innocent couple are 'naked of what you count nakedness', for example. He seems to enjoy the tactic of arousing sexual expectations only to deflect them; we do not learn until later that Adam and Eve were virgins throughout the period of innocence, intended to remain so for ever.[31] These playful ambushes and entrapments are presumably designed to serve Beaumont's didactic purpose—simultaneously exposing the erotic response and showing that it *can* exist in an innocent form, if only in conceit. Just as Eve, typologically, is a 'fair pipe' conveying '*Humanity* ... into *God* himself', so the emotional provocations around her may be connecting devices between the fallen reader and the state of innocence. These pipes are not always reliable, however. In many of his metaphors Beaumont seems to stray from the conscious manipulation of fallen ways of seeing and knowing, into the unwitting reproduction of worldly sensations and worldly 'knowingness'. In both Milton and Beaumont, for example, the breezes of Paradise actively contribute to the amorous excitement. But in Beaumont they behave like the

---

[30] (1702), VI. 223, 232-3. A similar effect is found in Sylvester's du Bartas: after praising (somewhat prematurely) the power of Adam and Eve's love to quench the fires of Venus, the poet then dwells on Eve's 'bosome (more than Lilly-white) / Two swelling Mounts of Ivorie panting light' (p. 291); cf. William Heale, *An Apologie for Women* (Oxford, 1609), pp. 55-6.)

[31] For example, the 'mighty Tides of flaming Loves and joys / In their first marriage-greeting', and the 'unspotted Pleasure's juncture' that involved not 'their amorous hands and lips alone' but 'a nearer dearer union', turn out to be purely spiritual; cf. (1702), VI. 249, 251, 246, 248, 321. This entrapment is not attempted in the 1648 version.

7. *Love Made in the First Age*

Sons of Belial, fighting each other for kisses, 'Imbracing with entirest liberty' the body of Eve, snatching up the odours, running with them 'from bed to bed', and at dawn 'return[ing] them back / To their own Lodgings'.[32] Beaumont thus embraces the asexual theory of the 'Hypocrites', but adorns it with the language and some of the mentality of the Courtly Amorists.

Beaumont's infatuation with his own conceits blinds him to the modish sensuality of his proclamations of pure Eros, and to the lush, over-civilized ornateness of his descriptions. His Eve is indeed 'the first-born *Queen of Gallantry*'. When Satan finally appears in Beaumont's narrative (personified as Envy), we are invited to recoil from a false and tainted vision, an 'ambitious Taste' that 'Disdains all Fair but in the noblest fashion'; but these words apply all too accurately to Beaumont's own descriptive style. When Pity enters the Cave of Oblivion to find a vision for the sleeping Adam, she searches among dreams both 'wanton' and 'chaste'; by the end of the Canto we are not sure which category best fits the poet's dream of Eve. The problem for Beaumont, as for Loredano, was this: how to appreciate the excellence, honour, and beauty of Eve in terms that do not give off an air of worldliness and expensiveness, an affinity with the 'Court Amours' and the 'bought smile of Harlots' that Milton so effectively places in satiric contrast to his own portrait of innocent eroticism.[33]

[iv]

Though I begin with a straightforward account of Milton's success as a 'sensuous and passionate' poet, I do not wish to present *Paradise Lost* as an untroubled erotic idyll, ignoring those moments when the reader is surprised by sin, or 'cited to examination'.[34] The issue may be defined in terms of Donne's paradox: does true Paradise depend on the serpent, or can it be described directly? Does the fall place absolute and severe limits on the capacity to imagine 'what lost Paradise relates' (another suggestive phrase from the divorce tracts), or can these barricades be breached? One

---

[32] (1702), VI. 220, 237, 170-1; 1648 has very little of this gallant personification, and no reference to typology.

[33] (1702), VI. 235, 253, 201; *PL* IV. 765-7. The 'wanton' dream does not appear in 1648, and Envy's aversion to the unfashionable 'Fair' was originally a disdain for humble 'fare' (1648, VI. 220): Beaumont thus puns on his own first draft.

[34] The phrase is used several times in the tragedy-drafts; 'surprised by sin' obviously alludes to the work of Fish.

influential school of Milton criticism effectively endorses the former view by stressing those passages that simulate a specifically fallen response, and so inveigle the reader into self-examination; in this rather Pascalian view, Milton consciously exploits the very problem that ruins the other versions of Genesis—the intrinsic fallenness of rhetoric and imagination, and the impossibility of directly apprehending the state of innocence. Other critics cleave to the opposite view, stressing Milton's optimistic faith in the powers of regeneration.[35] This critical diversity undoubtedly corresponds to a dichotomy within Milton himself that his eroticization of Paradise only deepens.

The confrontation with 'what lost Paradise relates' produces a painfully divided consciousness, yearning with strong 'intentions and desires' for Edenic happiness (as the divorce tracts had recognized), but also entangled or 'twisted and turned in the abyss of sin' (as Pascal had put it). The poetic medium is similarly divided: Milton was deeply aware of its fallen allure and its potential for 'ambushes', but he never entirely lost faith in a poetry that 'retains the sacred Promethean fire' and lifts our 'high-raised Phantasie', that could be a means of grasping hidden mysteries and an agent of reformation, particularly in readers of a 'soft and delicious temper'. Consequently, both 'fallen' and 'unfallen' responses are included when Milton comes to constitute the fit reader of *Paradise Lost*. The narrative design ensures that at first the former predominates: the epic of Satan is launched with such overwhelming power that by the fourth Book the reader is invaded or possessed by the Satanic viewpoint, and travels with him to encounter Paradise. But Milton then offers several models of response, by no means straightforwardly evil. Satan himself is unpredictably altered by the 'Airs' of Paradise, the unfallen Raphael provides a complication when he too reveals an erotic nature, and Milton's Adam and Eve are given a more intense, complex, and potentially troubled sexual life than any of their predecessors; the reader identifies with each of these figures in part, and thus experiences not a simple polarity of good and evil, sexuality and purity, but a suspension between fallen and unfallen sensuousness, a fluctuating affinity with both sides, sometimes guilty and sometimes comfortable. We are mortified by comparing the naked majesty of

[35] For a detailed account of M's theories of regeneration, see McColley, p. 136 n. 14.

Adam and Eve to the shame and tension of the present day, but we are also enticed, by descriptions that breathe 'the spirit of love and amorous delight', into the penetralia of their marriage. Like Adam in his conversation with Raphael, we are lifted up to speculate about the intimate life of higher beings, and encouraged to contemplate the ascent of Love, but we are also deterred from dreaming of other worlds; we are rebuked for our disorderly passions, but we find ourselves only 'half abasht'.

Milton is certainly not unwilling to present a depraved response, nor to address himself point-blank to fallen shame. After dwelling on Eve's 'coy submission' and 'Sweet reluctant amorous delay' he turns sharply to confront the issue of nakedness:

> Then was not guiltie shame, dishonest shame
> Of natures works, honor dishonorable,
> Sin-bred, how have ye troubl'd all mankind!   (IV. 313-15)

And after evoking the delights of conversation mingled with kisses—just before Eve leaves for the garden, shooting 'Darts of desire / Into all Eyes'—he exclaims 'O when meet now / Such pairs, in Love and mutual Honour joyn'd?' (VIII. 57-63) Do these expostulations convince us of the sinfulness of all sensuous responses, including Milton's own? On the contrary, the adjacent lines are a direct tribute to what he considered a relaxed and natural form of sexual delight, consistent with the Solomonic ideal of the divorce tracts, and his diction and characterization establish empathy rather than distance; the phrase 'nature's works' suggests a kind of soft primitivism, Eve's wittily understated eroticism ('from his Lip / Not Words alone pleas'd her') gives her the frankness of a Restoration heroine without the guardedness, and the significant plural 'all Eyes' shows that, if the masculine reader shares Milton's adoration at this point, then so do Raphael and Adam. Even the sad rhetorical question ('O when meet now such pairs?') points to several answers; the divorce tracts depend on the passionate conviction that, with the right combination of Miltonic encouragement, legalized divorce, and divine grace, such couples can indeed 'meet now'.

It may be objected that Milton had since abandoned the optimism of the revolutionary period, and its faith in achieving a Paradisal marriage in this world. In one important respect, however, *Paradise Lost* is more rather than less generous than the divorce tracts, and places more faith in the normal processes of sexuality. The attack on 'honor dishonorable' is not only a bold expropriation of the libertine Golden Age, but a redemptive echo of a savage passage in *Colasterion*, where he raged against any definition of matrimonial honour based on sexual fidelity, and any recognition that the strength of a marriage might depend on sexual compatibility: this is 'a boisterous and bestial strength, a dis-honourable honour'. Now the same oxymoron is again provoked by focusing on the genitals ('Nor those mysterious parts were there conceald'), but this time to proclaim their innocence and to foreshadow the great hymn to present and past wedded love. The breach between affectionate gesture and sexual consummation, once defended with all the disdain at Milton's command, is now healed, and the same phrase points towards fallen libido and the possibility of its transcendence.[36]

It is significant that some of the most languorous and intense moments in Milton's narrative should be punctuated by Satan himself, boiling over with sexual jealousy and 'fierce desire' when Eve leans against Adam, intruding into their bedroom in the form of a toad while they lie 'lulld by Nightingales', or gloating over 'the sweet recess of *Eve*' as she gardens alone. Milton's first illustrator exaggerated when he presented Satan as a horned devil and a masturbator (Fig. 4), but there *is* something pornographic in his erotic response.

His alliance with Asmodeus and Belial, his dalliance with Sin, and his response to the perfumes of Paradise (linked to the expulsion of the 'enamoured' Asmodeus from Tobit's bride), ensure that we already associate him with demonic copulation. Now, confronting unfallen sexuality directly, he seems to be trapped in a situation from Aretino; he is not so much the voyeur (who chooses and enjoys his position) as the initiate concealed behind a peephole, or perhaps the beldame crouching in the bedroom corner. Milton's contemporary reader would be 'cited to examination' at these moments, but would not be forced to align with Satan. If *Paradise Lost* were read jointly by the kind of married couple envisioned in the divorce tracts—Eve's account of her encounter with Adam

---

[36] *Prose* II. 728; *PL* IV. 299. Both passages may be seen as responses to 1 Cor. 12:23—'those members of the body which we think to be less honourable, upon these we bestow more abundant honour.'

4. After J. B. Medina, *Book IX* (detail), in Milton, *Paradise Lost* (London: J. Tonson, 1688)

leaves no doubt that unfallen sexuality runs strongly in the female as well as the male—their own experience would seem 'in some proportion' closer to the first couple's than to Satan's; if it were read by the inexperienced virgin or the frustrated husband (also characterized in the earlier prose), then the reader would be able to distinguish Satan's jealousy from the wholesome rage that 'hath not the least grain of a sin in it' (ch. 6 n. 33 above).

We may find fallenness where Milton least suspected it, of course: Satan's most intense outburst, for example, is triggered by Eve's 'submissive Charms' and Adam's smile of 'Superior Love', the least Paradisal aspect of their sexuality for those who do not accept the pre-subordinationist reading. Milton was probably unaware of the equation he implies here, but in most cases we can suppose a conscious intention to create scenes of judgement, not to convict the 'sensuous and passionate' reader of unalloyed depravity, but to show how human sexuality is poised on a scale between Satan and Adam, Sin and Eve—a necessary stage in realizing its potential for good. This process of discrimination and restitution is also enacted in the language of Paradise, where phrases first associated with Satan and Sin ('dalliance', 'enamoured', 'attractive grace') are restored to Adam and Eve.[37] The 'pure' marital joys of the godly couple are endorsed and encouraged by these passages in *Paradise Lost*, just as they are by the amorous writings of Solomon; they may be framed by Satanic libido (and its equivalent, fallen lust or 'Court Amours'), and they may be tinged with elegiac sorrow for their diminution by the fall, but they are not *negated* by these sad considerations. Indeed, to interpret 'pure' in a privational sense, and to assert that Adam and Eve felt nothing like what we conceive as sexuality, is to align with the 'Hypocrites' denounced in the hymn to Wedded Love; in Areopagitican terms, this would be not 'pure' but 'blank'.[38]

[37] *PL* 762, 765, 819, IV. 298, 338, V. 13; Sin's childbirths anticipate the painful curse on Eve after the fall (contrast also the 'kindly rupture' of eggs in VII. 419), and her repeated 'fleeing' from the lustful Death is echoed in Eve's hesitancy at the lake and her flight from Adam (II. 787-90, IV. 462-3, 482).
[38] *Prose* II. 515-16; the word 'blank' for M combined the associations of dismal nullity (*PL* III. 48) and the 'excrementall whitenesse' of hypocrisy (*Prose* II. 516, alluding to the dead and external surface of a whited sepulchre); cf. his tr. of Horace's 'speciosum pelle' as 'whited skin' (II. 639). For Fish, the point of M's erotic descriptions is that 'we cannot understand innocence at all', that our response is entirely fallen and entirely different from what Adam and Eve might have felt (pp. 105-7).

7. Love Made in the First Age

The redemptive element in Eros may even be detected within Satan himself. His seductive stratagem, in the dream-scene and in the fall itself, is to expropriate the resources of both pagan and Solomonic eroticism for his own evil purpose—exactly what Milton attempted in reverse.[39] But his approach to Edenic sexuality can also generate, for a moment at least, the opposite effect; the overwhelming delights of Eden begin to 'stir seeds of virtue' in him—the function that Milton had claimed for poetry—and he then fluctuates between amorous gentleness and renewed venom. He admits that he 'melts' on seeing the first couple, and 'could love' them, though this only exacerbates his jealousy and frustrated desire (IV. 389, 363, 505-11). The dream he creates for Eve (V. 26-93) is genuinely lyrical and Solomonic, however corrupt its conclusion; Satan seems to have abandoned the false magnificence of his earlier style, and imbibed a more human and domestic nature, in his attempt to find a tender, cool eroticism appropriate for Eve.

When he catches sight of Eve in Book IX, again, he becomes a momentary romance hero, struck by the *coup de foudre*; Eve's cloud of roses becomes a graphic equivalent of his rapture, like the hearts in comic-strips. Satan thus joins a series of characters in Milton's poetry who are ravished at a distance by the ideal woman—the poet in love with Emilia, Comus entranced by the singing of the Lady, the poet awe-struck by the singing of Leonora. Each of these scenes enacts a paradigm of the function of poetry and the possibility of a redeemed sensuousness. The Italian sonnets end by opposing divine grace to the 'disio amoroso' inspired by Emilia, and the depravity of Comus makes us suspect his rapture as the kind of devilish delusion that *Paradise Lost* teaches us to reject; but later in the masque the good spirit rescues the emotion by describing his own response to the Lady in equally ecstatic terms, and in the singing of Leonora Milton explicitly finds the presence of God.[40] Now Satan feels the redemptive power, not of female song, but of the whole female 'spirit of love and amorous delight'.

---

[39] The persuasive voice in the dream echoes Comus and the Cavalier 'fruition' topos, the flattering associations of Moon and female-worship derive from Satan's colleague Astarte, the sexual goddess of Syria (cf. I. 436-46 and later IX. 546-8), the pleading voice and the dewy-haired angel suggest the lover of S. of S. 5:2, and the sequence 'I rose as at thy call, but found thee not; / To find thee I directed then my walk' corresponds exactly to the verses following.

[40] Sonnet 2, ll. 13-14, Sonnet 3, ll. 13-14, *A Mask*, ll. 244-64 and 552-64, 'Ad Leonoram Romae canentem', ll. 4-10. Dennis H. Burden uses Comus's response as a paradigm of delusory and Satanic poetry; *The Logical Epic* (1967), pp. 60-2.

The beauty of Eve at first 'with rapine sweet bereav'd / His fierceness of the fierce intent it brought', leaving him 'stupidly good', an amorous fool like Loredano's Adam. This moment of susceptibility, of course, then fuels his hatred all the more 'the more he sees / Of pleasure not for him' (ll. 461-70). But the pleasure itself is unmistakably labelled 'good'. And even after he has recollected his hateful thoughts he appears to be struggling to suppress a genuine lover's tribute:

> Shee fair, divinely fair, fit Love for Gods,
> Not terrible, though terrour be in Love
> And beautie, not approached by stronger hate,
> Hate stronger, under shew of Love well feign'd
> The way which to her ruin now I tend.   (IX. 489-93)

The repetitions and contorted syntax of the last three lines directly imitate this struggle to force love into hatred, *Eros* into *Atē*. Satan's rhetoric here seems turned inward, to persuade himself. Later of course, after the resolution to hate, he is able to turn the 'shew of Love' into outwardly-directed rhetoric—the grotesque parody of Renaissance love-poetry which begins his seduction of Eve, ancestor of the 'Serenates' and 'Court Amours' so contemptuously dismissed in the earlier hymn to wedded love. But his previous speech is respectful and tender. Again he echoes the Song of Songs,[41] but this time he does so not as a manipulative persuasion, but in his private thoughts, in what proves to be his last soliloquy.

Milton's Satan is thus driven not only by vainglory and enmity towards God, but by thwarted love of Eve, and this gives him much of his energy and complexity. He is a uniquely Miltonic creation, a fallen erotic angel rather than an ithyphallic demon; his encounter with the human world makes him a complex Don Juan figure, burning with a desire for Eve that may at times be genuinely amorous, but which cannot be expressed except as an urge to destroy the sexual fulfilment of the happy married couple. The evidence for his attraction must be stated only lightly, to avoid the usual suggestions of corruption or collusion in Eve, but Adam recognizes both the theological and the erotic impulse; he is perceptive enough to guess that Satan aims not only 'to withdraw / Our fealtie from God' but also 'to disturb / Conjugal Love', and

[41] 'Who is she that looketh forth as the morning, fair as the moon, clear as the sun, and terrible as an army with banners?' (6:10)

he is able to infer from his own supreme happiness what the reader has already seen at first hand—'no bliss / Enjoy'd by us excites his envie more' (IX. 261-4).

This eroticization of Satan only reinforces the reader's amphibious condition, suspended between feelings of abashment and privilege. The tincture of heroic evil is replaced by a sense of affinity that is at once more seductive and more disturbing: Christian readers may be unsure whether it brings Satan closer to their regenerate selves, or whether it reveals their own corruption; male readers may feel that the conventionally feminine 'soft delicious temper' discovered both in Satan and themselves (specifically associated with the virtuous reader in Milton's earlier poetics) is endorsed rather than condemned, as a force capable of deflecting even the father of evil. The twentieth-century analyst will be rightly aware of the political insult buried within this emotional tribute to the 'female', but in the historical context—the crude misogyny of most contemporary versions of Genesis, and Milton's own neurotic expulsion of the feminine in the divorce tracts—it represents a striking revision of conventional gender-boundaries, and a bold attempt to reinsert the 'sensuous and passionate' into the Paradisal ideal.

Those critics who concentrate on the fallenness of Milton's Eden, whether they see it as a blunder or a deliberate stratagem, underestimate this capacity for sensuous directness. The intimacy of Milton's erotic Paradise certainly generates some tension in the reader, poised on the threshhold of the nuptial bower, encouraged to participate but excluded by 'reverence' and 'propriety'.[42] Some modern readers simplify or obliterate this balancing-effect, however, by identifying the intimate details themselves as fallen. Eve's coyness (more offensive than her submission for many critics), her veil of hair, the mysteriousness which surrounds sexual penetration, Eve's 'blushing like the morn' when she is first led to the bower, and Raphael's blush when Adam presses home his question—all these are taken to anticipate the fall too heavily. Privacy assumes a world already populated, half-veiling encourages voyeurism, modesty is a fig-leaf, amorous delay suggests a manipulative relation between the sexes, and as for blushing, we are told that it can only derive from an 'inner psychic tension' most inappropriate (though

[42] The opposite extreme is represented by William Kerrigan, who believes that the fit reader walks into the arch-parental bedroom hand-in-hand with Milton, as Adam entered it with Eve (*The Prophetic Milton* (Charlottesville, 1974), pp. 134-6).

delightfully 'fallen') in Eve, and most 'unfortunate' in an archangel. Indeed, 'the very fact that Milton can see the blush as part of Eve's charm is testimony to his own fallen state, but undermines the necessary contrast.'[43] These criticisms are not in themselves unreasonable, though they fail to mark the distinction between corrupt 'knowingness' and the experiential knowledge that Milton admits even into the state of innocence. Dryden's Adam and Eve, for example, describe their own erotic life in terms that come ludicrously close to the jaded and stylized routines of Restoration comedy.[44] But this half-ironic worldliness is quite foreign to *Paradise Lost*, where powerful emotion is never hedged with apology or cynicism; even the blush or flush is redefined as an appropriate response to sexual delight, and therefore as beautiful as, say, the roses that cover the naked limbs during sleep—indeed, one is a correlative for the other. Milton's experiential ethics, applied in *Areopagitica* with equal vigour to the unfallen as to the fallen state, make him include the possibility of guilty blushing as an evil by which the good is known; when Eve meets Raphael in all her nakedness we are told that 'no thought infirm / Alterd her cheek', and when she lies with 'glowing cheek' after her dream, and then looks 'startled' when she wakes to see Adam (reassuring him that he is the 'Sole' object of her thoughts, as if there had been another), the possibility of adulterous guilt is strongly suggested. But Adam's response to her flushed and tousled appearance dispels rather than reinforces this malign interpretation: 'with looks of cordial Love' he

> Hung over her enamour'd, and beheld
> Beautie, which whether waking or asleep
> Shot forth peculiar Graces.

In contrast, when Eve returns 'flushing' with distemper after eating the fruit, Adam's reaction is unambiguous horror. This clarifies rather than obliterates Milton's essential point: that intense physical responses like the blush exist in both guilty and innocent forms,

---

[43] Laurence Lerner, *Love and Marriage* (1979), p. 118; apart from this blushing, M's description of pre-lapsarian Eros leaves Prof. Lerner unmoved ('there is no denying that the unfallen love of Adam and Eve must seem cold to us', p. 117). Criticism of pre-lapsarian blushing assumes the Vulgate reading of Gen. 2:25—'ne erubescent'.

[44] e.g. *State of Innocence*, p. 436: 'Somewhat forbids me, which I cannot name, / For ignorant of guilt, I fear not shame: / But some restraining thought, I know not why, / Tells me, you long should beg, I long deny.'

and may be caused by healthy thoughts, such as those of the wedding night.[45] The point is affirmed from on high when Adam asks his question about angelic sexuality, Raphael, who as a seraph is largely composed of amorous flame, smiles and turns 'Celestial rosie red, Loves proper hue' (VIII. 619). There is no question of an archangel's being embarrassed, though Milton might trick us into thinking so at first. But it is only by confronting and pushing through our own assumptions of embarrassment that we realize, by contrast, what Milton is actually saying—that in the innocent world a fiery flush is the appropriate response not only to the private caresses of one's partner, but even to the images of ideal sexuality that come up in discourse.

Encouraged by Milton's 'sensuous' poetics and by his earlier insistence on the partial recoverability of Paradisal marriage, the fit audience of *Paradise Lost* can translate these models of erotic response—'at least in some proportion'—into the intimate 'conversation' of text and reader. Such a response authenticates and intensifies the fundamental struggle that runs throughout the Genesis-tradition and comes to a head in Milton: the conflict between pessimistic and optimistic theories of how human sexuality relates to Paradisal happiness. Milton's erotic imagination, though fully aware of the distortions of lust and the fallenness of conventional responses, nevertheless manages to bring to life a positive ideal of Edenic sexuality; he gives vividness and strength to both conflicting readings, hastening the collapse of Genesis by his own success. The 'energetick operation' of the poem, as Johnson called it, is not only cerebral but cardiovascular, and this power to move guarantees that we still read it when *Psyche* and *The State of Innocence* are no more than curiosities of literary history. It inspires a 'commotion strange'—Adam's phrase to describe his own desire for Eve—and though this complex of emotions will involve guilt, envy, 'fierce desire', and indignation, it will also be suffused with the 'spirit of love and amorous delight', with a sense of passion as a potentially redemptive force.

[45] V. 384-5, 10-28, IX. 887 (contrast VIII. 511). In his persuasive discussion of the dream (p. 220), Fish brings up from *Comus* (l. 210) the idea that seductive visions may 'startle' the innocent mind without damaging or 'astounding' it. Even if her flush were caused by a 'thought infirm'—and it is just as likely to be a physical reaction to Satan's venom—to be guilty Eve would have to approve it as well as experience it; Leopold Damrosch's perceptive discussion of sexuality in *PL* overstates the fallenness of dreaming (*God's Plot, Man's Stories* (1985), p. 107), led perhaps by the desire to make M more novelistic.

2. Passion and subordination

Milton's vision of pre-lapsarian sexuality, like the landscape of Paradise where it unfolds, is distinguished from all others by its capacity for 'growth and compleating'. Our sense of Milton's erotic universe grows throughout the central books of *Paradise Lost*, not only by accumulation of detail, but by an increasing awareness of complexity; each successive episode involves confrontation with a new form of erotic sensibility (Satan, Raphael) or a new aspect of the self revealed by passion, and the horizons of innocence expand to include the problematic. The discovery of redeemed sensuousness is part of a taxing enquiry into the 'prime institution' of Paradisal marriage, into the nature of human sexuality and its relation to the divine—the most important task for fallen humanity, condemned to sift like Psyche through the mingled grains of good and evil.[46] But the same struggle for truth—to foster rather than to recover their righteous pleasures—confronts the first couple. Understanding their sexual love, and discovering how to preserve it in a Paradise that must be shared with Satan, is therefore a central action of the poem, for the characters as much as for the readers.

The effect of continual discovery is generated by the narrative design itself, which builds up a texture of overlapping viewpoints, and thus subjects the passion of Adam and Eve to a refined scrutiny that anticipates the epistolary novel. Even the first description of the couple, a dramatic and didactic *tableau vivant* of Genesis 1 and 2, is framed by the presence of Satan, fluctuating between love, desire, and envy, straining to discover details that he can put to evil use: the obvious ideological function of lines such as 'Hee for God only, shee for God in him' and 'Not equal, as their sex not equal seemd' is undermined when we reflect that the only observer, the only subject to whom these qualities 'seemed' a product of 'their sex', is Satan himself. Indeed, the subjective impression of the couple receives an emphasis unusual even in Milton—'seemed' is repeated three times in the sentence introducing them, each time as a main verb—and the Satanic association of the word is increased by the remark that, since the fall, true sexual purity has been replaced by 'mere shows of seeming pure' (IV. 290-9, 316). The

---

[46] *Prose* II. 528, 587, 514. The image of the grains is one of several incompatible models of good and evil in *Areopagitica*; M sometimes assumes a dialectic interchange between good and evil, sometimes a simple 'mingling' of essentially distinct and immutable essences.

possibility of competing models of sexual identity, stirring even within this ostensibly monolithic description, is increased shortly afterwards when Eve recounts the first crisis of her life, the scene by the lake; she is forced to decide between two 'images' of erotic love, one 'watery' and narcissistic, the other substantial and reciprocal. As we have seen, the sexual bond emerges from this episode as a profounder and more complex phenomenon than was suggested in the original separation and limitation of functions ('For contemplation hee and valour formd, / For softness shee and sweet attractive grace'): both male and female are led by intense desire, both feel incomplete without a partner, and both devote their contemplative and active powers to realizing this drive. This sense of the reciprocity of the lovers and the interpenetration of intelligence, energy, and eroticism, absent from any other version of the Eden-myth, is confirmed in the dream-episode—where the problem is solved with exemplary lucidity and deepening affection—and in the successive events of Raphael's visit, including Adam's own account of his encounter with Eve and the 'commotion strange' of sexual passion.

[*ii*]

The long scene with Raphael (Books V-VIII) serves not only to feed audience and characters with necessary information, but to provide a social encounter in which the paradoxical attractiveness and innocence of unfallen sexuality can be tested, and its problems illuminated both in practice and in conversation. Milton is quite aware that the presence of an observer could impose a strain on his sexual idyll, and he is not afraid to evoke these tensions in order to shape them to his poetic purpose. The first evening's 'dalliance' is defined by contrast with the response of Satan, who grows more verminous the closer he edges to Eve; now she is approached by an unfallen archangel. In both cases the supernatural visitor is considered as an erotic subject, capable of a reaction that Milton characterizes as specifically male. (Female sensuousness is not ignored by Milton, as we have seen, but he renders it more indirectly.) The male reader's self-scrutiny, sometimes explicitly directed by the author, forms a counterpoint to the unfolding narrative of erotic discovery. Raphael's visit thus continues the complicated drama of Book IV, in which the triangular situation of Adam, Eve, and the newcomer is itself observed by the epic audience, which must include not only the solitary youth but also, given Milton's insistence on godly marriage as the highest form of human life, the couple reading together.

The confrontation of woman and angel involved a special hermeneutic problem—one that was all the deeper because it concerned primeval sexuality and the origin of evil. In some Hebrew scriptures, we have seen in chapter 1, the original fall occurs when the angels ('Sons of God') make love to the daughters of men and beget giants on them; a fragment of this story survives in Genesis 6:1-2, where it seems to provide the motive for exterminating the entire human race apart from Noah's family. The ingenuity of commentators was greatly taxed by this stupendous episode; most of them (though Donne is an exception) followed Augustine in wrongly interpreting 'Sons of God' as the elect, the godly part of the human race—though like Augustine they also asserted that devils could and often did copulate with wicked women.[47] But St. Paul, in a passage that greatly influenced Milton's depiction of Eve, might suggest that angels are meant: 'if a woman have long hair', he explains in 1 Corinthians 11:15, 'it is a glory to her, for her hair is given her for a covering,' and she needs to be covered—with a veil or similar sign of subjection if her own hair is cut—'because of the angels'.

Milton was quite uncertain about the meaning of this passage in Genesis 6, and the efforts of modern scholars to reduce him to orthodoxy are unsatisfactory. In *Paradise Lost* XI. 580-636 the seduction of the Sons of God, in their standard Augustinian meaning, provides an important episode in which Michael teaches Adam the need for sexual temperance. But in *De Doctrina* Milton quotes Genesis 6:1 approvingly, as an example of sound moral judgement in love. In the Limbo of *Paradise Lost* Book III the offspring of those 'ill-joyn'd Sons and Daughters' appear closely associated with births 'abortive, monstrous, or unkindly mixt' and with 'middle Spirits ... Betwixt th'Angelical and Human Kind', though the connection may be intended as a delusion. But in *Paradise Regain'd* Milton assumes quite unequivocally that the unholy couplings of Genesis 6 were in fact done by the supernatural Belial and his 'lusty crew', who then falsely named the perpetrators

---

[47] Cf. ch. 1 n. 17 above; Kirkconnell, pp. 486, 507-9; Augustine, *CG* III. 5 and XIV. 23, *De Trinitate*.XII. vii. 10; Luther, II. 10-11; Donne, *Sermons*, VIII. 107; Arnold Williams, *The Common Expositor* (Chapel Hill, 1948), pp. 117, 152.

'Sons of God'; since the character of evil, in Milton's universe, is a perversion of the good, then a purer version of such propensities must exist in all angels. Milton tells us explicitly that angels enjoy diffuse sexual intercourse among themselves, and that they can take on either sex and 'limb themselves' for their encounters with other beings. 'Sons of God' is thus a term which could refer to upright men, or to fallen angels, or to the highest spiritual beings—indeed, one of Satan's chief purposes in *Paradise Regain'd* is to find out which of these meanings applies to Christ, for 'Sons of God both Angels are and Men', and the phrase 'bears no single sence'.[48]

There are hints of this multiple signification at several points in *Paradise Lost*. The first description of the happy pair, in which Eve's 'wanton' hair, arranged 'as a vail down to the slender waist ... implied subjection,' concludes by linking their unveiled nakedness with the angels: 'So pass'd they naked on, nor shund the sight / Of God or Angel, for they thought no ill' (IV. 319-20). And when Raphael first meets Eve in all her splendour, lovelier than Venus displaying herself to Paris, a similar point is made: 'no vail / Shee needed, Vertue-proof' (V. 383-4). The primary stress, of course, is on the inner purity of the naked Eve (Adam's nudity passes without comment in the second example), but both descriptions evoke the possibility of a 'thought infirm' or susceptible response. Milton is apparently fascinated by the paradox of the veil that hides and reveals at once, simultaneously enhancing innocence and desirability. He found this piquant effect in a favourite episode of *The Faerie Queene*, where it is used by the wicked nymphs to inflame Sir Guyon; here it is reappropriated for innocence.[49] Just as Eve here is decked and undecked ('Undeckt, save with her self'), so she is somehow veiled and not veiled—veiled for the fallen but virtuous Sons of God who read the poem and appreciate the metaphorical allusion to what St. Paul would have to make literal, but unveiled for the angels who meet her in the flesh.

[48] *Prose* VI. 720 (Col. edn. XVII. 203) and cf. I. 552; *PL* III. 461-3, VI. 352; *PR* II. 178-81, IV. 197 and 517. For scholarly opinion, see notes on these passages in Fowler (which contradict the identification of 'Sons of God' with angels at V. 446-50) and *A Variorum Commentary on the Poems of John Milton*, IV, ed. Walter MacKellar (New York, 1975), p. 117.

[49] *FQ* II. xii. 63-8, esp. 64; several details of M's erotic Eden are borrowed from, and hence rebuild, Spenser's Bower of Bliss. For some fruitful speculations on the relation of M to Spenser, and of both poets to their female patronesses mortal and celestial, cf. Quilligan, ch. 4, 'The Gender of the Reader and the Problem of Sexuality'.

We are likely to wonder, as Adam does, what Raphael feels during this visit. The parallel with Venus on Mount Ida announces this as another scene of judgement, but the identity of the judge remains elusive. Is it the reader, the voyeur of three naked beings, or Adam, whose choice of Eve will soon set off an epic catastrophe worse than the Trojan war, or is it the newly-arrived Raphael himself? Even if we are unaware of the sexual capacity of the 'Sons of God', Milton has several times reminded us of the erotic associations of this archangel. Raphael is a seraph, whose natures were particularly suited to Love; he is selected for the visit because of his special interest in marital success (his later help to Tobit, already evoked when Satan first meets the scents of Paradise, is emphasized again at V. 221-3); and his arrival in Eden is heralded by an astonishing burst of sensuous imagery, a 'pouring forth' of 'enormous bliss' in the landscape (V. 296-7). He arrives, on the stroke of noon, just as 'the mounted Sun / Shot down direct his fervid Raies to warm / Earths inmost womb' (V. 300-2). Raphael's entrance is thus charged with sexual energy, and he leaves, with a noble exhortation to happiness and love, after a glowing response to Adam's frank curiosity about angelic Eros. And we have seen that at the midpoint of the conversation, when Eve leaves to go gardening, 'all Eyes'—which must include Raphael's—are struck with 'Darts of desire . . . to wish her still in sight'.

The characters in this naked *déjeuner sur l'herbe* are not waxwork figures of innocence, then, but powerful breathing beings who may inspire sensuous empathy and curiosity, as well as shame and tension at the contrast between their state and our own. Though the female reader is not necessarily excluded from this scene, which presents Eve as a creative and self-motivated artist as well as a passive object of desire—imaginative readers can in any case participate in the experience of the opposite gender vicariously, if not uncritically—Milton is here absorbed by an erotic response normally associated with the male: the frenzy caused by the submission of a beautiful woman. At one point this becomes quite explicit. The occasion is another of Milton's revisions of Spenser's Bower of Bliss, in which a moment of erotic sorcery is transplanted to Paradise with its sensuous root-structure intact. Whereas in Spenser it was the bathing nymphs who blush and display their nakedness, and 'Excesse' who offers the gentlemen an enchanted cup, now

7. Love Made in the First Age

>   at Table *Eve*
> Ministerd naked, and their flowing cups
> With pleasant liquors crown'd: O innocence
> Deserving Paradise! if ever, then,
> Then had the Sons of God excuse t'have been
> Enamour'd at the sight; but in those hearts
> Love unlibidinous reign'd, nor jealousie
> Was understood, the injur'd Lovers Hell.   (V. 443–50)

The emotional vehemence of this extraordinary passage does not exempt us from interpretative struggle. We are not allowed to fall back on the simple opposition of heavenly love to fallen lust, nor to rely on simple definitions of 'enamour'd' and 'Sons of God'. At first it seems that Love-unlibidinous and being-enamoured are mutually exclusive and morally polarized terms. We then recall, however, that Adam only a few hours earlier had 'hung over [Eve] enamour'd' (V. 13): it is possible of course that we assent to the murmuring voice that calls Adam foppish, uxorious, and already fallen, thus accusing either God or Milton of incompetence; but as regenerate readers we should have rescued the word from these associations and restored it to the state of innocence. (Augustine, we saw in chapter 2, believed that even words as tainted as *libido* and *concupiscentia* could be redeemed.) Since Adam can be innocent, 'unlibidinous', and 'enamour'd' at the same time, we are forced to replace our static dichotomy with a more complex dialectic.

The allusion to the 'Sons of God' is similarly multivalent and compressed. In the immediate context the phrase apparently refers to angelic as well as human susceptibility. The plural 'those hearts' shows that Milton is thinking of feelings shared by more than one admirer, and 'jealousie' is therefore applied first to both witnesses: Milton evokes, even as he denies it, a scenario like that of *Amphitryon*. We must assume in Raphael a loving but innocent desire for Eve, compared explicitly to the imprudent angels of Genesis 6, and implicitly to the jealousy and 'fierce desire' of Satan, the demonic copulator and Courtly Amorist—the sarcastic allusion to 'the injured Lover's Hell' encompasses both these roles. In the larger context, which includes the sober lesson of Book XI, 'Sons of God' refers to the upright man in a fallen world, the tribe of the author himself and the masculine part of his fit audience. In this quasi-confessional moment, Milton seems to be saying that Eve's 'sweet attractive grace' could have filled the highest beings, as well as the ordinary *homme moyen sensuel*, with a rush of amorous feeling, and that at the high points of his description such lunacy might be excused.[50]

In powerful outbursts of yearning such as this, Milton suffuses the Genesis-story with more personal, Proustian dreams of vanished happiness and an ideal mistress—a process already begun in the prose, but now given fuller voice. His tributes to an imagined Eve derive their special urgency from emotive repetition: her 'Subjection' (a fetish in the divorce tracts as well as here) is 'by her yielded, by him best receivd, / Yielded with coy submission ... '; her food (increasingly important to Milton himself in successive marriages) is designed to bring 'Taste after taste upheld with kindliest change'. The climactic moment when Eve serves as cupbearer or Ganymede, and the Sons of God are excused their passion, again produces a critically placed repetition, overflowing the line-ending and drowning out the conditional phrase: 'if ever, then, / Then ... ' At these peaks of excitement we see a naïve, transparent Milton, not the manipulator of fallen responses but the agent of unexamined passions. His presentation of Eve, a kind of surrogate courtship, is thus as personal as the invocations that tell of his blindness and misfortune, or the sonnet on his dead wife, or the private speculation that the desire of the Sons of God might have been entirely good.[51] As in his reckless divorce tracts, Milton bares his own emotion in order to revitalize the Paradise myth for the Sons of God among his own people. Here he seems to speak from a position of uneasy intimacy, both privileged and abashed; he is not quite a stranger in Paradise, and not quite a member of the innocent party, but he offers himself as the leader of the intruding group and the orchestrator of their tensions.

[*iii*]

The latent confessional impulse in Milton's relation of Edenic sexuality becomes explicit in Adam's conversation with Raphael (VIII. 251-630). Adam follows Eve's lead in reconstructing the pleasures and discoveries of his first waking hours: she first told of the triumph of love over hesitancy in their first meeting, crowned

---

[50] Lindenbaum (p. 287) treats this episode perceptively.

[51] *PL* IV. 309-10, V. 336, 446-7; M included specific culinary demands in his third marriage-contract. Cf. ch. 2 n. 106 above for another connection between sexual yielding and abundant food.

7. Love Made in the First Age

with immediate consummation; now Adam retells the same moment in similar terms, first diffident, then rising to a rapturous display of nuptial imagery. He then proceeds, with astonishing boldness, to tell Raphael how it feels to make love to Eve:

> [I] must confess to find
> In all things else delight indeed, but such
> As us'd or not, works in the mind no change,
> Nor vehement desire, these delicacies
> I mean of Taste, Sight, Smell, Herbs, Fruits, and Flowrs,
> Walks, and the melodie of Birds; but here
> Farr otherwise, transported I behold,
> Transported touch. Here passion first I felt,
> Commotion strange. (VIII. 523-31)

Adam's critical analysis and defence of his own passion comes at the climax of the most idyllic part of *Paradise Lost*; it is the intimate core to which the conversation with Raphael gradually moves. In his conversations with Eve Adam would 'solve high dispute / With conjugal Caresses' (VIII. 55-6); but now the same caresses *generate* high dispute, and reveal problems of their own. Eros and female subordination turn out to be doubly problematic, moreover: not only must Adam struggle with the same dialectic of emotion as the reader, but the 'solutions' of the poem do not quite match the complexity of its awareness of human sexuality, and do not quite reconcile the original contradictions of Genesis, now hatched by Milton's powerful imagination.

In all other enjoyments Adam describes himself as 'superior and unmov'd'; he means that he is distinct from and more advanced than the object that provides the delight, and that he is not 'moved' in his whole being, or 'transported' to a different realm of existence. This is quite in keeping with the dominion over the environment granted to mankind in Genesis 1. But in the presence of his fellow-human his very mind is changed, and he cannot separate his sensuous delight from his admiration for Eve's specifically human qualities—not just her beauty, but her dignity, intelligence, and completeness (VIII. 531-59). It is important to recall at this point that the text of Genesis says nothing whatever about male superiority or rule over the female, until the latter is imposed as a punishment after the fall. And the exegetical tradition, though it repeatedly violated the Scripture by assigning male dominance to the state of nature, was not unanimous; as we have seen in chapter 3,

Chrysostom insisted that Eve was not subordinated until her punishment, as did several English radicals, and the Lutheran *Enarrationes* describe primal equality in great detail—though they contradict themselves in different parts of the text. Milton was working with a divided heritage, and this is reflected in Adam's attempt to understand his love for Eve.

Adam begins, like any apprentice in the mysteries of Eros, by trying an inadequate dichotomy. Intellectually he 'understands' her to be what the divorce tracts say she is—an 'inferiour', inwardly less gifted and outwardly less like God than he is, a being made 'occasionally' as an afterthought; but in the penumbra of love he experiences her as intelligent, dignified, and 'absolute', 'in herself compleat', a being 'intended first', an autonomous and fully human counterpart to himself (VIII. 540-55). This latter vision, though it alarms the suprematist in Raphael and Milton, fits perfectly well with the 'fit help' promised in Genesis. Nor does Adam quite call her a superior. But he does lavish superlatives on her that balance ambiguously between egalitarian tribute and slavish gallantry. He forces a gap between what Eve ought to be and what she seems to be, between how he feels and what he knows he should be thinking; he then widens it by carelessly using a vocabulary of extreme moral turpitude, and digs it deeper with alarming explanations that seem to accuse God more than himself. He even toys with the idea that God had deliberately weakened him when He extracted Eve from his side, a notion that any Christian should find blasphemous— though Donne, as we saw in chapter 3, used it to adorn a wedding-sermon.

By creating an Adam who is conscious of being 'weak / Against the charm of Beauties powerful glance' (VIII. 532-3), Milton again focuses on a problem that had unwittingly compromised other versions of Genesis. In Loredano as well as in Milton Adam finds in Eve 'the summe of all his desires', but when Loredano attempts to praise God's handiwork in Eve, and pay tribute to her beauty and glory, he falls into a distinctively worldly and fallen attitude, a kind of gallant humanism with misogynistic undertones:

> Women have derived from heaven so sweet a Tyranny into their faces, that the denying them the subjection of all hearts is an effect rather of stupidity than of prudence. He that can resist the inchantments of a feminine beauty, either is no man, or is indued with qualities superiour to those of a Man.

7. Love Made in the First Age

Loredano effectively antedates the fall, accuses God of entrapment, and 'pleads Adam's excuse'. His condemnation of the fall is softened by a similar indulgence.[52] At these moments the author's attitude is indistinguishable from the flippancy of Adam's own reply to God's accusation: ' "Who can resist the power of beauty? ... He that can withstand the importunate solicitation of the fairest piece (*cosa*) that ever came out of thy hands, either knows not how to Love or deserves not to be Beloved." ' The fierce condemnation that Loredano showers on this speech of Adam's has very little moral authority, since he has already practically endorsed it in his own descriptions of Eve. In Milton a similar surrender to gallantry is 'placed' dramatically, checked by Raphael's frown, and scrutinized by Adam himself: he is not 'stupified' by his amorous experiences, but stimulated to keener self-analysis. Nevertheless, this process of discrimination—in Adam himself and in the reader—is achieved with difficulty, and the episode remains precariously poised on the edge of simplistic moralism and authorial confusion.

Adam's description of his passion presents us with a very mingled grain. Adam pours out his feelings in a torrent of praise for Eve, an overflow of the cup of earthly blessings; he ends, not by formulating a question about a problem, but by returning to the angelic radiance of his beloved. Nevertheless, what began as an indulgent 'confession' between friends soon takes on the tone of a real confession—*confess, weak, Nature faild in mee, too much of Ornament, degraded, folly*.[53] The vocabulary seems so wildly incompatible with the state of innocence, and so remote from the conversations we have actually witnessed between Adam and Eve, that we labour to apply the special mode of reading that we have already practised with 'dalliance', 'attractive grace', 'liquid lapse of falling streams', 'wanton', and 'enamoured'. We rescue *passion* and *commotion* from their Satanic associations by recalling that in *Areopagitica* 'passions' are the God-given seeds of virtue and

---

[52] 'What cannot women do in an amorous soule? What fortitude will not she conquer, what constancy will not she subdue, what Will will she not pervert, what impossibility will not she effect? He that, loving, is able to resist the violences of Woman, is either a God or hath the power of a God' (pp. 42-3); cf. pp. 21, 34-5. For a similar combination of gallantry and moralization, see Francesco Pona, *L'Adamo* (Verona, 1654), and William Davenant, *Gondibert* VI. 64.

[53] *PL* VIII. 523-59, and cf. IX. 2 'as with his Friend'. Just as M's Paradise can contain blushing without shame and wantonness without lust, so it can have confession without sin.

'commotions' are the marks of divine healing—and even 'vehemence' exists in a heroic Christ-like form.[54]

Other parts of Adam's confession resist improvement, however. His blame of 'Nature' for not making him more superior seems unduly fallen, especially when we notice that, even earlier in his narration, he had equated 'Nature' with the possibility of sinful thoughts in Eve. He seems to have been deluded into crude anthropomorphism when he says that Eve's 'outward' form is less in the image of God than his; not even Satan made this observation.[55] The terms 'degraded' and 'folly' seem themselves to degrade his partner even when he purports to exalt her. Both possible meanings of '[not] intended first' are dubious: we can agree that Eve is not planned as a ruler over him (as she was in van Helmont), but it is a gross presumption to declare that she was an afterthought, a being 'made / Occasionally' rather than intended from the first. The effect of these multiple doubts is to throw Adam's whole conceptual model into greater disarray than perhaps his author intended.

Does this mean that Raphael's reply is wholly correct? The archangel rebukes some of Adam's assumptions, but he endorses others. He is properly severe on Adam's blame of 'Nature', identical to the pusillanimous excuse he will offer when confronted with his crime. He agrees enthusiastically with Adam's disparagements of Eve, however, and proclaims her worthy of honour but 'less excellent' and of less ultimate value; he would certainly disagree with the critic who explains Eve's position as subordination without devaluation.[56] And he condemns 'Passion' with something of the

[54] *Prose* II. 527, 566; among the frequent praises of 'vehemence' in the prose of the 1640s, cf. I. 663, 874, 878, and in the divorce tracts II. 282, 301, 644, 664.

[55] *PL* VIII. 506, 543-6; cf. Satan's early observation: 'so lively shines / In *them* divine resemblance, and such grace / The hand that formed *them* on their shape hath poured' (IV. 363-5, my emphasis). M did perhaps assume that God had the appearance of a human male: certainly He always appears to Adam as a male, as does Raphael (whence Adam could deduce in his fallen anger that Heaven is peopled with 'Spirits Masculine', X. 890). But Adam's (and M's) uncertainty about how God appeared to Eve before she met Adam (n. 60 below), and the fact that God communicates directly to Eve while His messenger is instructing Adam in Books XI-XII, could suggest that God's manly looks are put on only for Adam, according to the principle of accommodation (i.e. we must conceive 'Him' the way 'He' chooses to communicate 'Himself' to us; *Prose* VI. 133-6). Cf. William Kerrigan, 'The Fearful Accommodations of John Donne', *ELR* IV (1974), esp. 340-6.

[56] *PL* VIII. 561-6; McColley, ch. 2 and *passim*. McColley argues that Adam and Eve should model their relationship on that of the divine Father and Son, learning submission-in-equality, obedience to a consubstantial being, and sacrificial love: but

austere anti-sexuality of the divorce tracts; love-making is no more than 'the sense of touch whereby mankind / Is propagated', and far from being of supreme value must be considered something given also to 'Cattel and each Beast'. (In the *Doctrine and Discipline of Divorce*, we recall, 'God does not principally take care for such cattell.') Passion, in Raphael's view, is entirely incompatible with Love, which here as in the earlier prose is conceived as a Platonic ascent:

> In loving thou dost well, in passion not,
> Wherein true Love consists not; love refines
> The thoughts, and heart enlarges, hath his seat
> In Reason, and is judicious, is the scale,
> By which the heav'nly Love thou maist ascend.
>
> (VIII. 588-92)

Adam must not remain 'sunk in carnal pleasure', which could have been provided by mating him with one of the beasts.

Adam's response to this rebuke is complex and divided: he is only 'half abasht', and he is stimulated to a more thorough and discriminating defence of erotic desire. A gulf thus opens between man and angel, and it is by no means certain who has the 'true authority'. Raphael expresses Milton's deeply held beliefs, of course: 'Passion' in the fallen world must be kept under because it is always ready to spring at the higher faculties and tear them down; as another impeccably orthodox speaker later puts it, once Reason is 'obscur'd or not obeyd', 'inordinate desires / And upstart Passions' snatch the government and reduce man to servitude—his previous condition, interestingly enough, having been equality (XII. 86-90). But Milton was just as serious about his vitalistic and experiential ethics, in which virtue is constituted by struggle with excess, and in which passions are implanted by God even in unfallen man, and must be 'known' to the full—'he had bin else a meer artificiall *Adam*'. He was serious, too, in his worship of pre-lapsarian Wedded Love. Aquinas had speculated that *passiones animae* could have existed in perfect harmony with reason, and that erotic feeling would have been all the more intense; Milton 'hatched' this hypothetical state, and gave it moral credibility by making conflict

---

God deliberately stimulates Adam's sense of the *dis*similarity of God and man in this area (in the testing-scene before the creation of Eve); and sacrificial love, supposing Adam had been told of it, would have encouraged his fall even more.

essential to the 'growth and compleating' of innocence. Adam's reply to Raphael draws on all these Miltonic beliefs.

He justifies himself to Raphael by drawing on the same sensationalist psychology that he used to explain Eve's dream:

> I to thee disclose
> What inward thence I feel, not therefore foild,
> Who meet with various objects, from the sense
> Variously representing; yet still free
> Approve the best. (VIII. 607-11)

Approval will still be granted, he assures Raphael, on subordinationist criteria: passion will be kept below reason and woman below man. But then he challenges the archangel's estimation of sexual desire, and so redeems some of the rhapsodic 'Passion' that had inspired his high valuation of Eve and thus caused the frowning interruption. He replies to Raphael's charge with a sense of mild superiority derived from the experience of married love:

> Neither her out-side formd so fair, not aught
> In procreation common to all kinds
> (Though higher of the genial Bed by far,
> And with mysterious reverence I deem)
> So much delights me as those graceful acts,
> Those thousand decencies that daily flow
> From all her words and actions mixt with Love.
> (VIII. 596-602)

Human eroticism is both 'higher' and more complex than the archangel realizes. Adam is right, then, to end this extraordinarily probing conversation by asking his preceptor about angelic sexuality, just as he had asked him about angelic eating at the very beginning. His goal is to discover whether heavenly love (which Raphael *can* describe at first hand) is indeed joined in a Platonic 'scale' to the highest sexual love between man and woman, and if so, whether this vertical dimension provides an adequate model for understanding his own feelings.

Milton knew from Matthew 22:30 that there is no marriage in heaven, and he seems to have agreed with Donne that angels do not and perhaps cannot know the mind of man; both the Chorus in 'Adam Unparadiz'd' and Satan in *Paradise Lost* display a curiosity to know more about the new creature. Angelic apprehension, like that of the pastoral swain, is intense but one-dimensional. Raphael is by no means an infallible guide: he has already vacillated on the important question of 'accommodation', and Book VII has already established that his knowledge is limited to the 'Priestly' part of Genesis, to the biological rather than the human aspect of creation. He there expressed the opinion that Milton denounced as 'crabbed' and 'rustic' in the divorce tracts: 'Male he created thee, but thy consort / Female for Race.'[57] Raphael's responses to Adam show us that angelic sexuality is like the angelic mind.

Milton's angels are not inaccessibly different from humans, but are another form of 'one first matter', more spirituous because nearer to God; they have the same digestive needs and the same sexual emotion, though they are not limited by specific organs:

> Whatever pure thou in the body enjoy'st
> (And pure thou wert created) we enjoy
> In eminence, and obstacle find none
> Of membrane, joynt, or limb, exclusive barrs:
> Easier than Air with Air, if Spirits embrace,
> Total they mix, Union of Pure with Pure
> Desiring; nor restrain'd conveyance need
> As Flesh to mix with Flesh, or Soul with Soul.
> (V. 469-90, VIII. 622-9)

These higher physical delights, reminiscent of the climactic aerial mingling that Shakespeare's Cleopatra only attains at her death, do indeed form a continuous scale with human sexuality. But it is not a simple or homogenous scale: each level of being has its own specific experiences, not necessarily less or worse than those above. Angels enjoy a distillate of human eroticism, but without its density and rootedness; their texture is 'liquid' rather than palpable and multifarious (VI. 348-52). They can 'limb themselves', but in love-making they evidently choose not to experience the constraint

---

[57] Donne, *Sermons*, X. 58, 82 (I owe this point to Arthur Barker); Fowler, introd.; *PL* III. 662-76, VII. 529-30; ch. 3 *passim* and 6. 2. iii above. Raphael's oft-quoted doctrine of accommodation (V. 564-74), which relies on the dualism of spirit and body and the ineffability of their connection, is undermined immediately by his own uncertainty (V. 574-6), and contradicted by the monism of his explanations of digestion (V. 404-500) and wounding (VI. 330-53). Several critics recognize that the archangel may not be a simple mouthpiece when the conversation turns to sexuality, e.g Lindenbaum, pp. 294-5 (a perceptive discussion), Aers and Hodge, pp. 144-8 (God deliberately gives Raphael an inadequate ideology in order to test Adam once again), and J. B. Broadbent (Raphael and Adam are both infuriatingly limited, but this only proves the fundamental seriousness of M's treatment of sexuality; *Some Graver Subject* (1960), pp. 244-6).

of limbs, which means they also forego the touch of breasts meeting through a veil of hair. They do not suffer 'exclusive barrs', but neither do they enjoy the exclusivity or 'sole propriety' that enriches the private love-making of Adam and Eve. They have Eros, but they do not have marriage. Angels—and earnest young men trying to gain a place at the Wedding-feast of the Lamb by keeping their virginity until their mid-thirties—are as it were Platonists by nature, but mature humans need a more complicated model. Unlike Raphael and Satan, Adam can be 'enamoured' and 'unlibidinous' at the same time; he glimpses the possibility that in a 'right temper' passion and love might be interfused rather than kept rigidly apart.

Adam is therefore not 'cleared' after this discussion of sexuality, as he was 'cleared' after his questions about astronomy, and as 'all was cleared' after Eve's dream. He is left suspended between two paradigms of the loving relationship, an embattled hierarchy of Reason and Passion, man and woman, and a vision of equality-in-difference. Raphael of course castigates Adam for yielding his very identity to a creature of less value:

> weigh with her thy self;
> Then value: Oft times nothing profits more
> Than self-esteem, grounded on just and right
> Well manag'd; of that skill the more thou know'st
> The more she will acknowledge thee her Head,
> And to realities yeild all her shows.   (VIII. 570-5)

Raphael's cynical condemnation is particularly appalling because, in equating Eve with 'shows', he declares her intrinsically fallen: when we first encountered her nakedness and sexual purity, Milton had explicitly contrasted it with 'sin-bred' hypocrisy—'shows instead, mere shows of seeming pure'; now he seems to agree with the archangel. But the poem itself allows us to challenge this authority. In the same narration, just before the nuptial dithyramb that leads to Raphael's interruption, we learn that Adam's most fervent desire is for an equal—a desire so deeply rooted in his being that it gives him the astonishing ability to argue down the Almighty within minutes of his creation; and his most rapturous eloquence is reserved for those moments (truly Paradisal to a non-hierarchic mind) where feeling and thought are harmonized and fused in sexual fulfilment with an 'absolute' human counterpart. Adam is divided between shame and pride at these feelings. A strict

Augustinian would probably call Adam's hierarchic determination *caritas* or 'good love', and dismiss his ecstatic and egalitarian passion as evil *libido*; but it is difficult to dismiss an experience conveyed with such transfiguring poetic power. Adam is only 'half abasht' by Raphael's rebuke because Raphael's model of Love is only half true.

The choice between ecstatic-egalitarian and patriarchal relationships is not simply a choice between good and evil, or between reason and passion; whatever Milton the ideologue would say, the poem itself presents both as moral systems based on self-knowledge and responsibility, and both appear to have been sanctioned by higher beings. Up to this point in the poem, in fact, Adam's experience has mostly encouraged him to think that God intends a fundamental equality and reciprocity between the sexes. At their first appearance, of course, the author's voice tells us that they 'seemed' to Satan 'not equal', because of their 'sex'. In its immediate context the phrase relates, rather loosely, to the image of God or 'true authority' that Satan senses in both man and woman, and in the larger context of the idyllic books, transformed by the semantics of Paradise, it comes to mean 'not identical' rather than essentially and ontologically different in value; as Adam observes, Eve is 'manlike but different sex'—a difference not necessarily marked by hierarchy.[58] Much of the accumulated experience of the poem supports the 'True Leveller' reading of Genesis: 'Man had Domination given him over the Beasts, Birds, and Fishes, but not one word was spoken in the beginning, that one branch of mankind should rule over other'; 'every single man, Male and Female, is a perfect Creature of himself.'[59] Milton's Eve is not 'perfect' in the sense of self-sufficient, of course, any more than Adam is; but compared with every other version she is an autonomous and well-rounded character, with specific counterparts to Adam's mental and physical skills, happily able to out-argue him in matters that concern her own sphere of expertise; even Raphael tells Adam that she 'sees when thou art seen least wise'. Nor can female inferiority be deduced from the 'beasts, birds and fishes' over whom the

---

[58] IV. 291–6, VIII. 471; the loose grammatical relationship of 'not equal' to the preceding lines can be seen by contrast with the sentence from *Tetrachordon* that M apparently echoes: woman shares the man's 'empire' over the universe, 'though not equally, yet largely' (ch. 6 n. 44 above).

[59] *The True Levellers Standard Advanced* (ch. 3 n. 21 above), also quot. (as a 'Leveller' belief, though it is in fact a Digger pamphlet) in McColley, p. 50.

human couple jointly rule. The vegetable kingdom displays some conventional emblems of female weakness, like the vine and the elm, but otherwise the physical environment is remarkably free of lessons in subordination: male dominance within the animal species is mentioned neither in Adam's first survey of the beasts in Book VIII, nor in the ample descriptions of Book IV, nor in the explicitly didactic Creation-story of Book VII—virtually the only creature to be given a symbolic application is the ant, 'Pattern of just equalitie perhaps'.[60] Most importantly of all, neither Eve nor Adam says a word about subordination or inferiority when they describe the most sacred moment of their lives, when God spoke directly to them and presented them with their mate.

Eve does, of course, provide one striking exception to this relatively egalitarian conception; she begins each of her speeches to Adam with a formal statement of the narrow Pauline interpretation of woman's role. Between her introduction in Book IV when Milton announces her 'submission', and Raphael's interruption in Book VIII, she herself is the only subordinationist voice in the poem. At times she even seems to embroider on her secondary role, attributing God-like features to Adam, and thus deepening the idolatry to which her author unwittingly condemned her from the first ('Hee for God only, shee for God in him'). Though Adam is taller and better at systematic reasoning, he is not 'Praeeminent by so much odds' that he must remain lonely, and he is not the 'Author' of Eve at all, unless the paper is the author of the book. If her formula of submission ('Unargu'd I obey; so God ordains') really does express the ideal, then we must condemn her when she corrects Adam's opinions about food-storage, and we must regard her as hopelessly corrupt when she argues for separate gardening, even though Milton insists she is 'yet sinless'. If God 'ordained' her obedience and inferiority, then He did so in a scene that neither Scripture nor Milton has recorded. 'Ordain' is a solemn word, referring to an eternal law decreed explicitly by God. The 'voice' that leads Eve to her husband (sometimes assumed to be God, sometimes a 'genial angel') is significantly devoid of gender, and defines marriage in terms of partnership and motherhood; and when Adam retells this scene, borrowing from conversations with Eve, he mentions only nuptial sanctity and marriage 'rites'—though

---

[60] *PL* V. 321–5, VIII. 578, VII. 487. Raphael's comment on Eve may also have a less flattering meaning: 'she notices your lapses.'

the voice combines several roles later assigned to father, priest, and mother, it does not dictate obedience.[61] When Raphael refers to the creation of 'female for race' he says nothing about subordination. And when Adam feels the 'intelligible flame' and demands a consort—the central moment from which grew Milton's entire conception of marriage both in the divorce tracts and in the epic— the relationship imagined by man and approved by God is described in egalitarian terms.

Adam's primal yearning is for an 'equal' partner. The reader may suspect either a divine trick or an authorial blunder here, remembering that Satan and Milton had conspired to pronounce Adam and Eve 'not equal'. The earlier declaration had been proved by the separation of male and female qualities, but in the intervening books this definition receded into the shadows, as contemplation and softness, valour and attractive grace, blend in what Heale had called 'a strange kinde of *Metamorphosis*'. Now the concept of equality is established with greater clarity:

> Among unequals what societie
> Can sort, what harmonie or true delight?   (VIII. 383–4)

Adam imagines a relationship not of bland identity but of reciprocity, an equal degree of creative tension, 'fellowship', and 'complacence'—which means not simply an 'object or source of pleasure' but a delight in the awareness of the other's pleasure.[62] In Genesis, moreover, it is God who pronounces it 'not good for man to be alone', but in *Paradise Lost* it is Adam himself who realizes this lack and imagines an equal partner, arguing down God's attempts to talk him out of it. The craving for partnership is so 'deeply graven', and so energetically maintained throughout the long wrestling-match with God, that it seems to define his whole being; he is unfinished without Eve. In the practice of dramatization, though not in his explicit ideological statements, Milton approaches the erotic ontogeny of Karl Barth (ch. 1 n. 2 above), assuming that humanity only exists in the relation of man

---

[61] *PL* IV. 445–8, 635–6; cf. IV. 467–76, IV. 712 and Fowler's note, VIII. 484–7.
[62] Fowler, note on VIII. 433; Nathanael Hardy, ch. 6 n. 41 above. McColley argues that, though Adam asks for an equal, he actually gets something else (p. 87, and cf. IX. 823); if so, this would bring M's God closer to the trickster of the original fable. It may be objected that M is using the sense recorded in *OED* 'equal' A.3 (fit in quantity, degree, or quality), but this meaning is only found in the construction with *to*.

to woman and woman to man. The notion that Eve is 'occasional', which implies that Adam's loneliness is an inessential mood, can barely stand beside this powerfully imagined vision.

When God congratulates Adam for passing this test, He too equates the urge for equal partnership with the essential discovery of self:

> Thus farr to try thee, *Adam*, I was pleas'd,
> And find thee knowing not of Beasts alone,
> Which thou hast rightly nam'd, but of thy self,
> Expressing well the spirit within thee free.
>
> (VIII. 437-40)

He then promises to create precisely what Adam has imagined: 'Thy likeness, thy fit help, thy other self, / Thy wish exactly to thy hearts desire' (VIII. 450-1). Female subordination and inferiority are never mentioned in this episode, astonishingly enough. Milton here, however locally, remains true to the original text, to the Lutheran vision of primal freedom for both sexes, and to the love of equality proclaimed in his own political writings (though not in his domestic treatises) and upheld by the archangel Michael in his teaching of Adam.

Proper self-knowledge, then, involves the discovery of the human capacity for egalitarian love, instituted in Paradise. But Raphael assumes, with fallen culture, that the principal business of married life is to obtain acknowledgements of superiority from the wife, and he in turn recommends the proper kind of self-knowledge to achieve this. And Christ, justly rebuking Adam's oily self-exoneration and transference of blame to Eve after the fall, asks

> Was shee thy God, that her thou didst obey
> Before his voice, or was shee made thy guide,
> Superior, or but equal, that to her
> Thou did'st resigne thy Manhood, and the Place
> Wherein God set thee above her made of thee,
> And for thee?

'Had'st thou known thy self aright', the judgement continues, Adam would have known that Eve's gifts were those of a subordinate, meant 'to attract thy Love, not thy Subjection' (X. 145-56). Adam has now forfeited the right, and temporarily the ability, to give an honest and courageous answer; but he could have replied, not in exoneration of his sin but in simple truth, that Eve was properly his 'guide' at times, that she was not his 'superior', but that God Himself had 'ordained' her as an equal, and had praised his self-knowledge when he demanded one. The ambiguous phrase 'or but equal' could set off a similar train of thought in the reader.

I am not suggesting that Milton intended to criticize or subvert the judgement of Raphael, Christ, and the divorce tracts; he undoubtedly believed that Eve's inferiority was so self-evident that she herself could spell it out. But his poem sees when he is seen least wise. Pre-subordination is a given, an axiom, an 'ideological imperative' that exists independently of evidence; but the act of expanding Eden into an almost novelistic universe brings it into the empirical sphere, and generates contrary evidence. Milton has succeeded in bringing to life, in the *praxis* of his art, two quite different models of the politics of love: one is drawn from the experience of being in love with an equal, and the mutual surrender of 'due benevolence', the other from the hierarchical arrangement of the universe, and the craving for male supremacy. His treatment of Genesis stands out from all others because his imagination responds generously to both of these, to the ecstatic egalitarian love of 'one flesh' as well as to the patriarchal love of superior and inferior; he has hatched the contradictions in the text and the tradition that elsewhere lie dormant. As Christ later points out, this brings 'Love' and 'Subjection' into potential conflict.

Adam's reply to Raphael attempts to solve the dichotomy his 'confession' has brought to light, by concentrating on the point where Love and Subjection touch. The 'words and actions' that make him enamoured of Eve are not just mixed with love, but 'mixt with Love / And sweet compliance'. Adam thus underlines those over-excited moments in the poem when desire is kindled by the acknowledgement of dominance, and encourages a distorting simplification of his marriage. As far as we can tell, the first couple lie 'side by side' when they make love, and in the morning Adam 'hangs over' his sleeping beloved more like Venus than Mars. But at other times he does assume a more dominant posture, sitting at the door of his bower while the 'mounted Sun' shoots his rays into the womb of the earth and Eve prepares lunch, or talking with his guest while Eve hangs back like a servant. (Milton cannot make up his mind whether Eve could hear Raphael's narrative at all.)[63]

---

[63] *PL* VIII. 602-3; IV. 741; V. 13 (cf. Lucretius, *De Rerum Natura*, I. 31-40), 299-302 (cf. Gen. 18:1). Eve sat 'retired in sight' during the conversation (in which Raphael

These patriarchal attitudes do not sum up the range of amorous emotion in the poem, however, and Adam's reply does not resolve the contradictions between the different modes of love it bodies forth. Indeed, his own impulse to 'say all', in this conversation with Raphael, has forced us to be aware of these discrepancies: we recall, for example, that at one of the most intense moments in Book IV, when Satan boils over with jealousy and desire, Milton has Adam 'Smile with superior Love' at Eve's 'meek surrender'; but we also remember Adam's confession to Raphael, that in the surges of love—precisely at moments like these—he has no feeling of superiority.

This irresolvable doubleness at the heart of Milton's apprehension of wedded love—a contradiction that lies dormant in Genesis and the Pauline tradition—may be traced even in the lines that first introduce the ideal couple. Let us recall again that Genesis gives the 'male and female' joint dominion over all the lower species (in chapter 1), but says nothing about masculine rule until it is imposed as a punishment after the fall. Milton deliberately evokes the former text when he introduces Adam and Eve as 'lords of all'—indeed, the whole account of sexual difference is offered as an explanation of their joint worthiness to rule over Paradise. Syntactically, Eve's 'softness' is as much a form of 'true authority', a manifestation of the image of God, as is Adam's 'valour'. His features and hair-arrangement 'declared / Absolute rule' and hers 'impli'd / Subjection, but requir'd with gentle sway' (IV. 300-8): the parallelism of syntax and allusion tells us that man and woman exercise their dominion in different ways, that Eve rules gently over her animals and Adam sternly—though we may also hear a courtly compliment to her sway over Adam here. Milton's actual meaning is then achieved by a violent swivelling. The subject of 'requir'd' turns out to be Adam, in defiance of all grammar, and 'Subjection' suddenly becomes the sexual and domestic surrender of Eve to him—'Yeilded' of course, 'with coy submission, modest pride, /

---

addresses Adam alone, referring to Eve as an absent third person, 'thy consort'), and leaves when she *sees* an abstruse look on Adam's face; later she claims that her entire knowledge of the Satanic threat comes from what Adam has retold her and from what she overheard, hiding behind a bush on her way back from gardening, of the closing stages of the talk on sexuality (VII. 529, VIII. 41, IX. 275-8). But at VII. 50-4 M says that Adam 'with his consorted Eve / The story heard attentive', and refers to the astonishment the war in Heaven provoked in '*their* thought' (my emphasis).

And sweet reluctant amorous delay' (IV. 309-11). Rhetorical slipperiness is not confined to Satan; despite Milton's praise of Paradisal 'simplicity' (IV. 318), his version of innocence has its sleights and contortions too. The exultant repetition, swelling epithets and langorous rhythm of these disturbingly beautiful lines may be interpreted, not just as an expression of Milton's ideal of pre-lapsarian love (intensified by his own slightly perverse sensibility), but as an attempt to cloud and soften the divergence between the text of Genesis and the tradition of exegesis—to solve high dispute with conjugal caresses.

3. The fall: 'casual fruition' and the problems of time

The troubled idyll of *Paradise Lost* depends on a distinctive combination of elements normally found apart: Milton's treatment is both strenuously confrontational and intensely lyrical. He will raise issues of which his literary contemporaries were barely conscious, making the struggle of opposing views the authenticating mark of freedom in Eden as well as in *Areopagitica*. But he will cloud the very problems his powerful and realistic imagination brings to light, enveloping the reader in an atmosphere of sweet amorous luxury. Though Milton may not be aware of this division of effect, it is an indispensable part of his attempt to build a coherent epic on a disintegrating foundation. If he is to express the original myth and its interpretative tradition with a fullness and authority 'unattempted yet in prose or rhyme' (I. 16), he must also express their inherent contradictions; he must persuade us that Adam and Eve are both sexual and innocent, both egalitarian and hierarchic, and (most difficult of all) both perfect and ready to fall.

Inducing a state of hypnotic lyrical suspension in the reader is not a luxury or an indulgence for Milton, as it might be for Keats, but a necessity. The impending catastrophe is larger and more intolerable than any other, and the epic structure needs an emotional counterweight. Author and reader both need to accommodate that desire to avert the fall that breaks out in the first line of Book IV—'O for that warning voice'—and this subjective 'amorous delay' may serve to assuage our inevitable sense of futility. And having chosen to give Adam and Eve a full sexual life, and having lodged them in Paradise for at least nine days, with frequent hints of a far longer residence, Milton is entirely at a loss to explain why God has not allowed Eve to conceive. We too must 'forget all time'.

In the state of love, Eve declares, 'All seasons and their change all please alike'. 'Seasons' suggests large units of time as well as the stages of the day, even when referring to the pre-lapsarian world: the migrating birds, for example, are created 'intelligent of seasons' in Book VII. Adam and Eve themselves seem to refer to memories of long duration. They have 'often' heard angels sing at midnight—a variation in their normal sleep-pattern—and Eve is 'oft wont' to dream of her husband and her work. Adam explains how 'words and deeds long past' combine with recent memories when we dream. Eve's beautiful account of her first meeting with Adam is introduced by 'That day I oft remember'—it is long enough ago for the cycle of memory and forgetting to have become habitual; Bentley's emendation to 'hour' rings entirely false. Enough time has elapsed, even by the day they meet Raphael, for Adam to think Eve has a full store-cupboard and for Eve to find which fruits improve with keeping, and we later see that she has a private flower-garden where she has planted, watered, and raised selected species during her infrequent departures to garden alone.[64]

What is true of *Othello* is even more true of *Paradise Lost*: there are quite simply two time-schemes, irreconcilable by the calendar, but corresponding to two aspects of subjectivity in love. Adam and Eve are at the same time young lovers, tragically snatched away after a few nights of love, and a mature couple; they recapitulate the landscape around them, in which '*Spring* and *Autumn* ... Danc'd hand in hand'. They inhabit Romance time, which 'contracts the day / To pitied beauty', and 'steals away / On downy feet'. Time in heaven, Raphael explains, is only 'applied to motion'. In the subjective heaven of unfallen love, time describes not a circle, which would strain credibility too far, but a gentle spiral or eddy that moves along a broadening river, an ideal day repeated with slight quickening variations. This is precisely the pattern traced out

---

[64] *PL* VII. 427; IV. 449, 680; V. 32, 113, 314-15, 322-5; IX. 437-8; XI. 273-9; *PL*, ed. Richard Bentley (1732), p. 122. Fowler's note to IV. 449 alludes to two of these time-indicators, but fails to account for them; M may well assume that the infused knowledge of Adam and Eve includes 'a ready-made understanding of seasonal change', but these passages refer to specific memories and the patterns of their recurrence in waking and sleeping—could this occur in the four days that Fowler gives them by the time of Books IV and V? Mary Nyquist provides a new perspective on this issue by relating these effects of suspended and divided time to mimetic and discursive discontinuities within the poem; cf. 'Reading the Fall: Discourse and Drama in *Paradise Lost*', *ELR* XIV (1984), esp. 199-206.

in Eve's amorous descant, 'With thee conversing I forget all time'.[65] That the river leads to a massive fall only increases the poignancy of this suspended time. We can never apprehend it except in the elegiac mode. The 'growth' of Paradise itself, moreover, will soon force an awareness of precisely the time-discrepancy that the idyllic books conceal. Early in Book IX Eve reports that the garden now grows all the more vigorously for their care of it, 'luxurious by restraint'—a valid botanical observation derived from her own expertise; 'one night or two' now undoes their whole day's labour (IX. 205-12). Adam's reply is breezily reassuring, but does not answer the point. His solution, that children will help them in the years to come, could not possibly keep pace with this rate of daily growth; and conception has not even begun.

[*ii*]

As he approaches the fall, Milton himself announces a change of literary mode: 'I now must change / These notes to tragic' (IX. 5-6). With this alteration comes a shift in time-consciousness and a more pessimistic attitude to conflict and difficulty. The garden-problem and the consequent debate on the division of labour forms a transition or pivot: it is the first scene of the new tragedy, but the characters are still explicitly 'sinless' and still inspired by the ideal of erotic love, dignity, and freedom built up in the earlier books. After the fall itself such a balancing is no longer possible, of course; but the transition from innocent to corrupt sexuality must still be done with appropriate complexity and realism, if it is to be convincing. When he came to depict the immediate effects of the fruit, moreover, he faced a specific problem inherited with his text: the requirements of exegesis and the resources of literary expression conflicted. Augustine, for example, tried his utmost to imagine a state of voluntary and delightful unfallen sexuality, and equated the immediate consequences of the fall with the eruption of lust. These speculations cannot be translated into literary form, however: the voluntary state is pure hypothesis, since human innocence lasted only a few hours; and the fall itself, with

---

[65] William Chamberlayne, *Pharonnida* (1659), 1st pagination, p. 151; *PL* V. 394-5, 580-1. Cf. Donne, *Sermons*, III. 247: 'though there be properly no eternity in this secular mariage [of Adam and Eve, and of their descendants], ... yet we may consider a kind of eternity, a kind of circle without beginning, without end, even in this secular mariage.'

its sudden rebellious tumescence of the sexual parts, could hardly be depicted without provoking scandal, shame, or ribald laughter—particularly if it is given the sensuous solidity and 'treatable smoothnesse' that Milton's poetics demanded.

The exegetes were themselves divided, moreover. As we have seen in chapter 4, the heterodox libertines and theosophists tended to equate the fall with sexuality itself. Most mainstream commentators, even when they accepted Augustine's version of innocence, chose not to dwell on the subject of sexuality; and though one or two suggested that the fall had immediate Priapic consequences, for the most part speculative links between sexuality and the fall are mentioned only as examples of Rabbinical excess. Calvin maintained that to ascribe the fall to appetite, lust, and the blandishments of Eve, rather than to an apostacy of the entire mind and soul, is trivial and childish; though the fig-leaves were placed over the genitals, it would have been more appropriate to have covered the mouth and eyes, which had sinned far more. (Donne, on the other hand, follows St. Bernard's amplification of Augustine—the penis is covered, and later circumcised, because it is the most rebellious organ and the ringleader of all the sins.) St. Paul may have taught that Adam was 'not deceived', which leaves us open to supply other motives—such as love of Eve, as Augustine suggests; but Calvin insists that he must have been deceived to some extent. His sin was intellectual disbelief and refusal of God's will, and compared to these titanic crimes the amorous or sensual element is negligible.[66]

Most literary and artistic versions, on the other hand, increase what Johnson called the 'human interest' by assuming that Satan is a seducer, that Eve's crime involves corrupt desire rather than intellectual hubris, and that she wins over Adam by erotic means. Many versions of Genesis use Eve's temptation as the occasion for diatribes against the female mind, accusing it of triviality, newfangledness, and even a love of what is prohibited and evil—qualities which, if really present in the unfallen creature, must impugn God's providence. These accusations, though sometimes

---

[66] Calvin 3:6, 3:7 (I. 152, 155, 159); Donne, *Sermons*, VI. 191-2; Augustine, *CG* XIV. 11; 2. 1. ii and 4. 3 above. Wolfgang E. H. Rudat, under the impression that Aug. thought unfallen man had erections, asserts that M's serpent simulates Adam's flourishing penis in order tŏ inspire envy in Eve ('Milton, Freud, St. Augustine: *Paradise Lost* and the History of Human Sexuality', *Mosaic* XV. ii (Spring, 1982), 108-22).

given to the father of lies, show every sign of authorial approval. Loredano, for example, speaks *in propria persona* when he asserts that Eve rushed to the tree as soon as she heard the prohibition: 'to forbid a woman, is to increase her appetite; he that denies her any thing, adds a spur to that desire, which is ardent in all things, but in things prohibited insatiable.' It was this curiosity, Loredano insists, that 'induced the Devill to tempt her' (though he also suggests that God created woman to make Adam sin, so that He could obtain more glory from His subsequent clemency—an argument that, in Milton's version of the myth, escaped even Satan).[67] Milton, in contrast, plants no such 'vain hopes, vain aimes, inordinate desires' in Eve; in fact, Satan has to exert all his 'Devilish art' to insert them as she dreams (IV. 801-8), and even then, as shrewder critics have noticed, his success is not proven.

Milton cannot entirely be cleared of the charges of 'Eve-baiting' levelled most memorably by Empson and since by many antimisogynist critics. There is clearly an undertone in the poem that points to the maleness of the good angels and accuses Eve of narcissism in the lake-episode, sensual weakness in the dream, perversity in gardening alone, and concupiscence in admitting Satan's courtly amours. It is not clear whether the connection between Eve and a woman who married a serpent-deity ('*Euryonome*, the wide- / Encroaching *Eve* perhaps') is Milton's own comment or part of the summary of the devils' lie (X. 581-2). Satan's false and courtly words do penetrate 'into the Heart of *Eve*' with gratuitous rapidity, though not with the sensual piquancy that Beaumont provides: 'Indeed his charms had open stole her heart / And delicately thrill'd their poison in' (1702, VI. 290). And Milton's classicizing similes do seem to hint at corrupt sexual connections, albeit less than Empson would claim. Eve is momentarily equated with Circe, Paradise is compared to places of violent seduction, and Satan reminds Milton of serpents who coupled with human matrons; he might therefore faintly suggest what Phineas Fletcher declares quite openly—that Eve mated with Satan to produce a sinful progeny.[68] But for the most part these possibilities

---

[67] pp. 23-4, 15 (but contrast p. 43, denouncing a similar sentiment); other examples of misogynistic satire can be found on almost every page. Cf. also Kirkconnell, pp. 68, 108-10, 269, 427, and Donne, *First Anniversary*, ll. 103-4; the fall shows that women 'were to good ends, and they are so still, / But accessory, and principal in ill.' The fullest discussion of misogyny in the literary versions of Gen. is found in McColley, ch. 5 *passim*.

[68] William Empson, *Some Versions of Pastoral* (1935; 2nd edn., 1966), pp. 142-6.

are no more than shadowy suggestions, and they will often reinforce rather than undermine Milton's distinctive vision of innocence; for example, the ominous sexual references that flank Eve's first entrance in the poem and her last unfallen exit from Adam (like '*Ceres* in her Prime, / Yet Virgin of *Proserpina* from *Jove*,' IX. 395-6) do not refer to voluntary copulation, as Empson suggests, but to rape in the true sense—the violent imposition of sex on a woman *against* her will. For Satan to be a rapist, his fury redoubled by 'tormenting' vulnerability, in no way compromises his victim. Erotic complicity between Eve and the snake may be suggested in other versions; in Samuel Pordage, for example, Satan chooses a Cavalier serpent who already

> Had gain'd *Eve's* love, or who it may be had
> Entwin'd about her naked neck, and play'd
> With her white hands, or favour'd in her lap.[69]

But Milton's Eve, incomparably more erotic in her relations with Adam, displays no such fetishism.

Nor does she use her sexuality to persuade Adam to eat the fruit. In most contemporary versions of Genesis Eve conquers his initial resistance by gradually increasing her erotic manipulative power. Illustrations of this persuasion are often flagrantly sexual (Figs. 5-6), and even the most benign portrayals of innocence may contain proleptic hints of sexual defection (Fig. 7).

Among literary versions Grotius manages this theme with some dignity, but most authors resort to the commonplaces of exasperated misogyny. Eve begins with 'a loving Glance, and modest smile, / (Those mighty Arms by which all females fight),' accuses Adam of never having properly loved her, threatens to leave him, pretends to be hurt (with theatrical asides to assure us of her dishonesty), and delivers the *coup de grâce* by bursting into 'teares, the wonted artifices with which women betray the honour, liberty, and safety of men'. Adam may experience an agonized conflict between Love and

---

151; *PL* IX. 521-2, 386-96, 505-10, IV. 268-79; Giles and Phineas Fletcher, *Poetical Works*, ed. Frederick S. Boas, II (Cambridge, 1909), 157. The allusion to Circe does seem to be either a blunder or what Empson would call a 'queer smack' at Eve, since M elsewhere uses Circe to blame the female for sexual enthralment, and since the terms of the comparison make Circe not an anti-Eve but a less commanding sorceress.

[69] Quot. in Kirkconnell, p. 427; his source is perhaps da Salandra's *Adamo Caduto*, where Satan actually chooses a snake that he sees playing in Eve's bosom (tr. in McColley, p. 162).

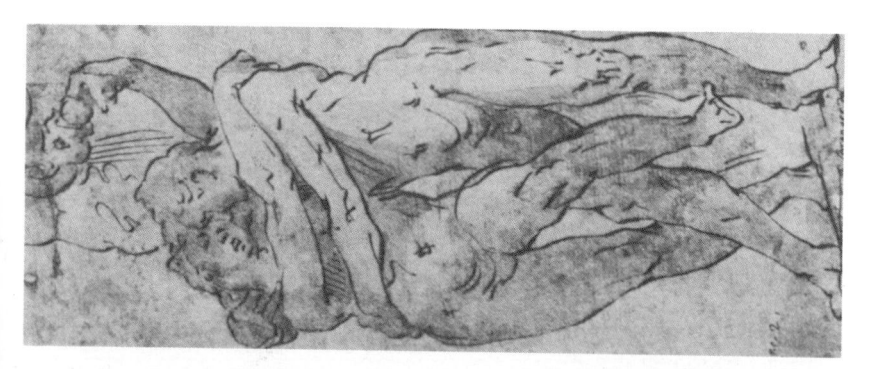

5. (*right*) Jan Gossaert Mabuse, *Adam and Eve*

6. (*far right*) After Bartholomaeus Spranger, *Adam and Eve*

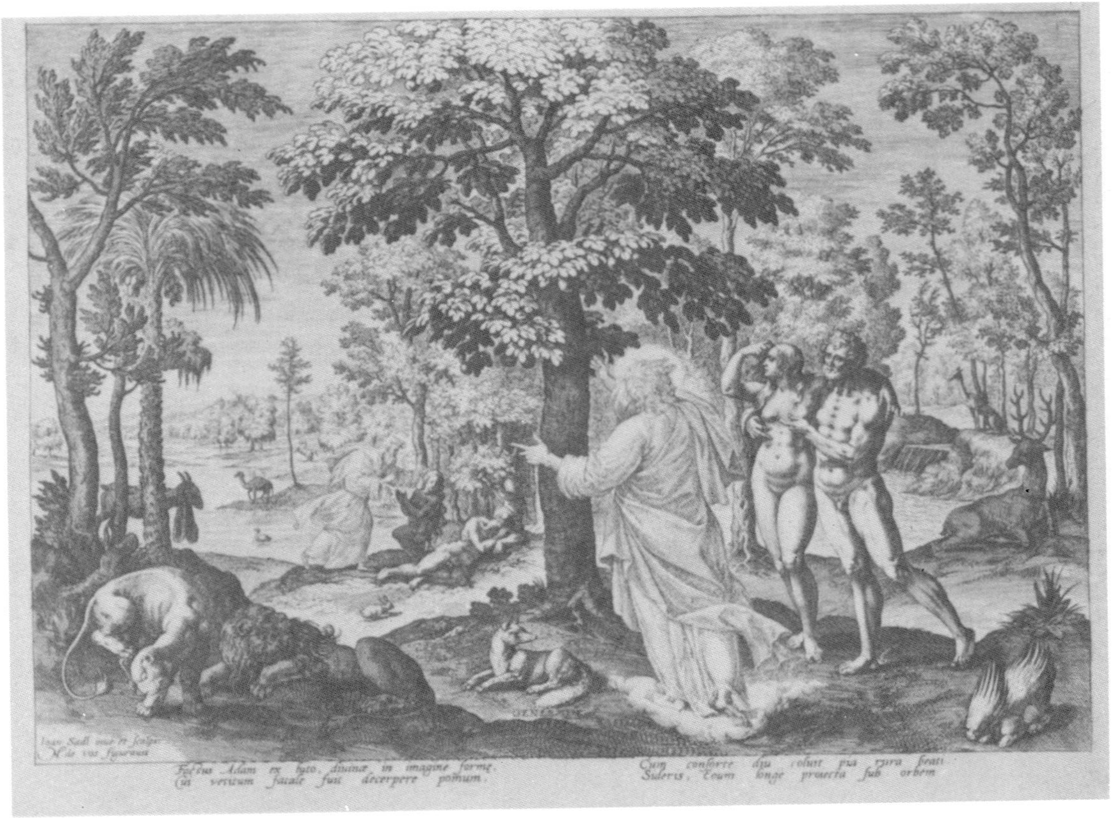

Duty, in the formal manner of the heroic drama, before launching into damnation with gallant bravado, or he may simply dissolve into helplessness before his blubbering wife. God's rebuke to Adam is then expanded into an explanation of female debility; in Sylvester's du Bartas, for example, the Almighty dismisses Eve as a 'wanton fondling', which makes us wonder why He should have created such an inadequate companion.[70]

Though the literary tradition presents the fall as a seduction, the consequences of eating the fruit are never sexual. Adam is immediately frantic and aghast, and in some cases demons actually leap from behind the bushes. The story remains magical and discontinuous, with sudden and unexpected changes of character. There is very little attempt to establish sexuality as an intrinsic part of human nature and to follow it through the stages of a complex transformation, as Milton does; sex is omitted from the state of innocence, suddenly appears in the debased form of Eve's blandishments, vanishes again at the moment of the fall, and then reappears at the conception of Cain, with brief remarks on the loss of virginity. Such careless treatment helps to explain the general weakness of the literary Genesis-tradition; we are moved to doubt either the author's understanding or the wisdom of providence.

Milton does his best to reconcile these divergences. By giving the forbidden fruit an intensely aphrodisiac effect, and then having the signs of shame first apparent in the face rather than in the genitals, he has ingeniously combined two strands of the exegetical tradition, and in the process has made Augustine's vision of the Priapic fall fit for literary presentation. In the process he has complicated the time-sequence and deepened the psychological level. The opening of Adam and Eve's eyes was normally assumed to come as soon as both had eaten the fruit, and Augustine adds that an immediate pruritus of the genitals plunged them into embarrassment, mortified that their bodies would no longer obey their minds; *Paradise Lost*, alone among literary depictions, shows their minds as well as their

---

[70] In Fig. 7, which unusually shows Adam and Eve embracing and strolling as they do in *PL*, Eve looks away towards the fruit while Adam listens to the prohibition, Adam's hand touches her breast with the same gesture that God uses to indicate the fruit, the lioness is scratching herself and turning away, and a rabbit is the closest animal to the creation of Eve. For literary examples, cf. Kirkconnell, pp. 68-9, 72, 180-4, 254-6, 327-31, 356 (i.e. Beaumont's 1702 *Psyche* misleadingly presented as the 1648 version), 468-70; Loredano, p. 34; Antonello Gerbi, *Il Peccato di Adamo ed Eva* (Milan, 1933), pp. 81-2 (Folengo and Aretino). Du Bartas's God limits Himself to calling Eve 'une folle' (*Works* III. 40).

bodies carried away in an eruption of desire, with the perception of nakedness dawning only after a drunken post-coital slumber. This rescues the erotic fall from Calvin's criticism, expanding it into a profound existential and psychic event. But Milton leans towards the narrative tradition and away from Calvin's revision when he affirms that Adam was 'not deceav'd, / But fondly overcome with Female charm' (IX. 998-9).

Milton would have agreed with Beaumont's charge that Adam was an 'effeminate' husband with an 'uxorious heart', and we can see from chapter 6 that Adam 'overcome with Female charm' matches the tender-hearted reformers 'overcome with harlot's language' and the uxorious Samson 'swayed by female usurpation'; some critics have even suggested that Adam's fault lies in not divorcing Eve on the spot. But Milton avoids the over-simplifications and discontinuities of his fellow poets' treatment of female charm. The changes induced by the fruit are naturally sudden, but they are not arbitrary: they are painfully recognizable distortions of the character of innocence. Nor does he lapse into misogynistic cliché. Having greatly augmented erotic life before the fall, Milton now reduces the erotic dimension of the persuasion-scene, and refuses to give Eve the usual manipulative gestures. (This restraint is all the more noticeable because, in *Samson Agonistes*, he does depict the female wiles that others had so readily ascribed to Eve.) Milton recognizes the possibility of dramatic tensions and lovers' quarrels, but he draws them off into an earlier scene, the gardening argument, where undertones of exasperation at Eve's persistence are absorbed by the continuing intelligence and nobility of the sentiments on both sides; this is, as Addison remarked, the sort of dispute they would have had even if they had remained unfallen. The misogynistic impulse, and the violent urge to divorce that leads Samson to expel his '*Hyaena*'-wife, are now recognized as the distemper of sin; Adam's denunciations of God for creating woman, and his furious expulsion of the 'Serpent' Eve, dramatically express the failure of introspection and the despair from which he must be rescued by Eve herself.[71]

[71] (1702), VI. 305, 308; *Milton: The Critical Heritage*, ed. John T. Shawcross (1970), p. 205; *SA* 748; *PL* X. 867. Separate gardening was already normal in their working lives, as we learn at V. 331-43 and VIII. 44-7, but M may have forgotten this. He also appears to equate the fallen Adam with the shorn Samson and Eve with the harlot Dalilah at *PL* IX. 1059-62; but in the epic simile, as Mary Nyquist persuasively argues (pp. 225-6), this misogynist equation may be a trap for the reader—strictly speaking, Dalilah corresponds to the 'lap of earth', and Samson

The immediate effect of the fruit is certainly to make Eve villainous. She embraces detestable doctrines: her desire to seize power by gaining 'what wants / In Female Sex, the more to draw his Love (IX. 821-2)' should offend feminists and male suprematists alike. She decides to give Adam the fruit for selfish and possessive reasons, and then lies about her feelings to him. Her evocations of the old pre-lapsarian love, and the echoes of 'With thee conversing I forget all time' that mingle both in her soliloquy and in her appeals to Adam, are bound to seem cynical. But by the time Adam declares his consent she appears to be sincerely moved. 'O glorious trial of exceeding Love' is not the tawdry lie that some critics have found it, but a sublime moment, resonant with a hymnic tone that anticipates the later scenes of *The Magic Flute*. Milton himself says that she

> for joy
> Tenderly wept, much won that he his Love
> Had so enobl'd, as of choice t'incurr
> Divine displeasure for her sake, or Death.   (IX. 990-3)

Neither these tears, nor her later tears of penitence and grief, are manipulative or dishonest.

Adam's fall is indeed chivalrous, and conforms to the highest standards of princely love-romance. He resolves immediately to join Eve, though fully aware of the transgression, and there is thus absolutely none of the persuasive weakening that enlivens other versions at the expense of their dignity. Instead, in Adam's private unspoken thoughts, we find a genuine expression of the emotions that Eve had dishonestly claimed—'agony of love till now not felt', and the desolation of losing, not just an abstract figure of Love or Companionship, but an irreplaceable individual. In Grotius it is Eve who cries 'non vivo sine te', but here it is Adam who is given the plangent lament, in lines whose beauty recalls the *che faro* of *Orpheus and Eurydice*:

> How can I live without thee, how forgo
> Thy sweet Converse and Love so dearly join'd,
> To live again in these wild Woods forlorn?
> Should God create another *Eve*, and I
> Another rib afford, yet loss of thee

not to the innocent male but to the guilty couple. (After I completed this book, Prof. Nyquist kindly sent me a full and richly speculative version of this argument, 'Textual Overlapping and Dalilah's Harlot-lap', forthcoming in *Renaissance Texts and Literary Theory*, ed. Patricia Parker and David Quint.)

> Would never from my heart; no, no, I feel
> The Link of Nature draw me: Flesh of Flesh,
> Bone of my Bone thou art, and from thy State
> Mine never shall be parted, bliss or woe.[72]

It may be that the omission of 'soul' from this version of 'flesh of my flesh' is significant, but to stress Adam's carnality is to reduce the complexity of our response. The entire experience of unfallen sexuality, the vast momentum of the idyllic books, flows through these lines, and our sympathies must run with this tide.

The nobility of the lovers in *Paradise Lost* has often been felt to undermine the moral and didactic effect of the poem, both in the eighteenth century and in more recent criticism, which has sometimes become a battle between defenders and denouncers of Adam and Eve. A more subtle approach recognizes the romantic appeal of 'O glorious trial of exceeding Love' and 'How can I live without thee', but insists that the reader must find in them, not the strains of genuine innocence or sincerity, but rather the delusive 'charm' of the Satanic poetry that 'suspended Hell' in Book II.[73] Milton has made it as difficult as possible to apply these hard criteria to this episode, however. It is not merely shallow sentimentality that forges a 'link of Nature' between Adam and ourselves. The effect of the 'treatable smoothnesse' of poetry, as Milton had defined it in his earlier prose, is to bathe us in ambrosia, to stir the softest part of our nature, and to 'set our affections in right tune'; the reader is still 'dissolved', still attuned to the 'Airs' of Paradise and to the acceptable ravishment of pre-lapsarian love.[74] Set against the solemn music of the love-sacrifice, the judgement pronounced on Adam—'fondly overcome with Female charm'—will seem discordant and mean.

'Fondness' has many times in Milton stood for the enchantment of love and poetry and their sway over 'better knowledge', and the word 'fondly' often resonates with an elegiac yearning and sympathy

[72] Kirkconnell, p. 204; *PL* IX. 961, 908–16. Puritan teaching on individual love would have condemned Adam here: William Gouge, for example, instructed the remarried widower to love his present wife and *not* to remain in love with his dead first wife—his love should be for the office and not the person (*Domesticall Duties*, 2nd edn. (1626), pp. 132–3, and contrast Hardy, ch. 2 n. 60 above).

[73] Burden, p. 164 and *passim*; cf. Frye, p. 79. We are clearly supposed to ponder what Adam should have done—the alternative is to sink into Adam's own naturalistic determinism—but the correct course is surely not outright divorce but reproof and intercession with God on Eve's behalf, as Fish suggests.

[74] C. S. Lewis expresses this well; the reader is an organ, on whom M plays 'the Paradisal stop' (cited in Fish, p. 303).

quite different from the contempt it expresses here. The beauties of 'Lycidas', for example, are framed by the sad recognition of the inadequacy of the poetic devices he has just deployed: 'Ay me, I fondly dream! . . . Let our frail thoughts dally with false surmise. / Ay me!' The divorce tracts warn against the 'desire' that teaches us 'fondly to think within our strength all that lost Paradise relates'; but the well-matched couple actually can attain a version of the dalliance of Paradise or the Song of Songs—'a kinde of ravishment and erring fondness in the entertainment of wedded leisures'. As judges, then, we must assent to Milton's harsh criticism of Adam, but as initiates into his vision of love we will find it coarse, and as listeners we will be jarred by the 'scrannel Pipe of wretched straw' that sounds in this line. Perhaps the most tragic result of the fall, for Milton and his readers, is this: the heights of poetic imagination and the glorious trials of moral duty can no longer blend together.[75]

[*iii*]

Having made such an unprecedented investment in pre-lapsarian sexuality, Milton must now find ways of relating it to the dramatic changes that accompany the fall. However divergent the requirements of poetics and ethics have become, Milton cannot simply let his vision of Eros evaporate; he chooses instead to divert its energies into large-scale parody, and to preserve its features even in the sinful state. The fall becomes a negative transfiguration rather than the abrupt alteration depicted by other poets. Just as the landscape of hell inverts the features of Paradise, so fallen sexuality—in the burning 'lust' that comes from eating the fruit, and in the later history of the human race revealed to Adam— recalls and perverts its innocent counterpart. And just as evil may appear in the 'hypocritical' form of Satan's angelic disguise or the reptilian shape to which he is transformed, so fallen sexuality may either be a fool's Paradise of simulated delights, such as we see in 'Court Amours', or the crude 'animal excretion' condemned in the divorce tracts. To continue the analogy with Miltonic landscape, human sexuality becomes either a 'curious knot' of artificial cultivation or 'an island salt and bare'.[76]

[75] 'Lycidas', ll. 56, 153-4 (and cf. 124); *Prose* II. 316, 597.
[76] Cf. *PL* III. 636-44, IV. 242, X. 510-19, XI. 834; the idea of creating a sensual mock-paradise appears in Henry More (ch. 4 n. 47 above). For the 'salt' side of M's sexuality, see the outrageous and aggressive puns of the *Defences*, some of them anticipated in the sixth Prolusion (Col. edn. XII. 244), where he explains that he does not want his '*sales*' (salty jokes) to be '*edentulos*' (lacking in teeth).

A network of correspondences and echoes therefore ties together the fallen and the unfallen eroticism of *Paradise Lost*. The phrase 'attractive grace', for example, applies first to Sin, and then to Eve, but reverts at the fall to Sin. 'Dalliance' describes first what passes between Sin and Satan, then the affectionate gestures of Adam and Eve, and thirdly the love-play of the unwise Solomon (evoked at the moment the serpent encounters Eve in her rose-garden), only to return to its first connotation in the aphrodisiac surge that follows the fall itself, when Adam 'gan Eve to dalliance move'. When Satan first sees Eve she wears her hair as a 'veil' and touches Adam with her 'swelling breast'; when he last meets her she is 'veild in a cloud of fragrance', and he tries to win her by fixedly comparing the forbidden 'Apples' to milk-swollen 'teats / of Ewe'. The scene takes place in 'the sweet recess of Eve', words which the context transfers from the 'Place' to the 'Person'; it is a private space which Eve had decorated with flowers, as she had decorated the 'close recess' of the nuptial bower. Eve is here 'Her self [the] fairest unsupported Flowr', which echoes the ominous comparison of Paradise to the place

> where *Proserpin* gathering flowers
> Her self a fairer Flowr by gloomie *Dis*
> Was gatherd.

This association of flowers and sexual violation heralds the first appearance of Eve in the poem, and after she eats the fruit Adam calls her 'deflowrd'—evoking with unconscious irony the libertine theory of Eve's seduction.[77] The long simile which frames this Satanic observation of Eve, in which his amorous vision is compared to the relief of a man 'long in populous City pent', delighted first by the fresh scent of the fields and then by a chance encounter with a fair virgin, reaches still further back: not only does it recall Satan's arrival in Paradise, with the 'sewers' of the city standing for the 'fishie fume' that repelled Asmodeus, but it also precisely re-enacts the fullest treatment of secular, autobiographical love in Milton's poetry—the youthful 'Elegia Septima'.[78]

[77] *PL* II. 762, IV. 298, X. 263; II. 819, IV. 338, IX. 443 and 1016; IV. 304 and 495, IX. 425 and 581-6; IX. 444, 456, IV. 708; IX. 432, IV. 269-71; IX. 901. The association of Proserpine with the endangered heroine appears also in a line of *A Mask* that M later cancelled (see Carey's note to 356-64).

[78] *PL* IX. 901, 445-56; 'Elegia Septima', ll. 51-101—in turn expanded from 'Elegia Prima', ll. 47-80, which also celebrates the beauties in the crowded streets of London. Cf. Edward Le Comte, 'Miltonic Echoes in Elegia VII', *ELR* XIV (1984), 191-7.

The scene immediately following the fall is especially thronged with echoes. The aphrodisiac intoxication of the fruit recalls the 'wingd' ascent to spirit that Raphael had promised as the reward for obedience, which in turn recalls the apotheosis of Eros in Plato's *Symposium* and the growth of the lovers' wings in *Phaedrus*. Milton may be intending an ironic comment on the intense physicality of this latter passage, which describes the pricking, throbbing, and melting of the wings as they begin to grow: after gorging themselves on the fruit, Adam and Eve

> swim in mirth, and fansie that they feel
> Divinitie within them breeding wings
> Wherewith to scorn the Earth: but that false Fruit
> Farr other operation first displaid,
> Carnal desire enflaming.

Even before this, we later learn, Sin had felt 'new strength within me rise, / Wings growing'. And Satan had already parodied the ascent in his dream for Eve, where she is first led to the fruit by a lover's voice, and then whisked into the air.[79]

The sexual arousal provoked by the fruit is clearly a morbid and evil inflammation; but the whole description is nevertheless permeated with echoes that tend to undermine our attempt to separate this burning and contagious 'Lust' from the unfallen sexuality of the earlier books. Eve's offering of forbidden fruit is 'elegant', but so was the meal she prepared for Raphael. Eve's eyes 'dart' contagious fire, but she already shot amorous 'Darts' in the state of innocence. Adam now burns with 'ardor', but his last gaze at the departing Eve was also 'ardent'. 'Play' and 'Loves disport' might seem immoral and frivolous unless we remember the breezes 'disporting' on the wedding night (and Wisdom 'playing' before the Lord). Adam 'seiz'd' her hand, but he had already 'seiz'd' it to conclude his first wooing. Though lust is elsewhere branded as 'effeminate', Adam here preserves the masculine role by taking the initiative and leading his wife, as he had done both on the wedding night and on the first occasion that we encounter them. Their arousal is sudden—though even 'sudden appetite' is legitimate in the unfallen state, as Adam's dream tells us—but, like the love-making of the first evening, it does occur at a time of day when

---

[79] *Symposium* 210-11; *Phaedrus* 251; *PL* IX. 1009-13, X. 243-4, V. 50-2, 86-90.

repose is appropriate and had been anticipated.[80] The place also bears a close resemblance to their nuptial bed: they couple on a bank 'with verdant roof imbowr'd', on the flowers that Homer chose for the nuptial couch of Jupiter and Juno—the second comparison of Adam and Eve to those fertile deities. Even if the place were not so appropriate, Milton had already, in his hymn to Wedded Love, condemned those Hypocrites who object to the 'place' of intercourse. In this first scene of fallen sexuality, then, the reader is confronted with the mingled grain of redeemed and vicious vocabulary, and must labour to separate them.[81]

Even if we extend the vista to include further episodes of fallen sexual behaviour, we still find these insistent echoes. The Sons of God in Book XI are enamoured, but so was Adam as he hung over his sleeping bride. They invoke '*Hymen*' for the 'Marriage Rites', allegedly a sign of false religion, but the heavenly choir had sung the 'Hymenean' over the 'Rites' of unfallen love. Even their indecent hurry to light the nuptial torch is matched by a detail from the innocent world, for on the original wedding night the nightingale 'bid haste' to do the same.[82] And when, in *Paradise Regain'd*, Belial proposes to tempt Christ with fair women, his eulogy of their power draws not only on the secular Ovidian love-poetry of Milton's youth, but on the splendours of his Eve. Belial's temptresses are 'skilled to retire, and in retiring draw / Hearts after them', just as Eve retired shooting 'Darts of desire' into the hearts of Raphael and Adam; he proposes a calculated replica of Eve's natural effect. When he extols their 'Virgin majesty with mild / And sweet allay'd', we are certain to recall 'the Virgin Majestie of *Eve*' in *Paradise Lost*. And when Satan dismisses Belial with a more contemptuous assessment of woman, he choses the very phrase that had entangled him with both Sin and Eve— 'attractive grace'.[83]

[80] *PL* IX. 1018, 1027, 1032, 1042, 1037; V. 335, IX. 397, VIII. 518, IV. 489; cf. Hagstrum, p. 39. Eve returns only slightly late for her noon appointment, when both food and rest were anticipated—a fact repeated by M with grave irony (IX. 400–7, and cf. 1027–8)—though of course this lateness means that Adam walks part of the way to meet her.
[81] *PL* IX. 1038–41; IV. 499–501, 745; cf. n. 46 above.
[82] *PL* XI. 583–90 (and cf. V. 446–8); V. 13, IV. 711 and 742, VIII. 518–20. Cf. *Prose* II. 249: 'many who have spent their youth chastly are in some things not so quick-sighted, while they hast too eagerly to light the nuptiall torch'—another link between M himself and the Biblical Sons of God.
[83] *PR* II. 159–62, 176; *PL* VIII. 61–2, IX. 270.

All these correspondences between fallen and unfallen sexuality suggest a deliberate and even self-conscious imitation, not only on the part of the author but on the part of the characters themselves. The dramatic irony of this self-consciousness measures the depth of the fall: Adam and Eve think they are deliberately re-enacting their love on a higher plane, but we can see it only as a travesty. Jean Hagstrum aptly observes that 'Miltonic love, unprotected as it is by ascetic prohibition, Stoic indifference, or Platonic denigration, is precisely the kind that might easily drive on toward lust' (p. 41). But the reverse is also true: the 'Lust' that inflames Adam and Eve immediately after the fall drives on towards the idyllic sexuality they have perpetually forfeited. This powerful scene, unique to Milton, shows the desperate attempt—before the intoxicating fumes of the fruit wear off, and their eyes are properly opened—to recapture the central experience of unfallen life.

[iv]

Fallen sexuality for Milton is not an entirely new experience, something visited on humanity or thrown in as a solace for the pains of expulsion—as it is in other retellings of the Genesis story. It is a version of Adam and Eve's established pattern, a cracked and hectic transcription of familiar music. It is not exactly 'the generalised and mechanical expression of the lust of a man for a woman, the woman being Eve because she is the only woman within reach' (Frye, p. 69); this is to underestimate the wicked accuracy of the allusions which tie both Adam's speech and Milton's narration to the *personal* history of the innocent couple. Nor can it adequately be explained as a reversion to animal lust in the absence of reason, as many critics assert; the fallen couple's sexual life is actually 'founded in Reason', like Wedded Love itself, though in a perverted way. Eve's sensory perception is heightened, and her heart made more 'ample', because she anticipates divine knowledge, the apotheosis of reason; Adam's desire for Eve is increased by appreciating her 'taste', 'sapience', and 'judicious palate', and by dwelling on the stimulus of prohibition. This libertine connoisseurship is obviously corrupt, but even in the state of innocence, Milton reminds us, love is 'judicious' and 'enlarges' the heart, and reason could be devoted to the art of enhancing the pleasures of the senses. The meal prepared for Raphael is a good example; Eve concentrates her mind on an 'elegant', selective, and well-structured combination of fruits, so as to 'bring / Taste after taste upheld with kindliest change'. It is no accident that Adam evokes that episode in his first speech of fallen seduction.[84]

Just as their eating habits pass from judicious 'delicacie' to corrupt gourmandise, so their erotic life passes from 'rationall burning' to the cerebral complications of libertinism. Fallen eroticism is not 'Sex' in the sense that Satan uses it when he pretends to speak as an animal—perhaps the first example of the modern usage of the word: 'I was at first as other Beasts . . . nor aught but food discern'd / Or Sex.' Adam and Eve are not 'coupled in the rites of nature by the meer compulsion of lust', or forced by appetite as Eve was in her dream; they adopt instead a pose of voluntary epicurism and sensual 'elegance'. The hand that 'seizes' Eve's is not now given the epithet 'gentle', but Adam's gentleness has been changed not into roughness but into the *genteel* mannerisms of the Court Amorist. This new eroticism is not at all like the debased sexuality so often denounced in the divorce tracts; theirs is not an animal 'mute kindlyness', but is rather 'cherisht and reincited' by speech. Sexual desire, far from acting 'what the soul complies not with', is urged on by the excited mind. A bad marriage was defined in the divorce tracts as a 'fleshly accustoming without the soul's union and commixture of intellectuall delight'; in the newly corrupted relationship of Adam and Eve, however, there is too much intellectual delight.[85]

Paradisal sexuality moved to a calm, full rhythm, orderly, 'seasonal', and passionate at the same time. The dynamics of fallen sexuality, in contrast, are at once too slack and too tense. Satanic desire is 'pent' up and 'bursts' forth, and even in its social form, revealed to Adam in his vision of the future, lust displays an ugly tension at the heart of its apparent ease. In the patterns of association that run through Milton's work, worldly erotic excitement is linked with the loose, undirected strolling of urban youths—whether the London girls ruefully celebrated in the Latin elegies, or the crowds in the proposed tragedy of Sodom, 'every one with his mistresse, or Ganymed, gitternning along the street or solacing on

---

[84] *PL* IV. 755; IX. 875, 1017–26; VIII. 590–1; V. 332–6. Eve also derives excitement from prohibition (IX. 753–4), but Adam greatly amplifies it ('ten')—a striking departure from the popular literary tradition (e.g. n. 67 above), which assumes that love of the prohibited is innately and even exclusively female.

[85] *PL* IX. 573–4, 1037 (contrast IV. 488–9); *Prose* II. 251, 739–40, 609, 339.

the banks of Jordan,' or the 'Bevy' of Daughters of Men in Book XI of *Paradise Lost*.[86]

This 'loose female Troupe', the ancestors of all conventionally 'feminine' and male-directed women, seduce the Sons of God with a continuous agitation of liquid and pointless gestures, being

> Bred only and completed to the taste
> Of lustfull appetence, to sing, to dance,
> To dress, and troll the Tongue, and roll the
> Eye.

Their fascinated victims let their eyes 'Rove without rein' until they are ironically 'Fast caught' in the snare; the soft, amorous, inconsequential movements of the Daughters of Men turn out to be sprung like a trap. Their masculine equivalents are the Sons of Belial, aimless rambling gangs with rape and violence coiled inside them, or the sybarites destroyed in the Flood, who gave themselves

> To luxury and riot, feast and dance,
> Marrying or prostituting, as befell,
> Rape or Adultery, as passing fair
> Allur'd them.

'Passing fair' is a conscious pun—also used by Belial when he proposes a sexual temptation for Christ—meant to evoke drifting constellations of Petrarchan beauties; and 'as befell' is an Anglo-Saxon homonym for the 'Casual fruition' of harlots and 'Court Amours', contrasted explicitly in Book IV, and implicitly throughout the poem, to the deliberate pleasures of Wedded Love.[87]

Adam's responses to the problems of fallen sexuality, however, are almost equally casual. His misogynistic accusations, both in the aftermath of the fall and in his response to the vision of the Daughters of Men, are rebuked implicitly by Milton—the 'soft words' of Eve are clearly preferred to the 'fierce passion' of woman-hating—and explicitly by the archangel Michael (X. 865-908, XI. 632-6). At the end of Book IX both Adam and Eve are locked in futile mutual accusation, but in Book X Eve progresses

---

[86] 'Elegia Prima' and 'Septima' (n. 78 above); *Prose* VIII. 559 (and for casual urban fornication cf. I. 849); *PL* XI. 582. M cannot conceal the attractiveness of this relaxed and aimless strolling; the ideal erotic marriage described in the divorce tracts, for example, fills the soul with the pleasures of 'wandring vacancy' even while providing a stable home (cf. ch. 6 n. 27 above).
[87] *PL* XI. 618-20, 596-7, 715-18; I. 497-505, IV. 765-70; *PR* II. 155. 'Loose female Troupe' is Addison's variant on XI. 614 (Shawcross, p. 215).

towards a larger perspective while Adam's blame of Eve deteriorates still further into misogyny. Even in the process of reconciliation to Eve, Adam reveals an immature and thoughtless attitude that, though it receives an approving comment from Milton, should strike a chill in the reader.

At this point in the poem we are inclined to trust Eve rather than Adam in matters of the heart. Eve makes a plain and humble confession of her fault, in striking contrast to Adam's rhetoric, and her speech 'Forsake me not thus, *Adam*' restores, in a muted form, the plangency of unfallen love-poetry—her *leitmotif* returns without ironic distortion. She is the first to break the icy deadlock of hatred, and her emotive plea for forgiveness initiates the process of repentance and creates a new kind of heroism suitable to the fallen world. The triumph of softness over stony-heartedness, brought about by female influence, had already been celebrated in Milton's secular love-poetry, where it is explicitly compared to divine grace; at the end of Book X, where the verbal repetitions suggest a plainer version of Eve's earlier aria, this theme is returned to God—but it is still an expression of love.[88]

During the course of their reconciling conversation, Eve proposes to eliminate the human race by sexual abstinence—or, if it proves too difficult

> Conversing, looking, loving, to abstain
> From Love's due Rites, Nuptial embraces sweet,
> And with desire to languish without hope,

to commit suicide (X. 993-5). Adam praises the sublimity of this new 'contempt of life and pleasure', but finds in her proposal only 'anguish and regret / For loss of life and pleasure overlov'd' (X. 1013-19). In these curt phrases he would sum up the entire experience of pre-lapsarian sexuality, so movingly invoked by Eve even in her despair. Adam goes through the same process that made the youthful Milton append to the amorous 'Elegia Septima' a recantation, boasting of the thick ice that renders his breast impregnable. Asceticism might be a necessary stage in his struggle, but it is clearly forced and naïve; when he later comes to witness the seduction of the Sons of God, his reaction is closer to the 'bent

---

[88] *PL* X. 125-44, 160-2, 914-44, 1086-104; cf. Sonnet 3, ll. 13-14. Joan M. Webber argues persuasively that Christ's quiet return to his mother's house in the final line of *Paradise Regain'd* shows a repudiation of masculinist values in the 'new Adam' ('The Politics of Poetry: Feminism and *Paradise Lost*', *MS* XIV (1980), p. 20).

of nature'—a childlike tendency to 'judge by pleasure' alone (XI. 597). He must be tutored out of both these extremes, towards a proper temperance and a proper appreciation of the exuberant pleasures of physical life.

[v]

The very close of *Paradise Lost* is also the point where protagonists, poet, and reader converge. Each has been through complicated struggles. The depiction of Adam and Eve has sometimes reinforced the Pascalian bewilderment, the sense of the remoteness of innocence, but it has also provoked a feeling of intimacy that is almost equally bewildering. The poet has sometimes been lost in private dreams, but sometimes speaks as the representative of a humanity broader than his 'Puritan' culture or his 'masculine' gender. There has always been some common ground between all those involved in 'what lost Paradise relates'. For all his supremacy, Milton has always been concerned with redeeming the 'soft' and 'sensuous', and towards the end he promotes the 'female' as a paradigm of the new heroism, according to the Christian confession 'I am made perfect in weakness'—a principle so important to him in his blindness that he adopted it as a personal motto.[89] For all his profound grief over the fall, he has consistently refused to exempt humanity, even at the height of its innocence, from the necessary dialectic of temperance.

Adam's final lesson thus reaches out beyond 'our first Parents', and beyond even the confines of the 'fit audience though few'. Milton's principle of temperance, as we have seen throughout this discussion of his prose and poetry, is based not on fugitive and cloistered virtue but on the constituent desires of humanity: 'wherefore did he create passions within us, pleasures round about us, but that these rightly temper'd are the very ingredients of vertu?' We have seen, too, that such virtue is meaningless without a deep, experiential, but somehow untainted knowledge of the whole, and even of the extreme. Milton's Adam and Eve have been blessed with strong passions and powerful apprehensions from the moment

---

[89] *The Life Records of John Milton*, ed. J. M. French, III (New Brunswick, 1954), 104–5, IV (1956), 118–19; M applies the words of Christ, as reported by St. Paul in 2 Cor. 12:9, to his own life. Ian Maclean shows that this verse was particularly associated with the heroism of females (conventionally 'weak', of course), including the Old Testament liberator Deborah (*The Renaissance Notion of Woman* (Cambridge, 1980), p. 21); M gave the name Deborah to the daughter whose birth killed his first wife.

of their creation—unlike their wretched cousins in du Bartas and Loredano and Beaumont—and though this involves them in a deeper fall, because they are responsible and complex beings, it also gives them the means of recovery. They must now retrain their imaginations to become readers of their past experience.

The Archangel Michael can explain some of the principles involved—he tells Adam, for example, that 'the Earth shall bear / More than enough, that temperance may be tried'—and he can provide instructive examples in his survey of history; but like Raphael he cannot directly help mankind *experience* their problems. To gain a properly human knowledge, Adam and Eve must draw on their own intelligence, and apply their own Paradisal resources to the fallen state. Their fallen life should begin where Milton's thoughts on marriage and divorce began—with the stubborn determination to recreate the Solomonic rapture, and the Edenic union of 'one flesh, one heart, one soul,' within the limits of practicality. They must relearn the arts of affectionate 'conversation' and erotic companionship. Their dialogue of reconciliation and their final hand-clasp reassure us that they have started this process, and Eve's last speech—

> but now lead on;
> In mee is no delay; with thee to goe
> Is to stay here   (XII. 614–16)

—suggests both heroic initiative and the Solomonic impulse of love: 'draw me after you, let us make haste.' They must learn to conduct their married life 'as much as may be' by the memory of lost Paradise, to locate Eden within their marriage. This involves, not sophisticated libertinism or contemptuous asceticism or naïve naturalism, all of which Adam passes through, but the rediscovery and internalization of those natural arts that made the landscape 'luxurious by restraint', that 'brought / Taste after taste upheld with kindliest change', and that made their marriage-bed a 'perpetual fountain of domestic sweets'.[90]

Milton establishes the character of innocence by transfiguring 'fallen' experience, not by suspending it in favour of a beautiful but inaccessible fantasy; he thus makes the vanished world ours and not merely his, 'within our strength' rather than merely a display

---

[90] *PL* XI. 804–5; IX. 209; V. 335–6. David Loewenstein's comments, here and elsewhere, have been greatly appreciated during the writing of this chapter.

of his own. The secular reader can appreciate the confluence, rare in the Christian tradition, of transcendent eroticism and natural passion; the godly reader, perhaps sitting with her spouse in the same intimate colloquy that Eve shared with Adam, can enjoy these conjugal caresses while still remaining obedient to the Lord. And at the end of the poem we may experience, 'at least in some proportion', a restoration of the Paradisal state: the gestures of lust had opened up an ironic distance between fallen sexuality and the Edenic Eros it parodies, and in registering these bitter echoes we are correspondingly alienated from our first parents; but the final moment of the poem, the first acting-out of the triumph of softness and reconciliation, re-establishes an intimacy that includes ourselves. The first step away from the barricaded garden begins the historical journey that leads to the writing of *Paradise Lost*, and the journey through that poem is itself a stage in regaining a Paradise within, private and imaginative; as John Dennis observed, the reader 'entertain'd with the accomplish'd Poem, is for a time at least restor'd to Paradise.'[91] Milton's epic, which alone among the versions of Genesis captures the restrained luxuriance of Paradisal experience, and properly includes sexuality in that experience, has thereby become a permanent feature for the religious and secular reader alike; it is now our own resource, our own 'perpetual fountain'.

---

[91] Ch. 5 n. 14 above. For the connection of history, sexuality, and the fall cf. Augustine *De Gen. ad Lit.* VIII. i. 2; he argues against those who 'assume that history, that is, the literal narrative of events, begins at the point where Adam and Eve, dismissed from Paradise, were joined in sexual union and begot children'—his point, however, is not that historicity and procreation are unconnected, but that they date back to the first creation.

Index

Abarbanel, Judah *see* 'Leone Ebreo'
Abrams, M. H. 149 n.
'*acclivitas*' (mystic ascent in sexual arousal) 81, 90, 94
Adam and Eve: as children or adolescents 15, 83, 138, 155, 159; asexual 28, 29, 55, 69, 82 n., 84, 98, 103, 128 n., 130, 131, 141, 143, 150–5, 158–64, 252, 254; both hermaphrodites 132 n., 163; duration of time in Paradise 19, 29, 104, 287–9 (*see also* fall); German-speaking 130 n.; intercourse without pregnancy 19, 30, 37, 231, 287–9; together during temptation 15, 97; with navels? 130
Adam: as author or creator 15, 34, 39, 112, 147; as author or creator of Eve 145, 282; as cuckold 168 (*see also* Eve, sexual accomplice of Satan); as rapist 153–4, 172; copulating with animals 22, 166, 173, 277; giving birth 143–5, 163; hermaphroditic 22, 39 n., 65, 66–71, 128, 129, 131, 132, 141, 143–6, 151, 155, 163; made of ether 134; spouses other than Eve 22, 297; transparent 143, 159, 163
'Adam' as pun on 'earth' 13 n., 14
Adamites (nudists) 37, 82, 84, 85, 88, 164, 185
Adams, Mary 85 n.
Addison, Joseph 140, 238 n., 296, 305 n.
Aers, David and Hodge, Bob 189 n., 199 n., 218 n., 230 n., 279 n.
Agrippa, Heinrich Cornelius 109–13, 127 n., 157–60, 163, 164, 166, 167, 169, 170, 172, 195 n.
Albertus Magnus 56 n.
Alexander of Hales 56 n.
allegory, Eden-story as 23, 27, 28, 40, 50, 65–9, 98, 121, 127, 128, 131–6, 137, 139, 140, 141, 149, 152, 162, 180, 255
Ambrose, St. 31
Ames, Richard 129 n.
Amphitryon (Plautus, Molière) 271
Anabaptists 80, 90, 133 n.

Anderdon, John 148 n.
androgyne *see* Adam, hermaphroditic, and Plato, *Symposium*
angels and angelic sexuality 12, 20–1, 24, 26, 28, 53, 55, 116 n., 125, 126, 143, 155, 158, 241, 249, 256, 257, 262, 264, 265, 267–72, 278–82, 291; limited capacity to understand humans 277, 281, 308
animals and animal sexuality 14, 15, 16, 22, 50, 58, 78, 100, 117, 118, 144, 150, 152, 163 n., 166, 173, 196, 197, 199, 202, 203, 215, 218, 227, 236, 241, 277, 278, 281, 286, 299, 303, 304
Anne of Denmark, consort of James I vi, 112
Answer to . . . the Doctor and Discipline of Divorce, An (author unknown) 93, 106, 196 n., 205, 213, 214, 220
Antinomianism 81, 83, 84–95, 185, 212
aphrodisiacs 77; forbidden fruit 150, 152 n., 153, 156, 157, 172, 242, 295, 301–3; mandrakes (Gen. 30) 19, 118 n., 165
Apocrypha and Pseudepigrapha: Armenian Book of Adam 21 n.; 2 Baruch 21; Dead Sea Scrolls 23; Ecclesiasticus 21, 23 n.; 1 Enoch 19 n.; 2 Enoch 156; 4 Esdras 21; Poimandres 156; Tobit 241, 258, 270, 300
Aquinas, St. Thomas 55–7, 58 n., 59, 72, 77, 101–2, 103, 106, 107, 162, 181, 194, 235, 277; Blackfriars eds. 102 n.
Aretino, Pietro 178, 199, 203, 248, 249, 258
Aristophanes (in Plato's *Symposium*) 66–8, 132
Aristotle 56, 101, 103, 118
Armstrong, Nancy 230 n.
asceticism 28, 40, 50, 51, 61, 64, 71, 77, 79, 82, 84, 87, 90, 91, 94, 158, 164, 166, 172, 194, 203, 204, 208, 252, 303, 306, 308
Ascham, Anthony 209 n.
Asmodeus 241, 258, 300
Astell, Mary 217 n.

Index

Augustine of Hippo, St. 3, 6, 8, 10, 27, 28–30, 31–3, 37, 40–62, 63, 64, 69, 72, 73, 82, 94, ch. 3 *passim*, 124, 126, 129, 130, 131, 134, 151, 160, 181, 197, 202, 204, 205, 212n., 221, 231, 235, 236, 237, 245, 254, 268, 271, 281, 289, 290, 295, 309n.; *see also* 'narrow-Augustinian' interpretation
Avitus 247
Avot de-Rabbi Nathan 128n.

Babington, Gervase 78, 115n.
Baer, Richard A. 65n.
Bailey, Margaret L. 148n.
Baluze, Étienne, ed. 81n.
Barcepha, Moses 156n.
Barker, Arthur E. 189n., 279n.
Barolsky, Paul 165n.
Baroni, Leonora 261
Barth, Karl 11, 12, 16n., 29, 179, 283
Bataille, Georges vi
Baxter, Richard, stoned 119
Bayle, Pierre 8, 11, 12, 23n., 28n., 29–31, 34n., 55, 66n., 68n., 78, 110n., 125, 129n., 130, 132n., 156, 159n., 163, 166n., 168., 172
Bayley, John 230n.
Beaumont, Joseph 1, 5, 21, 63–4, 251, 252–5, 265, 291, 295n., 296, 308
Belial and 'Sons of Belial' 167, 172, 204, 207, 247, 248, 258, 268, 302, 305
ben Levi, Jehoshua 34n.
Bentley, Richard 288
Bercher, William, tr. 110n.
Berington, Simon 137n.
Bernard of Clairvaux, St. 290
Best, Paul 103
Beverland, Adriaan 11, 37, 166–7, 169, 172
Beza, Theodore 220
Bible: Acts 6 n.; 1 Chronicles 90n.; Colossians 25n., 216, 218n.; 1 Corinthians 25, 26, 27, 54, 67, 68, 83, 197n., 209, 216, 258n., 268; 2 Corinthians 26n., 31n., 34, 94, 125n., 307n.; Deuteronomy 189, 191, 214; Ecclesiastes 92, 159; Ephesians 25, 27, 122, 216, 218n.; Exodus 16n.; Ezekiel 20, 43n., 139n.; Genesis *passim*; Habbakuk 92n.; Hebrews 25n., 197; Hosea 21, 25, 88n., 89, 116; Job 158; John 67; Jude 24; Leviticus 159; Luke 234; Malachi 211n.; Matthew 25, 52, 114, 118n., 188, 191, 203n., 220, 278; 2 Peter 24; Proverbs 23, 76, 126, 147, 155, 207, 233; Psalms 16, 33, 34n., 211n., 241n., 245; Revelation 25, 89, 122, 145, 209, 280; Romans 25, 43n., 217n.; 2 Samuel 90n.; Song of Songs v, 18n., 21, 27, 39, 62–4, 67, 68, 75–8, 79–80, 82, 83, 87, 89, 90, 91–2, 94, 107, 167, 206–10, 215, 233–5, 241, 260, 262, 299, 308; 2 Thessalonians 203n.; 1 Timothy 25, 26; Titus 83, 87, 93; *see also* Apocrypha, text of Bible
Blake, William 148
Bloom, Harold vi, viii
blushing 263–5, 270, 275n.
Boadicea 223n.
Boccaccio, Giovanni 53n.
Bodin, Jean 132, 134n., 160n., 162n.
Boehme, Jakob 6, 8, 31, 37, 80n., 142–9, 154–5, 156, 164, 171, 172, 173; present at fall 142; reputation of 148, 149
Bonaventure, St. 56n.
Borges, Jorge Luis 173
Bourignon, Antoinette 148, 163
Boyette, Purvis 230n., 238n.
Braden, Gordon 230n.
Broadbent, J. B. 279n.
Brodwin, Leonora L. 225n.
Brown, Peter 44n., 50n.
Browne, Sir Thomas 3, 125, 128–31, 141, 150, 156, 162, 163, 165
Brueggemann, Walter 14n., 17n.
Bruno, Giordano 178n.
Bucer, Martin 84n., 97, 189n., 190, 220n.
Buddha 160
Bullinger, Heinrich 117
Bullough, Geoffrey 246n.
Bunyan, John 85n., 117, 137
Burden, Dennis H. 261n., 298n.
Burton, Robert 82n., 85n.
Butler, Samuel 130, 141, 142, 148n.

Cain 11, 18n., 20, 21, 29, 48, 61, 133n., 137, 152, 156, 295
Calvert, Giles 92n.
Calvin, Jean 3, 6, 33n., 35n., 39n., 70n., 72, 73, 82–4, 85, 91n., 105–7, 118, 120–1, 124, 125, 126, 131, 132, 134, 142, 152n., 157, 164, 167, 197, 215n., 290, 296
Camerarius, Philip 162
Campanus, Johannes 80, 107, 117

Index

Care, Henry, tr. 110n., 111n., 160n.
Carew, Thomas 249–50
Carey, John 179n., 195n., 245n., 300n.
Carpocratians 87n.
Cassuto, Umberto 13n., 17n., 18, 20n.
Catharists 87n., 156
Cats, Jacob 79n., 236, 246–7
Cavalier poetry 73, 167, 181, 210n., 249–50, 261n.
celibacy 61, 115, 158, 161, 166, 178, 194, 280, 306
Celsus 65n.
Chamberlayne, William 289n.
Chandler, J., tr. 150n.
Charles I 181, 189, 223, 249
Chaucer, Geoffrey 76, 107n.
childbirth and procreation 11, 13, 17, 20, 22, 26, 27, 55, 62, 72, 85n., 87, 98, 99, 100, 101, 102, 103, 105, 113, 114, 120, 122, 130, 135, 138, 144, 147, 150, 158, 159, 161, 162, 171, 199, 235, 243, 252, 260n., 278, 309n.; asexual 129, 163, 172, 241 (*see also* Adam and Eve, asexual)
Christ: female 143; in Coppe's womb 89; remarks on sexuality, marriage, and divorce 21, 23, 24, 25, 27, 37, 42, 58, 75, 79, 83, 96, 110, 112n., 118, 143, 160, 162, 178, 183, 188, 189, 190, 196n., 201, 203n., 216, 220, 222, 227, 234, 284, 285, 302, 307n.
Chrysostom, St. John 106, 117, 274
Circe 224, 225, 227, 291
circumcision 18, 97, 109, 115n., 126, 128, 146, 153, 158, 290
Cirillo, A. R. 68n.
Clapam, David, tr. 110n.
Clark, Kenneth 141n.
Clarkson or Claxton, Laurence 88, 90–4, 133, 153n.
Cleanness 57, 77
Clement of Alexandria 82n., 87n., 98n.
Cohen, Kitty 238n.
Cokaigne, Land of 94n.
Coleridge, Samuel Taylor 148
Colie, Rosalie 110n.
Congreve, William 238
Coppe, Abiezer 88–94, 125n., 148n.
Coppens, Joseph 18n., 156n., 158n.
Cornelius Agrippa *see* Agrippa, Heinrich Cornelius
Cotton, Charles 167
Cranach, Lucas 168
Crasso, Nicolo 252

'crisis' v, 3, 133, 139, 141, 171, 175–6, 177, 247
Croese, Gerard 148n.
Crompton, Hugh, tr. 111n.

D'Israeli, Isaac 98n.
de Salandra, Serafino 247, 292n.
Damrosch, Leopold 53n., 144n., 265n.
Daniel, Glyn 138n.
Dante Alighieri 60n., 149n.
Davenant, William 275n.
Davies, Stevie 231n.
Davis, Charles 49n., 64
Deane, H. A. 32n., 42n., 44n.
Deborah 307n.
'deconstruction' vii–viii, 30, 31, 182n.
Dennis, John 184, 309
Descartes, René 68
Desmarets, R.-P. 86n.
Dido 46
Digby, Sir Kenelm 129n.
Diggers 86, 108, 132, 136, 281n.
Diotima 67, 146, 209
divorce 24, 37, 84, 93, 97, ch. 6 *passim*, 248, 251, 257, 296, 298n., 308; and 'hardness of heart' 220–1, 227; as cure for atheism 212; as expression of masculine freedom 188, 222, 225; as model for reader's response 229; as natural release 212; as principle of creation 201, 215, 227; as public benefaction 188, 227; as therapy 189, 212, 227; *see also* Milton, John, divorce tracts
Don Juan 262
Donne, John 3, 32, 68, 100, 103n., 120, 127, 128, 137n., 141, 165, 167n., 169–70, 195, 198, 206, 225, 247, 268, 274, 290, 291n.; *Sermons* 10, 32, 42n., 73n., 103n., 113, 116, 278, 289n.; 'Twickenham Garden' ii, v, 3, 10, 35, 169–70, 171, 251, 255
Douglas, Mary 224n.
Dronke, Peter 153n.
Dryden, John 30n., 81, 238, 243, 264, 265
du Bartas, Guillaume Saluste 1, 68, 127, 142, 186, 247, 254n., 295, 308
du Bosroger, Esprit 86n.
dualism ix, 150, 161, 188, 189, 196, 198, 200, 201, 204, 213
Duncan, Joseph E. 87n., 137n., 154n.
Dury, John 88n.
Dyer, Mary 85n.

Index

Ebreo, Leone *see* 'Leone Ebreo'
'Eden'; meaning 'pleasure' 13n., 21, 243n.
egalitarianism vi, viii–ix, 3, 8, 26, 27, 86, 87, 96, 100, 107–13, 115–17, 119–20, 121–3, 124, 132, 216–17, 222, 232, 273–87; and sexual 'due benevolence' (1 Cor. 7: 3) 26, 63, 74, 97, 100, 106, 118n., 122, 197, 200, 202, 216, 221–4, 233n., 236, 285
'eisegesis' v, vii, 12, 63n.
Eissa, Muhammad 160n.
Emilia (subject of Milton's Italian sonnets) 261
Empson, William 291, 292
Epiphanius 82n.
Erasmus, Desiderius 127n.
Eros, Platonic theories of v, vi, ix, 6, 7, 11, 23, 32, 39–40, 43, 48, 52, 54, 62, 65–71, 72, 73, 74, 86, 90, 96, 105, 111n., 132, 146, 154, 172, 184, 208–11, 213, 226n., 227, 231, 232–3, 237, 274, 277, 278, 280, 299, 301 (*see also* Plato, *Symposium*); linked to hatred by Milton 211
Escole des filles, L' (Jean Millot?) 68
Euripides 164
Eusebius 23n., 39n.
Evans, J. M. 19n., 21–3n., 154n., 156n., 247n.
Eve: and fellatio 165; as artist 34n., 242–3, 245–6, 270, 288, 301, 303; as Flesh 136, (*see also* allegory); as object of amorous dreaming 231, 234, 239, 250, 251, 255, 272; as vampire 114, 169, 225; bestial 70, 143, 145; created defective? 97, 101, 103, 104, 107, 113, 114, 120, 144–5, 149, 159, 274, 276, 280, 290, 295; erotic blandishments blamed for fall 157, 292, 295–6, 297; 'Eve-baiting' 291; fashioned out of Adam's womb 144; initiative in redemption 296, 305; penetrated by serpent's tail 156; procreating without man 150, 153; raped by Adam 153–4, 172; sexual accomplice of Satan 26, 91n., 98, 145, 153n., 155, 156, 162, 163, 168–9, 173, 264, 290, 291, 300; without soul 103, 108
'Eve': meaning 'mother of life' 13n., 17, 18, 109, 137n., 152; meaning 'serpent' 13n., 18

excretion 45, 58, 143, 162, 199, 202, 237, 299; semen as 195, 196, 198, 199
exegesis: and art 9, 31–7, 38–9, 141–2, 148, 175, 181, 183, 184, 190, 214, 289 (*see also* imagination); and emotion 31–3, 189–90, 193; and realism 124, 126, 131, 134, 138, 139, 141, 149, 155, 157, 193; 'leading out' v, 189, 191–2; self-defeating v, vii, viii, ch. 1 *passim*, 38, 62, 129, 174; visionary and prophetic vi, 6, 8, 31, 124, 130, 140, 141–56, 162, 164, 166, 170, 174, 175, 180, 184, 241, 290

fall, the: effects on the interpreter v, 2, 5, 6, 9, 14, 35, 37, 46–7, 60, 127, 141, 142, 151, 157, 176–80, 183, 185, 230, 247–8, 251, 253, 255–65, 270, 299; immediately following creation of Eve 19, 28, 29, 30, 55, 72, 247; not experienced outside Europe 129, 138; on a Friday 104n.; on 22 April 29; sexual implications 6, 20, 21, 31, 39, 43–5, 104, 141, 144–6, 150–72, 180, 198, 254, 289–309 (*see also* Tree of Life)
Fallon, Stephen 190n., 196n.
Familists ('Family of Love') 81n., 82n., 85, 87n., 90, 94n., 125n., 133n., 212
Farley, Benjamin W., tr. 83n.
Farwell, Marilyn R. 71n., 132n., 133n.
Fell Fox, Margaret 108
feminism and feminist readings of Genesis vi–vii, viii, 1, 14–16, 20, 37, 89n., 98, 106, 109–13, 115n., 118–19, 120–2, 132n., 150–4, 155, 157, 186n., 195n., 218, 297; *see also* egalitarianism, 'narrow-Augustinian' interpretation, 'presubordinationist' reading
Ficino, Marsilio 67, 68, 135
Fiorenza, Elizabeth S. 25n.
Fish, Stanley E. vi, viii, 183n., 218n., 238n., 255n., 260n., 265n., 298n.
Fleetwood, Edward, tr. 110n.
Fletcher, Phineas 155, 291
Flinker, Noam 85n., 91n.
Fludd, Robert 158, 159–61, 164
Foigny, Gabriel de 163
Folengo, Teofilo 295n.
food as parallel to sexuality 52, 58, 59, 94n., 242, 272, 303; *see also* aphrodisiacs
Forché, Carolyn 23n.

314   *Index*

Foucault, Michel vi, 8
Fowler, Alastair 247 n., 269 n., 279 n., 283 n., 288 n.
Fox, George 108
Franck, Sebastian 87, 89
Fränger, Wilhelm 82 n., 143 n.
Franklin, William 86
Fraser, Lady Antonia 97 n.
French, John Milton 307 n.
Fresch, Cheryl H. 153 n.
Freud, Sigmund 41
Frey, Nicholas 81 n.
Froula, Christine 23 n.
Frye, Roland M. 23 n., 73 n., 75 n., 77 n.
Frye, Northrop vi, 238 n., 298 n., 303

Gager, William 1
Ganymede 272, 304
Gardiner, Judith Kegan vii n.
Gataker, Thomas 73, 75 n., 76, 120 n., 195 n., 206
'Gawain-poet' *see Cleanness*
genital organs: absent before fall 143; as fifth column 44, 290, 295; beautiful in resurrection 54; growing like goitres after fall 158; hung upon Adam at fall 144–5; instruments of redemption 26, 146, 151; mouth-like before fall 163; movable like fingers 29, 45–6, 48, 55; praised 134, 258; useful only after fall 28
genres: 'apology for woman' 1, 109, 111, 112 n.; *ars amatoria* 73, 208, 233; Carte du Tendre 232; comedy 168, 252, 264; comic strip 261; courtesy book 112; dialogue 68, 236; dramatic interlude 147; elegy 289, 299; *enarratio* 27, 32, 33, 62; epic 5, 125, 128, 139, 142, 154, 156, 164, 171, 182, 184, 190, 232, 251, 252, 256, 270, 287; epistolary novel 266; fable 13, 16, 19, 24, 39, 67, 71, 125, 171; heroic play 295; hymn 13, 25, 33, 34, 297; idyll 243, 247, 248, 255, 267, 273, 281, 289, 298; lampoon 166, 203 n.; lyric (religious) 5, 63; lyric (secular) 167–70, 181, 209, 223, 241, 244, 248–51, 252, 261, 306; masque 249 n. (*see also* Milton, John, *Mask*); maxim 168; mock-treatise 165 n., 166; novel 285; opera 237, 245, 297, 306; Ovidian elegy 165, 209, 232, 241, 246, 301, 302, 304; palinode 306; paradox 103 n., 110, 111 n., 127, 157, 166; parody 299, 303, 309; pastoral 278; 'poema satyricon' 127, 165; pornography 68, 199, 258; romance 1, 137, 142, 171, 209, 224, 252, 261, 288, 297, 298; satire 129, 155, 162 n., 163, 185; sonnet 127, 223, 229, 240, 244, 245, 249 n., 261, 272; tragedy 214, 247, 255 n., 289, 304; Utopian fiction 163, 190; verse letter 169; wedding-sermon 74, 76, 113–16, 169, 195, 274
Gerbi, Antonello 156 n., 159 n., 161 n., 295 n.
Gilbert, Sandra M. 186 n.
Ginzburg, Louis 128 n.
Gnostics and Gnostic interpretations of Edenic sexuality 23, 28, 85, 88, 132 n., 141–2, 154, 155, 156 n., 163, 164, 172, 197, 207, 248; Sophia 144, 147, 154, 155, 207, 301
Golden Age, related to Eden-story 23, 107, 112, 167, 169, 248–50, 258
Goodwin, Thomas 115 n.
Gouge, William, vi, 74–6, 118–20, 298 n.
Graves, Robert 21–3 n.
Gregory of Nyssa 55, 78
Greville, Fulke 127
Grotius, Hugo 68, 79 n., 195 n., 236, 246, 292, 297
Guillory, John 175 n.

H., Lady M. 1
Hagstrum, Jean H. viii, 44 n., 45 n., 46 n., 49 n., 199 n., 217 n., 218 n., 230 n., 302 n., 303
Halkett, John 73 n., 106 n., 108 n., 115 n., 116 n., 119 n., 189 n., 195 n., 205 n., 206 n., 210 n., 220 n., 222 n., 226 n., 230 n.
Hall, Joseph 110 n.
Hall, Thomas 85 n.
Haller, William and Malleville 73 n., 74 n., 108 n., 119 n., 190 n., 195 n., 198 n.
Ham 19
Hamilton, Alistair 87 n., 93 n., 133 n.
Hardy, Nathanael 76–7, 219 n., 283 n., 298 n.
Hartlib, Samuel 88 n.
Haydn, Hiram 83 n.
Heale, William 1–3, 7, 97, 101, 111, 112–13, 115, 117, 207 n., 219, 230, 254 n., 283
Hegel, G. W. F. 148

Helmont, Franciscus Mercurius van 148, 163, 164
Helmont, Jean-Baptiste van 37, 148, 149–55, 156, 161, 164, 172, 276
'help meet', interpretations of 11, 14, 16, 26, 69, 85, 99, 100, 102, 105–6, 108, 114, 116, 121, 130, 153, 159, 189, 201, 214, 215, 218, 235, 274
Henkel, A. and Schöne, A. 68 n.
Henrietta Maria, consort of Charles I 223
Hermetic philosophy 154–6, 158, 159, 164
Herodotus 223 n.
Hesiod 65 n.
Heydon, John 108, 116, 207
Hieron, Samuel 97 n.
Hildegarde of Bingen 153 n.
Hill, Christopher viii, 84 n., 85 n., 87 n., 88 n., 91 n., 92 n., 94 n., 108, 115 n., 133 n., 153 n., 199 n., 203 n., 211 n.
Hobbes, Thomas 233
Hodge, Bob *see* Aers, David
Hoffman, Melchior 81 n.
Homer 302
Homines Intelligentiae 81 n.
homosexuality 19, 40, 54, 67, 96, 132, 304
homunculus 161, 162
Hooker, Edith, homunculus grower 161 n.
Hooker, Richard 119
Horace 187 n., 260 n.
Huartes, Juan 103
Huguelet, Theodore L. 210 n.
Hume, David 86
Hutchinson, Anne 85 n.
Hutin, Serge 149 n.
Hutterites 82 n., 118

iconoclasm and 'casting down imaginations' (2 Cor. 10: 5) 12, 31, 34, 125, 175, 183, 185, 228, 231
ideologies of gender v, viii, 3, 8, 97, 100, 106, 113, 117–18, 119, 122, 123, 131, 138, 174, 186, 217–24, 229, 231, 237, 239, 246, 263, 266, 274, 276, 278, 280, 283, 290, 305; and sexual excitement 235, 260, 285; subverted in *PL?* 281–7
'image of God': differentiated by gender 13, 14, 26, 58, 59, 106, 108, 115, 119, 121, 138, 154, 172, 217–18, 276, 281, 286; in genitals 151, 160
imagination 11, 12, 30, 31, 33–5, 37, 46, 51, 62, 70, 124–31, 140, 142, 143, 146–9, 155, 170–1, 174, 175, 183 n., 184, 185, 186, 232, 240 n., 256, 299, 307; 'evil' (Gen. 6: 5 and 8: 21) 3, 6, 10, 20, 30, 31, 33, 34, 39, 61, 91, 140, 174, 245
indeterminacy or indecipherability of Scripture vii, 3, 5, 6, 10–12, 13, 16–20, 27, 29, 30, 31, 35, 37, 46, 131, 138, 152, 174, 193, 195 n.
Irenaeus 15 n., 23 n., 154
Islam 12, 22, 55, 85, 118, 160 *see also* Koran

Jackson, A. V. Williams 23 n.
James I 113
James, Robert 159 n., 161 n.
Jauss, Hans Robert vi
John Damascene, St. 55
Johnson, Samuel 141, 182, 230, 231, 265, 290
Jonas, Hans 23 n., 28 n., 88 n., 156 n.
Jonson, Ben 34 n., 130 n.
Junia 217 n.
Jurieu, Pierre 137 n.
Justin Martyr 98 n.

Kearns, Edward J. 181 n.
Keats, John 224, 239, 287
Kelly, Henry Ansgar 43 n., 57 n., 107 n.
Kelso, Ruth 110 n.
Kerrigan, William W. 180 n., 230 n., 263 n., 276 n.
Kidderminster; Baxter stoned in 119
Kierkegaard, Søren 229
Kirkconnell, Watson 247 n.; tr. 68 n., 236 n., 246 n., 268 n., 291 n., 292 n., 295 n., 298 n.
Knott, John R. 182 n.
Koran 12
Krailsheimer, A. J. 162 n.
Kristeva, Julia vi, 63 n.
Kuntz, Marion L. D. 89 n., 132 n.; tr. 160 n.
L'Adamite, ou le Jesuite insensible (author unknown) 86 n.
La Mothe Le Vayer, François de 166, 172
Laclos, Pierre Choderlos de 49
Ladurie, Emmanuel Le Roy 87 n.
Lamont, William M. 119 n.
Landy, Marcia 231 n.
Lanier, Emilia vi, 111–13
Lapeyrère, Isaac de 133 n., 136–40
Lapide, Cornelius a 63 n.
Latitudinarianism 136

Index

Law, William 142n., 148
Lawrence, D. H. 226
Le Comte, Edward 199n., 203n., 209n., 218n., 222n., 223, 230n., 300n.
Leach, Edmund 18n.
Lead, Jane 148
Leah 19
'Leone Ebreo' (Judah Abarbanel) 66–71, 73, 75, 125, 129, 131n., 141, 154, 156, 161
'Leonora' (singing praised by Milton) see Baroni, Leonora
Lerner, Laurence 73n., 75n., 195n., 226n., 264n.
Levin, Harry 250n.
Lewalski, Barbara K. 231n.
Lewis, C. S. 298n.
libertinism and scepticism vi, 11, 49, 50, 61, 64, 68, 70, 71, 84, 89, 114, 125–6, 130, 131, 132, 133, 134, 150, 152, 164–73, 175, 180, 190, 197, 203, 210–12, 248–51, 258, 290, 300, 303, 305–8 (*see also* Belial; Milton, John, and 'Court Amours'; Spiritual Libertines); *libertins érudits* 4, 136, 166
Lilith 22, 224
Lindenbaum, Peter 22n., 45n., 48n., 230n., 247n., 272n., 279n.
Locke, John 151
Loewenstein, David A. 125n., 224n., 228n., 308n.
Loists see Spiritual Libertines
Lombard, Peter 107, 115
Loredano, Giovanni Francesco 35n., 168n., 251–2, 255, 262, 274–5, 291, 295n., 308
Lot 19, 20
Lovelace, Richard 73, 167, 249–50
Lucretius 241, 285n.
Luther, Martin 6–7, 32, 33, 34, 37, 58–62, 63, 72, 78, 96, 98, 105, 107, 120–4, 126, 131, 153, 191, 195n., 206, 216, 222, 236, 245, 268n., 274, 284

Mabuse, Jan Gossaert Fig. 5
Maclean, Ian 101n., 107n., 110n., 307n.
Madan, Falconer 1n.
Mandeville, Bernard 169n.
Manicheanism 23n., 28, 49, 50, 159
Marcus, Jane 16n.
Margaret of Austria 110

Margaret of Navarre, court of 83n.
marriage, affected by interpretation of Eden-story 2, 6–7, 17, 21, 22, 24, 49, 57, 62, 69, 70, 72–9, 80, 83, 87, ch. 3 *passim*, 133, 139, 153, 164, 166, 171, 174, 176, ch. 6 *passim*, 232, 233, 248, 250, 257, 265, 299, 308; *see also* wedding-ceremony
Martin, Andrew 19n.
Marvell, Andrew 71, 169
McColley, Diane Kelsey 15n., 78, 107n., 110n., 117n., 119n., 163n., 218n., 230n., 256n., 276n., 281n., 283n., 291n., 292n.
McLoughlin, Daniel 165n.
Mechthild of Magdeburg 143n.
Medina, Giovanni Battista Fig. 4
Meeks, Wayne A. 25n.
menstruation 46, 151–2, 158, 159n., 160, 161, 212
Michelangelo 165
Michelet, Jules 86n.
Middleton, Thomas 82n.
Miller, Leo 81n.
MILTON, JOHN v–ix, 1, 4, 8, 9, 12, 21n., 29, 30, 32, 37, 57, 64, 70–1, 72–3, 75, 77–9, 87, 90, 92–5, 97, 105–6, 108, 114, 118, 121, 123, 125, 128, 132, 138, 139, 141, 142, 149, 154–6, 163, 164, 166–7, 171–4, chs. 5–7 *passim*
  Areopagitica 9, 71n., 92, 154, 171, 172, ch. 5 *passim*, 190, 199, 203, 204, 208, 209, 210, 211, 228, 229, 232, 243, 249, 251, 260, 264, 266, 275, 287, 307; divorce tracts vi, 4, 7, 25n., 37, 69, 75, 77, 84, 108, 110n., 115, 120, 139, 140, 154, 166, 176, 182, 184, 186, ch. 6 *passim*, 232–7, 248, 255, 256, 257–8, 263, 272, 276n., 277, 279, 283, 285, 299, 302n., 304, 305n., 308; *Mask, A* 177, 179n., 180, 181, 184, 185, 207n., 209n., 222, 227, 244, 245, 250, 261, 265n., 300n.; *Paradise Lost* v, 2, 4n., 19n., 25, 30, 33, 35n., 38, 39, 41, 53, 54–5, 57, 61, 64, 75n., 82n., 84, 94, 103n., 113, 116n., 120, 122, 125, 127, 129, 130, 139, 152n., 155, 157, 162, 163, 167, 176, 178, 180, 182, 186, 199, 207, 208, 217, 218, 222n., 225n., 228, 229, ch. 7 *passim*, Fig. 4; *Paradise Regained* 178, 185, 268, 302, 306n.; *Samson Agonistes* 164, 185, 214, 215n., 224–5, 227–8, 296

MILTON, JOHN (*cont.*):
  and 'Court Amours' 61, 237, 248, 249, 255, 260, 262, 271, 291, 299, 305; and illicit sexuality in general 196, 197, 205, 208, 211, 212, 213, 215, 223, 224–5, 227, 251 n., 305; and 'manliness' 188, 213, 215–27, 284, 296; ethics of confrontation 4, 9, 92, ch. 5 *passim*, 248, 277; fear of sexual thralldom (bondage, slavery) 218, 220–7, 292 n.; female aspects of 187, 224 n., 263, 306, 307; reappropriation of sensuousness 241, 248–51, 258, 261; 'salt' humour 299; temperance ch. 5 *passim*, 190, 214, 228, 306, 307, 308; violence or 'vehemence' 214, 227–9, 232, 238, 244 n., 260, 276, 296, 301; vitalism 4, 183–8, 199, 210, 232, 277 (*see also* text, literary, as 'life blood')
Moll, John, tr. 162 n.
monism ix, 53, 54, 198–204, 211, 213, 240, 279
Montaigne, Michel de 38, 45, 54 n., 219
More, Sir Thomas 190
More, Alexander 223
More, Henry 4, 32, 85, 89, 90, 133–6, 140, 149, 156, 299 n.
Moss, Jean D. 81 n.
Muggletonians 87 n., 91 n., 153 n., 162 n.
Münster (Anabaptist rising) 80, 82, 118
'My One Flesh' (London radical group) 92

'narrow-Augustinian' interpretation of Eve 28, 58 n., ch. 3 *passim*, 130, 161, 164, 181, 195, 204–6, 210, 215, 279
Nauert, Charles G. 158 n.
Naylor, James 86
Needham, Marchamont 88 n.
'nefesogli' (humans born without copulation) 160
Neville, Henry 103 n.
Newman, Barbara 153 n.
Newton, Judith vii n.
Newton, Thomas 238 n.
Niclaes, Henry 81 n., 85 n., 92 n.
Nierembergus, Johannes Eusebius 34 n.
Noah 19, 20, 268
Nogarola, Isotta 109
Nohrnberg, James 22 n., 45 n., 68 n.
Nygren, Anders 41 n.
Nyquist, Mary 15 n., 33 n., 288 n., 296 n.

O'Meara, John J. 45 n.
Olsen, V. Norskov 105 n., 189 n.
Origen 23 n., 39 n., 64, 65, 70, 131, 134
Original Sin 18, 29, 43–4, 48, 87, 128, 129, 162, 166, 174, 245; *see also* Cain
Osborne, Francis 166, 203 n.
Ovid 1, 73

P., Mrs. T. 89 n.
Pagel, Walter 137 n., 150 n., 153 n., 161 n.
Pagels, Elaine 23 n., 132 n., 217 n.
Paget, Nathan 87
Palaeologus, Jakob 136
Pandora 23
Paracelsus and Paracelsan concepts 142, 150, 154, 158–9, 160–1, 162, 163, 166
Paraeus, David 72 n., 106, 220, 236
Parker, Patricia 238 n.
Parker, W. R. 93 n., 94 n., 110 n., 190 n., 205 n., 225 n.
Parliament of Wômen, The (author unknown) 85 n.
Pascal, Blaise 5, 6, 32, 130, 156, 178, 181, 186, 256, 307
Passieri, Marcantonio Fig. 3
Patrides, C. A., ed. 141 n.
patronesses, influence of vi, 1, 110, 112, 113, 186, 269 n.; charismatic 'New Eve' 87, 89 n.
Paul, St., and Pauline doctrines 16 n., 21–3, 31 n., 34 n., 42, 43, 54, 63, 64, 75, 80, 81 n., 83, 84, 89, 93, 96–9, 104, 106, 107, 110, 121, 138, 156, 158, 168, 196, 197, 200, 202, 203, 209, 216, 217, 221, 224, 234, 268, 269, 282, 286, 290, 307 n.
Peczenik, Fanny 16 n., 231 n.
Pelagianism 49, 57, 136
Penn, William 88 n.
Pererius, Benedictus 72 n., 103 n.
Peter Martyr (Vermigli) 105
Petronius 178
Philips, John 84
Phillips, John A. v n., 18 n., 22 n.
Philo Judaeus 23 n., 65, 98, 131 n., 135, 156, 162
Physiologus 156
Picards 82 n.
Pico della Mirandola, Giovanni 66
Pintard, René 137 n., 166 n.
Plato 65, 72, 73, 129, 181, 209, 211, 232,

301; *Symposium* v, ix, 17, 22, 23, 39–41, 62, 65–71, 131, 209, 211, 301
Plotinus 65
pollution *see* sexuality, as 'abomination'
polygamy 80, 82, 118
Pona, Francesco 275 n.
Pope, Alexander 166
Popkin, Richard H. 133 n., 137 n.
Pordage, Samuel and John 148, 149 n., 292
Potter, George R., ed. 114 n.
Poulain de la Barre, François 108, 168 n.
Pre-Adamites 133, 136–9, 140
'presubordinationist' reading of the creation of Eve 18 n., 22, 25–6, ch. 3 *passim*, 216, 235, 260, 273, 282, 285
'protevangelium' (promise of a Saviour deduced from Gen. 3: 15) 12, 59, 61, 129, 152
Proust, Marcel 231, 235, 250, 272
Prynne, William 251 n.
Purchas, Samuel 111
Puritanism and 'Puritan Art of Love' vi, 7, 73–9, 90, 94, 108, 109, 115–18, 120, 194, 204, 208, 209, 211 n., 298 n.

Quakers 85, 86, 96, 108
Quilligan, Maureen 94 n., 175 n., 233 n., 244 n., 269 n.

R., L. 85 n., 168 n.
Rabbinical commentary on Genesis 21–3, 30, 34, 66, 67, 69, 73, 78, 115, 127, 128, 156, 162, 166, 168, 172, 236 n., 238 n., 290
Rabelais, François 68, 128, 129, 162, 165
Rachel 19
Rad, Gerhard von 14 n., 16 n., 18 n.
radicalism and 'Radical Reformation' vi, ix, 5, 75, 79–95, 105, 107–8, 117, 122, 132–3, 136–7, 139, 140, 148, 149, 167, 175–6, 177, 180, 183, 211 n., 213, 228, 274, 281
Radzinowicz, Mary Ann 218 n., 228 n.
Raine, Kathleen 144 n., 149 n.
Ranters 37, 40, 84–94, 136, 164, 168, 177
Rapaport, Herman 182 n.
Raphael *see* angels
Rashi 19 n.
Reay, Barry 91 n.
'reception' and readers' response vi, viii, 5–9, 31, 47, 48, 182, 183, 188, 228, 248, 251, 254, 255–65, 267, 270–2, 275, 287, 296 n., 299, 307–9; as angelic encounter 231, 257; as divorce 229; separating 'mingled grain' 266, 275, 302; 'soft and delicious' 182, 187, 241, 256, 260, 261, 263, 265, 287, 298, 307, 309
Rembrandt frontispiece, 140–1, 142, 175, 229
resurrection of the flesh 28, 42, 51–5, 116 n., 143
'rib', interpretation of 10, 22, 59, 73, 100, 107, 111 n., 112–15, 117, 119, 121, 126, 130, 164, 225, 231
Ricoeur, Paul vi
Rivet, André 105, 236
Robinson, John A. T. 43 n.
Rochester, John Wilmot, earl of 210, 248
Rogers, Daniel 108
Roman de la Rose (Jean Le Meung) 76, 107 n.
Rosenburg, Joel W. 18 n.
Rothmann, Bernard 118
Rous, Francis 79
Rudat, Wolfgang E. H. 290 n.
Rykwert, Joseph 242

Sadelaer, Jan I Figs. 1, 2, 7
Salden, Willem 137 n.
Salkeld, John 103–4, 113–15, 121
Salmasius, Claude 223
Salmon, Joseph 88 n.
Sarasin, Jean-François 168–9, 171
Sartre, Jean-Paul 19
Satan 12, 21, 24, 91 n., 98, 100, 125, 129, 153 n., 154, 155, 158, 162, 168, 171, 173, 222, 233, 238, 253, 255, 256, 258–63, 266, 269, 270, 271, 278, 280, 281, 286, 287, 290, 291, 300, 301, 302, 304; as artist 147, 148; as exegete 131, 283; as rapist 155, 292, 300
Schelling, F. W. J. von 148
'scholastic synthesis' of Genesis and Aristotle 101, 107, 118
Scholem, Gerschom S. 86 n.
Schöne *see* Henkel, A.
Schottus, Gaspar 34 n.
Schultze, Anne J. 85 n.
Schwartz, Regina 224 n.
Screech, Michael A. 89 n.
Secker, William 96, 108, 115 n., 218 n.
sects associated with sexual irregularities 82, 85, 90, 93, 175, 212; *see also* Adamites, Anabaptists, Carpocratians, Cathars, Familists, Gnostics, Homines Intelligentiae,

sects (*cont.*):
  Hutterites, 'My One Flesh', Picards, Ranters, Spiritual Libertines, Turlupins
serpent, sexual implications of v, 19, 21, 22, 70, 98, 132, 135, 145–7, 155, 156–9, 162, 165, 170, 290n., 291–2
Seth 20, 161
sexuality and sexual practices; as 'abomination' or pollution vii, 8, 20, 27, 72, 144–7, 155, 159, 162, 163, 164, 172, 189, 194, 197–203, 210, 222, 223, 226, 229, 232, 236, 258; as creativity 26, 50, 70, 147, 154, 161; as disease 60, 70, 200; as dissolution 225–7; buggery 85n., 88; communal copulation 81, 82, 84, 85n., 86, 89, 91–2, 164, 237; entailing death 151, 156, 159, 169, 195, 198, 203, 226, 260n.; in response to landscape 237–44, 270, 299, 299, 302, 308; more intense before fall 51, 56, 59, 77, 135n., 194, 235, 277; nocturnal emissions 22, 226; pagan and Near-Eastern 18n., 44, 166, 172, 223, 237, 261, 291, 302; solitary 231, 235, 250, 258, 261; voyeurism 258, 263, 270; *see also* genital organs, homosexuality
Shakespeare, William 149n., 164, 169, 238, 246, 279, 288
Shawcross, John T., ed. 141n., 172n., 190n., 296n., 305n.
Showalter, Elaine viin.
Sidney, Sir Philip 1, 35, 39, 125, 126, 182
Simpson, Evelyn M., ed. 32n., 114n., 137n.
Sin, Milton's figure of 155, 162, 164, 258, 260, 300, 301, 302
Sinibaldus, Giovanni Battista 200n.
Smith, Henry 76, 106n., 115
Smith, Nigel, ed. 84n., 87n., 88n.
Smith, Hilda 16n., 108n., 117n.
Socrates 67, 68n., 146, 209
Sodom 20, 57, 304
Solomon *see* Bible: Ecclesiastes, Proverbs, Song of Songs
'Sons of God' (sexual partners of 'daughters of men' in Gen. 6:2) 20, 126, 153n., 240, 268–72, 302, 305, 306; *see also* angels
Sowernam, Esther (pseud.) 115n.
Sparrow, John, tr. 142n., 145n.
Speght, Rachel 115n.
Spenser, Edmund 177–8, 181, 234, 252, 269n., 270
Spinoza, Baruch 41
spirits, sexual relations with 22, 153n., 155, 160, 166, 203, 258, 268, 291; *see also* angels
Spiritual Libertines 37, 40, 82–4, 85, 89, 91, 93, 124, 125, 142, 157, 190
Spranger, Bartholomaeus Fig. 6
Steele, Sir Richard 163n.
Steinberg, Leo 165n.
Stewart, Stanley 63n.
Stone, Harold 137n.
Strauss, Leo 137n.
Struck, Wilhelm 149n.
Stubbs, Phillip 165n.
Stubs, M. 84n.
succubae *see* spirits
Sutcliffe, Anne 162
Swan, Jim 231n.
Swan, John 29n., 115n.
Swetnam, Joseph 115n.
Swift, Jonathan 82, 156, 211n.
Sylvester, Joshua 68, 128n., 254n., 295

Tarabotti, Arcangela 110n.
Tasso, Torquato 249
Taylor, Thomas 119
Taylor, Jeremy 195n.
Taylor, John H., ed. 99n.
Tennenhouse, Leonard 230n.
Teresa of Avila, St. 153n.
text of Bible: division into 'Priestly' and 'Jahwist' segments 13–14, 19, 30, 65, 136, 137; 'loosening' 131, 136, 140, 166; modification punished by death 98; seen as corrupt 37, 133, 137n., 166
text, literary: as act of divorce 214; as agent of restitution 6, 142, 147, 184, 188, 213, 248, 252, 256–65, 271, 308, 309; as 'amorous descant' or emotive music 183n., 184, 188, 237, 243–6, 289, 297, 298, 303, 306; as 'assertion' 182, 184; as body 1, 4, 133; as expression of rage 214–15, 219, 228, 229; as guide to enjoyment 208, 233, 257, 260; as journey or 'walk' 2–4, 5, 8, 10, 39, 96, 188, 230, 253; as 'life blood' or vital force 4, 181, 183–4, 188, 191, 211, 232, 246; as perfume 245; as 'stroking' 184, 189, 229; as therapy 214, 235; conveying experiential knowledge 180–3, 185,

208, 211, 229, 307; generative power 160; resistant to ideology 106; 'sensuous and passionate' 182, 184, 189, 208, 210, 232, 235, 242, 253, 255, 261, 263, 265, 290, 307
Theodoretus 82n., 85n.
theosophy *see* exegesis, visionary
Thomas, Keith 103n., 161n.
Thompson, Roger 86n., 203n.
Thorowgood, G. 226n.
Tickell, John 88n., 125n., 148n.
Titanic hubris 29n., 70n., 148, 154
Titian 234
Tomasinus, J. P. Fig. 3
Trapp, J. B. 141n.
Tree of Life, sexual interpretation of 11, 18, 19, 69, 128, 152, 156–9, 165, 167, 170
Trible, Phyllis 14n., 16n., 18n., 21n., 63n.
Tryon, Thomas 148
Turlupins 82n.
Turner, James G. viii
Tymme, Thomas 72
Tyndale, William 34

'uncleanness' *see* sexuality; as 'abomination'

Vawter, Bruce 18n.
Verstegen, Richard 130n.
Villars, Nicolas Pierre Henri de Montfaucon de 166
Virgil 45, 46, 51, 198, 203, 241
visual depictions of Genesis 22, 37, 140, 165, 168, 258, 290, 292, Figs. 1, 2, 4–7
Vives, Juan Luis 153, 205n.
Voltaire 39, 156, 171
Vondel, Joost van den 247
Vos, Martin de Figs. 1, 2, 7

Warburton, William 190
Ward, Edward 129n., 165n.
Webber, Joan M. 306n.
Webster, Charles 148n., 149n.
wedding-ceremony in Eden 22, 26, 87, 236, 241, 242, 244, 246–8, 273, 301, 302; combined with funeral 169, 195, 247
Weemes, John 115n., 118, 216n.
Westermann, Claus 16n., 18n.
Whately, William 74–5, 76, 109n., 118, 195n., 198, 204n.
White Christopher 141n.
Wilkinson, C. H., ed. 73n.
Williams, Arnold 72n., 82n., 106n., 115n., 131n., 162n., 177n., 268n.
Williams, George Huntston 80n., 81n., 82n., 86n., 87n., 88n., 93n., 118n., 133n., 137n.
Williams, Norman Powell 15n., 18n., 20n., 21n., 24n., 34n., 98n., 131n., 156n.
Williams, Selma R. 85n.
Willis, Gladys J. 189n.
Wind, Edgar 66n., 68n.
Winstanley, Gerrard 37, 86, 92n., 108n., 132, 133, 137, 140
Winthrop, John 85n.
Wood, Anthony à 88n.
Woodbridge, Linda 110n., 112n.
Woolf, Virginia viii, 186, 217, 231

Xenophon 209

Yeats, W. B. 215

Zeno of Verona, St. 158n.
Zevi, Sabbatai 86
Zoroaster 137n.